C

A Reference Manual

THIRD EDITION

Samuel P. Harbison

Guy L. Steele Jr.

Tartan Laboratories

Prentice Hall Software Series

PRENTICE HALL, Englewood Cliffs, NJ 07632

Library of Congress Cataloging-in-Publication Data

Harbison, Samuel P.
    C, a reference manual / Samuel P. Harbison, Guy L. Steele, Jr. --
3rd ed.
        p.   cm.
    Includes index.
    ISBN 0-13-110941-3 (case ed.) :   . -- ISBN 0-13-110933-2
(paper ed.) :
    1. C (Computer program language)   I. Steele, Guy. II. Title.
QA76.73.C15H38   1991
005.13'3--dc20   90-43586
                                                         CIP

Editorial/production supervision: *Colleen Brosnan*
Cover design: *Bruce Kenselaar*
Manufacturing buyers: *Linda Behrens/Patrice Fraccio*

Ada is a registered trademark of the U.S. Government, Ada Joint Program Office. DEC, DECSYSTEM 20, PDP, VAX, and VMS are trademarks of Digital Equipment Corporation. IBM is a registered trademark of International Business Machines Incorporated. UNIX is a trademark of Bell Laboratories. Microsoft is a registered trademark of Microsoft Corporation. Lattice is a trademark of Lattice, Incorporated. Intel is a trademark of Intel Corporation.

© 1991 by Prentice-Hall, Inc.
A Division of Simon & Schuster, Inc.
Englewood Cliffs, New Jersey 07632

The author and publisher of this book have used their best efforts in preparing this book. These efforts include the development, research, and testing of the theories and programs to determine their effectiveness. The author and publisher make no warranty of any kind, expressed or implied, with regard to these programs or the documentation contained in this book. The author and publisher shall not be liable in any event for incidental or consequential damages in connection with, or arising out of, the furnishing, performance, or use of these programs.

Printed in the United States of America

10 9 8 7 6

ISBN 0-13-110941-3
ISBN 0-13-110933-2 {PBK}

Prentice-Hall International (UK) Limited, *London*
Prentice-Hall of Australia Pty. Limited, *Sydney*
Prentice-Hall Canada Inc., *Toronto*
Prentice Hall Hispanoamericana, S.A., *Mexico*
Prentice-Hall of India Private Limited, *New Delhi*
Prentice-Hall of Japan, Inc., *Tokyo*
Simon & Schuster Asia Pte. Ltd., *Singapore*
Editora Prentice-Hall do Brasil, Ltda., *Rio de Janeiro*

Contents

Preface

This text is a reference manual for the C programming language. Our aim is to provide a complete discussion of the language, the run-time libraries, and a style of C programming that emphasizes correctness, portability, and maintainability.

We expect our readers to already understand basic programming concepts, and many will have previous experience with C. In keeping with a reference format, we have presented the language in a "bottom-up" order: the lexical structure, the preprocessor, declarations, types, expressions, statements, functions, and the run-time libraries. We have included many cross-references in the text so that readers can begin at any point.

With the third edition of *C: A Reference Manual* we have fully integrated the descriptions of "traditional C" and the American National Standard X3.159–1989— "ANSI C." Many popular C compilers—including, for example, Microsoft C for the IBM PC—have been moving toward the ANSI C language for some time. Even if these compilers are not fully ANSI conforming as we write this, programmers using them are better served by books that fully cover ANSI C.

For the majority of programmers still using non-ANSI conforming implementations, we have not short-changed traditional C. We have retained the descriptions of various shortcomings and variations in pre-ANSI compilers so that programmers may avoid the less portable language areas if desired. We have been careful to note where ANSI C and traditional C differ and have given suggestions for writing programs that are portable between the two languages.

We have also taken the opportunity afforded by this edition to make more extensive changes in the text. We added study problems to most chapters in part 1 so that readers may test their understanding of the language. We added various tables to highlight language features and make the text more readable. Finally, we added many examples that illustrate the use of the library facilities in part 2. To keep the book to a reasonable length, we shortened some tedious discussions of minor technical points, and we eliminated two chapters at the end of part 1 that contained a separate discussion of ANSI C and a large C example program. The ANSI C description is now integrated into the main text, and there are many software engineering textbooks that treat the problems of building large software systems in more depth.

This book grew out of our work at Tartan Laboratories developing a family of C compilers for a wide range of computers, from micros to supermainframes. We wanted the compilers to be well documented, to provide precise and helpful error diagnostics, and to generate exceptionally efficient object code. A C program that compiles correctly with one compiler must compile correctly under all the others, insofar as the hardware differences allow.

In spite of C's popularity, and the increasing number of primers and introductory texts on C, we found that there was no description of C precise enough to guide us in designing the new compilers. Similarly, no existing description was precise enough for our programmer/customers, who would be using compilers that analyzed C programs more thoroughly than was the custom. In this text we have been especially sensitive to language features that affect program clarity, object code efficiency, and the portability of programs among different environments, both UNIX and non-UNIX.

ACKNOWLEDGMENTS

This edition was greatly improved by comments from reviewers Jeffrey Esakov of the University of Pennsylvania, Alan J. Filipski of Arizona State University, and Frank J. Wagner of the University of Cincinnati. Marcia Horton at Prentice Hall has been an excellent guide for the book and the authors over the past seven years.

We also wish to thank our colleagues who helped in the writing, editing, and production of this book in its various editions: Michael Angus, Mady Bauer, Larry Breed, Sue Broughton, Alex Czajkowski, Robert Firth, David Gaffney, Steve Gorman, Dennis Hamilton, Chris Hanna, Ken Harrenstien, Rex Jaeschke, Don Lindsay, Tom MacDonald, Peter Nelson, Joe Newcomer, Kevin Nolish, David Notkin, Peter Plamondon, P. J. Plauger, Roger Ray, Larry Rosler, David Spencer , and Barbara Steele.

Some of the example programs in this book were inspired by algorithms appearing in the following works, which we recommend to anyone seriously interested in programming: Beeler, Michael, Gosper, R. William, and Schroeppel, Richard, *HAKMEM*, AI Memo 239 (Massachusetts Institute of Technology Artificial Intelligence Laboratory, February 1972); Bentley, Jon Louis, *Writing Efficient Programs* (Prentice-Hall, 1982); Bentley, Jon Louis, "Programming Pearls" (monthly column appearing in *Communications of the ACM* beginning August 1983); Kernighan, Brian W., and Ritchie, Dennis M., *The C Programming Language* (Prentice-Hall, 1978); Knuth, Donald E, *The Art of Computer Programming* Volumes 1–3 (Addison-Wesley, 1968, 1969, 1973, 1981); and Sedgewick, Robert, *Algorithms* (Addison-Wesley, 1983). We are indebted to these authors for their good ideas.

Sam Harbison
Guy Steele

PART 1
The C Language

1

Introduction

C is a member of the "ALGOL family" of algebraic programming languages, and is more similar to languages such as PL/I, Pascal, and Ada, and less similar to BASIC, FORTRAN, or Lisp. A collection of papers, *Comparing & Assessing Programming Languages Ada, C, and Pascal*, edited by Alan R. Feuer and Narain Gehani (Prentice-Hall, 1984) discusses the similarities and differences found in C, Pascal, and Ada.

Dennis Ritchie designed the C language at Bell Laboratories in about 1972, and its ancestry dates from ALGOL 60 (1960), through Cambridge's CPL (1963), Martin Richards's BCPL (1967) and Ken Thompson's B language (1970) at Bell Labs. Although C is a general-purpose programming language, it has traditionally been used for systems programming. In particular, the popular UNIX operating system is written in C. Now widely available on both UNIX and non-UNIX systems, C is increasingly popular for applications that must be ported to different computers.

C's popularity is due to several factors. First, C provides a fairly complete set of facilities for dealing with a wide variety of applications. It has all the useful data types, including pointers, structures, and strings. There is a rich set of operators and control structures. C also has a standard run-time library that includes useful functions for input/output, storage allocation, string manipulation, and other purposes.

Second, C programs are efficient. C is a small language, and its data types and operators are closely related to the operations provided directly by most computers. Said another way, there is only a small "semantic gap" between C and the computer hardware.

Third, C programs are generally quite portable across different computing systems. Although C allows the programmer to write nonportable code, the uniformity of most C implementations makes it relatively easy to move applications to different computers and operating systems.

Finally, there is a growing number of C programs and C programmers. The UNIX operating system provides a large set of tools that improve C programming productivity and can serve as starting points for new applications. Because UNIX has been used in universities for several years, many students have C and UNIX experience.

Unfortunately, some of the very characteristics of C that account for its popularity can also pose problems for programmers. For example, C's smallness is due in large part to its lack of "confining rules," but the absence of such rules can lead to error-prone programming habits. To write well-ordered programs, the C programmer often relies on a set of stylistic conventions that are not enforced by the compiler. As another example, to allow C compilers to implement operations efficiently on a variety of computers, the precise meaning of some C operators and types is intentionally unspecified. This can create problems when moving a program to another computer.

In spite of the inelegancies, the bugs, and the confusion that often accompany C, it has withstood the test of time. It remains a language in which the experienced programmer can write quickly and well. Millions of lines of code testify to its usefulness.

1.1 WHO DEFINES C?

Although there were many introductions to C at the time we wrote this book, there were no detailed descriptions of the C language.

The traditional (pre-standard) language reference is the book *The C Programming Language*, by Brian Kernighan and Dennis Ritchie (Prentice-Hall, 1978). In fact, it is not uncommon to see references to "K&R C." However, after the book was published the language continued to evolve in small ways; some features were added and some were dropped. Usually a consensus was reached on these features, although this consensus was not always documented. Many new implementations of C added their own variations to the language. When we use the phrase "the original definition of C" in this book, we mean specifically Kernighan and Ritchie's definition, before the post-1978 changes. When we speak of "traditional C," "modern C," or "pre-ANSI C," we include the generally accepted extensions in use just prior to the ANSI standard. .

When textbooks on a language cannot answer your detailed questions, you can try writing an appropriate C program and see what it does. Many C compilers are based on the Portable C Compiler (PCC) written at Bell Laboratories, and this compiler has become a de facto standard for the traditional language. The problem is, of course, that PCC has errors like other compilers, and these errors are often in the areas of the language where clarification would be useful.

In 1982 the American National Standards Institute (ANSI) formed a technical subcommittee on C language standardization, X3J11, to propose a standard for the C language and run-time libraries. The standard, which we refer to as "ANSI C," was formally adopted in 1989 as *American National Standard X3.159-1989*. The standardization effort involved a large number of commercial C implementors—including ourselves—and their discussions helped to clarify existing practices as well as to map out the new language. Many parts of this book have benefited from these discussions. The characteristics of ANSI C are discussed in section 1.2.

ANSI C was developed at the same time as the UNIX operating system standard known as POSIX (IEEE Std. 1003.1–1988, *Portable Operating System Interface for Computer Environments*). Because of the historical connection between C and UNIX, some effort was made to ensure that the C and POSIX standards were compatible, especially in the run-time library. The POSIX standard does not require the use of ANSI C; in fact, the POSIX standard is language-independent. POSIX facilities can be provided in both ANSI C and traditional C environments.

This book describes ANSI C, traditional C, and the original definition of C as they are implemented by commercial compilers on the larger computers. We do not consider language subsets found on the smallest microcomputers. Where compilers tend to differ in their implementations, we describe the common variations. Where certain C features tend to lead to bad programming practices, we do not hesitate to suggest a better way to use the language.

1.2 ANSI C

In large part, ANSI C codifies existing practice by C programmers and tries not to invalidate the large body of C programs. In a few areas the Standard extends the language to overcome specific shortcomings, but the "spirit of C" is usually preserved. The Standard allows—but does not require—a programmer to write portable programs. In many places, the Standard simply makes the description of C more precise.

At the same time, ANSI C is not a minor change to C. Some authorities have estimated that ANSI C is about twice as "big" as traditional C. They arrive at this figure by looking at the size of the language definition and the sizes of conforming compilers and run-time libraries. The effect of a few of the new features is pervasive, and the clarification of some difficult areas in the base language adds to the complexity.

If you are a C programmer, do not be discouraged. The vast majority of C programs use well-understood language features and will port to ANSI C with little or no changes.

Both C programs and C implementations can *conform* to ANSI C. A C program is said to be *strictly conforming* to ANSI C if that program uses only the features of the language and library described in the Standard. The program's operation must not depend on any aspect of the C language that the Standard characterizes as unspecified, undefined, or implementation-defined.

There are two kinds of conforming implementations—hosted and freestanding. A C implementation is said to be a *conforming hosted implementation* if it accepts any strictly conforming program. A *conforming freestanding implementation* is one that accepts any strictly conforming program that uses no library facilities other than those provided in the header files `float.h`, `limits.h`, `stdarg.h`, and `stddef.h`. (Chapter 10 lists the contents of these header files.) This kind of conformance is meant to accommodate C implementations for embedded systems or other target environments with minimal run-time support (for example, no file system).

A *conforming* program is one that is accepted by a conforming implementation. Thus, a conforming program can depend on some nonportable, implementation-defined features of a conforming implementation, whereas a strictly conforming program cannot depend on those features (and so is maximally portable).

Conforming implementations may provide extensions that do not change the meaning of any strictly conforming program. This allows implementations to add library routines and define their own #pragma directives, but not to introduce new reserved identifiers or change the operation of standard library functions.

Compiler vendors continue to provide non-conforming extensions that their customers have grown used to. Compilers enable (or disable) these extensions with special switches.

1.3 AN OVERVIEW OF C PROGRAMMING

A C *program* is composed of one or more *source files*, or *translation units*, each of which contains some part of the entire C program—typically some number of external functions. Common declarations are often collected into *header files* and are included into the source files with a special command (section 3.4). One external function must be named main (section 20.1); by convention this will be the first function executed.

A C compiler independently processes each source file and translates the C program text into instructions understood by the computer. The compiler "understands" the C program and analyzes it for correctness. If the programmer has made an error the compiler can detect, the compiler issues an error message. Otherwise, the output of the compiler is usually called *object code* or an *object module*.

When all source files are compiled, the object modules are given to a program called the *linker*. The linker resolves references between the modules, adds functions from the standard run-time library, and detects some programming errors such as the failure to define a needed function. The linker is typically not specific to C; each computer system has a standard linker that is used for programs written in many different languages. The linker produces a single executable program, which can then be invoked, or "run."

Although most computer systems go through these steps, they may appear different to the programmer. For instance, suppose a program to be named prog consists of the two C source files proga.c and progb.c. (The ".c" in the file names is a common convention for C source files.) The file proga.c might contain these lines:

```
void hello()
{
    printf("Hello!\n");
}
```

The header file for proga.c, named proga.h (also by convention), contains:

```
extern void hello();
```

File `progb.c` contains the main program, which simply calls function `hello`:

```
#include "proga.h"
main()
{
    hello();
}
```

On a UNIX system, compiling, linking, and executing the program takes only two steps:

```
% cc -o prog proga.c progb.c
% prog
```

The first line compiles and links the two source files, adds any standard library functions needed, and writes the executable program to file `prog`. The second line then executes the program, which prints:

```
Hello!
```

With Microsoft C on an IBM PC, the sequence might be:

```
C:> CL PROGA.C PROGB.C
C:> PROGA
Hello!
```

In this book we are not concerned with the details of building C programs; readers should consult their own computer system and C compiler documentation.

1.4 SYNTAX NOTATION

When specifying the C language syntax, terminal symbols are printed in fixed type and are to appear in the program exactly as written. Nonterminal symbols are printed in italic type; they are spelled beginning with a letter and can be followed by zero or more letters, digits, or hyphens:

expression   argument-list   declarator

Syntactic definitions are introduced by the name of the nonterminal being defined followed by a colon. One or more alternatives then follow on succeeding lines:

character :

> *printing-character*
> *escape-character*

When the words "one of" follow the colon, this signifies that each of the terminal symbols following on one or more lines is an alternative definition:

digit : one of

> 0   1   2   3   4   5   6   7   8   9

Optional components of a definition are signified by appending the suffix *opt* to a terminal or nonterminal symbol:

enumeration-constant-definition :

> *enumeration-constant enumeration-initializer*$_{opt}$

initializer :

> *expression*
> {   *initializer-list* , $_{opt}$ }

2

Lexical Elements

This chapter describes the lexical structure of the C language; that is, the characters that may appear in a C source file and how they are collected into lexical units, or tokens.

2.1 CHARACTER SET

A C source file is a sequence of characters selected from a character set. A C compiler may use any character set as long as it includes at least the following standard characters:

1. the 52 uppercase and lowercase alphabetic characters:

    ```
    A B C D E F G H I J K L M N O P Q R S T
    U V W X Y Z a b c d e f g h i j k l m
    n o p q r s t u v w x y z
    ```

2. the 10 decimal digits:

    ```
    0 1 2 3 4 5 6 7 8 9
    ```

3. the blank or space character

4. the 29 graphic characters shown in the table on the next page.

Graphic characters

Char	Name	Char	Name	Char	Name
!	exclamation pt.	+	plus	"	double quote
#	number sign	=	equal	{	left brace
%	percent	~	tilde	}	right brace
^	circumflex	[	left bracket	,	comma
&	ampersand	]	right bracket	.	period
*	asterisk	\	backslash	<	less than
(	left parenthesis	|	vertical bar	>	greater than
)	right parenthesis	;	semicolon	/	slash
–	hyphen or minus	:	colon	?	question mark
_	underscore	'	apostrophe		

There must also be some way of dividing the source program into lines; this can be done with a character or character sequence or with some mechanism outside the source character set (for example, an end-of-record indication).

Additional characters are sometimes used in C source programs, including:

1. the five formatting characters corresponding to the ASCII characters backspace (BS), horizontal tab (HT), vertical tab (VT), form feed (FF), and carriage return (CR).
2. extra graphic characters not needed in the standard character set, including the characters $ (dollar sign), @ (at-sign), and ` (accent grave).

The formatting characters are treated as spaces and do not otherwise affect the source program. The extra graphic characters may appear only in comments, character constants, and string constants.

As will be seen from the previous discussion, C has a much larger source character set than do most other programming languages. ANSI C has defined a set of trigraphs to allow C programs to be written in a restricted character set.

References   trigraphs in ANSI C 2.1.4; character constants 2.7.3; comments 2.2; character encodings 2.1.3; character escape codes 2.7.6; string constants 2.7.4; target character set 2.1.1

2.1.1 Execution Character Set

The character set interpreted during the execution of a C program is not necessarily the same as the one in which the C program is written. Characters in the execution character set are represented by their equivalents in the source character set or by special character escape sequences that begin with the backslash \ character.

In addition to the standard characters mentioned above, the execution character set must also include:

1. a null character that must be encoded as the value 0
2. a newline character that is used as the end-of-line marker

The null character is used to mark the end of strings; the newline character is used to divide character streams into lines during input/output. (It must appear to the programmer as if this newline character were actually present in text streams in the execution environment. However, the run-time library implementation is free to simulate them. For instance, newlines could be converted to end-of-record indications on output, and end-of-record indications could be turned into newlines on input.)

As with the source character set, it is common for the execution character set to include the formatting characters backspace, horizontal tab, vertical tab, form feed, and carriage return. Special escape sequences are provided to represent these characters in the source program.

These source and execution character sets are the same when a C program is compiled and executed on the same computer. However, occasionally programs are cross-compiled; that is, compiled on one computer (the host) and executed on another computer (the target). When a compiler calculates the compile-time value of a constant expression involving characters, it must use the target computer's encodings, not the more natural (to the compiler writer) source encodings.

References   character constants 2.7.3; character encodings 2.1.3; constant expressions 7.11; escape characters 2.7.5; standard characters 2.1; text streams Ch. 15

2.1.2 Whitespace and Line Termination

In C source programs the blank (space), end-of-line, vertical tab, form feed, and horizontal tab (if present) are known collectively as whitespace characters. (Comments, discussed below, are also whitespace.) These characters are ignored except insofar as they are used to separate adjacent tokens or when they appear in character or string constants. Whitespace characters may be used to lay out the C program in a way that is pleasing to a human reader.

The end-of-line character or character sequence marks the end of source program lines. In some implementations, the formatting characters carriage return, form feed, and (or) vertical tab additionally terminate source lines and are called line break characters. Line termination is important for the recognition of preprocessor control lines. The character following a line break character is considered to be the first character of the next line. If the first character is itself a line break character, then another (empty) line is terminated, and so forth.

A source line can be continued onto the next line by ending the first line with a backslash (\) character or with the ANSI C trigraph ??/. The backslash and end-of-line marker are removed to create a longer, *logical source line*. This convention has always been valid in preprocessor command lines and within string constants, where it is most useful and portable. ANSI C, and many non-ANSI implementations, generalize it to apply to any source program line. This splicing of source lines conceptually occurs before preprocessing and before the lexical analysis of the C program, so that even tokens may be split across lines:

```
if (a==b) x=1; el\
se x=2;
```

If an implementation treats any nonstandard source characters as whitespace or line breaks, it should handle them exactly as it does blanks and end-of-line markers, respectively. ANSI C suggests that an implementation do this by translating all such characters to some canonical representation as the first action when reading the source program. However, programmers should probably beware of relying on this by, for example, expecting a backslash followed by a form feed to be eliminated.

Most C implementations impose a limit on the maximum length of source lines both before and after splicing continuation lines. ANSI C requires implementations to permit logical source lines of at least 509 characters.

References   character constants 2.7.3; preprocessor lexical conventions 3.2; string constants 2.7.4; tokens 2.3; trigraphs 2.1.4

2.1.3 Character Encodings

Each character in a computer's (execution) character set will have some conventional encoding; that is, some numerical representation on the computer. This encoding is important because C converts characters to integers, and the values of the integers are the conventional encodings of the characters. All of the standard characters listed earlier must have distinct, nonnegative integer encodings.

A common C programming error is to assume a particular encoding is in use when, in fact, another one holds. For example, the C expression `'Z'-'A'+1` computes one more than the difference between the encodings of Z and A and might be expected to yield the number of characters in the alphabet. Indeed, under the ASCII character set encodings the result is 26, but under the EBCDIC encodings, in which the alphabet is not encoded consecutively, the result is 41.

References   source and target character sets 2.1.1

2.1.4 Trigraphs

A set of trigraphs is included in ANSI C so that C programs may be written using only the ISO 646-1083 Invariant Code Set, a subset of the seven-bit ASCII code set. The trigraphs, introduced by two consecutive question mark characters, are listed in the table below. (Trigraphs are not customary in non-ANSI compilers.)

ANSI Trigraphs

Trigraph	Replaces	Trigraph	Replaces
??(	[	??)	]
??<	{	??>	}
??/	\	??!	|
??'	^	??-	~
??=	#		

The translation of trigraphs in the source program occurs before lexical analysis (tokenization) and before the recognition of escape characters in string and character constants. Only these exact nine trigraphs are recognized; all other character sequences (e.g., ??&) are left untranslated. A new character escape, \?, is available to prevent the interpretation of trigraph-like character sequences. Two examples are shown in the table below. In the first example, a backslash is used to prevent the interpretation of ??! as a trigraph. In the second example, two backslashes are supplied so that one appears in the output string, according to the escape character convention.

Trigraph examples

Traditional C string	Trigraph form	Result
`"What??!"`	`"What?\?!"`	`What??!`
`"Backslash: \\"`	`"Backslash: ??/??/"`	`Backslash: \`

References   character sets 2.1; escape characters 2.7.5; string concatenation 2.7.4

2.1.5 Multibyte Characters

In order to accommodate foreign alphabets that may contain a very large number of characters, ANSI C introduces wide characters and multibyte characters. A *wide character* is a binary representation of an element of a large character set. It has the integer type `wchar_t` in header file `stddef.h`.

A *multibyte character* is the external representation of a wide character in either the source or execution character set. It has the form of a normal C character string. The mapping between external, multibyte characters and internal, wide characters is implementation-defined and can be different in the source and execution character sets.

A wide character string (i.e., a sequence of wide characters) can be represented externally by a multibyte character string (i.e., a sequence of multibyte characters). Multibyte characters may appear in comments, string constants, and character constants.

For example, if a `write_foreign` function expected a multibyte character string, a call to it might look like this:

```
write_foreign("\033\111ZBC\001");
```

The string literal contains a hypothetical multibyte encoding of Japanese characters. The `\033` and `\0111` codes might "shift" the interpreter into the proper state for interpreting the characters `ZBC`, and the code `\001` might restore the shift state to its default value.

The ANSI C language has extensions to allow the explicit specification of wide character constants and strings, and the run-time library has facilities for translating between wide and multibyte characters.

References   character constant 2.7.3; comments 2.2; multibyte conversion facilities 11.7, 11.8; string constants 2.7.4; wide character 2.7.3; wide string 2.7.4

2.2 COMMENTS

A comment in a C program begins with an occurrence of the two characters /* not within a character or string constant and ends with the first subsequent occurrence of the two characters */. Comments may contain any number of characters and are always treated as whitespace. For example, the following program contains six legal C comments:

```
/********************************************/
/*/ Program to compute the squares of    /*/
/*/ the first 10 integers                /*/
/********************************************/
void Squares()   /* no arguments */
{
    int i;
    /*
        Loop from 1 to 10,
        printing out the squares
    */
    for (i=1; i<=10; i++)
        printf("%d squared is %d\n",i,i*i);
}
```

Comments are removed by the compiler before preprocessing or lexical analysis, so line breaks inside comments do not terminate preprocessor commands. For example, the two #define commands below have the same effect:

```
#define ten (2*5)

#define ten /* ten:
               one greater than nine
            */ (2*5)
```

ANSI C specifies that all comments are to be replaced by a single space character for the purposes of further translation of the C program, but many current implementations do not insert any white space. This affects the behavior of the preprocessor and is discussed in section 3.3.9.

A few non-UNIX C implementations implement "nestable comments," in which each occurrence of /* inside a comment must be balanced by a subsequent */. This implementation is not standard, and programmers should not depend on it. For a program to be acceptable to both implementations of comments, no comment should contain the character sequence /* inside it.

To cause the compiler to ignore large parts of a C program, it is best to enclose the parts to be removed with the preprocessor commands

```
#if 0
...
#endif
```

rather than to insert comment delimiters. This avoids having to worry about comments in the enclosed source text (unless the comments span the preprocessor commands).

References `#if` preprocessor command 3.5.1; preprocessor lexical conventions 3.2; whitespace 2.1

2.3 TOKENS

The characters making up a C program are collected into lexical tokens according to the rules presented in the rest of this chapter. There are five classes of tokens: operators, separators, identifiers, reserved words, and constants.

The compiler always forms the longest tokens possible as it collects characters in left-to-right order, even if the result does not make a legal C program. Some examples of tokenization are listed in the table below.

Token parsing

Characters	C Tokens
`forwhile`	`forwhile`
`b>x`	`b, >, x`
`b->x`	`b, ->, x`
`b--x`	`b, --, x` [1]
`b---x`	`b, --, -, x`

[1] Even though this is illegal but **b, -, -, x** is not.

Adjacent tokens may be separated by whitespace characters or comments. To prevent confusion, an identifier, reserved word, integer constant, or floating-point constant must always be so separated from a following identifier, reserved word, integer constant, or floating-point constant. (In a macro body, separating tokens with comments rather than whitespace characters may cause "token merging.")

References comments 2.2; constants 2.7; identifiers 2.5; reserved words 2.6; token merging 3.3.9; whitespace characters 2.1

2.4 OPERATORS AND SEPARATORS

The operator and separator tokens in C are usefully divided into several groups, as shown in the table below.

Operators and separators

Token class	Tokens
Simple operators	! % ^ & * − + = ~ | . < > / ?
Compound assignment operators	+= −= *= /= %= <<= >>= &= ^= |=
Other compound operators	−> ++ −− << >> <= >= == != && ||
Other separator characters	( ) [ ] { } , ; :

In traditional C, the compound assignment operators are considered to be two separate tokens (the operator and =), and so can be separated by whitespace. In ANSI C the operators are single tokens, and it is better programming style to write them that way.

References compound assignment operators 7.9.2

2.5 IDENTIFIERS

An identifier, also called a *name* in C, is a sequence of letters, digits, and underscores. An identifier must not begin with a digit, and it must not have the same spelling as a reserved word:

identifier :
>>> *underscore*
>>> *letter*
>>> *identifier following-character*

following-character :
>>> *letter*
>>> *underscore*
>>> *digit*

letter : one of
>>> A B C D E F G H I J K L M
>>> N O P Q R S T U V W X Y Z
>>> a b c d e f g h i j k l m
>>> n o p q r s t u v w x y z

underscore :

>>> _

digit : one of
>>> 0 1 2 3 4 5 6 7 8 9

Two identifiers are the same when they are spelled identically, including the case of all letters. That is, the identifiers abc and aBc are distinct.

In addition to avoiding the spelling of the reserved words, a C programmer must guard against inadvertently duplicating a name used in the standard libraries. ANSI C specifically reserves these identifiers for their indicated uses, and further reserves for implementations all names beginning with an underscore; programmers should avoid creating such identifiers.

The original description of C specified that two identifiers spelled identically up to the first eight characters would be considered the same even if they differed in subsequent characters. For example, the identifiers countless and countlessone would be considered the same identifier. ANSI C requires implementations to permit a minimum of 31 significant characters in identifiers, and this limit is met or exceeded by many current C implementations. Longer names tend to improve program clarity and thus reduce errors. The use of underscores and mixed letter case make long identifiers more readable:

```
averylongidentifer
AVeryLongIdentifier
a_very_long_identifier
```

An external identifier—one declared with storage class extern—may be subject to additional restrictions on particular computer systems. These identifiers have to be processed by other software, such as debuggers and linkers, which may have more restrictive limits on identifiers. For maximum portability, keep external identifiers no more than six characters long and do not depend on case sensitivity.

When a C compiler permits long internal identifiers but the target computer requires short external names, the preprocessor may be used to hide these short names. In the example below, an external error-handling function has the short and somewhat obscure name eh73, but the function is referred to by the more readable name error_handler. This is done by making error_handler a preprocessor macro that expands to the name eh73.

```
#define error_handler eh73
extern void error_handler();
...
error_handler("nil pointer error");
```

Some compilers permit characters other than those specified above to be used in identifiers. The dollar sign ($) is often allowed in identifiers so that programs can access special non-C library functions provided by some computing systems.

References #define (preprocessor macros) 3.3; external names 4.2.9; extern storage class 4.3; reserved words 2.6

2.6 RESERVED WORDS

The following identifiers have been reserved in various versions of the C language and must not be used as program identifiers when they are reserved. Some C implementations have additional reserved words, but this is not permitted in ANSI conforming implementations, because it could cause an ANSI-conforming program to become invalid.

C Reserved Words

asm[1]	default	float	register	switch
auto	do	for	return	typedef
break	double	fortran[1]	short	union
case	else	goto	signed[3]	unsigned
char	entry[1]	if	sizeof	void[2]
const[3]	enum[2]	int	static	volatile[3]
continue	extern	long	struct	while

[1] Traditionally reserved, but omitted from ANSI C.
[2] In most modern compilers, and ANSI C.
[3] New to ANSI C.

A reserved word may be used as a preprocessor macro name, although doing so is usually poor style. As an example of a reasonable use, the following macro definition could be appropriate when a non-ANSI C compiler does not implement the void type:

```
#define void int
```

References   #define (preprocessor macros) 3.3; identifiers 2.5; void type specifier 5.9

2.7 CONSTANTS

The lexical class of constants includes four different kinds of constants: integers, floating-point numbers, characters, and strings:

> *constant* :
>> *integer-constant*
>> *floating-point-constant*
>> *character-constant*
>> *string-constant*

Such tokens are called literals in other languages, to distinguish them from objects whose values are constant (that is, not changing) but that do not belong to lexically distinct classes. An example of these latter objects in C is enumeration constants, which belong to the lexical class of identifiers. In this book, we use the traditional C terminology of "constant" for both cases.

Every constant is characterized by a value and a type. The formats of the various kinds of constants are described in the following sections.

References   character constant 2.7.3; enumeration constants 5.5; floating-point constant 2.7.2; integer constant 2.7.1; string constant 2.7.4; tokens 2.3; value 7.3

2.7.1 Integer Constants

Integer constants may be specified in decimal, octal, or hexadecimal notation:

> *integer-constant* :
>> *decimal-constant*   *integer-suffix*$_{opt}$
>> *octal-constant*   *integer-suffix*$_{opt}$
>> *hexadecimal-constant*   *integer-suffix*$_{opt}$
>
> *decimal-constant* :
>> *nonzero-digit*
>> *decimal-constant* *digit*
>
> *octal-constant* :
>> `0`
>> *octal-constant* *octal-digit*
>
> *hexadecimal-constant* :
>> `0`x *hex-digit*
>> `0`X *hex-digit*
>> *hexadecimal-constant*   *hex-digit*
>
> *digit* : one of
>> `0  1  2  3  4  5  6  7  8  9`
>
> *nonzero-digit* : one of
>> `1  2  3  4  5  6  7  8  9`
>
> *octal-digit* : one of
>> `0  1  2  3  4  5  6  7`
>
> *hex-digit* : one of
>> `0  1  2  3  4  5  6  7  8  9`
>> `A  B  C  D  E  F  a  b  c  d  e  f`
>
> *integer-suffix* :
>> *long-suffix* *unsigned-suffix*$_{opt}$
>> *unsigned-suffix* *long-suffix*$_{opt}$
>
> *long-suffix* : one of
>> `l  L`
>
> *unsigned-suffix* : one of   (ANSI C)
>> `u  U`

These are the rules for determining the radix of an integer constant:

1. If the integer constant begins with the letters 0x or 0X, then it is in hexadecimal notation, with the characters a through f (or A through F) representing 10 through 15.
2. Otherwise, if it begins with the digit 0, then it is in octal notation.
3. Otherwise, it is in decimal notation.

An integer constant may be immediately followed by the one of the letters l or L to indicate a constant of type long. (The lower case letter l can be easily confused with the digit 1 and should be avoided.) ANSI C also permits the suffix letters u or U to indicate an unsigned constant. Originally, C also allowed the digits 8 and 9 in octal constants, but they have been eliminated in ANSI C.

The type of an integer constant depends on its size, on its radix, on whether a suffix letter is present, and on type representation decisions made by the particular C implementation. Furthermore, the rules for determining the type are different in ANSI C. Both the traditional and new rules are shown in the table below.

Types of integer constants

Constant	Conventional type[1]	ANSI C type[1]
dd...d	int long int	int long int unsigned long int
0*dd...d* 0X*dd...d*	unsigned int long int	int unsigned int long int unsigned long int
*dd...d*U 0*dd...d*U 0X*dd...d*U	*not applicable*	unsigned int unsigned long int
*dd...d*L 0*dd...d*L 0X*dd...d*L	long int	long int unsigned long int
*dd...d*UL 0*dd...d*UL 0X*dd...d*UL	*not applicable*	unsigned long int

[1]   The chosen type is the first one from the appropriate group that can represent the value of the constant without overflow.

The value of an integer constant is always nonnegative in the absence of overflow. If there is a preceding minus sign, it is taken to be a unary operator applied to the constant, not part of the constant itself.

The ANSI C rules differ subtly from those found in most current implementations: under the new rules constants without suffixes may have an unsigned type and therefore force expressions to use unsigned arithmetic. If type `long` has a 32-bit, two's-complement representation, the following program determines the rules in effect:

```
#define K 0xFFFFFFFF /* -1 in 32-bit, 2's compl. */
int main()
{
    if (0<K) printf("K is unsigned (ANSI C)\n");
    else printf("K is signed (traditional C)\n");
    return 0;
}
```

To illustrate some of the subtleties of integer constants, assume that in some implementation type `int` uses a 16-bit two's-complement representation, and that type `long` uses a 32-bit two's-complement representation. We list in table 2–1 some interesting integer constants, their true mathematical values, their types—conventional and under the ANSI rules—and the actual C representation used to store the constant.

Table 2–1: Assignment of types to integer constants

C constant notation	True value	Conventional type	ANSI C type	Actual representation
0	0	int	unsigned	0
32767	$2^{15}-1$	int	int	0x7FFF
077777	$2^{15}-1$	int	int	0x7FFF
32768	2^{15}	long int	long int	0x00008000
0100000	2^{15}	int[1]	unsigned int	0x8000
65535	$2^{16}-1$	long int	long int	0x0000FFFF
0xFFFF	$2^{16}-1$	int[1]	unsigned int	0xFFFF
65536	2^{16}	long int	long int	0x0001FFFF
0x10000	2^{16}	long int	long int	0x0001FFFF
2147483647	$2^{31}-1$	long int	long int	0x7FFFFFFF
0x7FFFFFFF	$2^{31}-1$	long int	long int	0x7FFFFFFF
2147483648	2^{31}	long int[1]	unsigned long int	0x80000000
0x80000000	2^{31}	long int	unsigned long int	0x80000000
4294967295	$2^{32}-1$	long int[1]	unsigned long int	0xFFFFFFFF[1]
0xFFFFFFFF	$2^{32}-1$	long int[1]	unsigned long int	0xFFFFFFFF
4294967296[2]	2^{32}	*undefined*	*undefined*	0
0x100000000[2]	2^{32}	*undefined*	*undefined*	0

[1] This type cannot represent the value, causing overflow.
[2] These values are outside the representation capability of the implementation, which need not allow them in a program.

If the value of a decimal constant exceeds the largest integer representable in type `long`, or if the value of an octal or hexadecimal constant exceeds the largest integer representable in type `unsigned long`, the result is undefined. Many C compilers will silently substitute another value for the constant.   In ANSI C, integer type representational information is provided in the header file `limits.h`.

An interesting point to note from this table is that integers in the range 2^{15} through $2^{16}-1$ will have positive values when written as decimal constants but negative values when written as octal or hexadecimal constants (and cast to type `int`). In spite of these anomalies, the programmer will rarely be "surprised" by the values of integer constants because the representation of the constants is the same even though the type is in question.

References   conversions of integer types 6.2.3; integer types 5.1; `limits.h` 5.1.1; overflow 7.2.2; unary minus operator 7.5.3; unsigned integers 5.1.2

2.7.2 Floating-point Constants

Floating-point constants may be written with a decimal point, a signed exponent, or both. A floating-point constant is always interpreted to be in decimal radix. ANSI C allows a suffix letter (*floating-suffix*) to designate constants of types `float` and `long double`. Without a suffix the type of the constant is `double`:

> *floating-constant* :
>> *digit-sequence   exponent   floating-suffix*$_{opt}$
>> *dotted-digits   exponent*$_{opt}$ *floating-suffix*$_{opt}$

> *floating-suffix* : one of   (ANSI only)
>> f   F   l   L

> *exponent* :
>> e *sign-part*$_{opt}$ *digit-sequence*
>> E *sign-part*$_{opt}$ *digit-sequence*

> *sign-part* : one of
>> +   −

> *dotted-digits* :
>> *digit-sequence*   .
>> *digit-sequence*   .   *digit-sequence*
>> . *digit-sequence*

> *digit-sequence* :
>> *digit*
>> *digit digit-sequence*

> *digit* : one of
>> 0 1 2 3 4 5 6 7 8 9

The value of a floating-point constant is always nonnegative in the absence of overflow. If there is a preceding minus sign, it is taken to be a unary operator applied to the constant, not part of the constant itself. If the magnitude of the floating-point constant is too great or too small to be represented, the result is unpredictable. Some compilers will warn the programmer of the problem, but most will silently substitute some other value that can be represented. In ANSI C the floating-point limits are recorded in the header file float.h.

Examples of floating-point constants are shown in the table below.

Floating-point constants		
0.	3e1	3.14159
.0	1.0E-3	1e-3
1.0	.00034	2e+9
1.0f[1]	1.0e67L[1]	0E1L[1]

[1] ANSI C only.

References   double type 5.2; float.h 5.2; overflow and underflow 7.2.2; sizes of floating-point types 5.2; unary minus operator 7.5.3

2.7.3 Character Constants

A character constant is written by enclosing one or more characters in apostrophes. A special escape mechanism is provided to write characters or numeric values that would be inconvenient or impossible to enter directly in the source program. ANSI C allows the character constant to be preceded by the letter L to specify a wide character constant:

character-constant :
         ' *c-char-sequence* '
       L' *c-char-sequence* '   (ANSI C)

c-char-sequence :
         c-char
         c-char-sequence c-char

c-char :
               any source character except the apostrophe ',
                  backslash \, or newline character
               escape-character

The apostrophe, backslash, and newline characters may be included in character constants by using escape characters, as described in section 2.7.5. It is a good idea to use escapes for any character that might not be easily readable in the source program, such as the formatting characters. Character constants containing more than a single character or escape are called multibyte characters.

Character constants not preceded by the letter L have type int. It is typical for such a character constant to be a single character or escape code (section 2.7.7), and the value of the constant is the integer encoding of the corresponding character in the target character set or the value of the numeric escape code. The resulting integer value is computed as if it had been converted from an object of type char. For example, if type char were implemented as an 8-bit signed type, the character constant '\377' would undergo sign extension and thus have the value −1. The value of a character constant is implementation defined if:

1. there is no corresponding character in the target character set
2. more than a single character appears in the constant
3. if a numeric escape has a value not represented in the target character set

Below are some examples of single-character constants along with their (decimal) values under the ASCII encodings.

Examples of character constants

Character	Value	Character	Value	Character	Value
`'a'`	97	`'A'`	65	`'%'`	37
`' '`	32	`'?'`	63	`'8'`	56
`'\r'`	13	`'\0'`	0	`'\23'`	19
`'"'`	34	`'\377'`	255	`'\\'`	92

ANSI C wide character constants, designated by the prefix letter L, have type `wchar_t`, an integral type defined in the ANSI C header file `stddef.h`. Their purpose is to allow C programmers to express characters in alphabets (e.g., Japanese) that are too large to be represented by type `char`. Wide character constants typically consist of a sequence of characters and escape codes that together form a single multibyte character. The value of a wide character constant is implementation-defined if it contains more than a single multibyte character. If multibyte characters uses a shift-state encoding, the character constant must begin and end in the initial shift state.

Some C implementations permit character constants that contain more than a single character. (ANSI permits this implementation-defined behavior.) Since most computers represent integers in a storage area big enough to hold several characters, character constants such as `'ABCD'` can be a convenient way to specify a complete integer. The use of this feature, if available, can result in portability problems, not only because integers have different sizes on different computers but also because computers differ in their "byte ordering," that is, the order in which characters are packed into words. For example, the figure below shows the difference in the value produced by left-to-right packing and right-to-left packing:

'ABCD': left-to-right packing   'ABCD': right-to-left packing

`'A'`	`'B'`	`'C'`	`'D'`
0x41	0x42	0x43	0x44

`'D'`	`'C'`	`'B'`	`'A'`
0x44	0x43	0x42	0x41

Integer value: 0x41424344   Integer value: 0x44434241

References ASCII characters App. A; byte order 6.1.2; character encodings 2.1; `char` type 5.1.3; escape characters 2.7.5; formatting characters 2.1; multibyte characters 2.1.5; wchar_t 11.1

2.7.4 String Constants

A string constant is a (possibly empty) sequence of characters enclosed in double quotes. The same escape mechanism provided for character constants can be used to express the characters in the string:

string-constant :
        " *s-char-sequence*$_{opt}$ "
        L" *s-char-sequence*$_{opt}$ "   (ANSI C)

s-char-sequence :
        s-char
        s-char-sequence *s-char*

s-char :
        any source character except the double quote ",
           backslash \, or newline character
        escape-character

The double quote, backslash, and newline characters may be included in character constants by using escape characters, as described in section 2.7.5. It is a good idea to use escapes for any character that might not be easily readable in the source program, such as the formatting characters. Some examples of string constants are shown below.

Examples of string constants
```
""
"\""
"Total expenditures: "
"Copyright 1982 Tartan Laboratories Incorporated.\
All rights reserved."
"Comments begin with '/*'.\n"
```

For each string constant of *n* characters (not prefixed by the letter L) there will be at run time a statically allocated block of *n*+1 characters whose first *n* characters are initialized with the characters from the string and whose last character is the null character, `'\0'`. This block is the "value" of the character constant, and its type is "char [*n*+1]." For example, the value of `sizeof("abcdef")` is 7, not 6. (Use `strlen`, section 13.4, to find a string's length.)

If a string constant appears anywhere except as an argument to `sizeof` or as an initializer of a character array, the conversions that are usually applied to arrays come into play, and these conversions change the string from an array of characters to a pointer to the first character in the string, which has type "char *" or "pointer to char." Therefore string constants can and do appear in contexts that require character pointers, such as this declaration, which initializes a character pointer p with the address (0xF8A0) of the block in memory containing the string constant:

Note that the value of a single-character string constant and the value of a character constant are quite different. The former is a memory address and the latter is the integer representation of the character:

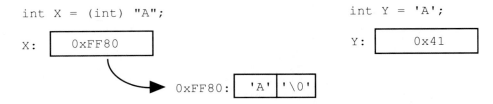

A string constant prefixed by the letter `L` is an ANSI C wide string constant and is of type "array of `wchar_t`." Its contents designate a sequence of characters from an extended target character set, such as might be used for a language like Japanese. The wide string is expressed in the source language as a sequence of multibyte characters in an implementation-defined manner. If multibyte characters use a shift-state encoding, the wide string constant must start and end in the initial shift state.

Portability There are two ways in which existing C programs may be affected by the ANSI C rules for string constants. First, ANSI C allows implementations to place string constants in regions of memory that are protected against modification. It is known that some UNIX library routines (e.g., `mktemp`) modify their string arguments—which are often string constants—and in this way some C programs implicitly require string constants to be in writable memory. However, when a pointer to a writable string must be used, it is better style and more portable to initialize an array of characters than to establish a pointer to a string constant:

```
char p1[] = "abcdef"; /* p1[i] is always writable */
char *p2 = "ghijkl";   /* p2[i] may not be writable */
```

Second, ANSI C allows implementations to use the same storage for two strings that contain the same characters. C implementations traditionally have allocated a distinct block of storage for every string constant.

Here is a simple program that discriminates the various implementations of strings:

```
char *string1, *string2;
int main() {
    string1 = "abcd";
    string2 = "abcd";
    if (string1==string2)
        printf("Strings are shared.\n");
    else
        printf("Strings are not shared.\n");
    /* The following statement may cause a runtime error
       if string constants are not writable. */
    string1[0] = '1';
    if (*string1=='1')
        printf("Strings writable\n");
    else
        printf("Strings not writable\n");
    return 0;
}
```

In ANSI C the programmer can specify strings that are not to be writable by storing them in arrays of type "const char []":

```
const char die_message[] = "?Internal Error\n";
```

Continuation   A string constant is normally written on one source program line. If a string is too long to fit conveniently on one line, all but the final source lines containing the string can be ended with a backslash \ character, in which case the backslash and end-of-line character(s) are ignored. This allows string constants to be written on more than one line. (Some implementations also remove leading whitespace characters from the continuation line, although it is incorrect to do so.)

ANSI C automatically concatenates adjacent string constants and adjacent wide string constants, placing a single null character at the end of the last string. Therefore, an alternative to using the \ continuation mechanism in ANSI C programs is to break a long string into separate strings. A wide string constant and a normal string constant cannot be concatenated in this way. Here are examples of the two forms of continuation:

```
char s1[] =
    "This long string is acc\
eptable to all C compilers.";
char s2[] =
    "This long string is permissible "
    "in ANSI C."
```

A newline character (i.e., the end of line in the execution character set) may be inserted into a string by putting the escape sequence \n in the string constant; this should not be confused with line continuation within a string constant.

References   array types 5.4; const type specifier 4.4.4; versions from array types 6.2.7; escape characters 2.7.5; initializers 4.6; mktemp facility 15.16; multibyte characters 2.1.5; pointer types 5.3; preprocessor lexical conventions 3.2; sizeof operator 7.5.2; whitespace characters 2.1; usual unary conversions 6.3.3; `wchar_t` 11.1

2.7.5 Escape Characters

Escape characters can be used in character and string constants to represent characters that would be awkward or impossible to enter in the source program directly. The escape characters come in two varieties: "character escapes," which can be used to represent some particular formatting and special characters, and "numeric escapes," which allow a character to be specified by its numeric encoding:

    escape-character :
        \ *escape-code*

    escape-code :
        character-escape-code
        octal-escape-code
        hex-escape-code   (ANSI C)

    character-escape-code : one of
        `n  t  b  r  f`
        `v  \  '  "`
        `a  ?`   (ANSI C)

    octal-escape-code :
        octal-digit
        octal-digit   octal-digit
        octal-digit octal-digit octal-digit

    hex-escape-code :
        x *hex-digit*
        hex-escape-code hex-digit   (ANSI C)

The meanings of these escapes are discussed in the following sections.

If the character following the backslash is neither an octal digit, the letter x, nor one of the character escape codes listed above, the result is undefined. Traditionally, the the backslash is ignored; in ANSI C the lowercase letters are reserved for future language features and the uppercase letters are reserved for implementation-specific extensions.

2.7.6 Character Escape Codes

Character escape codes are used to represent some common special characters in a fashion that is independent of the target computer character set. The characters that may follow the backslash, and their meanings, are listed below.

Character escape codes

Escape code	Translation	Escape code	Translation
a[1]	alert (e.g., bell)	v	vertical tab
b	backspace	\	backslash
f	form feed	'	single quote
n	newline	"	double quote
r	carriage return	?[1]	question mark
t	horizontal tab		

[1] ANSI C addition.

The code \a is typically mapped to a "bell" or other audible signal on the output device (ASCII control-G). The \? escape is needed to obtain a question mark character in the rare circumstances in which it might be mistaken as part of a trigraph.

The quotation mark, ", may appear without a preceding \ in character constants and the apostrophe, ', may appear without \ in string constants.

To show how the character escapes can be used, here is a small program that counts the number of lines (actually, the number of newline characters) in the input. The function getchar returns the next input character until the end of the input is reached, at which point getchar returns the value of the macro EOF defined in stdio.h:

```
#include <stdio.h>
main()        /* Count the number of lines in the input. */
{
    int next_char;
    int num_lines = 0;
    while ((next_char = getchar()) != EOF)
        if (next_char == '\n')
            ++num_lines;
    printf("%d lines read.\n",num_lines);
}
```

References   character constants 2.7.3; EOF 15.1; getchar facility 15.6; stdio.h 15.1; string constants 2.7.4; trigraphs 2.1.4

2.7.7 Numeric Escape Codes

Numeric escape codes allow any value of type unsigned char to be expressed by writing the value directly in octal or—in ANSI C—hexadecimal notation. (ANSI C prohibits values outside the range of unsigned char.) Up to three octal digits or any number of hexadecimal digits may be used to express the encoding. (The octal notation is sufficient for characters represented by up to nine bits on the target computer.) For instance, under the ASCII encodings, the character 'a' may be written as '\141' and the character '?' as '\77'. The null character, used to terminate strings, is always written as \0. The value of a numeric escape that does not correspond to a character in

the execution character set is implementation-defined. The following short code segment
illustrates the use of numeric escape codes:

```
int inchar;
...
for (;;) {
    inchar = receive();
    if (inchar == '\0') continue;        /* Ignore */
    if (inchar == '\004') break;         /* Quit */
    if (inchar == '\006') reply('\006'); /* ACK */
    else reply('\025');                  /* NAK */
    }
```

There are two reasons for the programmer to be cautious when using numeric escapes. First, of course, the use of numeric escapes may depend on character encodings
and therefore be nonportable. It is always much better to hide escape codes in macro
definitions so that they are easy to change:

```
#define NUL '\0'
#define EOT '\004'
#define ACK '\006'
#define NAK '\025'
```

Second, the syntax for numeric escapes is very delicate; an octal escape code
terminates when three octal digits have been used or when the first character that is not an
octal digit is encountered. Therefore, the string "\0111" consists of two characters,
\011 and 1, and the string "\090" consists of three characters, \0, 9, and 0.
Hexadecimal escape sequences also suffer from the termination problem, especially since
they can be of any length; to stop an ANSI C hexadecimal escape in a string, break the
string into pieces:

```
"\xabc"       /* This string contains one character. */
"\xab" "c"    /* This string contains two characters. */
```

Some non-ANSI C implementations provide hexadecimal escape sequences that, like the
octal escapes, permit only up to a fixed number of hexadecimal digits.

References   character constant 2.7.3; #define 3.3; macro definitions 3.3; null character
2.1; string constant 2.7.4; target character set 2.1

2.8 EXERCISES

1.   Which of the following are lexical tokens?
     (a)   reserved words   (e)   trigraphs
     (b)   comments   (f)   wide string constants
     (c)   whitespace   (g)   parentheses
     (d)   hexadecimal constants

2.   Assume the following strings of source characters were processed by an ANSI C compiler. Which strings would be recognized as a sequence of C tokens? How many tokens would be found in each case? (Don't worry if some of the token sequences could not appear in a legal C program.)
     (a)   `X++Y`   (f)   `x**2`
     (b)   `-12uL`   (g)   `"X??/"`
     (c)   `1.37E+6L`   (h)   `B$C`
     (d)   `"String ""FOO"""`   (i)   `A*=B`
     (e)   `"String+\"FOO\""`   (j)   `while##DO`

3.   Eliminate all the comments from the following C program fragment.
     ```
     /**/*/*"*/*/*"//*//**/*/
     ```

4.   An ANSI C compiler must perform each of the following actions on an input program. In what order are the actions performed?
          collecting characters into tokens
          removing comments
          converting trigraphs
          processing line continuation

5.   Some poor choices for program identifiers are shown below. What makes them poor choices?
     (a)   `pipesendintake`   (c)   `O77U`
     (b)   `Const`   (d)   `SYS$input`

3

The C Preprocessor

The C preprocessor is a simple macro processor that conceptually processes the source text of a C program before the compiler proper reads the source program. In some implementations of C, the preprocessor is actually a separate program that reads the original source file and writes out a new "preprocessed" source file that can then be used as input to the C compiler. In other implementations, a single program performs the preprocessing and compilation in a single pass over the source file.

3.1 PREPROCESSOR COMMANDS

The preprocessor is controlled by special preprocessor command lines, which are lines of the source file beginning with the character #. Lines that do not contain preprocessor commands are called lines of source program text. The preprocessor commands are shown in table 3–1.

The preprocessor removes all preprocessor command lines from the source file and makes additional transformations on the source file as directed by the commands, such as expanding macro calls that occur within the source program text. The resulting preprocessed source text must then be a valid C program.

The syntax of preprocessor commands is completely independent of (though in some ways similar to) the syntax of the rest of the C language. For example, it is possible for a macro definition to expand into a syntactically incomplete fragment, as long as the fragment makes sense (that is, is properly completed) in all contexts in which the macro is called.

Table 3–1: Preprocessor commands

Command	Meaning	Sec.
`#define`	Define a preprocessor macro.	3.3
`#undef`	Remove a preprocessor macro definition.	3.3.5
`#include`	Insert text from another source file.	3.4
`#if`	Conditionally include some text, based on the value of a constant expression.	3.5.1
`#ifdef`	Conditionally include some text, based on whether a macro name is defined.	3.5.3
`#ifndef`	Conditionally include some text, with the sense of the test opposite that of `#ifdef`.	3.5.3
`#else`	Alternatively include some text, if the previous `#if`, `#ifdef`, `#ifndef`, or `#elif` test failed.	3.5.1
`#endif`	Terminate conditional text.	3.5.1
`#line`	Supply a line number for compiler messages.	3.6
`#elif`[1]	Alternatively include some text based on the value of another constant expression, if the previous `#if`, `#ifdef`, `#ifndef`, or `#elif` test failed.	3.5.2
`defined`[1]	Preprocessor function that yields 1 if a name is defined as a preprocessor macro and 0 otherwise; used in #if and #elif.	3.5.5
unary # operator[2]	Replace a macro parameter with a string constant containing the parameter's value.	3.3.8
binary ## operator[2]	Create a single token out of two adjacent tokens.	3.3.9
`#pragma`[2]	Specify implementation-dependent information to the compiler.	3.7
`#error`[2]	Produce a compile-time error with a designated message.	3.8

[1] Not originally part of C, but now common.
[2] New in ANSI C.

3.2 PREPROCESSOR LEXICAL CONVENTIONS

The preprocessor does not parse the source text, but it does break it up into tokens for the purpose of locating macro calls. The lexical conventions of the preprocessor are somewhat different from the compiler proper; the preprocessor recognizes the normal C tokens, and additionally recognizes as "tokens" other characters that would not be recognized as legal in C proper. This enables the preprocessor to recognize file names, the presence and absence of whitespace, and the location of end-of-line markers.

A line beginning with # is treated as a preprocessor command; the name of the command must follow the # character. ANSI C permits whitespace to precede and follow the # character on the same source line, but some older compilers do not. A line whose only non-whitespace character is a # is termed a "null directive" in ANSI C and is treated the same as a blank line. Older implementations may behave differently.

The remainder of the line following the command name may contain arguments for the command if appropriate. If a preprocessor command takes no arguments, then the remainder of the command line should be empty except perhaps for whitespace characters or comments. Many pre-ANSI compilers silently ignore all characters following the expected arguments (if any); this can lead to portability problems. The arguments to preprocessor commands are generally subject to macro replacement.

Preprocessor lines are recognized before macro expansion. Therefore, if a macro expands into something that looks like a preprocessor command, that command will not be recognized by the preprocessor in ANSI C or most other C compilers. (Unfortunately, some UNIX implementations violate this rule.) For example, the result of the following code is *not* to include the file math.h in the program being compiled:

```
/* This example doesn't work as one might think! */
#define GETMATH #include <math.h>
GETMATH
```

Instead, the expanded token sequence

```
# include < math . h >
```

is merely passed through and compiled as (erroneous) C code.

As noted in section 2.1.2, all source lines (including preprocessor command lines) can be continued by preceding the end-of-line marker by \. For example:

```
#define err(flag,msg)   if (flag) \
    printf(msg)
```

is the same as

```
#define err(flag,msg)   if (flag) printf(msg)
```

Also, if a line ends with \ the following line will never be treated as a preprocessor command line, even if its first non-whitespace character is #. In the following example, if the \ character immediately precedes the end-of-line marker, the second define command will be ignored:

```
#define BACKSLASH \
#define ASTERISK *
```

As explained in section 2.2, the preprocessor treats comments as whitespace, and line breaks within comments do not terminate preprocessor commands.

References   comments 2.2; line termination and continuation 2.1; tokens 2.3

3.3 DEFINITION AND REPLACEMENT

The #define preprocessor command causes a name (identifier) to become defined as a macro to the preprocessor. A sequence of tokens, called the body of the macro, is associated with the name. When the name of the macro is recognized in the program source text or in the arguments of certain other preprocessor commands, it is treated as a call to that macro; the name is effectively replaced by a copy of the body. If the macro is defined to accept arguments, then the actual arguments following the macro name are substituted for formal parameters in the macro body. For example, if a macro sum with two arguments is defined by

```
#define sum(x,y)   x+y
```

then the preprocessor replaces the source program line

```
result = sum(5,a*b);
```

with

```
result = 5+a*b;
```

The preprocessor does not distinguish reserved words from other identifiers, and so it is possible, in principle, to use a C reserved word as the name of a preprocessor macro, but to do so is usually bad programming practice. Macro names are never recognized within comments or string constants.

3.3.1 Simple Macro Definitions

The #define command has two forms, depending on whether or not a left parenthesis, (, immediately follows the name to be defined. The simpler form has no left parenthesis there:

```
#define name sequence-of-tokens
```

A macro defined in this manner takes no arguments. It is invoked merely by mentioning its name. When the name is encountered in the source program text or other appropriate context, the name is replaced by the body (the associated *sequence-of-tokens*).

The simple form of macro is particularly useful for introducing named constants into a program, so that a "magic number" such as the length of a table may be written in exactly one place and then referred to elsewhere by name. This makes it easier to change the number later. For example:

```
#define BLOCK_SIZE   0x100
#define TRACK_SIZE   (16*BLOCK_SIZE)
#define EOF          '\004'
#define ERRMSG       "*** Error %d: %s.\n"
```

The syntax of the `#define` command does not require an equal sign or any other special delimiter token after the name being defined. The body starts right after the name. A typical programming error is to include an extraneous equal sign:

```
/* Probably wrong: */
#define NUMBER_OF_TAPE_DRIVES = 5
```

This is a legal definition but causes the name `NUMBER_OF_TAPE_DRIVES` to be defined as "= 5" rather than as "5". If one were then to write the source program line

```
count = NUMBER_OF_TAPE_DRIVES;
```

it would be expanded to

```
count = = 5; /* Illegal. */
```

which is syntactically illegal. For similar reasons, also be careful to avoid an extraneous semicolon:

```
#define NUMBER_OF_TAPE_DRIVES 5 ;     /* Probably wrong. */
```

An important use of simple macro definitions is to isolate implementation-dependent restrictions on the names of externally defined functions and variables. An example of this appears in section 2.5.

References   compound assignment operators 7.9.2; operators and separators 2.4

3.3.2 Defining Macros with Parameters

The more complex form of macro definition declares the names of formal parameters within parentheses, separated by commas:

```
#define name(name1, name2, ..., namen) sequence-of-tokens
```

The left parenthesis must immediately follow the name of the macro with no intervening whitespace. (If whitespace separates the left parenthesis from the macro name, the definition is considered to define a macro that takes no arguments and has a body beginning with a left parenthesis.)

The names of the formal parameters must be identifiers, no two the same. There is no requirement that any of the parameter names be mentioned in the body (though normally they all will be mentioned).

A macro defined in this manner takes as many actual arguments as there are formal parameters. The macro is invoked by writing its name, a left parenthesis, then one actual argument token sequence for each formal parameter, then a right parenthesis. The actual argument token sequences are separated by commas. For example:

```
#define product(x,y)   ((x)+(y))
...
return product(a+3,b);
```

When the macro is invoked, whitespace may appear between the macro name and the left parenthesis or in the actual arguments.

A macro can have zero formal parameters:

```
#define getchar()   getc(stdin)
```

When such a macro is invoked, an empty actual argument list must be provided:

```
while ((c=getchar()) != EOF) ...
```

This kind of macro is useful to simulate a function that takes no arguments.

An actual argument token sequence may contain parentheses if they are properly nested and balanced and may contain commas if each comma appears within a set of parentheses (this restriction prevents confusion with the commas that separate the actual arguments). Parentheses and commas may also appear freely within character-constant and string-constant tokens and are not counted in the balancing of parentheses and the delimiting of actual arguments. For example, the arguments to the product macro above could be function calls:

```
int f(), g();
...
return product( f(a,b), g(a,b) );
```

Braces and subscripting brackets may also appear within macro arguments, but they cannot contain commas and do not have to balance. For example, suppose we define a macro that takes as its argument an arbitrary statement:

```
#define insert(stmt)   stmt
```

The invocation

```
insert( {a=1; b=1;} )
```

works properly, but if we change the two assignment statements to a single statement containing two assignment expressions:

```
insert( {a=1, b=1;} )
```

then the preprocessor will complain that we have too many macro arguments for insert. To fix the problem we would have to write:

```
insert( {(a=1, b=1);} )
```

Some (deficient) preprocessor implementations do not permit the actual argument token list to extend across multiple lines unless the lines to be continued end with a \.

When a complex macro call is encountered, the entire macro call is replaced, after parameter processing, by a processed copy of the body. Parameter processing proceeds as follows. Actual argument token strings are associated with the corresponding formal parameter names. A copy of the body is then made in which every occurrence of a formal parameter name is replaced by a copy of the actual argument token sequence associated with it. This copy of the body then replaces the macro call. The entire process of replacing a macro call with the processed copy of its body is called *macro expansion*; the processed copy of the body is called the *expansion* of the macro call.

As an example, consider this macro definition, which provides a convenient way to make a loop that counts from a given value up to (and including) some limit:

```
#define incr(v,l,h)    \
    for ((v) = (l); (v) <= (h); (v)++)
```

For example, to print a table of the cubes of the integers from 1 to 20, we could write

```
main()
{   int j;
    incr(j, 1, 20)
        printf("%2d %6d\n", j, j*j*j);
}
```

The call to the macro incr is expanded to produce this loop:

```
for ((j) = (1); (j) <= (20); (j)++)
```

The liberal use of parentheses ensures that complicated actual arguments will not be misinterpreted by the compiler. (See section 3.3.6.)

References   whitespace 2.1.2

3.3.3 Rescanning of Macro Expressions

Once a macro call has been expanded, the scan for macro calls resumes at the beginning of the expansion so that names of macros may be recognized within the expansion for the purpose of further macro replacement. Note that macro replacement is not performed on any part of a `#define` command, not even the body, at the time the command itself is processed and the macro name defined. Macro names are recognized within the body only after the body has been expanded for some particular macro call. Macro replacement is also not performed within the actual argument token strings of a complex macro call at the time the macro call is being scanned. Macro names are recognized within actual argument token strings only during the rescanning of the expansion, assuming that the corresponding formal parameter in fact occurred one or more times within the body (thereby causing the actual argument token string to appear one or more times in the expansion). For example, given the following definitions:

```
#define plus(x,y)    add(y,x)
#define add(x,y)    ((x)+(y))
```

The invocation of these macros is expanded as shown in the following table.

Macro expansion steps

Step	Result
1. (original)	`plus(plus(a,b),c)`
2.	`add(c,plus(a,b))`
3.	`((c)+(plus(a,b)))`
4.	`((c)+(add(b,a)))`
5. (final)	`((c)+(((b)+(a))))`

Macros appearing in their own expansion—either immediately or through some intermediate sequence of nested macro expansions—are not reexpanded in ANSI C. This permits a programmer to redefine a function in terms of its old definition. The following macro changes the definition of the square root function to handle negative arguments in a different fashion than is normal:

```
#define sqrt(x)    ((x)<0 ? sqrt(-x) : sqrt(x))
```

Older C preprocessors traditionally do not detect this recursion, and will attempt to continue the expansion until they are stopped by some system error.

3.3.4 Predefined Macros

Preprocessors for ANSI C are required to define five special macros that take no arguments. The name of each begins and ends with two underscore characters.

Predefined macros

Macro	Value
__LINE__ [1]	The line number of the current source program line, expressed as a decimal integer constant.
__FILE__ [1]	The name of the current source file, expressed as a string constant.
__DATE__	The calendar date of the translation, expressed as a string constant of the form "Mmm dd yyyy". Mmm is as produced by asctime.
__TIME__	The time of the translation, expressed as a string constant of the form "hh:mm:ss", as returned by asctime.
__STDC__	The decimal constant 1, if and only if the compiler is an ANSI conforming implementation.

[1] These macros are common in non-ANSI implementations also.

None of these predefined macros may be redefined by the programmer. The values of __TIME__ and __DATE__ must remain constant throughout the compilation. The values of the __LINE__ and __FILE__ macros are established by the implementation but are subject to alteration by the #line directive (section 3.6). They are useful in certain kinds of error messages:

```
if (n != m)
    fprintf(stderr,"Internal error: line %d, file %s\n",
        __LINE__, __FILE__ );
```

Implementations routinely define additional macros to communicate information about the environment, such as the type of computer for which the program is being compiled. For example, a compiler targeted to the DEC Vax-11 computer might predefine a macro named vax so that the programmer could write

```
#ifdef vax
    VAX-specific-code
#endif
```

Exactly which macros are defined is implementation-dependent, although UNIX implementations customarily predefine unix. Unlike the built-in macros, these macros may be undefined. ANSI C requires predefined macro names to begin with a leading underscore followed by either an uppercase letter or another underscore.

References asctime facility 20.3; fprintf 15.11; #ifdef preprocessor command 3.5.3; #if preprocessor command 3.5.1; undefining macros 3.3.5

3.3.5 Undefining and Redefining Macros

The #undef command can be used to make a name be no longer defined:

```
#undef name
```

This command causes the preprocessor to forget any macro definition of name. It is not
an error to undefine a name that is currently not defined. Once a name has been
undefined, it may then be given a completely new definition (using #define) without
error. Macro replacement is not performed within #undef commands.

The "benign" redefinition of macros is allowed in ANSI C and many other implementations. That is, a macro may be redefined if the new definition is the same, token for
token, as the existing definition. The redefinition must include whitespace in the same
locations as in the original definition, although the particular whitespace characters can
be different. In the example below, the redefinition of NULL is allowed, but neither
redefinition of FUNC is legal. (The first includes whitespace not in the original definition,
and the second changes two tokens.)

```
# define NULL 0
# define FUNC(x)  x+4
# define NULL        0   /* null pointer */
# define FUNC(x)  x + 4
# define FUNC(y)  y+4
```

We think programmers should avoid depending on benign redefinitions. It is generally
better style to have a single point of definition for all program entities, including macros.
Some older implementations of C may not allow any kind of redefinition. When the
programmer for legitimate reasons can't tell if a previous definition exists, the #ifndef
command can be used to test for an existing definition so that a redefinition can be
avoided:

```
#ifndef MAXTABLESIZE
#define MAXTABLESIZE 1000
#endif
```

This idiom is particularly useful with UNIX C and other implementations that allow
macro definitions in the command that invokes the C compiler. For example, the
following UNIX invocation of C provides an initial definition of the macro
MAXTABLESIZE as 5000. The C programmer would then check for the definition as
shown above:

```
cc -c -DMAXTABLESIZE=5000 prog.c
```

Although disallowed in ANSI C, a few preprocessor implementations handle
#define and #undef so as to maintain a stack of definitions. When a name is rede-
fined with #define, its old definition is pushed onto a stack and then the new definition
replaces the old one. When a name is undefined with #undef, the current definition is
discarded and the most recent previous definition (if any) is restored.

References #define command 3.3; #ifdef and #ifndef command 3.5.3

3.3.6 Precedence Errors in Macro Expansions

Macros operate purely by textual substitution of tokens. Parsing of the body into declarations, expressions, or statements occurs only after the macro expansion process. This can lead to surprising results if care is not taken. Consider this macro definition:

```
#define SQUARE(x) x*x
```

The idea is that SQUARE takes an argument expression and produces a new expression to compute the square of that argument. For example, SQUARE(5) expands to 5*5. However, the expression SQUARE(z+1) expands to z+1*z+1, which is parsed as z+(1*z)+1 rather than the expected (z+1)*(z+1). As a rule, it is safest to always parenthesize each parameter appearing in the macro body. The entire body, if it is syntactically an expression, should also be parenthesized:

```
#define SQUARE(x) ((x)*(x))
```

The outer parentheses are needed to prevent misinterpretation of an expression such as (short) SQUARE(z+1).

> **References**   cast expressions 7.5.1; precedence of expressions 7.2.1

3.3.7 Side Effects in Macro Arguments

Macros can also produce problems due to side effects. Consider the macro SQUARE shown above and also a function square that does (almost) the same thing:

```
int square(x)
    int x;
{
    return x*x;
}
```

The function, unlike the macro, can square only integers, not floating-point numbers. Also, calling the function is likely to be somewhat slower at run time than using the macro. But these differences are less important than the question of side effects. In the program fragment

```
a = 3;
b = square(a++);
```

the variable b gets the value 9 and the variable a ends up with the value 4. However, in the superficially similar program fragment

```
a = 3;
b = SQUARE(a++);
```

the variable b may very well get the value 12 and the variable a may end up with the value 5, because the expansion of the last fragment is

```
a = 3;
b = ((a++)*(a++));
```

(We say that 12 and 5 "may" be the resulting values of b and a because C implementations are free to evaluate the expression ((a++)*(a++)) in several different ways. See section 7.12.)

When a function such as square is used, the argument expression is evaluated exactly once, so any side effects of the expression occur exactly once. When a macro, such as SQUARE, is used, an actual argument may be textually replicated and therefore executed more than once, and side effects may occur more than once. Macros must be used with care to avoid such problems.

References   increment operator ++ 7.4.4

3.3.8 Converting Tokens to Strings

There is a mechanism in ANSI C to convert macro parameters (after expansion) to string constants.   Before this, programmers had to depend on a "loophole" in many C preprocessors that achieved the same result in a different way.

In ANSI C, the # token appearing within a macro definition is recognized as a unary "stringization" operator that must be followed by the name of a macro formal parameter. During macro expansion, the # and the formal name are replaced by the corresponding actual argument enclosed in string quotations. For example, after preprocessing and string concatenation the ANSI C source text

```
#define TEST(a,b) printf( #a "<" #b "=%d\n", (a)<(b) )
TEST(0,0xFFFF);
```

becomes

```
printf("0<0xFFFF=%d\n", (0)<(0xFFFF) );
```

When creating the string, each sequence whitespace in the macro formal's expansion is replaced by a single space character, and any embedded quotation or backslash characters are preceded by a backslash character to preserve their meaning in the string. Therefore, if the TEST macro above were invoked as TEST('\n',10), the result would be

```
printf("'\\n'<10=%d\n", ('\n')<(10) );
```

A similar result can be obtained in the many (not all) current implementations of C that recognize macro formal parameter names within string and character constants. (ANSI C disallows such recognition.) In these implementations, the TEST macro would be written this way:

```
#define TEST(a,b) printf( "a<b=%d\n", (a)<(b) )
```

The result of expanding `TEST(0,0xFFFF)` would probably be the same as in the ANSI C case, but the expansion of `TEST('\n',10)` would almost certainly be missing the extra backslash and the output of the `printf` function would be garbled.

```
printf("'\n'<10=%d\n", ('\n')<(10) );
```

The handling of whitespace in non-ANSI implementations is also likely to vary from compiler to compiler—another reason to avoid depending on this feature except in ANSI C implementations.

3.3.9 Token Merging in Macro Expansions

Merging of tokens to form new tokens in ANSI C is controlled by the presence of a "merging" operator, `##`, in macro definitions. In a macro replacement list—before rescanning for more macros—the two tokens surrounding any `##` operator are combined into a single token. (If they do not form a legal token, the result is undefined.) Consider this source text:

```
#define TEMP(i)  temp ## i
TEMP(1) = TEMP(2);
```

After preprocessing, this becomes

```
temp1 = temp2;
```

As with the conversion of macro arguments to strings (section 3.3.8), programmers can obtain something like this merging capability through a loophole in many non-ANSI C implementations. Although the original definition of C explicitly described macro bodies as being sequences of tokens, not sequences of characters, nevertheless many C compilers expand and rescan macro bodies as if they were character sequences. This becomes apparent primarily in the case where the compiler also handles comments by eliminating them entirely (rather than by replacing them with a space), a situation exploited by some cleverly written programs. Consider the following example:

```
#define INC ++
#define TAB internal_table
#define INCTAB table_of_increments
#define CONC(x,y) x/**/y
CONC(INC,TAB)
```

The "proper" interpretation of the body of `CONC` is as a sequence of the tokens `x` and `y`, separated by a comment or a space. The comment does, in all implementations, serve to separate `x` and `y` so that they are recognized as formal parameters of the macro `CONC`. The call `CONC(INC,TAB)` ought to expand to the sequence of tokens `INC TAB`, which will in turn expand to `++ internal_table`. However, those implementations that simply eliminate comments and that rescan macro bodies as character sequences rather than token sequences will often expand the call `CONC(INC,TAB)` into the character sequence (and token) `INCTAB`. This will then expand into `table_of_increments`, which is a very different thing altogether. Non-ANSI implementations vary in this area, so depending on such implicit concatenation of tokens renders a program nonportable. ANSI C requires comments to be replaced by a single space character, which prevents this "accidental" merging of tokens.

>   **References**   increment operator ++ 7.5.8

3.3.10 Other Problems

Some implementations of C do not perform stringent error checking on macro definitions and calls, including permitting an incomplete token in the macro body to be completed by text appearing after the macro call. For example, the following fragment

```
#define FIRSTPART "This is a split
...
printf(FIRSTPART string.");  /* Yuk! */
```

will, after preprocessing, result in compiling the source text

```
printf("This is a split string.");
```

The lack of error checking by certain implementations does not make clever exploitation of that lack legitimate. ANSI C reaffirms that macro bodies must be sequences of well-formed tokens.

3.4 FILE INCLUSION

The `#include` preprocessor command causes the entire contents of a specified source text file to be processed as if those contents had appeared in place of the `#include` command. The `#include` command has the following three forms in ANSI C:

```
# include < h-char-sequence >
# include " q-char-sequence "
# include   preprocessor-tokens                                  (ANSI C)
```

h-char-sequence :
>   any sequence of characters except > and end-of-line

q-char-sequence :
>   any sequence of characters except " and end-of-line

preprocessor-tokens :
>   any sequence of C tokens—or non-whitespace characters
>   that cannot be interpreted as tokens—that does not begin with < or "

In the first two forms of `#include`, the characters between the delimiters should be a file name in some implementation-defined format. There should be only whitespace after the closing `>` or `"`. These two forms of `#include` are supported by all C compilers. The file name is subject to trigraph replacement in ANSI C and source-line continuation, but no other processing of the characters occurs.

In third form of `#include`, the *preprocessor-tokens* undergo normal macro expansion and the result must match one of the first two forms (including the quotes or angle brackets). This form of `include` is seen less often, and may not be implemented or may be implemented in a different fashion in non-ANSI compilers. Here is one way to use this form of `include`:

```
#if some_thing==this_thing
#   define IncludeFile "thisname"
#else
#   define Includefile <thatname>
#endif
...
#include Includefile
```

This style can be used to localize customizations, but programmers interested in compatibility with older compilers should instead place `#include` commands at the site of the `#define` commands above:

```
#if some_thing==this_thing
#   include "thisname"
#else
#   include <thatname>
#endif
```

File names delimited by quotes and file names delimited by angle brackets differ in how the specified file is located by the C implementation. Both forms search for the file in a set of (possibly different) implementation-defined places. Typically, the form

```
#include <filename>
```

searches for the file in certain "standard" places according to implementation-defined search rules. These standard places usually contain the implementation's own header files, such as `stdio.h`. The form

```
#include "filename"
```

will also search in the standard places, but usually after searching some "local" places, such as the programmer's "current" directory. Often, implementations have some standard way outside of the C language for specifying the set of places to search for these files. The general intent is that the `"..."` form is used to refer to header files written by the programmer, whereas the `<...>` form is used to refer to standard implementation files.

An included file may itself contain #include commands. The permitted depth of such #include nesting is implementation dependent, but most implementations will allow nesting to at least five or six levels. The location of included files can affect the search rules for nested files.

Consider the situation depicted below. We are compiling a C program, first.c, in the file system directory near. The first included file, second.h, is specified to be in another directory, far. The header file second.h in turn includes a file, third.h, with no specified directory. Will the implementation choose the file third.h in the original "current" directory, near, or will it choose the file with the same name in the directory of the file containing the #include, far?

Our UNIX C compiler would find far/third.h; the original description of C seems to expect that near/third.h should be found. We think near/third.h is the better choice for an implementation, but this is not mandated by ANSI C.

References   string constants 2.7.4; trigraphs 2.1.4

3.5 CONDITIONAL COMPILATION

The preprocessor conditional commands allow lines of source text to be passed through or eliminated by the preprocessor on the basis of a computed condition.

3.5.1 The #if, #else, and #endif Commands

The following preprocessor commands are used together to allow lines of source text to be conditionally included in or excluded from the compilation: #if, #else, and #endif. They are used in the following way:

```
#if  constant-expression
     group-of-lines–1
#else
     group-of-lines–2
#endif
```

The *constant-expression* is subject to macro replacement and must evaluate to a constant arithmetic value. Restrictions on the expression are discussed in section 7.11.1. A "group of lines" may contain any number of lines of text of any kind, even other preprocessor command lines, or no lines at all. The `#else` command may be omitted, along with the group of lines following it; this is equivalent to including the `#else` command with an empty group of lines following it. Either group of lines may also contain one or more sets of `#if-#else-#endif` commands.

A set of commands such as shown above is processed in such a way that one group of lines will be passed on for compilation and the other group of lines will be discarded. First the constant-expression in the `#if` command is evaluated. If its value is not 0, then *group-of-lines–1* is passed through for compilation and *group-of-lines–2* (if present) is discarded. Otherwise, *group-of-lines–1* is discarded; and if there is an `#else` command, then *group-of-lines–2* is passed through; but if there is no `#else` command, then no group of lines is passed through. The constant expressions that may be used in a `#if` command are described in detail in sections 3.5.4 and 7.11.

A group of lines that is discarded is not processed by the preprocessor. Macro replacement is not performed and preprocessor commands are ignored. The one exception is that, within a group of discarded lines, the commands `#if`, `#ifdef`, `#ifndef`, `#elif`, `#else`, and `#endif` are recognized for the sole purpose of counting them; this is necessary to maintain the proper nesting of the conditional compilation commands. (This recognition in turn implies that discarded lines are scanned and broken into tokens and that string constants and comments are recognized and must be properly delimited.)

If an undefined macro name appears in the constant-expression of `#if` or `#elif`, it is replaced by the integer constant 0. This means that the commands "`#ifdef` *name*" and "`#if` *name*" will have the same effect as long as the macro name, when defined, has a constant, arithmetic, nonzero value. We think it is much clearer to use `#ifdef` or the defined operator in these cases, but ANSI C also supports this use of `#if`.

References   `defined` 3.5.5; `#elif` 3.5.2; `#ifdef` 3.5.3

3.5.2 The #elif Command

The `#elif` command is present in ANSI C and in the more modern pre-ANSI compilers as well. It is convenient because it simplifies sequential preprocessor conditionals.

The `#elif` command is like a combination of `#else` and `#if`. It is used between `#if` and `#endif` in the same way as `#else` but has a constant expression to evaluate in the same way as `#if`. It is used in the following way:

```
#if  constant-expression-1
    group-of-lines-1
#elif  constant-expression-2
    group-of-lines-2
#elif  constant-expression-3
    group-of-lines-3
...
#elif  constant-expression-n
    group-of-lines-n
#else
    last-group-of-lines
#endif
```

A set of commands such as shown above are processed in such a way that at most one group of lines will be passed on for compilation and all other groups of lines will be discarded. First the *constant-expression-1* in the `#if` command is evaluated. If its value is not 0, then *group-of-lines-1* is passed through for compilation and all other groups of lines up to the matching #endif are discarded. If the value of the *constant-expression-1* in the `#if` command is 0, then the *constant-expression-2* in the first `#elif` command is evaluated; if that value is not 0, then *group-of-lines-2* is passed through for compilation. In the general case, each *constant-expression-i* is evaluated until one produces a nonzero value; the preprocessor then passes through the group of lines following the command containing the nonzero constant expression, ignoring any other constant expressions in the command set, and discards all other groups of lines. If no *constant-expression-i* produces a nonzero value and there is an `#else` command, then the group of lines following the `#else` command is passed through; but if there is no `#else` command, then no group of lines is passed through. The constant expressions that may be used in a `#elif` command are the same as those used in a `#if` command (see sections 3.5.4 and 7.11).

Within a group of discarded lines, `#elif` commands are recognized in the same way as `#if`, `#else`, and `#endif` commands, for the sole purpose of counting them; this is necessary to maintain the proper nesting of the conditional compilation commands.

Macro replacement is performed within the part of a command line that follows an `#elif` command, so macro calls may be used in the constant-expression.

While the `#elif` command is very convenient when it is appropriate, its functionality can be duplicated using only `#if`, `#else`, and `#endif`. For example, this set of commands:

```
#if  constant-expression-1
    group-of-lines-1
#elif  constant-expression-2
    group-of-lines-2
#else
    last-group-of-lines
#endif
```

can be rewritten in this way:

```
#if  constant-expression–1
    group-of-lines–1
#else
#if  constant-expression–2
    group-of-lines–2
#else
    last-group-of-lines
#endif
#endif
```

3.5.3 The #ifdef and #ifndef Commands

The `#ifdef` and `#ifndef` commands can be used to test whether a name is defined as a preprocessor macro. A command line of the form

```
#ifdef  name
```

is equivalent in meaning to

```
#if 1
```

when *name* has been defined and is equivalent to

```
#if 0
```

when *name* has not been defined or has been undefined with the `#undef` command. The `#ifndef` command has the opposite sense; it is true when the *name* is not defined and false when it is.

Note that `#ifdef` and `#ifndef` test names only with respect to whether they have been defined by `#define` (or undefined by `#undef`); they take no notice of names appearing in declarations in the C program text to be compiled. (Some C implementations allow names to be defined with special compiler command-line arguments.)

The `#ifndef` and `#ifdef` commands have come to be used in several stylized ways in C programs. First, it is a common practice to implement a preprocessor-time enumeration type by having a set of symbols of which only one is defined. For example, suppose that we wish to use the set of names VAX, PDP11, and CRAY2 to indicate the computer for which the program is being compiled. One might insist that all these names be defined, with one being defined to be 1 and the rest 0:

```
#define VAX 0
#define PDP11 0
#define CRAY2 1
```

One could then select machine-dependent source code to be compiled in this way:

```
#if VAX
    VAX-dependent code
#endif
#if PDP11
    PDP11-dependent code
#endif
#if CRAY2
    CRAY2-dependent code
#endif
```

However, the customary method defines only one symbol:

```
#define CRAY2 1
    /* None of the other symbols are defined. */
```

Then the conditional commands test whether each symbol is defined:

```
#ifdef VAX
    VAX-dependent code
#endif
#ifdef PDP11
    PDP11-dependent code
#endif
#ifdef CRAY2
    CRAY2-dependent code
#endif
```

Another use for the `#ifdef` and `#ifndef` commands is to provide default definitions for macros. For example, a library file might provide a definition for a name only if no other definition has been provided:

```
#ifndef TABLE_SIZE
#define TABLE_SIZE 100
#endif
...
static int internal_table[TABLE_SIZE];
```

A program might simply include this file:

```
#include <table.h>
```

in which case the definition of TABLE_SIZE would be 100, both within the library file itself and after the `#include`; or the program might provide an explicit definition first:

```
#define TABLE_SIZE 500
#include <table.h>
```

in which case the definition of TABLE_SIZE would be 500 throughout.

It is a common C programming error to test whether a name is defined by writing "#if name" instead of "#ifdef name" or "#if defined(name)." The incorrect form often works because the preprocessor replaces any name in the #if expression that is not defined as a macro with the constant 0. Therefore, if name is not defined all three forms are equivalent. However, if name is defined to have the value 0 then "#if name" will be false even though the name is defined. Similarly, if name is defined with a value that is not a legal expression, then "#if name" will cause an error.

References   #define 3.3; defined operator 3.5.5; #include 3.4; preprocessor lexical conventions 3.2; #undef 3.3

3.5.4 Constant Expressions in Conditional Commands

The expressions that may be used in #if and #elif commands are described in section 7.11.1. They include integer constants and all the integer arithmetic, relational, bitwise, and logical operators.

3.5.5 The defined Operator

The defined operator, new to C and incorporated into ANSI C, can be used in #if and #elif expressions but nowhere else. An expression in one of the two forms

```
defined name
defined( name )
```

evaluates to 1 if *name* is defined in the preprocessor, and 0 if it is not. This allows the programmer to write

```
#if defined(VAX)
```

instead of

```
#ifdef VAX
```

The defined operator may be more convenient to use because it is possible to build up complex expressions, such as this:

```
#if defined(VAX) && !defined(UNIX) && debugging
...
```

3.6 EXPLICIT LINE NUMBERING

The #line preprocessor command advises the C compiler that the source program was generated by another tool and indicates the correspondence of places in the source program to lines of the original user-written file from which the C source program was produced. The #line command may have one of two forms. The form

> # line *n* " *filename* "

indicates that the next source line was derived from line *n* of the original user-written file named by *filename*. *n* must be an integer constant. The form

> # line *n*

indicates that the next source line was derived from line *n* of the user-written file last mentioned in a #line command. Finally, if the #line command does not match either of the forms above, it is interpreted as

> # line *preprocessor-tokens*

Macro replacement is performed on the argument token sequence, and the result must match one of the two previous forms of #line.

The information provided by the #line command is used in setting the values of the predefined macros __LINE__ and __FILE__. Otherwise, its behavior is unspecified and compilers may ignore it. Typically, the information is also used in diagnostic messages. Some tools that generate C source text as output will use #line so that error messages can be related to the tool's input file instead of the actual C source file.

Some implementations of C allow the preprocessor to be used independently of the rest of the compiler. Indeed, sometimes the preprocessor is a separate program that is executed to produce an intermediate file that is then processed by the "real" compiler. In such cases the preprocessor may generate new #line commands in the intermediate file; the compiler proper is then expected to recognize these even though it does not recognize any other preprocessor commands. Whether the preprocessor generates #line commands is implementation dependent. Similarly, whether the preprocessor passes through, modifies, or eliminates #line commands in the input is also implementation dependent.

Older versions of C allow simply "#" as a synonym for the #line command, allowing this form:

> # *n filename*

This syntax is considered obsolete and is not permitted in ANSI C, but many implementations continue to support it for the sake of compatibility.

References   __FILE__ 3.3.4; __LINE__ 3.3.4

3.7 PRAGMA DIRECTIVE

The #pragma command is new in ANSI C. Any sequence of tokens can follow the command name:

    # pragma *preprocessor-tokens*

The #pragma directive can be used by C implementations to add new preprocessor functionality or to provide implementation-defined information to the compiler. No restrictions are placed on the information that follows the #pragma command, and implementations should ignore information they do not understand. The argument to #pragma is subject to macro expansion.

There is obviously the possibility that two implementations will place inconsistent interpretations on the same information, so it is wise to use #pragma conditionally. The following code checks that the proper compiler (tcc), computer, and standard-conforming implementation are in use before issuing the #pragma command:

```
#if defined(_TCC) && defined(__STDC__) && defined(vax)
#pragma builtin(abs),inline(myfunc)
#endif
```

There is not yet any agreement on standard pragmas. The table below shows some that have begun to appear in C implementations. We have not attempted to show the arguments to the pragmas, if any.

Examples of pragmas

Pragma name	Purpose
align, pack	Control alignment of structures.
extend	Allow language extensions, e.g., more keywords.
optimize	Control optimization level.
debug	Control generation of debug information.
rom	Create code that can run in read-only memory.
small, medium, compact, large	Select memory model (section 6.1.5).
list, xref, pagelength	Control the program listing.
inline, intrinsic	Compile functions with fast calling conventions.
check stack	Generate code to detect call stack overflow.

References   defined 3.5.3; memory models 6.1.5; #if 3.5.1

3.8 ERROR DIRECTIVE

The #error directive is new in ANSI C. Any sequence of tokens can follow the command name:

    # error *preprocessor-tokens*

The #error directive produces a compile-time error message that will include the argument tokens, which are subject to macro expansion.

   The #error directive is most useful in detecting programmer inconsistencies and violations of constraints during preprocessing. Here are some examples:

```
#if defined(A_THING) && defined(NOT_A_THING)
#error "Inconsistent things!"
#endif

#include "sizes.h"    /* defines SIZE */
...
#if (SIZE % 256) != 0
#error "SIZE must be a multiple of 256!"
#endif
```

   References   defined 3.5.3; #if 3.5.1

3.9 EXERCISES

1.   Which of the following ANSI C macro definitions are (probably) wrong? Why? Which definitions might cause problems in traditional C?
     (a) `#define ident (x)  x`   (c) `#define PLUS +`
     (b) `# define FIVE = 5;`   (d) `#definevoid int`

2.   Below are shown some macro definitions and invocations. How would each macro invocation be expanded by ANSI C and by traditional C?

Definition	*Invocation*
(a) `#define sum(a,b) a+b`	`sum(b,a)`
(b) `#define paste(x,y) x/**/y`	`paste(x,4)`
(c) `#define str(x) # x`	`str(a book)`
(d) `#define free(x) x?free(x):NULL`	`free(p)`

3.   Two header files and a C program file are shown below. If the C preprocessor is applied to the program file, what will be the result?

```
/* File blue.h */       /* file red.h */        /* file test.c */
int blue = 0;           #ifndef __red__         #include "blue.h"
#include "red.h"        #define __red__         #include "red.h"
                        #include "blue.h"
                        int red = 0;
                        #endif
```

4.   A friend shows you the following definition for a macro that is supposed to double its numeric argument. What is wrong with the macro? Rewrite the macro so that it operates correctly.
         `#define DBL(a)    a+a`

5.   In the following ANSI C program fragment, what is the expansion of `M(M)(A,B)`?
         ```
         #define M(x)      M ## x
         #define MM(M,y)   M = # y
         M(M)(A,B)
         ```

6. Write a sequence of preprocessor directives that will cause an ANSI C program to fail to compile if the macro SIZE has not been defined, or if it has been defined but it has a value that is not in the range 1 through 10.

7. Give an example of a sequence of characters that is a single token to the preprocessor but not to the C compiler proper.

8. What is wrong with the following program fragment:

```
if (x != 0)
    y = z/x;
else
    # error "Attempt to divide by zero, line " __LINE__
```

4

Declarations

To *declare* a *name* in the C language is to associate an identifier with some C object, such as a variable, function, or type. The names that can be declared in C are

- variables
- functions
- types
- type tags

- structure and union components
- enumeration constants
- statement labels
- preprocessor macros

Except for statement labels and preprocessor macros, all identifiers are declared by their appearance in C *declarations*. Variables, functions, and types appear in *declarators* within declarations, and type tags, structure and union components, and enumeration constants are declared in certain kinds of *type specifiers* in declarations. Statement labels are declared by their appearance in a C function, and preprocessor macros are declared by the #define preprocessor command.

Declarations in C are difficult to describe for several reasons. First, they involve some unusual syntax that may be confusing to the novice. For example, the declaration

```
int (*f)();
```

declares a pointer to a function returning an integer.

Second, many of the abstract properties of declarations, such as scope and extent, are more complicated in C than in other programming languages. Before jumping into the actual declaration syntax, we will discuss these properties in section 4.2.

Finally, some aspects of C's declarations are difficult to understand without a knowledge of C's type system, which is described in chapter 5. In particular, discussions of type tags, structure and union component names, and enumeration constants are left to that chapter, although some properties of those declarations will be discussed here for completeness.

References   enumeration type 5.5; #define preprocessor command 3.3; statement labels 8.3; structure types 5.6; type specifiers 4.4; union types 5.7

4.1 ORGANIZATION OF DECLARATIONS

Declarations may appear in several places in a C program, and where they appear affects the properties of the declarations. A C source file, or *translation unit*, consists of a sequence of *top-level declarations* of functions, variables, and other things. Each function has *parameter declarations* and a *body*; the body in turn may contain *blocks* (compound statements). A block may contain a sequence of *inner declarations*.

The basic syntax of declarations is shown below. A discussion of function definitions is deferred until chapter 9.

> *declaration* :
> > *declaration-specifiers initialized-declarator-list* ;
>
> *declaration-specifiers* :
> > *storage-class-specifier   declaration-specifiers*$_{opt}$
> > *type-specifier   declaration-specifiers*$_{opt}$
> > *type-qualifier   declaration-specifiers*$_{opt}$
>
> *initialized-declarator-list* :
> > *initialized-declarator*
> > *initialized-declarator-list* , *initialized-declarator*
>
> *initialized-declarator* :
> > *declarator   initializer-part*$_{opt}$

Semantic rules will prohibit certain syntactically valid declarations, depending on the location and form of the declaration. At most one storage class specifier and one type specifier may appear in the *declaration-specifiers*, although a single type specifier may be formed of several tokens (e.g., unsigned long int). Each of the two type qualifiers can appear at most once in the *declaration-specifiers*.

Within these constraints, type specifiers, storage class specifiers, and type qualifiers can appear in any order in *declaration-specifiers*. However, it is customary to put any storage class specifier first, followed by any type qualifiers, and finally the type specifiers. In the following example, i and j have the same type and storage class, but the declaration of i is better style.

```
unsigned volatile long extern int const j;
extern const volatile unsigned long int i;
```

References   declarators 4.5; expressions ch. 7; function definitions ch. 9; initializers 4.6; statements ch. 8; storage class specifiers 4.3; type specifiers and qualifiers 4.4

4.2 TERMINOLOGY

This section establishes some terminology used to describe declarations.

4.2.1 Scope

The *scope* of a declaration is the region of the C program text over which that declaration is active. In C, identifiers may have one of the six scopes listed in table 4–1.

Table 4–1: Identifier scopes

Kind	Active region of declaration
Top-level identifiers	Extends from its declaration point (section 4.2.3) to the end of the source program file.
Formal parameters in function definitions	Extends from its declaration point to the end of the function body.
Formal parameters in function prototypes[1]	Extends from its declaration point to the end of the prototype.
Block (local) identifiers	Extends from its declaration point to the end of the block.
Statement labels	Encompasses the entire function body in which it appears.
Preprocessor macros	Extends from the `#define` command that declares it through the end of the source program file, or until the first `#undef` command that cancels its definition.

[1] New in ANSI C.

Nonpreprocessor identifiers declared within a function or block are often said to have *block scope*, or *local scope*. Identifiers in prototypes have *prototype scope*. Statement labels have *function scope*. All other identifiers have *file scope*.

The scope of every identifier is limited to the C source file in which it occurs. However, some identifiers can be declared to be *external*, in which case the declarations of the same identifier in two or more files can be linked as described in section 4.8.

References `#define` preprocessor command 3.3; external names 4.8; prototypes ch. 4; `#undef` preprocessor command 3.3

4.2.2 Visibility

A declaration of an identifier is *visible* in some context if a use of the identifier in that context will be bound to the declaration; that is, the identifier will have an association made with that declaration. A declaration might be visible throughout its scope, but it may also be *hidden* by other declarations whose scope and visibility overlap that of the first declaration. For example, in the following program, the declaration of `foo` as an integer variable is hidden by the inner declaration of `foo` as a floating-point variable. The outer `foo` is hidden only within the body of function `main`.

```
int foo = 10; /* foo defined at the top level */
main()
{
    float foo; /* this foo hides the outer foo */
    ...
}
```

In C, declarations at the beginning of a block can hide declarations outside the block. For one declaration to hide another, the declared identifiers must be the same, must belong to the same *overloading class*, and must be declared in two distinct scopes, one of which contains the other.

In ANSI C, the scope of formal parameter declarations in a function definition is the same as the scope of identifiers declared at the beginning of the block that forms the function body. This means that the following redeclaration of x is an error:

```
int f(x)
    int x;
{
    long x = 34;      /* illegal? */
    return x;
}
```

However, some earlier implementations of C have considered the parameter scope to enclose the block scope, thus permitting the redeclaration and hiding of the parameter x. (And probably allowing a troublesome programming error to go undetected.)

   References   block 8.4; overloading class 4.2.4; parameter declarations 9.3; top-level declarations 4.1

4.2.3 Forward References

An identifier may not normally be used before it is fully declared. To be precise, we define the *declaration point* of an identifier to be the position of the identifier's lexical token in its declaration. Uses of the identifier after the declaration point are permitted. In the example below, the integer variable, intsize, can be initialized to its own size because the use of intsize in the initializer comes after the declaration point:

```
static int intsize = sizeof(intsize);
```

When an identifier is used before it is completely declared, a *forward reference* to the declaration is said to occur. C permits forward references in three situations:

1. A statement label may appear in a goto statement before it appears as a label, since its scope covers the entire function body:

```
if (error) goto recover;
...
recover:
    CloseFiles();
```

2. An incomplete structure, union, or enumeration type may be declared, allowing
    it to be used for some purposes before it is fully defined. See section 5.6.1.
3. A function can be declared separately from its definition, either with a declara-
    tion or implicitly by its appearance in a function call. See sections 4.7 and 5.8.

Illegal forward references are illustrated in the following example. The
programmer is attempting to define a self-referential structure with a `typedef` declaration. In this case, the last occurrence of `cell` on the line is the declaration point, and
therefore the use of `cell` within the structure is illegal.

```
typedef struct { int Value; cell *Next; } cell;
```

The correct way to declare such a type is by use of a structure tag, S, which is defined on
its first appearance and then used later within the declaration:

```
typedef struct S { int Value; struct S *Next; } cell;
```

See also the later discussions of *implicit declarations* (section 4.7) and *duplicate declarations* (section 4.2.5).

References   duplicate declarations 4.2.5; function types 5.8; goto statement 8.10; implicit
declarations 4.7; pointer types 5.3; structure types 5.6

4.2.4 Overloading of Names

In C and other programming languages, the same identifier may be associated with more
than one program entity at a time. When this happens, we say that the name is *overloaded*, and the context in which the name is used determines the association that is in
effect. For instance, an identifier might be both the name of a variable and a structure
tag. When used in an expression, the variable association is used; when used in a type
specifier, the tag association is used.

There are five *overloading classes* for names in C. (We sometimes refer to them as
name spaces.) They are listed and described in the table on the following page.

These overloading rules differ slightly from those in the original definition of C.
First, the original definition of C put statement labels in the same name space as ordinary
identifiers, and enough compilers still follow this rule that the programmer should be
aware of it and consider not using the same name for a label and a variable.

Overloading classes

Class	Included identifiers
Preprocessor macro names	Because preprocessing logically occurs before compilation, names used by the preprocessor are independent of any other names in a C program.
Statement labels	Named statement labels are part of statements. Definitions of statement labels are always followed by : (and are not part of `case` labels). Uses of statement labels always immediately follow the reserved word `goto`.
Structure, union, and enumeration tags	These tags are part of structure, union, and enumeration type specifiers and, if present, always immediately follow the reserved words `struct`, `union`, or `enum`.
Component names	Component names are allocated in name spaces associated with each structure and union type. That is, the same identifier can be a component name in any number of structures or unions at the same time. Definitions of component names always occur within structure or union type specifiers. Uses of component names always immediately follow the selection operators `.` and `->`.
Other names	All other names fall into an overloading class that includes variables, functions, typedef names, and enumeration constants.

Second, the original definition of C allocated all structure and union component names from a single name space instead of separate name spaces for each type. Thus, if x was a component of one structure type, it couldn't be the member of another structure type. There were complicated rules that allowed identifiers to be in more than one structure if their offsets in the structure were identical. Fortunately, this is now rarely seen in C compilers and has been corrected in the current language definitions.

When a name is overloaded with several associations, each association has its own scope and may be hidden by other declarations independent of other associations. For instance, if an identifier is being used both as a variable and a structure tag, an inner block may redefine the variable association without altering the tag association.

References   component names 5.6.3; duplicate definition 4.2.5; enumeration tags 5.5; goto statement 8.10; selection operators 7.4.2; statement labels 8.10; structure tags 5.6; structure type specifiers 5.6; typedef names 5.10; union tags 5.7; union type specifiers 5.7

4.2.5 Duplicate Declarations

It is illegal to make two declarations of the same name (in the same overloading class) in the same block or at the top level. Such declarations are said to *conflict*. In the following example, the two declarations of howmany are conflicting but the two declarations of str are not (because they are in different name spaces):

```
extern int howmany;
extern char str[10];
typedef double howmany();
extern struct str {int a, b;} x;
```

There are two exceptions to the prohibition against duplicate declarations. First, any number of external (*referencing*) declarations for the same name may exist, as long as the declarations assign the same type to the name in each instance. This exception reflects the belief that declaring the same external library function twice should not be illegal.

Second, if an identifier is declared as being external, that declaration may be followed with a *definition* (section 4.8) of the name later in the program, assuming that the definition assigns the same type to the name as the external declaration(s). This exception allows the user to generate legal forward references to variables and functions. For instance, in the following example we define two functions, f and g, that reference each other. Normally, the use of f within g would be an illegal forward reference. However, by preceding the definition of g with an external declaration of f, we give the compiler enough information about f to compile g. (Without the initial declaration of f, a one-pass compiler could not know when compiling g that f returns a value of type double rather than int.)

```
extern double f();

double g(x, y)
    double x, y;
{
    ... f(x-y) ...
}

double f(z)
    double z;
{
    ... g(z, z/2.0) ...
}
```

There is a deficiency in this mechanism. Variables that are the subject of forward references from within the same file must be declared extern, when they could otherwise have storage class static. Some compilers, when they see an external declaration followed by a static definition of the same name, will guess (correctly or not) what is going on and not generate an external reference at link time.

References   defining and referencing declarations 4.8; extern storage class 4.3; forward references 4.2; overloading class 4.2; static storage class 4.3

4.2.6 Duplicate Visibility

Because C's scoping rules specify that a name's scope begins at its declaration point rather than at the head of the block in which it is defined, a situation can arise in which two nonconflicting declarations can be referenced in different parts of the same block.

In the example below there are two variables named i referenced in the block labeled B—the integer i declared in the outer block is used to initialize the variable j, and then a floating-point variable i is declared, hiding the first i.

```
{
    int i = 0;
    ...
    B:  {
            int j = i;
            float i = 10.0;
            ...
        }
}
```

The reference to i in the initialization of j is ambiguous. Which i was wanted? Most compilers will do what was (apparently) intended; the first use of i in block B is bound to the outer definition, and the redefinition of i then hides the outer definition for the remainder of the block. We consider this usage to be bad programming style; it should be avoided.

4.2.7 Extent

Variables and functions, unlike types, have an existence at run time; that is, they have storage allocated to them. The *extent* of these objects is the period of time that the storage is allocated.

An object is said to have *static extent* when it is allocated storage at or before the beginning of program execution and the storage remains allocated until program termination. In C, all functions have static extent, as do all variables declared in top-level declarations. Variables declared at the beginning of blocks may have static extent, depending on the declaration.

An object is said to have *local extent* when (in the case of C) it is created upon entry to a block or function and is destroyed upon exit from the block or function. If a variable with local extent has an initializer, the variable is initialized each time it is created. Formal parameters have local extent, and variables declared at the beginning of blocks may have local extent, depending on the declaration. A variable with local extent is called *automatic* in C.

Finally, it is possible in C to have data objects with *dynamic extent*; that is, objects that are created and destroyed explicitly at the programmer's whim. However, dynamic objects must be created through the use of special library routines such as *malloc* and are not viewed as part of the C language itself.

References auto storage class 4.3; initializers 4.6; malloc function 16.1; static storage class 4.3; storage allocation functions ch. 16

4.2.8 Initial Values

Allocating storage for a variable does not necessarily establish the initial contents of that storage. Most variable declarations in C may have *initializers*, expressions used to set the initial value of a variable at the time that storage is allocated for it. If an initializer is not specified for a variable, its value after allocation is unpredictable.

It is important to remember that a static variable is initialized only once and that it retains its value even when the program is executing outside its scope. In the following example, two variables, L and S, are declared at the head of a block and both are initialized to 0. Both variables have local scope, but S has static extent while L has local (automatic) extent. Each time the block is entered, both variables are incremented by one and the new values printed.

```
{
    static int S = 0;
    auto int L = 0;
    L = L + 1;
    S = S + 1;
    printf("L = %d, S = %d\n", L, S);
}
```

What values will be printed? If the block is executed many times, the output will be this:

```
L = 1, S = 1
L = 1, S = 2
L = 1, S = 3
L = 1, S = 4
...
```

There is one dangerous feature of C's initialization of automatic variables declared at the beginning of blocks. The initialization is guaranteed to occur only if the block is entered normally; that is, if control flows into the beginning of the block. Through the use of statement labels and the goto statement, it is possible to jump into the middle of a block; if this is done, there is no guarantee that automatic variables will be initialized. The same is true when case or default labels are used in conjunction with the switch statement to cause control to be transferred into a block. In the following example, for instance, the initialization of variable sum will not occur when the goto statement transfers control to label L, causing erroneous behavior.

```
goto L;
...
{
        static int vector[10] = {1,2,3,4,5,6,7,8,9,10};
        int sum = 0;
    L:
        /* Add up elements of "vector". */
        for ( i=1; i<10; i++ ) sum += vector[i];
            printf("sum is %d", sum);
}
```

References goto statement 8.10; initialization of variables 4.6; storage classes 4.3; switch statement 8.7

4.2.9 External Names

A special case of scope and visibility is the *external* variable or function. An external object is treated just like a static object in the file containing its declaration. However, an identifier declared to be external is *exported* to the linker, and if the same identifier is similarly declared in another program file, the linker will ensure that the two files reference the same object (variable or function).

External names are usually declared at the top level of a C program and therefore have file scope. However, implementations differ on how external names declared within a block are handled. For example, the following program fragment is acceptable to many C compilers; it declares an external name within a block and then uses it outside the block:

```
{
    extern int E;
    ...
}
E = 1;
```

According to normal block-scoping rules the declaration should not be visible outside the block, but many implementations of C implicitly give E file scope and so compile this fragment without error. ANSI C requires the declaration to have block scope, but does not state that the above fragment should be illegal. Technically, the behavior of an implementation in this case is undefined, thus permitting a conforming implementation to accept the program. We think programmers should treat this fragment as a programming error even if the compiler accepts it and the run time behavior is correct.

It is indisputably an error if two external declarations (in the same file or different files within the same program) specify different types for the same identifier . In the following program, the two declarations of X do not conflict in the source file, although their behavior at run-time is undefined:

```
int f()
{
    extern int X;
    return X;
}
...
double g()
{
    extern double X;
    return X;
}
```

References   external name conventions 2.5; external name definition and reference 4.8; scope 4.2.1; visibility 4.2.2

4.2.10 Compile-time Objects

So far the discussion has focused mainly on variables and functions, which have an existence at run time. However, the scope and visibility rules apply equally to identifiers associated with objects that do not necessarily exist at run time: typedef names, type tags, and enumeration constants. When any of these identifiers are declared, their scope is the same as that of a variable defined at the same location.

References   enumeration constants 5.5; scope 4.2.1; structure type 5.6; typedef name 5.10; visibility 4.2.2

4.3 STORAGE CLASS SPECIFIERS

We now proceed to examine the pieces of declarations: storage class specifiers, type specifiers, declarators, and initializers.

A storage class specifier determines the extent of a declared object (except for `typedef`, which is special). At most one storage class specifier may appear in a declaration. It is customary for storage class specifiers (if any) to precede type specifiers or qualifiers (if any) in declarations. In fact, both ANSI and traditional C allow them to occur in any order, although ANSI C considers this to be an obsolescent feature.

storage-class-specifier : one of
```
          auto  extern  register  static  typedef
```

The meanings of the storage classes are given in table 4–2. Note that not all storage classes are permitted in every declaration context.

Table 4–2: Storage class specifiers

Specifier	Usage
auto	Permitted only in declarations of variables at the heads of blocks. It indicates that the variable has local (automatic) extent. (Because this is the default, auto is rarely seen in C programs.)
extern	May appear in declarations of external functions and variables, either at the top level or at the heads of blocks. It indicates that the object declared has static extent and its name is known to the linker. See section 4.8.
register	May be used for local variables or parameter declarations. It is equivalent to auto, except that it provides a hint to the compiler that the object will be heavily used and should be allocated in a way that minimizes access time.
static	May appear on declarations of functions or variables. On function definitions, it is used only to specify that the function name is not to be exported to the linker. On function declarations, it indicates that the declared function will be defined—with storage class static— later in the file. On data declarations, it always signifies a defining declaration that is not exported to the linker. Variables declared with this storage class have static extent (as opposed to local extent, signified by auto).
typedef	Indicates that the declaration is defining a new data type rather than a variable or function. The name of the new data type appears where a variable name would appear in a variable declaration, and the new data type is the type that would have been assigned to the variable name. (See section 5.10.)

ANSI C allows register to be used with any type of variable or parameter, but it is not permitted to compute the address of such an object, either explicitly (with the & operator) or implicitly (e.g., by converting an array name to a pointer when subscripting the array). Many non-ANSI C compilers behave differently:

- They may restrict the use of register to objects of scalar types.
- They may permit the use of & on register objects.
- They may implicitly widen small objects declared with register, e.g., treating the declaration register char x as if it were register int x.

Implementations are permitted to treat the register storage class specifier the same as the auto specifier. However, programmers can expect the use of register on one or two heavily used variables in a function to increase performance. Using `register` on many declarations is likely to be ineffective or counterproductive. The use of `register` with highly optimizing compilers is likely to have less effect, since those compilers already allocate variables to registers as necessary.

References   address (`&`) operator 7.5.6; formal parameter declarations 9.3; initializers 4.6; subscripts 7.4.1; top-level declarations 4.1; typedef names 5.10

4.3.1 Default Storage Class Specifiers

If no storage class specifier is supplied with a declaration, one will be assumed based upon the declaration context, as shown below.

Default storage class specifiers

Location of declaration	Kind of declaration	Default storage class
Top level	All	`extern`
Function parameter	All	none (that is, "not `register`")
Block head	Functions	`extern`
Block head	Non-functions	`auto`

Omitting the storage class specifier on a top-level declaration may not be the same as supplying `extern`, as discussed in section 4.8. As a matter of good programming style, we think programmers should supply the storage class `extern` when declaring an external function inside a block. The `auto` storage class is never seen in C programs; it is always defaulted.

References   blocks 8.4; parameter declarations 9.3; top-level declarations 4.1, 4.8

4.3.2 Examples of Storage Class Specifiers

Table 4–3 shows an implementation of the heapsort algorithm for sorting the contents of an array. It is beyond the scope of this book to explain how it works in detail. We remark only that the algorithm regards the array as a binary tree such that the two subtrees of element `b[k]` are elements `b[2*k]` and `b[2*k+1]`, and that a heap is a tree such that every node contains a number that is no smaller than any of the numbers contained by that node's descendants. The code is a practical example of the use of storage class specifiers.

The main function is `heapsort`; it must be visible to users of the sort package, and so it has the default storage class, namely `extern`. The auxiliary function `adjust` does not need to be externally visible, and so it is declared `static`. The speed of the `adjust` function is crucial to the performance of the sort, and so its local variables have been given storage class `register` as a hint to the compiler. The formal parameter n is also referred to repeatedly within `adjust`, and so it is also specified with storage class `register`. The other two formal parameters for `adjust` are referred to only once and are defaulted to "not register." The local variables of function `heapsort` do not impact performance as much as those in adjust; they have been given the default storage class, auto.

Table 4–3: Heapsort

```
/* Heapsort. */

#define SWAP(x, y) (temp = (x), (x) = (y), (y) = temp)

static void adjust(v, m, n)
    int v[], m;
    register int n;
/*
    If v[m+1] through v[n] is already in heap form,
    this puts v[m] through v[n] into heap form.
*/
{
    register int *b, j, k, temp;
    b = v - 1;    /* b is "1-origin", customary in heapsort,
                       i.e., v[j] is the same as b[j-1] */
    j = m;
    k = m * 2;
    while (k <= n) {
        if (k < n && b[k] < b[k+1]) ++k;
        if (b[j] < b[k]) SWAP(b[j], b[k]);
        j = k;
        k *= 2;
    }
}


/* Sort v[0]…v[n-1] into increasing order. */
void heapsort(v, n)
    int v[], n;
{
    int *b, j, temp;
    b = v - 1;
    /* Put the array into the form of a heap. */
    for (j = n/2; j > 0; j--)
        adjust(v, j, n);
    /* Repeatedly extract the largest element and
       put it at the end of the unsorted region. */
    for (j = n-1; j > 0; j--) {
        SWAP(b[1], b[j+1]);
        adjust(v, 1, j);
    }
}
```

4.4 TYPE SPECIFIERS AND QUALIFIERS

Type specifiers provide some of the information about the data type of the program identifiers being declared. Additional type information is supplied by the declarators. Type specifiers may also define (as a side effect) type tags, structure and union component names, and enumeration constants.

The type qualifiers, `const` and `volatile`, are new in ANSI C and specify additional properties of types that are relevant only when accessing objects of the type through lvalues (section 7.1):

> *type-specifier* :
>> *enumeration-type-specifier*
>> *floating-point-type-specifier*
>> *integer-type-specifier*
>> *structure-type-specifier*
>> *typedef-name*
>> *union-type-specifier*
>> *void-type-specifier*
>
> *type-qualifier* :
>> `const`
>> `volatile`

Examples of type specifiers include:

```
void                  union { int a; char b; }
int                   enum {red, blue, green}
unsigned long int     char
my_struct_type        float
```

The type specifiers are described in detail in chapter 5, and we will defer further discussion of particular type specifiers until then. However, there are a few general issues surrounding type specifiers that will be discussed here.

References   declarators 4.5; enumeration type specifier 5.5; floating-point type specifier 5.2; integer type specifier 5.1; lvalue 7.1; structure type specifier 5.6; type qualifiers 4.4.3; typedef name 5.10; union type specifier 5.7; void type specifier 5.9

4.4.1 Default Type Specifiers

C allows the type specifier in a variable declaration or function definition to be omitted, in which case it defaults to `int`. One often sees this in function definitions:

```
/* Sort v[0]…v[n-1] into increasing order. */
sort(v, n)
    int v[], n;
{
    …
}
```

This is bad programming style in modern C. Older compilers did not implement the
void type, so a rationale behind omitting the type specifier on function definitions was
to indicate to human readers that the function didn't really return a value (although the
compiler had to assume that it did). The modern style is to declare those functions with
the void type:

```
/* Sort v[0]…v[n-1] into increasing order. */
void sort(v, n)
    int v[], n;
{
    …
}
```

When using a compiler that doesn't implement void, it is much nicer to define void
yourself and then use it explicitly than to omit the type specifier entirely:

```
/* Make "void" be a synonym for "int". */
typedef int void;
```

At least one compiler we know of actually reserves the identifier void but doesn't
implement it. For that compiler, the preprocessor definition

```
#define void int
```

is one of the few cases in which using a reserved word as a macro name is justified.

The declaration syntax (section 4.1) requires declarations to contain a storage class
specifier, a type specifier, a type qualifier, or some combination of the three. This
requirement avoids a syntactic ambiguity in the language. If all specifiers and qualifiers
were defaulted, the declaration

```
extern int f();
```

would become simply

```
f();
```

which is syntactically equivalent to a statement consisting of a function call. We think
that the best style is to always include the type specifier and to allow the storage class
specifier to default, at least when it is auto.

A final note for LALR(1) grammar aficionados: both the storage class specifier and the type specifier can be omitted on a function definition, and this is very common in C programs, as in

```
main()
{
    ...
}
```

There is no syntactic ambiguity in this case, because the declarator in a function declaration must be followed by a comma or semicolon, whereas the declarator in a function definition must be followed by a left brace.

      References declarations 4.1; function definitions 9.1; void type specifier 5.9

4.4.2 Missing Declarators

The following discussion deals with a subtle point of declarations and type specifiers. Type specifiers that are structure, union, or enumeration definitions have a side effect of defining new types. For example, the type specifier

```
struct S { int a, b; }
```

defines a new structure type S with components a and b. The type can be referenced later by using just the specifier

```
struct S
```

When using these specifiers, it makes sense to omit all the declarators from the declaration, so that the whole declaration consists of just a type definition:

```
struct S { int a, b; };
```

The C grammar permits this, and so do all C compilers. However, the grammar also permits some nonsensical variations on this declaration. Most C compilers will not notice these variations, although they are clearly programming errors.

    The first variation is omitting the type tag, as in

```
struct { int a, b; };
```

This is clearly nonsensical because without a tag it is impossible to refer to the type later in the program.

    The second variation is including a storage class specifier, which will be ignored:

```
static struct S { int a, b; };
```

This may mislead the programmer into thinking that a later declaration of the form

```
struct S x,y;
```

will cause x and y to have the storage class static. It won't.

The final nonsensical variation is using a type specifier that has no side effects:

```
int ;
```

References   enumeration types 5.5; declarators 4.5; structure types 5.6; type specifiers 4.4; union types 5.7

4.4.3 Type Qualifiers

The type qualifiers const and volatile are new in ANSI C. An identifier declared using one or both of these qualifiers is said to have a *qualified type*; there are three different qualified *versions* of each unqualified type, corresponding to the presence of the qualifier const, volatile, or both. None of the three qualified versions is compatible with the others or with the unqualified type.

Type qualifiers specify additional properties of types that are relevant only when accessing objects through lvalues with those qualified types. When used in a context that requires a value rather than a designator, the qualifiers are eliminated from the type. That is, in the expression L=R, the type of the right operand of = always has an unqualified type, even if R was declared with type qualifiers. The left operand, however, keeps its qualification, since it is used in lvalue context.

When using a C compiler that does not support type qualifiers, you can supply the following macro definitions so that the use of the type qualifiers will not cause the compilation to fail. Of course, the qualifiers will also have no effect.

```
#ifndef __STDC__
#define const /*nothing*/
#define volatile /*nothing*/
#endif
```

References   #ifndef 3.5.3; __STDC__ 11.3; type compatibility 5.11

4.4.4 Const

The type qualifier const may be used with other type specifiers and qualifiers—including structure, union, and enumeration type specifiers and volatile—or it may be used alone, in which case the additional specifier int is assumed. Members of structures can also be qualified with const.

An lvalue expression of a const-qualified type cannot be used to modify an object. That is, such an lvalue cannot be used as the left operand of an assignment expression or the operand of an increment or decrement operator. The intent is to use the const qualifier to designate objects whose value is unchanging, and to have the C compiler attempt to ensure that the programmer does not change the value. For example, the following declaration specifies that `ic` is to be an integer with the constant value 37:

```
const int ic = 37;
...
ic = 5; /* Illegal */
ic++;   /* Illegal */
```

The `const` qualifier can also appear in pointer declarators to make it possible to declare both "constant pointers" and "pointers to constant data":

```
int * const const_pointer;
const int *pointer_to_const;
```

The syntax may be confusing: constant pointers and constant integers, for example, have the type qualifier `const` in different locations. The appearance also changes when `typedef` names are used; the constant pointer `const_pointer` in the previous example may also be declared

```
typedef int *int_pointer;
const int_pointer const_pointer;
```

or equivalently

```
int_pointer const const_pointer;
```

A "pointer to constant data" may be assigned to, but the object to which it points cannot be. Expressions with this type can also be generated by applying the address operator `&` to values of `const`-qualified types:

```
const int *pc; /* pointer to a constant integer */
int *p, i;
const int ic;
pc = p = &i; /* OK */
pc = &ic;    /* OK */
*p = 5;      /* OK */
*pc = 5;     /* Illegal */
```

To protect the integrity of constant data, assigning a value of type "pointer to `const` T" to an object of type "pointer to T" is allowed only by using an explicit cast. Continuing the previous example:

```
pc = &i;          /* OK */
pc = p;           /* OK */
p = &ic;          /* Illegal */
p = pc;           /* Illegal */
p = (int *)&ic;   /* OK */
p = (int *)pc;    /* OK */
```

The language rules for `const` are not foolproof; that is, they may be bypassed or overridden if the programmer tries hard enough. For instance, the address of a constant object can be passed to an external function without a prototype. However, implementations are permitted to allocate static objects of `const`-qualified types in read-only storage, so that attempts to alter the objects could cause run-time errors, as shown in this program fragment:

```
static const int * pc;
static int * p;
static const int ic = 0;
...
pc = &ic;         /* OK */
p = (int *)pc;    /* Legal, but dangerous */
*p = 5;           /* Legal, but may cause a run-time error */
```

References assignment expression 7.9; increment and decrement expressions 7.4; pointer declarators 4.5.2

4.4.5 Volatile

The type qualifier `volatile` may be used with other type specifiers and qualifiers—including structure, union, and enumeration type specifiers and `const`—or may be used alone, in which case the additional specifier `int` is assumed.

The `volatile` type qualifier informs the ANSI C implementation that certain objects can have their values altered in ways not under control of the implementation. That is, any object (strictly speaking, any lvalue expression) of a `volatile`-qualified type should not participate in optimizations that would increase, decrease, or delay any references to, or modifications of, the object.

To be more precise, ANSI C introduces the notion of *sequence points* in C programs. A sequence point exists at the completion of all expressions that are not part of a larger expression; that is, at the end of expression statements, control expressions `if`, `switch`, `while`, and `do` statements, each of the three control expressions in the `for` statement, `return` statement expressions, and initializers. Additional sequence points are present in function calls immediately after all the arguments are evaluated, in the logical AND (`&&`) and OR (`||`) expressions, and before the conditional operator (`?:`) and the comma operator (`,`).

References to and modifications of volatile objects must not be optimized across sequence points, although optimizations between sequence points are permitted. Extra references or modifications can be generated at any time. For example, consider the following program fragment:

```
extern int f();
auto int i,j;
...
i = f(0);
while (i) {
    if (f(j*j)) break;
}
```

If the variable i were not used again during its lifetime, then traditional C implementations would be permitted to rewrite this program fragment as

```
if (f(0)) {
    i = j*j;
    while( !f(i) ) ;
}
```

The first assignment to i was eliminated, and i was reused as a temporary variable to hold j*j, which is evaluated once outside the loop. If the declaration of i and j were

```
auto volatile int i,j;
```

then these optimizations would not be permitted. However, we could write the loop as shown below, eliminating one reference to j before the sequence point at the end of the if statement control expression:

```
i = f(0);
while (i) {
    register int temp = j;
    if (f(temp*temp)) break;
}
```

The new syntax for pointer declarators allows the declaration of type "pointer to volatile ...." References to this kind of pointer may be optimized, but references to the object to which it points cannot be. Assigning a value of type "pointer to volatile *T*" to an object of type "pointer to *T*" is allowed only when an explicit cast is used. For example:

```
volatile int * pv;
int *p;
pv = p;          /* OK */
p = pv;          /* Illegal */
p = (int *)pv; /* OK */
```

The most common use of volatile is to provide reliable access to special memory locations used by the computer hardware or by asynchronous processes such as

interrupt handlers. Consider the following typical example. A computer has three special
hardware locations:

Address	Use
0xFFFFFF20	Input data buffer
0xFFFFFF24	Output data buffer
0xFFFFFF28	Control register

The control register and input data buffer can be read by a program but not written;
the output buffer can be written but not read. The third least significant bit of the control
register is called "input available"; it is set to 1 when data have arrived from an external
source, and it is set to 0 automatically when these data are read out of the input buffer by
the program (after which time the contents of the buffer are undefined until "input
available" becomes 1 again). The second least significant bit of the control register is
called "output available"; when the external device is ready to accept data, the bit is set to
1. When data are placed in the output buffer by the program the bit is automatically set to
0 and the data are written out. Placing data in the output buffer when the control bit is 0
causes unpredictable results.

The function `copy_data` below copies data from the input to the output until an
input value of 0 is seen. The number of characters copied is returned. There is no
provision for overflow or other error conditions:

```
typedef unsigned long datatype, control type, counttype;
#define CONTROLLER/
    ((const volatile controltype * const) 0xFFFFFF28)
#define INPUT_BUF/
    ((const volatile datatype * const) 0xFFFFFF20)
#define OUTPUT_BUF /
    ((volatile datatype * const)  0xFFFFFF24)
#define input_ready ((*CONTROLLER) & 0x4)
#define output_ready ((*CONTROLLER) & 0x2)

counttype copy_data()
{
    counttype count = 0;
    datatype temp;
    for(;;) {
        while (!input_ready) ;    /* Wait for input */
        temp = *INPUT_BUF;
        if (temp == 0) return count;
        while (!output_ready) ;   /* Wait to do output */
        *OUTPUT_BUF = temp;
        count++;
    }
}
```

References   pointer declarators 4.5

4.5 DECLARATORS

Declarators introduce the name being declared and also supply additional type information. No other programming language has anything quite like C's declarators:

> *declarator* :
> > *pointer-declarator*
> > *direct-declarator*
>
> *direct-declarator* :
> > *simple-declarator*
> > (*declarator*)
> > *function-declarator*
> > *array-declarator*

The different kinds of declarators are described in the following sections.

4.5.1 Simple Declarators

Simple declarators are used to define variables of arithmetic, enumeration, structure, and union types:

> *simple-declarator* :
> > *identifier*

Suppose that *S* is a type specifier and that *id* is any identifier. Then the declaration

> *S* *id* ;

indicates that *id* is of type *S*. The *id* is called a simple declarator. Examples of simple declarators are shown in the table below.

Examples of simple declarators

Declaration	Type of x
`int x;`	integer
`float x;`	floating-point
`struct S { int a;`	structure of two
`          float b; } x;`	components

Simple declarators may be used in a declaration when the type specifier supplies all the typing information. This happens for arithmetic, structure, union, enumeration, and void types, and for types represented by typedef names. Pointer, array, and function types require the use of more complicated declarators. However, every declarator includes an identifier, and we thus say that a declarator "encloses" an identifier.

References   type specifiers 4.4; structure types 5.6; typedef names 5.10

4.5.2 Pointer Declarators

Pointer declarators are used to declare variables of pointer types. The *type-qualifier-list* in the following syntax is new in ANSI C; in older compilers it is omitted:

> *pointer-declarator* :
> > *pointer direct-declarator*
>
> *pointer*:
> > $\star$ *type-qualifier-list*$_{opt}$
> > $\star$ *type-qualifier-list*$_{opt}$ *pointer*
>
> *type-qualifier-list* :   (ANSI C)
> > *type-qualifier*
> > *type-qualifer-list type qualifier*

Suppose that *D* is any declarator enclosing the identifier *id*, and that the declaration "*S D ;* " indicates that *id* has type "... *S*." Then the declaration

> *S ⋆D ;*

indicates that *id* has type "...pointer to *S*." For example, in the three declarations of x in the table below, *id* is x, *S* is int, and "..." is, respectively, "", "array of," and "function returning."

Examples of pointer declarators

Declaration	Type of x
int *x;	pointer to integer
int *x[];	array of pointers to integers
int *x();	function returning a pointer to an integer

It's harder to explain than it is to learn.

The optional *type-qualifier-list* in pointer declarators is allowed only in ANSI C. When present, the qualifiers apply to the pointer, not to the object pointed to. In the following declarations, ptr_to_const is a (variable) pointer to a constant integer, whereas const_ptr is a constant pointer to a (variable) integer:

```
const int * ptr_to_const;
int * const const_ptr;
```

References   array declarators 4.5.3; const type qualifier 4.4.4; function declarators 4.5.4; pointer types 5.3; type qualifiers 4.4.3

4.5.3 Array Declarators

Array declarators are used to declare objects of array types:

array-declarator :
        direct-declarator [*constant-expression*$_{opt}$]

constant-expression :
        expression

If *D* is any declarator enclosing the identifier *id*, and if the declaration "*S D;* " indicates that *id* has type "… *S*," then the declaration

S (*D*) [*e*] ;

indicates that *id* has type "… array of *S*."   (The parentheses may often be elided according to the precedence rules in constructing declarators; see section 4.5.5.)   The integer constant expression *e*, if present, specifies the number of elements in the array.

    For example, in the three declarations in the table below, *id* is *x*, *S* is int, and "…" is, respectively, "", "pointer to," and "array of."

Examples of array declarators

Declaration	Type of x
int (x)[5];	array of integers
int (*x)[5];	pointer to an array of integers
int (x[5])[5];	array of array of integers

    Type qualifiers may appear in the declaration of an object of array type, but the qualifiers apply to the elements rather than the array itself.   That is, the declaration const int a[10] is a declaration of an array of constant integers, not a constant array of integers.

    C's arrays are always "0-origin"; that is, the array

int A[3];

consists of the elements A[0], A[1], and A[2].   The number of elements in an array must be greater than 0, although some popular C compilers do not check this.

    As in the example above, higher-dimensioned arrays are declared as "arrays of arrays." For example:

int judges_scores[10][2];
int checker_board[8][8];

The length of the array, a constant expression, may be omitted as long as it is not needed to allocate storage. It is not needed when:

1. The object being declared is a formal parameter of a function.
2. The declarator is accompanied by an initializer from which the length of the array can be deduced.

3. The declaration is not a defining occurrence; that is, it is an external declaration
    that refers to an object defined elsewhere.

An exception to these cases is that the declaration of any *n*-dimensional array must
include the sizes of the last *n*–1 dimensions so that the accessing algorithm can be
determined. For example:

```
static int vector[5];        /* defining occurrence */
char prompt[]="Yes or No?";  /* can deduce size */
extern matrix[][10];         /* external, but last
                                dimension must be supplied */
```

For more information, see section 5.4.

References   array types 5.4; constant expressions 7.11; formal parameters 9.3; initializers
4.6; referencing and defining declarations 4.8; type qualifiers 4.4.3

4.5.4 Function Declarators

Function declarators are used to declare or define functions, and to declare types that
have function pointers as components:

> *function-declarator :*
> > *direct-declarator*   (*parameter-type-list*)   (ANSI C)
> > *direct-declarator*   (*identifier-list*$_{opt}$)
>
> *parameter-type-list* :
> > *parameter-list*
> > *parameter-list* , . . .
>
> *parameter-list* :
> > *parameter-declaration*
> > *parameter-list* , *parameter-declaration*
>
> *parameter-declaration* :
> > *declaration-specifiers declarator*
> > *declaration-specifiers abstract-declarator*$_{opt}$
>
> *identifier-list :*
> > *identifier*
> > *parameter-list* , *identifier*

If *D* is any declarator enclosing the identifier *id*, and if the declaration "*S D ;* " indicates
that *id* has type "... *S*," then the declaration

> *S* (*D*) (*P*) ;

indicates that *id* has type "... function returning *S* with parameters *P*." The parentheses
around D can be omitted in most cases according to the precedence rules in constructing

declarators (section 4.5.5). The presence of *parameter-type-list* in the declarator syntax indicates that the declarator is in the form of an ANSI C prototype. Without it, the declarator is in traditional form, which is accepted by both traditional and ANSI C compilers. Some examples of function declarators are shown below:

Examples of function declarators

Declaration	Type of x
`int x();`	function with unspecified parameters returning an integer
`int x(double, float);`	function taking a `double` and a `float` parameter and returning an integer (prototype)
`int x(double d, float f);`	same as the preceding declarator
`int (*x)();`	pointer to a function with unspecified parameters returning an integer
`int (*x[])(int,...);`	array of pointers to functions that take a variable number of parameters beginning with an integer and return an integer (prototype)

Function declarators are subject to several constraints depending on whether they appear in a function definition or as part of an object or function type declaration. Table 4–4 shows the possible forms of a function declarator, indicates whether it is in traditional C form or ANSI C prototype form, whether it can appear in a function definition

Table 4–4: Function declarators

Syntax	Form	Appears in	Parameters specified
f()	traditional	definitions	no parameters
f()	traditional	type declarations	any number of parameters
f(x, y,..., z)	traditional	definitions	fixed[1]
f(void)	prototype	either	no parameters
f(T_x, T_y,..., T_z)	prototype	type declarations	fixed
f(T_x, T_y,..., T_z, ...)	prototype	type declarations	fixed, plus extras[2]
f(T_x x, T_y y,..., T_z z)	prototype	either	fixed
f(T_x x, T_y y,..., T_z z, ...)	prototype	either	fixed, plus extras[2]

[1] It is possible to have additional, unspecified parameters, except in ANSI C.

[2] The number and type of the extra parameters are unspecified.

or in a function type declaration, and what parameter information is specified. In the table, the notation T_x x refers to the syntax "*declaration-specifiers declarator*," that is, a parameter type declaration that includes the parameter name, x. T_x refers to "*declaration-specifiers abstract-declarator$_{opt}$*," that is, a parameter type declaration that omits the parameter name.

The declaration and use of functions are discussed in more detail in chapter 9. Variable-length parameter lists are accessed with the facilities in the `stdarg.h` or `varargs.h` header files.

References   abstract declarator 5.12; array declarators 4.5.3; defining and referencing declarations 4.8; function types and declarations 5.8; function definitions 9.1; pointer declarators 4.5; `stdarg.h` and `varargs.h` 11.4

4.5.5 Composition of Declarators

Declarators can be composed to form more complicated types, such as "5-element array of pointers to functions returning int," which is the type of `ary` in this declaration:

```
int (*ary[5])();
```

The only restriction on declarators is that the resulting type must be a legal one in C. The only types that are *not* legal in C are:

1. Any type including `void` except in the form of "...function returning `void`" or (in ANSI C) "pointer to `void`."
2. "Array of function of ...." Arrays may contain pointers to functions, but not functions themselves.
3. "Function returning array of ...." Functions may return pointers to arrays, but not arrays themselves.
4. "Function returning function of ...." Functions may return pointers to other functions, but not the functions themselves.

When composing declarators, the precedence of the declarator expressions is important. Function and array declarators have higher precedence than pointer declarators, so that "`*x()`" is equivalent to "`*(x())`" ("function returning pointer ...") instead of "`(*x)()`" ("pointer to function returning ..."). Parentheses may be used to group declarators properly. Here are some examples of declarator composition:

Examples of declarator composition

Declaration	Type of x
`int   x();`	function returning an integer
`int (*x)();`	pointer to a function returning an integer
`void (*x)();`	pointer to a function returning no result
`void *x();`[1]	function returning "pointer to `void`"

[1] ANSI C only.

Although declarators can be arbitrarily complex, it is better programming style to factor them into several simpler definitions. That is, rather than writing

```
int *(*(*(*x)())[10])();
```

write instead

```
typedef int *(*print_function_ptr)();
typedef print_function_ptr (*digit_routines)[10];
digit_routines (*x)();
```

(The variable x is a pointer to a function returning a pointer to a 10-element array of pointers to functions returning pointers to integers, in case you wondered.)

Early C compilers had an upper limit of 6 on the depth of declarator nesting. Modern C compilers allow at least a depth of 12, which is also the minimum depth that ANSI-conforming implementation must provide.

The rationale behind the syntax of declarators is that they mimic the syntax of a use of the enclosed identifier. For instance, if you see the declaration

```
int *(*x)[4];
```

then the type of the expression

```
*(*x)[i]
```

is int.

References   array types 5.4; function types 5.8; pointer to void 5.3.2; pointer types 5.3; void type specifier 5.9

4.6 INITIALIZERS

The declaration of a variable may be accompanied by an initializer that specifies the value the variable should have at the beginning of its lifetime. The full syntax for initializers is

initializer :
> *assignment-expression*
> { *initializer-list* , *opt* }

initializer-list :
> *initializer*
> *initializer-list* , *initializer*

The optional trailing comma inside the braces does not affect the meaning of the initializer.

The initializers permitted on a particular declaration depend on the type and storage class of the object to be initialized and on whether the declared object has static or automatic storage class. The options are listed in table 4–5 and presented in more detail in the following sections. Declarations of external objects should not have initializers unless they are defining occurrences.

Table 4–5: Form of initializers

Storage	Type	Initializer expression	Default initializer
static	scalar	constant	0, 0.0, or null pointer
static	array[1] or structure	brace-enclosed constants	recursive default for each component
static	union[2]	constant	default for the first component
automatic	scalar	any	none
automatic	array[1,2]	brace-enclosed constant	none
automatic	structure[2]	brace-enclosed constant, or a single non-constant expression of the same structure type	none
automatic	union[2]	constant, or a single non-constant expression of the same union type	none

[1] The array may have an unknown size; the initializer determines the size.
[2] ANSI C; older implementations may not permit initializations of these objects.

The "shape" of an initializer—the brace-enclosed lists of initializers—should match the structure of the variable being initialized. The language definition specifies that the initializers for scalar variables may optionally be surrounded by braces, although such braces are logically unnecessary. We recommend that braces be reserved to indicate aggregate initialization. There are special rules for abbreviating initializers for aggregates.

Historical note: C originally had a syntax for initializers in which the = operator was omitted, and some current C compilers accept this syntax for compatibility. Users of these compilers, when they accidentally omit a comma or semicolon in a declaration (e.g., "int a b;"), get an obscure error message about an illegal initializer. ANSI C does not support this obsolete syntax.

The following sections explain the special requirements for each type of variable.

References   automatic and static lifetime 4.2; declarations 4.1; external objects 4.8; static storage class 4.3

4.6.1 Integers

The form of an initializer for an integer variable is

> *declarator = expression*

The initializing expression must have a type that would be permitted in a simple assignment to the initialized variable; the usual assignment conversions are applied.   If the variable is static or external, the expression must be constant. If the variable is automatic or register, any expression is permitted.   For example:

```
static int Count = 4*200;
extern int getchar();

main()
{
    int ch = getchar();
    ...
}
```

The default initializer for a static integer is 0.

References   constant expression 7.11; integer types 5.1; static and automatic extent 4.2; usual assignment conversions 6.3.2

4.6.2 Floating-point

The form of an initializer for a floating-point variable is

> *declarator = expression*

The initializing expression must have a type that would be permitted in a simple assignment to the initialized variable; the usual assignment conversions are applied.   If the variable is static or external, the expression must be constant. If the variable is automatic or register, any expression is permitted.   For example:

```
static void process_data(K)
    double K;
{
    static double epsilon = 1.0e-6;
    auto float fudge_factor = K*epsilon;
    ...
}
```

ANSI C specifically permits floating-point constant expressions in initializers. Some older C compilers have been known to balk at complicated floating-point constant expressions.

The default initialization of static, floating-point variables is 0.0. This value might not be represented on the target computer as an object whose bits are zero. ANSI C compilers must initialize the variable to the correct representation for 0.0, but most older C compilers always initialize static storage to zero bits.

References   arithmetic types ch. 5; constant expressions 7.11; floating-point constant 2.7.2; floating-point types 5.2; static and automatic extent 4.2; unary minus operator 7.5.3; usual assignment conversions 6.3.2

4.6.3 Pointers

The form of an initialization of a pointer variable is

declarator = *expression*

The initializing expression must have a type that would be permitted in a simple assignment to the initialized variable; the usual assignment conversions are applied.   If the variable is static or external, the expression must be constant. If the variable is automatic or register, any expression is permitted.

Constant expressions used as initializers of pointer type *PT* may be formed from the following elements.

1. An integral constant expression with the value 0, or such a value cast to type void *. These are null pointer constants, usually referred to by the name NULL in the standard library.

   ```
   #define NULL ((void *)0)
   double *dp = NULL;
   ```

2. The name of a static or external function of type "function returning *T*" is converted to a constant of type "pointer to function returning *T*."

   ```
   extern int f();
   static int (*fp)() = f;
   ```

3. The name of a static or external array of type "array of *T*" is converted to a constant of type "pointer to *T*."

   ```
   char ary[100];
   char *cp = ary;
   ```

4. The & operator applied to the name of a static or external variable of type *T* yields a constant of type "pointer to *T*."

   ```
   static short s; auto short *sp = &s;
   ```

5. The `&` operator applied to an external or static array of type "array of T," subscripted by a constant expression, yields a constant of type "pointer to T."

```
float PowersOfPi[10];
float *PiSquared = &PowersOfPi[2];
```

6. An integer constant cast to a pointer type yields a constant of that pointer type, although this is not portable.

```
long *PSW = (long *) 0xFFFFFFF0;
```

Not all compilers accept casts in constant expressions.

7. A string literal yields a constant of type "pointer to `char`" when it appears as the initializer of a variable of pointer type.

```
char *greeting = "Type <cr> to begin ";
```

8. The sum or difference of any expression shown for cases 3 through 7 above and an integer constant expression.

```
static short s;
auto short *sp = &s + 3, *msp = &s - 3;
```

In general, the initializer for a pointer type must evaluate to an integer or to an address plus (or minus) an integer constant. This limitation reflects the capabilities of most linkers.

The default initialization for static pointers is the null pointer. In the (rare) case that null pointers are not represented by an object whose bits are zero, ANSI C specifies that the correct null pointer value must be used. Most older C compilers simply initialize static storage to zero bits.

References   & address operator 7.5.6; array types 5.4; conversions involving pointers 6.2.7; function types 5.8; integer constants 2.7; pointer declarator 4.5; pointer types 5.3; string constants 2.7; usual assignment conversions 6.3.2

4.6.4 Arrays

If I_j is a constant expression that is an allowable initializer for objects of type T, then

$$\{ \ I_0 \ , \ I_1 \ , \ ... , \ I_{n-1} \ \}$$

is an allowable initializer for type "n-element array of T." The initializer Ij is used to initialize element j of the array (zero origin). For example:

```
int ary[4] = { 0, 1, 2, 3 };
```

Multidimensional arrays follow the same pattern, with initializers listed by row. (The last subscript varies most rapidly in C.)

```
int ary[4][2][3] =
            { { { 0,  1,  2},  { 3,  4,  5} },
              { { 6,  7,  8},  { 9, 10, 11} },
              { {12, 13, 14},  {15, 16, 17} },
              { {18, 19, 20},  {21, 22, 23} } };
```

Arrays of structures (section 4.6.6) may be initialized analogously:

```
struct {int a; float b;} a[3] = { {1,  2.5},
                                  {2,  3.9},
                                  {0, -4.0} };
```

Static and external arrays may always be initialized in this way. ANSI C permits the initialization of automatic arrays using constant component expressions, but older compilers are likely to reject any initialization of automatic arrays because the feature was not in the original definition of C.

Array initialization has a number of special rules. First, the number of initializers may be less than the number of array elements, in which case the remaining elements are initialized to their default initialization value. That is, the initializations

```
float ary[5] = { 1, 2, 3 };
int mat[3][3] = { {1, 2}, {3} };
```

are equivalent to

```
int ary[5] = { 1.0, 2.0, 3.0, 0.0, 0.0 };
int mat[3][3] = { {1, 2, 0},
                  {3, 0, 0},
                  {0, 0, 0} };
```

This is true for both static and automatic initializations. On the other hand, if the number of initializers is greater than the number of elements, it is an error.

Second, the bounds of the array need not be specified, in which case the bounds are derived from the length of the initializer. For example:

```
int squares[] = { 0, 1, 4, 9 };
```

is the same as

```
int squares[4] = { 0, 1, 4, 9 };
```

Third, string literals may be also be used to initialize variables of type "array of char." In this case, the first element of the array is initialized by the first character in the string, and so forth. The string's terminating null character, '\0', will be stored in

the array if there is room or if the size of the array is unspecified. The string may
optionally be enclosed in braces. Thus, the initializations

```
char x[5]   = "ABCDE";
char str[]  = "ABCDE";
char q[5]   = {"A"};
```

are the same as

```
char x[5]    = { 'A', 'B', 'C', 'D', 'E' }; /* No '\0'! */
char str[6]  = { 'A', 'B', 'C', 'D', 'E', '\0' };
char q[5]    = { 'A', '\0', '\0', '\0', '\0' };
```

It is an error if the string is too long for a character array of specified size.

An array whose element type is compatible with `wchar_t` can be initialized by a
wide string literal in the same way.

Finally, a list of strings can be used to initialize an array of character pointers:

```
char *astr[] = { "John", "Bill", "Susan", "Mary" };
```

References   array types 5.4; character constants 2.7; character types 5.1.3; pointer types 5.3;
string constants 2.7; wide strings 2.7.4

4.6.5 Enumerations

The form of initializers for variables of enumeration type is

   declarator = *expression*

The initializing expression must have a type that would be permitted in a simple
assignment to the initialized variable; the usual assignment conversions are applied.   If
the variable is static or external, the expression must be constant. If the variable is
automatic or register, any expression is permitted.   Good programming style suggests
that the type of the initializing expression should be the same enumeration type as the
variable being initialized. For example:

```
static enum E { a, b, c } x = a;
auto enum E y = x;
```

References   cast expressions 7.5.1; constant expressions 7.11; enumeration types 5.5; usual
assignment conversions 6.3.2

4.6.6 Structures

If a structure type T has n named components of types T_j, $j=1,\ldots,n$, and if I_j is an
initializer that is allowable for an object of type T_j then

$$\{ I_1 , I_2 , ..., I_n \}$$

is an allowable initializer for type *T*. Unnamed bit field components do not participate in initialization. The initializers I_j must always be constant expressions. For example:

```
struct S {int a; char b[5]; double c; };
struct S x = { 1, "abcd", 45.0 };
```

Static and external variables of structure types can be initialized by all C compilers. Automatic and register variables of structure types can be initialized in ANSI C, and either of two forms may be used.   First, a brace-enclosed list of constant expressions can be used, as for static variables. Second, an initialization of the form

declarator = *expression*

may be used, where *expression* is of the same structure type as the variable being initialized.

As with array initializers, structure initializers have some special abbreviation rules. In particular, if there are fewer initializers than there are structure components, the remaining components are initialized to their default initial values. Thus, given the structure declaration

```
struct S1 {int a;
           struct S2 {double b;
                      char c; } b;
           int c[4]; };
```

the initialization

```
struct S1 x = { 1, {4.5} };
```

is the same as

```
struct S1 x = { 1, { 4.5, '\0' }, { 0, 0, 0, 0 } };
```

If there are too many initializers for the structure, it is an error.

A few older C compilers are deficient in not allowing the initialization of structures containing bit fields.

References   bit fields 5.6.5; constant expressions 7.11; structure types 5.6

4.6.7 Unions

ANSI C allows the initialization of union variables. (Traditional C does not.) The initializer for a static, external, automatic, or register union variable must be a brace-enclosed constant expression that would be allowable as an initializer for an object of the type of the first component of the union. The initializer for an automatic or register union may alternatively be any single expression of the same union type. These two initializer forms are shown below for the union variables x and y:

```
enum Greek { alpha, beta, gamma };
union U {
        struct { enum Greek tag; int Size; } I;
        struct { enum Greek tag; float Size; } F;
     };
static union U x = {{ alpha, 42 }};
auto union U y = x;
```

The only remaining C types are function types and void. Since variables of these types cannot be declared, the question of initialization is moot.

References   static extent 4.2; union types 5.7

4.6.8 Eliding Braces

C permits braces to be dropped from initializer lists under certain circumstances, although it is usually clearer to retain them. The general rules are listed below.

1. If a variable of array or structure type is being initialized, the outermost pair of braces may *not* be dropped.
2. Otherwise, if an initializer list contains the correct number of elements for the object being initialized, the braces may be dropped.

The most common use of these rules is in dropping inner braces when initializing a multidimensional array:

```
int matrix[2][3] = { 1, 2, 3, 4, 5, 6 };
        /* same as: { {1, 2, 3}, {4, 5, 6} } */
```

Many C compilers treat initializer lists casually, permitting too many or too few braces. We advise keeping initializers simple and using braces to make their structure explicit.

4.7 IMPLICIT DECLARATIONS

An external function used in a function call need not have been declared previously. If the compiler sees an identifier *id* followed by a left parenthesis, and if *id* has not been previously declared, then a declaration is implicitly entered in the innermost enclosing scope of the form:

```
extern int id();
```

(Some non-ANSI conforming implementations may declare the identifier at the top level rather than in the innermost scope.)

Allowing functions to be declared in this way is poor programming style and may lead to errors, particularly those concerning incorrect return types. For example, if a pointer-returning function, such as `malloc` (section 16.1), is allowed to be implicitly declared as

```
extern int malloc();
```

rather than the correct

```
extern char *malloc();    /* returns (void *) in ANSI C */
```

then calls to `malloc` will probably not work if the types `int` and `char *` are represented differently. Suppose type `int` occupies two bytes and pointers occupy four bytes. When the compiler sees

```
int *p;
...
p = (int *) malloc(sizeof(int));
```

it generates code to extend what it thought was a two-byte value returned by `malloc` to the four bytes required by the pointer. The effect is that only the low half of the address returned by `malloc` is assigned to p, and the program begins to fail when enough storage has been allocated to cause `malloc` to return addresses larger than $0xFFFF$.

4.8 EXTERNAL NAMES

An important issue with external names is ensuring consistency among the declarations of the same external name in several files. For instance, what if two declarations of the same external variable specified different initializations? For this and other reasons, it is useful to distinguish a single *defining declaration* of an external name within a group of files. The other declarations of the same name are then considered *referencing declarations*; that is, they reference the defining declaration.

It is a well-known deficiency in C that defining and referencing occurrences of external variable declarations are difficult to distinguish. In general, compilers use one of four models to determine when a top-level declaration is a defining occurrence.

4.8.1 The Initializer Model

The presence of an initializer on a top-level declaration indicates a defining occurrence; all others are referencing occurrences. There must be a single defining occurrence among all the files in the C program.

4.8.2 The Omitted Storage Class Model

In this scheme, the storage class `extern` must be explicitly included on all referencing declarations, and the storage class must be omitted from the single defining declaration for each external variable. The defining declaration can include an initializer, but it is not required to do so. (It is illegal to have both an initializer and the storage class `extern` in a declaration.) This solution is probably the most common one, and the one adopted in ANSI C.

4.8.3 The Common Model

This scheme is so named because it is related to the way multiple references to a FORTRAN COMMON block are merged into a single defining occurrence in some FORTRAN implementations. Both defining and referencing external declarations have storage class `extern`, whether explicitly or by default. Among all the declarations for each external name in all the object files linked together to make the program, only one may have an initializer. At link time, all external declarations for the same identifier (in all C object files) are combined and a single defining occurrence is conjured, not necessarily associated with any particular file. If any declaration specified an initializer, that initializer is used to initialize the data object. (If several declarations did, the results are unpredictable.)

This solution is the most painless for the programmer and the most demanding on system software.

4.8.4 Mixed Common Model

This model is a cross between the "omitted storage class" model and the "common" model. It is used in many versions of UNIX.

1. If `extern` is omitted and an initializer is present, a definition for the symbol is emitted. Having two or more such definitions among all the files comprising a program results in an error at link time or before.
2. If `extern` is omitted, and no initializer is present, a "common" definition (a la FORTRAN) is emitted. Any number of common definitions of the same identifier may coexist.
3. If `extern` is present, the declaration is taken to be a reference to a name defined elsewhere. It is illegal for such a declaration to have an initializer. If the identifier so declared is never actually used, the compiler will not issue an external reference to the linker.

If no explicit initializer is provided for the external variable, the variable is initialized as if the initializer had been the integer constant 0.

4.8.5 Summary and Recommendations

Table 4–6 shows the interpretation of a top-level declaration according to the model for external references in use.

Table 4–6: Interpretation of top-level declarations

Top-level declaration	Initializer	Model Omitted storage class	Common	Mixed common	Recom- mended
`int x;`	Reference	Definition	Definition or reference	Definition or reference	(Don't use)
`int x = 0;`	Definition	Definition	Definition	Definition	Definition
`extern int x;`	Reference	Reference	Definition or reference	Reference	Reference
`extern int x = 0;`	Definition	Reference	Definition	(Illegal)	(Don't use)

To remain compatible with the most compilers, we recommend following these rules:

1. Have a single definition point (source file) for each external variable; in the defining declaration, omit the `extern` storage class and include an explicit initializer:

   ```
   int errcnt = 0;
   ```

2. In each source file or header file referencing an external variable defined elsewhere, use the storage class `extern` and do not include an initializer:

   ```
   extern int errcnt;
   ```

Independent of the defining/referencing distinction, an external name should always be declared with the same type in all files making up a program. The C compiler cannot verify that declarations in different files are consistent in this fashion, and the punishment for inconsistency is erroneous behavior at run time. The `lint` program, usually supplied with the C compiler in UNIX systems, can check multiple files for consistent declarations.

4.8.6 Unreferenced External Declarations

Although not required by the C language, it is customary to ignore declarations of external variables or functions that are never referenced. For example, if the declaration "`extern double fft();`" appears in a program, but the function `fft` is never used, then no external reference to the name `fft` is passed to the linker. Therefore, the function `fft` will not be loaded with the program, where it would take up space to no purpose.

4.9 EXERCISES

1. The definition of a static function `P` is shown below. What will be the value of `P(6)`, if `P` has never been called before? What will `P(6)` be the second time it is called?

```
static int P(x)
    int x;
{
    int i = 0;
    i = i+1;
    return i*x;
}
```

2. The following program fragment shows a block containing various declarations of the name `f`. Do any of the declarations conflict? If so, cross out declarations until the program is legal, keeping as many different declarations of `f` as possible.

```
{
    extern double f();
    int f;
    typedef int f;
    struct f {int f,g;};
    union f {int x,y;};
    enum {f,b,s};
    f: ...
}
```

3. The following program fragment declares three variables named `i` with types `int`, `long`, and `float`. On which lines is each of the variables declared and used?

```
 1 int i;
 2 void f(i)
 3     long i;
 4 {
 5     long l = i;
 6     {
 7         float i;
 8         i = 3.4;
 9     }
10     l = i+2;
11 }
12 int *p = &i;
```

4. Write C declarations that express the following English statements. Use prototypes for function declarations.

(a) P is an external function that has no parameters and returns no result.

(b) i is a local integer variable that will be heavily used and should be optimized for speed.

(c) LT is a synonym for type "pointer to character."

(d) Q is an external function with two arguments and no result. The first, i, is an integer and the second, cp, is a string. The string will not be modified.

(e) R is an external function whose only argument, p, is a pointer to a function that takes a single 32-bit integer argument, i, and returns a pointer to a value of type double. R returns an integer value.

(f) STR is a static, uninitialized character string that should be modifiable and hold up to 10 characters, not including the terminating null character.

(g) STR2 is a character string initialized to the string literal that is the value of the macro INIT_STR2. Once initialized, the string will not be modified.

(h) IP is a pointer to an integer, initialized with the address of the variable i.

5.   The matrix m is declared as int m[3][3]; the first subscript specifies the row number and the second subscript specifies the column number. Write an initializer for m that places ones in the first column, twos in the second column, and threes in the third column.

5

Types

A *type* is a set of *values* and a set of *operations* on those values. For example, the values of an integer type consist of integers in some specified range, and the operations on those values consist of addition, subtraction, inequality tests, and so forth. The values of a floating-point type include numbers represented differently from integers, and a set of different operations: floating-point addition, subtraction, inequality tests, and so forth.

We say a variable or expression "has type *T*" when its values are constrained to the domain of *T*. The types of variables are established by the variable's declaration; the types of expressions are given by the definitions of the expression operators.

The C language provides a large number of built-in types, including integers of several kinds, floating-point numbers, pointers, enumerations, arrays, structures, unions, and functions.

It is useful to organize C's types into the categories shown in figure 5–1. The `void` type has no values and no operations. The *integral types* include all forms of integers, characters, and enumerations. The *arithmetic types* include the integral and floating-point types. The *scalar types* include the arithmetic types, pointer types, and enumerated types. The *function types* are the types "function returning...." *Aggregate types* include arrays and structures. *Union types* are created with the `union` specifier.

All of C's types are discussed in this chapter. For each type, we indicate how objects of the type are declared, the range of values of the type, any restrictions on the size or representation of the type, and what operations are defined on values of the type.

References array types 5.4; character types 5.1.3; declarations 4.1; enumerated types 5.5; floating-point types 5.2; function types 5.8; integer types 5.1; pointer types 5.3; structure types 5.6; union types 5.7; void type 5.9

5.1 INTEGER TYPES

C provides a larger number of integer types and operators than do most programming languages. The variety reflects the different word lengths and kinds of arithmetic

C Types

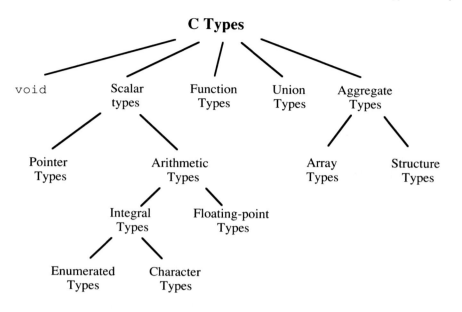

Figure 5–1: Type categories

operators found on most computers, thus allowing a close correspondence between C programs and the underlying hardware. Integer types in C are used to represent:

1. signed or unsigned integer values, for which the usual arithmetic and relational operations are provided
2. bit vectors, with the operations AND, OR, XOR, and left and right shifts
3. boolean values, for which zero is considered "false" and all nonzero values are considered "true," with the integer 1 being the canonical "true" value
4. characters, which are represented by their integer encodings on the computer

ANSI C requires implementations to use a binary encoding of integers; this is a recognition that many low-level C operations are not describable in any portable fashion on computers with non-binary representations.

It is convenient to divide the integer types into three classes: signed types, unsigned types, and characters. Each of these classes has a set of type specifiers that can be used to declare objects of the type.

> *integer-type-specifier* :
> > *signed-type-specifier*
> > *unsigned-type-specifier*
> > *character-type-specifier*

References   assignment conversions 6.3.2; binary operators 7.6; bitwise not operator ~ 7.5.5; bitwise operators |, ^, and & 7.6.6; character constants 2.7; constant expressions 7.11; declarations 4.1; integer constants 2.7; relational operators 7.6.4, 7.6.5; shift operators << and >> 7.6.3; unary minus operator − 7.5.3

5.1.1 Signed Integer Types

C provides the programmer with three sizes of signed integer types, denoted by the type specifiers short, int, and long in nondecreasing order of size. Each type can be named in several equivalent ways; in the syntax below, the equivalent names are shown for each of the three types.

signed-type-specifier :
```
        short or short int or signed short or signed short int
        int or signed int or signed
        long or long int or signed long or signed long int
```

The keyword signed is new in ANSI C, and can be omitted for compatibility with other C implementations. The only time the presence of signed might affect the meaning of a program is in conjunction with type char and with bit fields in structures; in that case a distinction can be made between a signed integer and a "plain integer," i.e., one written without signed. Here are some examples of typical declarations of signed integers:

```
short i, j;
long int l;
static signed int k;
```

The C language does not specify the range of integers that the integral types will represent, except to say that type int may not be smaller than short and long may not be smaller than int. Many implementations represent characters in 8 bits, type short in 16 bits, and type long in 32 bits, with type int using either 16 or 32 bits depending on the implementation. ANSI C requires implementations to use at least these widths.

The precise range of values representable by a signed integer type depends not only on the number of bits used in the representation but also on the encoding technique. By far the most common binary encoding technique for integers is called *two's-complement notation*, in which a signed integer represented with n bits will have a range from -2^{n-1} through $2^{n-1}-1$ encoded in the following fashion:

1. The high-order (leftmost) bit of the word is the sign bit. If the sign bit is 1, the number is negative; otherwise, the number is positive.
2. Positive numbers follow the normal binary sequence:

$$0 = 000...0000_2$$
$$1 = 000...0001_2$$
$$2 = 000...0010_2$$
$$3 = 000...0011_2$$
$$4 = 000...0100_2 \quad \text{(etc)}$$

In an n-bit word, omitting the sign bit, there are $n-1$ bits for the positive integers, which can represent the integers 0 through $2^{n-1}-1$.

3. To negate an integer, complement all the bits in the word and then add 1 to the result. Thus, to form the integer -1, start with 1 ($00...0001_2$); complement the bits ($11...1110_2$); and add 1 ($11...1111_2 = -1$).

4. The maximum negative value, $10...0000_2$ or -2^{n-1}, has no positive equivalent; negating this value produces the same value.

Other binary integer encoding techniques are *one's-complement notation*, in which negation simply complements all the bits of the word, and *sign magnitude notation*, in which negation involves simply complementing the sign bit. These alternative notations have a range from $-(2^{n-1}-1)$ through $2^{n-1}-1$; they have one less negative value and two representations for zero (positive and negative). All three notations represent positive integers identically.

ANSI C requires that implementations document the ranges of the integer types in the header file limits.h, and also specifies the maximum representable range a C programmer can assume for each integer type in all ANSI-conforming implementations. The symbols that must be defined in limits.h are shown in the table below. Implementations can substitute their own values, but they must not be less in absolute magnitude than the values shown, and must have the same sign. Therefore, an ANSI-conforming implementation cannot represent type int in only 8 bits, nor can a strictly conforming C program depend on, say, the value $-32,768$ being representable in type short. (This is to accommodate computers that use a one's-complement representation of binary integers.) The contents of limits.h is shown in table 5-1; programmers using older implementations can create a limits.h file for their implementation.

To keep programs as portable as possible, it is best not to depend on type int being able to represent integers outside the range $-32,767$ to $32,767$. Use type long if this range is insufficient. It is usually good style to define special integer types with typedef, based on the needs of each particular program. For example:

```
/* invdef.h
   Inventory definitions for the XXX computer.
*/
typedef short part_number;
typedef int   order_quantity;
typedef long  purchase_order;
```

In addition to making the program more readable, this technique makes it easy to adapt to computers with differing integer sizes by changing the definitions in only one file.

References   bit fields in structures 5.6.5; declarations 4.1; integer constants 2.7.1; `signed` type specifier 5.1.1; type conversions ch. 6; `typedef` 5.10

Table 5-1 Values defined in limits.h (ANSI C)

Name	Minimum value	Meaning
CHAR_BIT	8	width of `char` type, in bits
SCHAR_MIN	−127	minimum value of `signed char`
SCHAR_MAX	127	maximum value of `signed char`
UCHAR_MAX	255	maximum value of `unsigned char`
SHRT_MIN	−32,767	minimum value of `short int`
SHRT_MAX	32,767	maximum value of `short int`
USHRT_MAX	65,535	maximum value of `unsigned short`
INT_MIN	−32,767	minimum value of `int`
INT_MAX	32,767	maximum value of `int`
UINT_MAX	65,535	maximum value of `unsigned int`
LONG_MIN	−2,147,483,647	minimum value of `long int`
LONG_MAX	2,147,483,647	maximum value of `long int`
ULONG_MAX	4,294,967,295	maximum value of `unsigned long`
CHAR_MIN	SCHAR_MIN or 0[1]	minimum value of `char`
CHAR_MAX	SCHAR_MAX or UCHAR_MAX[2]	maximum value of `char`

[1] If type `char` is signed by default, then SCHAR_MIN, else 0.
[2] If type `char` is signed by default, then SCHAR_MAX, else UCHAR_MAX.

5.1.2 Unsigned Integer Types

For each of the signed integer types there is a corresponding unsigned type that occupies the same amount of storage but has a different integer encoding. The unsigned type is specified by preceding the corresponding signed type specifier with the keyword `unsigned` (replacing the keyword `signed` if it was present).

unsigned-type-specifier :
        `unsigned short int`$_{opt}$
        `unsigned int`$_{opt}$
        `unsigned long int`$_{opt}$

In each case the keyword `int` is optional and does not affect the meaning of the type specifier. Choosing from among the unsigned types involves the same considerations already discussed with respect to the signed integer types.

    All unsigned types use straight binary notation, regardless of whether the signed types use two's-complement, one's-complement, or sign magnitude notation; the sign bit is treated as an ordinary data bit. Therefore an n-bit word can represent the integers 0 through 2^n-1. Most computers are easily able to interpret the value in a word using either signed or unsigned notation. For example, when the two's-complement notation is used, the bit pattern $11\ldots1111_2$ can represent either −1 (using the signed notation), or 2^n-1 (using the unsigned notation). The integers from 0 through $2^{n-1}-1$ are represented identically in both signed and unsigned notations. The particular ranges of the unsigned types in an ANSI C implementation is documented in the header file `limits.h`.

Whether an integer is signed or unsigned affects the operations performed on it. All arithmetic operations on unsigned integers behave according to the rules of modular (congruence) arithmetic modulo 2^n. So, for example, adding 1 to the largest value of an unsigned type is guaranteed to produce 0. Overflow is not possible.

Expressions that mix signed and unsigned integers are forced to use unsigned operations. Section 6.3.4 discusses the conversions performed, and chapter 7 discusses the effect of each operator when its arguments are unsigned. These conversions can be surprising. For example, because unsigned integers are always nonnegative, you would expect that the following test would always be "true":

```
unsigned int u;
...
if (u > -1) ...
```

However, it is always "false"! The (signed) –1 is converted to an unsigned integer before the comparison, yielding the largest unsigned integer, and the value of u cannot be greater than that integer.

Historical note: The original definition of C provided only a single unsigned type, `unsigned`. It is now customary for C implementations to provide the full range of unsigned types, and these types are mandated in ANSI C.

References   integer conversions 6.2.3; constants 2.7; `limits.h` 5.1.1; signed types 5.1.1

5.1.3 Character Types

The character type in C is an integral type; that is, values of the type are integers and can be used in integer expressions:

```
character-type-specifier :
        char
        signed char
        unsigned char
```

There are three varieties of character types: signed, unsigned and plain. Each occupies the same amount of storage but may represent different values. The signed and unsigned representations used are the same as used for the signed and unsigned integer types. The plain character type corresponds to the absence of both `signed` and `unsigned` in the type specifier. The `signed` keyword is new in ANSI C, so in C implementations not recognizing the keyword, there are only two varieties of character types: unsigned and plain. An array of characters is C's notion of a "string." Typical declarations involving characters are shown below:

```
static char greeting[7];          /* 7-character string */
char *prompt;                     /* pointer to a character */
char padding_character = '\0';    /* single character */
```

The representation of the character types depends upon the nature of the character and string processing facilities on the target computer. The character type has some special characteristics that set it apart from the normal signed and unsigned types. For example, the plain char type may be signed, unsigned, or a mixture of both. For reasons of efficiency, C compilers are free to treat type char in one of three ways:

1. Type char may be a signed integral type, equivalent to signed char.
2. Type char may be an unsigned integral type, equivalent to unsigned char.
3. Type char may be a "pseudo-unsigned" integral type; that is, it can contain only nonnegative values but it is treated as if it were a signed type when performing the usual unary conversions.

If a true unsigned character type is needed, the type unsigned char can be specified. If a true signed type is needed, the type signed char can be specified. For example, if type char uses an 8-bit, two's-complement representation, given the declarations

```
unsigned char uc = -1;
signed char sc = -1;
char c = -1;
int i=uc, j=sc, k=c;
```

then i must have the value 255 and j must have the value −1 in all ANSI C implementations. However, it is implementation-defined whether k has the value 255 or −1. If your older C implementation does not recognize the keyword signed, or does not permit unsigned char, you are stuck with the ambiguous plain characters.

The signedness of characters is an important issue because the standard I/O library routines, which normally return characters from files, return a negative value when the end of the file is reached. (The negative value, often −1, is specified by the macro EOF in the standard header files.) The programmer should always treat these functions as returning values of type int, since type char may be unsigned. For example, the following program is intended to copy characters from the standard input stream to the standard output stream until an end-of-file indication is returned from getchar. The first three definitions are typically supplied in the standard header file stdio.h:

```
extern int getchar();
extern void putchar();
#define EOF -1   /* Could be any negative value */
```

```
void copy_characters()
{
    char ch; /* Incorrect! */
    while ((ch = getchar()) != EOF)
        putchar(ch);
}
```

However, this function will not work when `char` is unsigned or pseudo unsigned. To see this, assume the `char` type is represented in 8 bits and the `int` type in 16 bits, and that two's-complement arithmetic is used. Then, when `getchar` returns −1, the assignment `ch=getchar()` assigns the value 255 (the low-order 8 bits of −1) to `ch`. The loop test is then `255!=-1`, and if type `char` is pseudo unsigned, this (signed) comparison will evaluate to "true." If type `char` is unsigned the usual conversions will cause −1 to be converted to an unsigned integer, yielding the (unsigned) comparison `255!=65535`, which still evaluates to "true." Thus, the loop never terminates. Changing the declaration of `ch` to "`int ch;`" makes everything work fine.

To improve readability, you can define a "pseudo-character" type to use in these cases. For example, the following rewriting of `copy_characters` uses a new type, `character`, for characters that are represented with type `int`:

```
typedef int character;
...
void copy_characters()
{
    character ch;
    while ((ch = getchar() ) != EOF)
        putchar(ch);
}
```

A second area of vagueness about characters is their size. In the above example, we assumed they occupied 8 bits, and this assumption is almost always valid (although it is still unclear if their values range from 0 to 255 or from −128 to 127). However, a few computers may use 9 bits or even 7 bits. Programmers should be cautious. ANSI C requires that implementations document the range of their character types in the header file `limits.h`.

References   bit fields 5.6.5; character constants 2.7.3; character set 2.1; EOF 15.1; `getchar` 15.6; integer types 5.1; integer conversions 6.2.3; limits.h 5.1.1

5.2 FLOATING-POINT TYPES

C's floating-point numbers (sometimes called "real" numbers) come in two sizes: single and double precision, or `float` and `double`:

floating-type-specifier :
```
        float
        double
        long double
```
(ANSI C)

The type specifier `long double` is new in ANSI C. The type specifier `long float` is permitted in older implementations as a synonym for `double`, but it was never popular and has been eliminated in ANSI C. Here are some typical declarations of objects of floating-point types:

```
double d;
static double pi;
float coefficients[10];
long double epsilon;
```

The use of `float`, `double`, and `long double` is analogous to the use of `short`, `int`, and `long`. Prior to ANSI C, all implementations were required to convert all values of type `float` to type `double` before any operations were performed (see section 6.3.4), so using type `float` was not necessarily more efficient than using type `double`. In ANSI C, operations can now be performed using type `float`.

C does not dictate the sizes to be used for the floating-point types, or even that they be different. The programmer can assume that the values representable in type `float` are a subset of those in type `double`, which in turn are a subset of those in type `long double`. Some C programs have depended on the assumption that the type `double` can accurately represent all values of type `long`; that is, that converting an object of type `long` to type `double` and then back to type `long` results in exactly the original `long` value. While this is likely to be true, it is not required.

Most of the arithmetic and logical operations may be applied to floating-point operands. These include arithmetic and logical negation; addition, subtraction, multiplication, and division; relational and equality tests; logical AND and OR; assignment; and conversions to and from all the arithmetic types.

Any computer floating-point number x can be written as

$$x = s \times b^e \times \sum_{k=1}^{p} f_k \times b^{-k} \qquad e_{min} \leq e \leq e_{max}$$

where

s is the sign (± 1)
b is the base or radix of the representation (typically 2, 8, 10, or 16)
e is the exponent value
p is the number of base-b digits in the significand
f_k are the significand digits, $0 \leq f_k < b$

ANSI C requires that the characteristics of the floating-point types be documented in the header file `float.h.`; table 5-2 lists the symbols that must be defined. Symbols whose

Table 5-2 Values defined in `float.h` (ANSI C)

Name	Minimum	Meaning
FLT_RADIX[1]	2	the value of the radix, b
FLT_ROUNDS[1]	*none*	rounding mode: -1: indeterminable; 0: toward 0; 1: to nearest; 2: toward $+$ infinity; 3: toward $-$ infinity[2]
FLT_EPSILON	10^{-5}	the minimum $x>0.0$ such that $1.0+x \neq x$
DBL_EPSILON	10^{-5}	
LDBL_EPSILON	10^{-5}	
FLT_DIG	6	the number of decimal digits of precision
DBL_DIG	10	
LDBL_DIG	10	
FLT_MANT_DIG	*none*	p, the number of base-b digits in the significand
DBL_MANT_DIG		
LDBL_MANT_DIG		
FLT_MIN	10^{-37}	the minimum normalized positive number
DBL_MIN	10^{-37}	
LDBL_MIN	10^{-37}	
FLT_MIN_EXP	*none*	e_{min}, the minimum negative integer x such that b^{x-1} is in the range of normalized floating-point numbers
DBL_MIN_EXP		
LDBL_MIN_EXP		
FLT_MIN_10_EXP	-37	minimum x such that 10^x is in the range of normalized floating-point numbers
DBL_MIN_10_EXP	-37	
LDBL_MIN_10_EXP	-37	
FLT_MAX	10^{+37}	maximum representable finite number
DBL_MAX	10^{+37}	
LDBL_MAX	10^{+37}	
FLT_MAX_EXP	*none*	e_{max}, the maximum integer x such that b^{x-1} is a representable finite floating-point numbers
DBL_MAX_EXP		
LDBL_MAX_EXP		
FLT_MAX_10_EXP	37	maximum x such that 10^x is in the range of representable finite floating-point numbers
DBL_MAX_10_EXP	37	
LDBL_MAX_10_EXP	37	

[1] `FLT_RADIX` and `FLT_ROUNDS` apply to all three floating-point types.
[2] Other values are implementation-defined.

names begin with FLT document type float, names beginning with DBL refer to type double, and names beginning with LDBL refer to type long double. Also shown are the minimum magnitudes for each symbol, that is, the minimum requirements for range and precision of the floating-point types.

A common floating-point representation used by many microprocessors is given by the *IEEE Standard for Binary Floating-Point Arithmetic* (ANSI/IEEE Std 754–1985). The models for 32-bit single and 64-bit double precision floating-point numbers under that standard (adjusted to the ANSI C notational conventions) are

$$x_{float} = s \times 2^e \times \sum_{k=1}^{24} f_k \times 2^{-k} \quad -125 \le e \le +128$$

$$x_{double} = s \times 2^e \times \sum_{k=1}^{53} f_k \times 2^{-k} \quad -1021 \le e \le +1024$$

The values from float.h corresponding to these types are shown below. The floating-point constants of type float use the ANSI C suffix F to denote their type.

IEEE floating-point characteristics

Name	FLT_*name* value	DBL_*name* value
RADIX	2	*not applicable*
ROUNDS	*implementation-defined*	*not applicable*
EPSILON	1.19209290E-07F	2.2204460492503131E-16
DIG	6	15
MANT_DIG	24	53
MIN	1.17549435E–38F	2.2250738585072014E–308
MIN_EXP	–125	–1021
MIN_10_EXP	–37	–307
MAX	3.40282347E+38F	1.7976931348623157E+308
MAX_EXP	128	1024
MAX_10_EXP	38	308

References   floating-point constants 2.7.2; floating-point conversions 6.2.4; floating-point representations 6.1.1

5.3 POINTER TYPES

For any type *T*, a pointer type "pointer to *T*" may be formed. Pointer types are referred to as *object pointers* or *function pointers*, depending on whether *T* is an object type or a function type. A value of pointer type is the address of an object or function of type *T*. The declaration of pointer types is discussed in section 4.5.2. For example:

```
int *ip;        /* ip: a pointer to an object of type int */
char *cp;       /* cp: a pointer to an object of type char */
int (*fp)();    /* fp: a pointer to a function returning
                   an integer */
```

The two most important operators used in conjunction with pointers are the address operator, `&`, which creates pointer values, and the indirection operator, `*`, which dereferences pointers to access the object pointed to. In the following example, the pointer `ip` is assigned the address of variable `i` (`&i`). After that assignment, the expression `*ip` refers to the same object denoted by `i`:

```
int i, j, *ip;
ip = &i;
i = 22;
j = *ip;
    /* j now has the value 22 */
*ip = 17;
    /* i now has the value 17 */
```

Other operations on pointer types include assignment, addition of integers, subtraction, relational and equality tests, logical AND and OR, addition and subtraction of integers, and conversions to and from integers and other pointer types.

The size of a pointer is implementation-dependent and in some cases varies depending on the type of the object pointed to. For example, data pointers may be shorter or longer than function pointers (section 6.1.5). There is not necessarily any relationship between pointer sizes and the size of any integer type, although it is common to assume that type `long` is at least as large any pointer type.

In ANSI C, pointer types may be qualified by the use of the type qualifiers `const` or `volatile`. The qualification of a pointer type (if any) can affect the operations and conversions that are possible with it.

References   address operator `&` 7.5.6; arrays and pointers 5.4.1; assignment operators 7.9; cast expressions 7.5.1; conversions of pointers 6.2.7; `if` statement 8.5; indirection operator `*` 7.5.7; pointer declarators 4.5.2; type qualifiers 4.4.3; `volatile` type qualifier 4.4.5

5.3.1 Generic Pointers

The need for a generic data pointer that can be converted to any object pointer type arises frequently in C. In traditional C, it is customary to use type `char *` for this purpose, casting these generic pointers to the proper type before dereferencing them. Further details are given in section 6.2, where pointer conversions are discussed. The problem with this use of `char *` is that the compiler cannot check that programmers always convert the pointer type properly.

ANSI C introduces the type `void *` as a "generic pointer." It has the same representation as type `char *` for compatibility with older implementations, but the language treats it differently. Generic pointers cannot be dereferenced with the `*` or subscripting operators. Any pointer to an object or incomplete type (but *not* to a function type) can be converted to type `void *` and back without change. (Type `void *` is considered to be neither an object pointer nor a function pointer.) For example:

```
void *generic_ptr;
int *int_ptr;
char *char_ptr;
generic_ptr = int_ptr;        /* OK */
int_ptr = generic_ptr;        /* OK */
int_ptr = char_ptr;           /* Illegal in ANSI C */
int_ptr = (int *) char_ptr; /* OK */
```

Generic pointers provide additional flexibility in using function prototypes. When a function has a formal parameter that can accept a pointer of any type, the formal should be declared to be of type `void *`. If the formal is declared with any other pointer type, the actual argument must be of the same type, since different pointer types are not assign compatible in ANSI C. For example, the `strcpy` facility copies character strings and therefore requires arguments of type `char *`:

```
char *strcpy(char *s1, const char *s2);
```

On the other hand, `memcpy` can take a pointer to any type and so uses `void *`:

```
void *memcpy(void *s1, const void *s2, size_t n);
```

References   assign compatibility 6.3.2; `const` type specifier 4.4; `memcpy` facility 14.3; `strcpy` facility 13.3

5.3.2 Null Pointers and Invalid Pointers

C has a special "null pointer" value that explicitly points to no object or function. The null pointer may be written as the integer constant `0`, `0L` (when pointers are larger than type `int`), or (in ANSI C) as `(void *)0`. The macro `NULL` is defined to be one of these constants in standard header files—`stddef.h` in ANSI C and `stdio.h` in most other implementations. The null pointer, like the integer value 0, has the value "false" in boolean expressions, so tests for the null pointer can be abbreviated . For example, the statement

```
if (ip) i = *ip;
```

is a common shorthand notation for

```
if (ip != NULL) i = *ip;
```

It is good programming style to be sure that all pointers have the value `NULL` when they are not designating a valid object or function.

It is also possible to create *invalid pointers*, that is, pointer values that are not null but also do not designate a proper object or function. Invalid pointers can be created by casting arbitrary integer values to pointer types, by deallocating the storage for an object to which a pointer refers (as by using the `free` facility), or by using pointer arithmetic to produce a pointer outside the range of an array. An attempt to dereference an invalid pointer may cause a run-time error.

In conjunction with pointer arithmetic, C does require that the address of an object one past the last object of an array be defined, although such an address can still be invalid to dereference. This requirement makes it easier to use pointer expressions to walk through arrays. For example, the following loop uses the address just beyond the end of an array, although it never attempts to dereference that address:

```
int array[N];   /* the last object address is &array[N-1] */
int *p;
…
for (p=&array[0]; p<&array[N]; p++)
    …
```

This requirement may restrict implementations for a few target computers that have discontiguous addressing architectures, reducing by one object the maximum length of an array. On such computers it may be impossible to perform arithmetic on pointers that do not fall within a contiguous area of memory, and only by allocating an array is the programmer guaranteed that the memory is contiguous..

References integer constants 2.7.1; pointer arithmetic 7.6.2; `stddef.h` facility 11.1; `void * ` type 5.3.1

5.3.3 Some Cautions with Pointers

Many C programmers assume that all pointer types (actually, all addresses) have a uniform representation. On common byte-addressed computers all pointers are typically simple byte addresses occupying, say, one word. Conversions among pointer and integer types on these computers require no change in representation and no information is lost.

In fact, the C language does not require such nice behavior. Section 6.1 discusses the problems in more detail, but here is a brief summary:

1. Pointers are often not the same size as type `int`, and sometimes not the same size as type `long`. Sometimes the size is a compiler option.
2. Character pointers can be larger than other kinds of pointers, or may use bits in their representation that are not used (and may or may not be ignored) in other kinds of pointers.
3. Function pointers and data pointers may have significantly different representations, including different sizes.

The programmer should always use explicit casts when converting between pointer types, and should be especially careful that pointer arguments given to functions have the correct type expected by the function. In ANSI C, `void` `*` can be used as a generic object pointer, but there is no generic function pointer.

References   casts 7.5.1; `malloc` function 16.1; pointer conversions 6.2.7

5.4 ARRAY TYPES

If *T* is any C type except `void` or "function returning…," the array type "array of *T*" may be declared. Values of this type are sequences of elements of type *T*. All C arrays are 0-origin. For example, the array declared

```
int A[3];
```

consists of the elements `A[0]`, `A[1]`, and `A[2]`. In the following example, an array of integers (`int`s) and an array of pointers (`ptrs`) are declared, and each of the pointers in `ptrs` is set equal to the address of the corresponding integer in `ints`:

```
int ints[10], *ptrs[10], i;
for (i = 0; i < 10; i++)
    ptrs[i] = &ints[i];
```

The memory size of an array (in the sense of the `sizeof` operator) is always equal to the length of the array in elements multiplied by the memory size of an element.

An array type of unknown size is called an *incomplete type*. A variable of such a type can be declared, but must later have the type completed by supplying a second declaration that includes the array bounds:

```
extern int a[];    /* a has an incomplete array type */
...
int a[10];         /* the type of a is now complete */
```

An incomplete type can be specified only for a top-level identifier, since these are the only declarations that can be duplicated. Objects of incomplete types cannot be allocated storage, but pointers to them can be created and used. An incomplete array type can also be used as the type of a function parameter, because all array types in parameter declarations are converted to pointer types.

References   array declarators 4.5.3; sizeof operator 7.5.2; storage units 6.1.1

5.4.1 Arrays and Pointers

In C there is a close correspondence between types "array of *T*" and "pointer to *T*." First, when an array identifier appears in an expression, the type of the identifier is converted from "array of *T*" to "pointer to T," and the value of the identifier is converted to a pointer to the first element of the array. Thus, in

```
int a[10], *ip
ip = a;
```

the value a is converted to a pointer to the first element of the array. It is exactly as if we had written

```
ip = &a[0];
```

This rule is one of the usual unary conversions. The only exception to this conversion rule is when the array identifier is used as an operand of the sizeof operator, in which case sizeof returns the size of the entire array, not the size of a pointer to the first array element.

Second, array subscripting is defined in terms of pointer arithmetic. That is, the expression

```
a[i]
```

is defined to be the same as

```
*((a) + (i))
```

where a is converted to &a[0] under the usual unary conversions. This definition of subscripting also means that a[i] is the same as i[a], and that any pointer may be subscripted just like an array; it is up to the programmer to ensure that the pointer is pointing into an appropriate array of elements:

```
double d,*dp;
...
d = dp[4];
```

References address operator & 7.5.6; addition operator + 7.6.2; array declarators 4.5.3; conversions of arrays 6.3.3; indirection operator * 7.5.7; pointer types 5.3; sizeof operator 7.5.2; subscripting [ ] 7.4.1; usual unary conversions 6.3.3

5.4.2 Multidimensional Arrays

Multidimensional arrays are declared as "arrays of arrays," such as in the declaration

```
int matrix[10][10];
```

which declares matrix to be a 10-by-10 element array of int. The language places no limit on the number of dimensions an array may have.

Multidimensional arrays are stored in row-major order, that is, in such a way that the last subscript varies most rapidly. For example, the elements of the array int t[2][3] are stored (in increasing addresses) as

```
t[0][0], t[0][1], t[0][2], t[1][0], t[1][1], t[1][2]
```

The conversions of arrays to pointers happens analogously for multidimensional arrays. For example, if t is a 2-by-3 array as defined above, then the expression t[1][2] is expanded to *(*(t+1)+2), which is evaluated as shown in the following table.

Evaluation of *(*(t+1)+2)

Step	Subexpression	Subexpression value
1.	t	a 2-by-3 array, which is converted immediately to a pointer to the first 3-element subarray
2.	t+1	a pointer to the second 3-element subarray
3.	*(t+1)	the second 3-element subarray of integers, which is immediately converted to a pointer to the first integer in that subarray
4.	*(t+1)+2	a pointer to the third integer in the second 3-element subarray
5.	*(*(t+1)+2)	the third integer in the second 3-element subarray; t[1][2]

In general, any expression A of type "i-by-j-by-...-by-k array of T" is immediately converted to "pointer to j-by-...-by-k array of T."

References   addition operator + 7.6.2; array declarators 4.5.3; indirection operator * 7.5.7; pointer types 5.3; subscripting 7.4.1

5.4.3 Array Bounds

Any time that storage for an array is allocated, the size of the array must be known. However, because subscripts are not normally checked to lie within declared array bounds, it is possible to omit the size (that is, use an incomplete array type) when declaring an external, singly dimensioned array defined in another module or when declaring a singly dimensioned array that is a formal parameter to a function. (See section 4.5.) For instance, the following function, sum, returns the sum of the first n elements of an external array, a, whose bounds are not specified:

```
extern int a[];

int sum(n)
    int n;
{
    int i, s = 0;
    for (i = 0; i < n; i++)
        s += a[i];
    return s;
}
```

It is common when passing arrays to functions to omit the bounds information on the formal parameter:

```
int sumarray(array,arraylength)
    int arraylength, array[];
{ … }
```

In this example the parameter `array` could also be declared as "`int *array`", which would more accurately reflect the implementation but less clearly indicate the intent.

When multidimensional arrays are used, it is necessary to specify the bounds of all but the first dimension, so that the proper address arithmetic can be calculated:

```
extern int matrix[][10]; /* ?-by-10 array of int */
```

If such bounds are not specified, the declaration is in error.

References   array declarators 4.5.3; defining and referencing declarations 4.8; indirection operator * 7.5.7; omitted array bounds 4.5; pointer types 5.3; subscripting 7.4.1

5.4.4 Operations

The only operation that can be performed directly on an array value is the application of the `sizeof` operator. The array must be bounded. The result of such an operation is the number of storage units occupied by the array. For an n-element array of type T, the result of the `sizeof` operator is always equal to n times the result of `sizeof` applied to the type T.

In all other contexts, such as subscripting, the array value is actually treated as a pointer, and so operations on pointers may be applied to the array value.

References   array declarators 4.5.3; conversions from array to pointer 6.2.7; pointer types 5.3; `sizeof` operator 7.5.2; subscripting 7.4.1

5.5 ENUMERATED TYPES

Enumerated types are a recent addition to C; similar concepts occur in other languages, including Pascal and Ada. The syntax for declaring enumerated types is shown below:

enumeration-type-specifier :
      enumeration-type-definition
      enumeration-type-reference

enumeration-type-definition :
      enum   *enumeration-tag$_{opt}$* { *enumeration-definition-list* }

enumeration-type-reference :
      enum   *enumeration-tag*

enumeration-tag :
        identifier

enumeration-definition-list :
        enumeration-constant-definition
        enumeration-definition-list , *enumeration-constant-definition*

enumeration-constant-definition :
        enumeration-constant
        enumeration-constant = *expression*

enumeration-constant :
        identifier

An enumerated type in C is a set of integer values represented by identifiers called *enumeration constants*. The enumeration constants are specified when the type is defined and have type `int`. Each enumerated type is represented by an implementation-defined integer type and is compatible with that type. Thus, for the purposes of type checking, an enumerated type is just one of the integer types, and when the C language permits an integer expression in some context an enumeration constant or a value of an enumerated type can be used instead.

For example, the declaration

```
enum fish { trout, carp, halibut } my_fish, your_fish;
```

creates a new enumerated type, `enum fish`, whose values are `trout`, `carp`, and `halibut`. It also declares two variables of the enumerated type, `my_fish` and `your_fish`, which can be assigned values with the assignments

```
my_fish = halibut;
your_fish = trout;
```

Variables or other objects of the enumerated type can be declared in the same declaration containing the enumerated type definition or in a subsequent declaration that mentions the enumerated type with an "enumerated type reference." For example, the single declaration

```
enum color { red, blue, green, mauve }
    favorite, acceptable, least_favorite;
```

is exactly equivalent to the two declarations

```
enum color { red, blue, green, mauve } favorite;
enum color acceptable, least_favorite;
```

and to the four declarations

```
enum color { red, blue, green, mauve };
enum color favorite;
enum color acceptable;
enum color least_favorite;
```

The enumeration tag, `color`, allows an enumerated type to be referenced after its definition. Although the declaration

```
enum { red, blue, green, mauve }
   favorite, acceptable, least_favorite;
```

defines the same type and declares the same variables, the lack of a tag makes it impossible to introduce more variables of the type in later declarations. Enumeration tags are in the same overloading class as structure and union tags, and their scope is the same as that of a variable declared at the same location in the source program.

Identifiers defined as enumeration constants are members of the same overloading class as variables, functions, and typedef names. Their scope is the same as that of a variable defined at the same location in the source program. In the following example, the declaration of `shepherd` as an enumeration constant hides the previous declaration of the integer variable `shepherd`. However, the declaration of the floating-point variable `collie` causes a compilation error, because `collie` is already declared in the same scope as an enumeration constant.

```
int shepherd = 12;
{
   enum dog_breeds {shepherd, collie};
      /* Hides outer declaration of the name "shepherd" */
   float collie;
      /* Illegal redefinition of the name "collie" */
}
```

Enumerated types are implemented by associating integer values with the enumeration constants, so that the assignment and comparison of values of enumerated types can be implemented as integer assignment and comparison. Integer values are associated with enumeration constants in the following way:

1. An explicit integer value may be associated with an enumeration constant by writing

    enumeration-constant = expression

    in the type definition. The expression must be a constant expression of integral type, although some compilers may also allow expressions involving previously defined enumeration constants, as in

```
enum boys { Bill = 10,
            John = Bill+2,
            Fred = John+2 };
```

2. The first enumeration constant receives the value 0 if no explicit value is specified.
3. Subsequent enumeration constants without explicit associations receive an integer value one greater than the value associated with the previous enumeration constant.

For example, given the declaration

```
enum sizes { small, medium=10, pretty_big, large=20 };
```

the values of `small`, `medium`, `pretty_big`, and `large` will be 0, 10, 11, and 20, respectively.

Any signed integer value representable as type `int` may be associated with an enumeration constant. Positive and negative integers may be chosen at random, and it is even possible to associate the same integer with two different enumeration constants. For instance, the following definition is legal:

```
enum people { john=1, mary=19, bill=-4, sheila=1 };
```

but then the expression

```
john == sheila
```

is "true," which is not intuitive.

Although the form of an enumerated type definition is suggestive of structure and union types, with strict type checking, in fact enumerated types in ANSI C (which is the definition given in this book) act as little more than slightly more readable ways to name integer constants. As a matter of style, we suggest that programmers treat enumerated types as different from integers and not mix them in integer expressions without using casts. In fact, some UNIX C compilers implement a weakly typed form of enumerations in which some conversions between enumerated types and integers are not permitted without casts.

References   cast expressions 7.5.1; identifiers 2.5; overloading classes 4.2.4; scope 4.2.1; structure tags 5.6; union tags 5.7

5.6 STRUCTURE TYPES

The structure types in C are similar to the types known as "records" in other programming languages. They are collections of named *components* (also called "members" or "fields") that can have different types. One way of looking at structures is that they allow the programmer to create *abstract data types*. Structures can be defined to encapsulate related data objects—the values of the abstract type—and functions can be written to manipulate the values—the operations on the type.

A programmer who wanted to implement complex numbers might define a structure `complex` to hold the real and imaginary parts as components `real` and `imag`. The first declaration below defines the new type, and the second declares two variables, `x` and `y`, of that type:

```
struct complex {
    double real;
    double imag;
};
struct complex x,y;
```

real	imag
double	double

struct complex

A function `new_complex` can be written to create a new object of the type. Note that the selection operator (`.`) is used to access the components of the structure:

```
struct complex new_complex(r, i)
    double r, i;
{
    struct complex new;
    new.real = r;
    new.imag = i;
    return new;
}
```

Operations on the type, such as `complex_multiply`, can also be defined:

```
struct complex complex_multiply(a, b)
    struct complex a,b;
{
    struct complex product;
    product.real=(a.real * b.real - a.imag * b.imag);
    product.imag=(a.real * b.imag + a.imag * b.real);
    return product;
}
```

Here is the general syntax for structure declarations:

structure-type-specifier :
   structure-type-definition
   structure-type-reference

structure-type-definition :
   struct *structure-tag$_{opt}$* { *field-list* }

structure-type-reference :
        `struct` *structure-tag*

structure-tag :
        identifier

field-list :
        component-declaration
        field-list component-declaration

component-declaration :
        type-specifier component-declarator-list `;`

component-declarator-list :
        component-declarator
        component-declarator-list `,` *component-declarator*

component-declarator :
        simple-component
        bit-field

simple-component :
        declarator

bit-field :
        declarator$_{opt}$ `:` *width*

width :
        expression

Each structure type definition introduces a new structure type, different from all others. If present in the definition, the structure tag is associated with the new type and can be used in a subsequent structure type reference. For instance, the single declaration

```
struct complex { double real, imag; } x, y;
```

is equivalent to the two declarations

```
struct complex { double real, imag; };
struct complex x, y;
```

5.6.1 Structure Type References

The use of a type specifier of the syntactic classes *structure-type-definition* or *union-type-definition* (section 5.7) introduces the definition of a new type. The scope of the definition (and the type tag, if any) is from the declaration point to the end of the innermost block containing the specifier. The new definition explicitly overrides (hides) any definition of the type tag in an enclosing block.

The use of a type specifier of the syntactic classes *structure-type-reference* or *union-type-reference* (section 5.7) without a preceding definition in the same or enclosing scope is allowed when the size of the structure is not required, including when declaring:

1. pointers to the structure
2. a typedef name as a synonym for the structure

The use of this kind of specifier introduces an "incomplete" definition of the type and type tag in the innermost block containing the use. For this definition to be completed, a *structure-type-definition* or *union-type-definition* must appear later in the same scope.

As a special case, the occurrence of a *structure-type-reference* or *union-type-reference* in a declaration with no declarators hides any definition of the type tag in any enclosing scope and establishes an incomplete type. For example, consider the following correct definition of two self-referential structures in an inner block:

```
{
    struct cell;
    struct header { struct cell   *first; … };
    struct cell   { struct header *head;  … };
    …
}
```

The incomplete definition "`struct cell;`" in the first line is necessary to hide any definitions of the tag `cell` in an enclosing scope. The definition of `struct header` in the second line automatically hides any enclosing definitions, and its use of `struct cell` to define a pointer is legal. The definition of `struct cell` on the third line completes the information about `cell`.

An incomplete type declaration also exists within a *structure-type-definition* or *union-type-definition*, from the first mention of the new tag until the definition is complete. This allows a single structure type to include a pointer to itself:

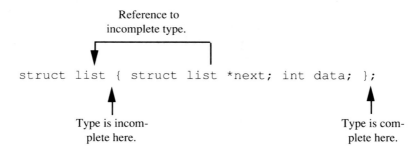

References   declarations 4.1; declarators 4.5; duplicate visibility 4.2.2; scope 4.2.1; selection operator . 7.4.2; type equivalence 5.11

5.6.2 Operations on Structures

The operations provided for structures may vary from compiler to compiler. All C compilers provide the selection operators `.` and `->` on structures, and newer compilers now allow structures to be assigned, to be passed as parameters to functions, and to be returned from functions. (With older compilers, assignment must be done component by component, and only pointers to structures may be passed to and from functions.)

It is not permitted to compare two structures for equality. An object of a structure type is a sequence of components of other types. Because certain data objects may be constrained by the target computer to lie on certain addressing boundaries, a structure object may contain "holes," storage units that do not belong to any component of the structure. The holes would make equality tests implemented as a wholesale bit-by-bit comparison unreliable, and component-by-component equality tests might be too expensive. (Of course, the programmer may write component-by-component equality functions.)

In any situation where it is permitted to apply the unary address operator & to a structure to obtain a pointer to the structure, it is also permitted to apply the operator to a component of the structure to obtain a pointer to the component; that is, it is possible for a pointer to point into the middle of a structure. An exception to this rule occurs with components defined to be bit fields. Components defined as bit fields will in general not lie on machine-addressable boundaries, and therefore it may not be possible to form a pointer to a bit field. The C language therefore forbids such pointers.

References   address operator 7.5.6; assignment 7.9; bit fields 5.6.5; equality operator ==
7.6.5; selection operator . and -> 7.4.2; type equivalence 5.11

5.6.3 Components

A component of a structure may have any type except "function returning..." and void. Structures may not contain instances of themselves, although they may contain pointers to instances of themselves. That is:

```
struct S {
    int a;
    struct S next; /* illegal! */
};
```

is illegal, but

```
struct S {
    int a;
    struct S *next;
};
```

is permitted.

The names of structure components are defined in a special overloading class associated with the structure type. That is, component names within a single structure must be distinct, but they may be the same as component names in other structures and may be the same as variable, function, and type names. For example, consider the following sequence of declarations:

```
int x;
struct A { int x; double y; } y;
struct B { int y; double x; } z;
```

The identifier x has three nonconflicting declarations: it is an integer variable, an integer component of structure A, and a floating-point component of structure B. These three declarations are used, respectively, in the expressions

```
x
y.x
z.x
```

If a structure tag is defined in one of the components, as T is in

```
struct S {
    struct T {int a, b; } x;
};
```

then the scope of T extends to the end of the block in which structure S is defined. (If S is defined at the top level, so is T.)

A historical note: The original definition of C specified that all components in all structures were allocated out of the same overloading class, and therefore no two structures could have components with the same name. (An exception was made when the components had the same type and the same relative position in the structures!) This interpretation is now anachronistic, but you might see it mentioned in older documentation or actually implemented in some old compilers.

References   overloading classes 4.2.4; scope 4.2.1

5.6.4 Structure Component Layout

Most programmers will be unconcerned with how components are packed into structures. However, C does give the programmer some control over the packing. C compilers are constrained to assign components increasing memory addresses in a strict order, with the first component starting at the beginning address of the structure itself. There is no difference in component layout between the structure

```
struct { int a, b, c; };
```

and the structure

```
struct { int a; int b, c; };
```

Both put a first, b second, and c last in order of increasing addresses, as pictured below.

In general, given two pointers p' and q to components within the same structure, p < q will be true if and only if the declaration of the component to which p points appears earlier within the declaration of the structure type than the declaration of the component to which q points. For example:

```
{
    struct vector3 { int x, y, z; } s;
    int *p, *q, *r;
    ...
    p = &s.x;
    q = &s.y;
    r = &s.z;
    /* At this point (p < q), (q < r),
        and (p < r) are all true. */
    ...
}
```

Holes, or padding, may appear between any two consecutive components in the layout of a structure if necessary to allow proper alignment of components in memory. The bit patterns appearing in such holes are unpredictable, and may differ from structure to structure or over time within a single structure.

5.6.5 Bit Fields

C allows the programmer to pack integer components into spaces smaller than the compiler would ordinarily allow. These integer components are called bit fields and are specified by following the component declarator with a colon and a constant integer expression that indicates the width of the field in bits. For example, the following structure has three components, a, b, and c, occupying four, five, and seven bits, respectively:

```
struct S{
    unsigned a:4;
    unsigned b:5, c:7;
};
```

A bit field of n bits can represent unsigned integers in the range 0 through 2^n-1, and signed integers in the range -2^{n-1} through $2^{n-1}-1$, assuming a two's-complement representation of signed integers. The original definition of C permitted only bit fields of type unsigned, but ANSI C permits bit fields to be of type unsigned int, `signed int`, or just `int`, termed unsigned, signed, and "plain" bit fields. Some C implementations allow bit fields of any integer type, including `char`.

Bit fields are typically used in machine-dependent programs that must force a data structure to correspond to a fixed hardware representation. The precise manner in which components (and especially bit fields) are packed into a structure is implementation-dependent but is predictable for each implementation. The intent is that bit fields should be packed as tightly as possible in a structure, subject to the rules discussed later in this section. The use of bit fields is therefore likely to be nonportable. The programmer should consult the implementation documentation if it is necessary to lay out a structure in memory in some particular fashion, and then verify that the C compiler is indeed packing the components in the way expected.

Here is an example of how bit fields can be used to create a structure that matches a predefined format. Below is the layout of a 32-bit word treated as a virtual address on a hypothetical computer. The word contains fields for the segment number, page number, and offset within a page, plus a "supervisor" bit and an unused bit:

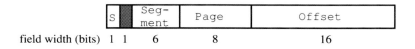

```
                          Seg-
                    S     ment     Page            Offset

field width (bits)  1  1    6        8               16
```

To duplicate this layout, we first have to know if our computer packs bit fields left to right or right to left, that is, whether it is a "big endian" or a "little endian." (See section 6.1.2.) If packing is right to left, the appropriate structure definition is

```
typedef struct {
    unsigned Offset      : 16;
    unsigned Page        : 8;
    unsigned Segment     : 6;
    unsigned UNUSED      : 1;
    unsigned Supervisor  : 1;
} virtual_address;
```

On the other hand, if packing is left to right, the appropriate structure definition is

```
typedef struct {
    unsigned Supervisor  : 1;
    unsigned UNUSED      : 1;
    unsigned Segment     : 6;
    unsigned Page        : 8;
    unsigned Offset      : 16;
} virtual_address;
```

The signedness of a plain integer bit field follows the signedness of plain characters; that is, a plain integer bit field may actually be implemented as a signed, unsigned, or pseudo-unsigned type. (See section 5.1.3.) Signed and unsigned bit fields must be implemented to hold signed and unsigned values. Consider the effect of the following ANSI C declarations on a two's-complement computer:

```
struct S { unsigned ubf:3;
           signed sbf:3;
           int bf:3; } x = { -1, -1, -1 };
  ...
{ int i = x.ubf, j = x.sbf, k = x.bf; ...
```

The value of i must 7 and the value of j must be −1, but the value of k may be either 7 or −1.

Compilers are free to impose constraints on the maximum size of a bit field and to specify certain addressing boundaries that bit fields cannot cross. These alignment restrictions are usually related to the natural word size of the target computer. When a field is too long for the computer, the compiler will issue an appropriate error message. When a field would cross a word boundary, it may be moved to the next word.

An unnamed bit field may also be included in a structure to provide "padding" between adjacent components. For instance, the following structure places component a in the first four bits of the structure, followed by two bits of padding, followed by the component b in six bits. (Assuming a basic word size of 16 bits, a final four bits will also be unused at the end of the structure. See section 5.6.7.)

```
struct S {
   unsigned a : 4;
   unsigned   : 2;
   unsigned b : 6;
};
```

Specifying a length of 0 for an unnamed bit field has a special meaning—it indicates that the following component should begin on the next boundary appropriate to its type. ("Appropriate" is not specified further; in ANSI C, it is the next int-sized unit.) That is, in the following structure the component b should begin on a natural addressing boundary (for example, 16 bits) following component a. The new structure occupies twice as much storage as the old one:

```
struct S {
   unsigned a : 4;
   unsigned   : 0;
   unsigned b : 6;
};
```

Unnamed bit fields cannot be referenced and their contents at run time are not predictable.

The address operator & may not be applied to bit-field components, since many computers cannot address arbitrary-sized fields directly.

References   address operator & 7.5.6; alignment restrictions 6.1.3; byte order 6.1.2; enumerated types 5.5; signed types 5.1.1; unsigned types 5.1.2

5.6.6 Portability Problems

There are several ways in which depending on packing strategies is dangerous. First, computers differ on the alignment constraints on data types. For instance, a 4-byte integer on some computers must begin on a byte boundary that is a multiple of four, whereas on other computers the integer can (and will) be aligned on the nearest byte boundary.

Second, the restrictions on bit-field widths will be different. Some computers have a 16-bit word size, which limits the maximum size of the field and imposes a boundary that fields cannot cross. Other computers have a 32-bit word size, and so forth.

Third, computers differ in the way fields are packed into a word, that is, in their "byte ordering." On the Motorola 68000 family of computers, characters are packed left to right into words, from the most significant bit to the least significant bit. On DEC VAX and Intel 80X86 computers, characters are packed right to left, from the least significant bit to the most significant bit. As seen in the `virtual_address` example in the previous section, different structure definitions are needed for computers with different byte ordering.

We know of two situations that seem to justify the use of bit fields:

1. A predefined data structure must be matched exactly so it can be referenced in a C program. (These programs may not be portable anyway.)
2. An array of structured data must be maintained, and its large size requires that its components be packed tightly to conserve memory.

Programmers may wish to consider an alternative way to access packed data structures that does not involve the use of `struct` definitions. By using the C bitwise operators to perform masking and shifting functions, it is possible to access bit fields in a way that is not sensitive to byte ordering. For example, consider the problem of accessing the `Page` field in the `virtual_address` structure. Since this 8-bit field is located 16 bits from the low-order end of the word, it can be accessed with the following code:

```
unsigned V;   /* formatted as a virtual_address */
int Page
...
Page = (V & 0xFF0000) >> 16;
```

This is equivalent to the the more readable structure component access `Page=V.Page`, but the mask-and-shift approach is *not* sensitive to the computer's byte ordering, as is the definition of `virtual_address`. The masking and shifting operations are demonstrated below for `V==0xb393352e` (`Page==0x93`):

```
10110011100100110011010100101110    V

00000000111111110000000000000000    0xFF0000

00000000100100110000000000000000    V&0xFF0000

00000000000000000000000010010011    (V&0xFF0000)>>16
```

Similar operations may be used to set the value of a bit field. There may be little difference in the run-time performance of these two access methods.

References   alignment restrictions 6.1.3; bitwise operators 7.6.6; byte order 6.1.2; shift operators 7.6.3

5.6.7 Sizes of Structures

The size of an object of a structure type is the amount of storage necessary to represent all components of that type, including any unused padding space between or after the components. The rule is that the structure will be padded out to the size the type would occupy as an element of an array of such types. (For any type T, including structures, the size of an n-element array of T is the same as the size of T times n.) Another way of saying this is that the structure must terminate on the same alignment boundary on which it started; that is, if the structure must begin on an even byte boundary, it must also end on an even byte boundary.

For example, on a computer that starts all structures on an address that is a multiple of 4 bytes, the length of the following structure will be a multiple of four (probably exactly four), even though only two characters are actually used:

```
struct S {
    char c1;
    char c2;
};
```

Bytes: 1   1   2

The alignment requirement for a structure type will be at least as stringent as for the component having the most stringent requirements. For example, on a computer that requires all objects of type `double` to have an address that is a multiple of 8 bytes, the length of the following structure is probably 24 bytes, even though only 18 bytes are declared:

```
struct S {
    double value;
    char name[10];
};
```

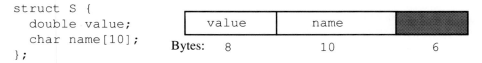

Bytes: 8   10   6

Six extra units of padding are needed at the end to make the size of the structure a multiple of the alignment requirement, eight. If the padding were not used, then in an array of such structures not all of the structures would have the value component aligned properly to a multiple-of-eight address.

Alignment requirements may cause padding to appear in the middle of a structure. If the order of the components in the previous example is reversed, the length remains 24 but the unused space appears between the components so that the value component may be aligned to an address that is a multiple of 8 bytes relative to the beginning of the structure:

```
struct S {
  char name[10];
  double value;
};
```

name		value

Bytes: 10   6   8

Any object of the structure type will be required to have an address that is a multiple of eight, and so the value component of such an object will always be properly aligned.

5.7 UNION TYPES

The syntax for defining union types is almost identical to that for defining structure types:

union-type-specifier :
        union-type-definition
        union-type-reference

union-type-definition :
        union *union-tag$_{opt}$* { *field-list* }

union-type-reference :
        union *union-tag*

union-tag :
        identifier

The syntax for defining components is the same as that used for structures. In traditional C, bit fields are not permitted in unions, but in ANSI C they are.

As with structures and enumerations, each union type definition introduces a new union type, different from all others. If present in the definition, the union tag is associated with the new type and can be used in a subsequent union type reference. Forward references and incomplete definitions of union types are permitted with the same rules as structure types.

A component of a union may have any type except "function returning..." and void. Also, unions may not contain instances of themselves, although they may contain pointers to instances of themselves. As in structures, the names of union components are defined in a special overload class associated with the union type. That is, component names within a single union must be distinct, but they may be the same as component names in other unions and may be the same as variable, function, and type names.

5.7.1 Union Component Layout

Each component of a union type is allocated storage starting at the beginning of the union. For example, here is a union with three components, all effectively overlaid in memory:

```
union U {
   double d;
   char c[2];
   int i;
};
```

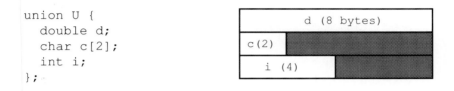

A union can contain only one of its component values at a time.

An object of a union type will begin on a storage alignment boundary appropriate for any contained component. More precisely, if we have the following union type and object definitions:

```
static union U {
   ...
   int C;
   ...
} object, *P = &object;
```

then the following two equalities hold:

```
(union U *) &(P->C)   == P
&(P->C)   == (int *) P
```

Furthermore, these equalities hold no matter what the type of the component C and no matter what other components in the union precede or follow C.

References   alignment restrictions 6.1.3

5.7.2 Sizes of Unions

The size of an object of a union type is the amount of storage necessary to represent the largest component of that type, plus any padding that may be needed at the end to raise the length up to an appropriate alignment boundary. The rule is that the union will be padded out to the size the type would occupy as an element of an array of such types. Recall that for any type T, including unions, the size of an n-element array of T is the same as (the size of T)$\cdot n$. Another way of saying this is that the structure must terminate on the same alignment boundary on which it started; that is, if the structure had to begin on an even byte boundary, it must end on an even byte boundary.

Note that the alignment requirement for a union type will be at least as stringent as for the component having the most stringent requirements. For example, on a computer that requires all objects of type `double` to have an address that is a multiple of 8 bytes, the length of the following union will be 16, even though the size of the longest component is only 10:

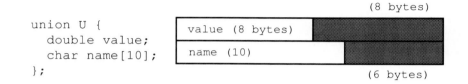

```
union U {
    double value;
    char name[10];
};
```

Six extra units of padding are needed to make the size of the union a multiple of the alignment requirement, eight. If the padding were not used, then in an array of such unions not all of the unions would have the `value` component aligned properly to a multiple-of-eight address.

5.7.3 Using Union Types

C's union type is somewhat like a "variant record" in other languages. Like structures, unions are defined to have a number of components. Unlike structures, however, a union can hold at most one of its components at a time; the components are conceptually overlaid in the storage allocated for the union. If the union is very large, or if there is a large array of the unions, then the storage savings can be significant.

For example, suppose we want an object that can be *either* an integer or a floating-point number, depending on the situation. We define union `datum`:

```
union datum {
    int i;
    double d;
};
```

and then define a variable of the union type:

```
union datum u;
```

To store an integer in the union, we write

```
u.i = 15;
```

To store a floating-point number in the union, we assign to the other component

```
u.d = 88.9e4;
```

A component of a union should be referenced only if the last assignment to the union was through the same component. C provides no way to inquire which component of a union was last assigned; the programmer either can remember or can encode explicit data tags to be associated with unions.

A *data tag* is an object associated with a union that holds an indication of which component is currently stored in the union. The data tag and union can be enclosed in a common structure. For example, we can replace the union

```
union widget {
    long count;
    double value;
    char name[10];
} x;
```

by

```
enum widget_tag { count_widget,
                  value_widget,
                  name_widget };

struct WIDGET {
  enum widget_tag tag;
  union { long count;
          double value;
          char name[10]; } data;
} x;

/* Make "widget" a name for "struct WIDGET". */
typedef struct WIDGET widget;
```

The size of the `widget` structure is 24 bytes, which is caused by the assumption that objects of type `double` must be aligned on 8-byte boundaries. They layout is shown below:

If, as is common, objects of type `double` can be placed on 4-byte boundaries, then `widget`'s length will be only 16 bytes.

To assign an integer to the union, we write

```
    x.tag = count_widget;
    x.data.count = 10000;
```

To assign a floating point number, we write

```
    x.tag = value_widget;
    x.data.value = 3.1415926535897932384;
```

To assign a string, we can use the `strncpy` library function:

```
    x.tag = name_widget;
    strncpy(x.data.name, "Millard", 10);
```

Below is a portable function that can discriminate among the possibilities for the union. `print_widget` can be called without regard to which component was last assigned:

```
    void print_widget(w)
        widget w;
    {
        switch(w.tag) {
            case count_widget:
                printf("Count %ld\n", w.data.count);
                break;
            case value_widget:
                printf("Value %f\n", w.data.value);
                break;
            case name_widget:
                printf("Name \"%s\"\n", w.data.name);
                break;
        }
    }
```

5.7.4 (Mis)using Union Types

Unions are used in a nonportable fashion any time a union component is referenced when the last assignment to the union was not through the same component. Programmers sometimes do this to "reach under" C's type system and discover something about the computer's underlying data representation (itself a nonportable concept). For example, to discover how a floating-point number is represented:

1.   Create a union with floating-point and integer components of the same size:

```
        ┌─────────────────┐
        │ float (4 bytes) │
        ├─────────────────┤
        │ int   (4 bytes) │
        └─────────────────┘
```

2. Assign a value to the floating-point component.
3. Read the value of the integer component and print it out as, say, a hexadecimal number.

Here is an example of a function that does just this, assuming types `float` and `int` have the same length:

```
void print_rep( f )
    float f;
{
    union { float f; int i } f_or_i;
    f_or_i.f = f;
    printf("The representation of %12.7e is %#010x\n",
        f_or_i.f, f_or_i.i );
}
```

When `print_rep(1.0)` is called, the output on our Motorola 68020-based workstation is

```
The representation of 1.0000000e+00 is 0x003f800000
```

Notice that a cast operation cannot be used to discover the underlying representation. The cast operator in C converts its operand to the closest value in the new representation; `(int) 1.0` is 1, not `0x003f800000`.

References   cast expression 7.5.1; enumerations 5.5; overloading 4.2.4; scope 4.2.1; `switch` statement 8.7; `strncpy` facility 13.3; structures 5.6

5.8 FUNCTION TYPES

The type "function returning *T*" is a function type, where *T* may be any type except "array of…" or "function returning…." Said another way, functions may not return arrays or other functions, although they can return pointers to arrays and functions.

Functions may be introduced in only two ways. First, a function definition can create a function object, define its parameters and return value, and supply the body of the function. For example, `square` is an object of function type:

```
int square(x)
    int x;
{
    return x*x;
}
```

More information about function definitions is given in section 9.1.

Second, a function declaration can introduce a reference to a function object defined elsewhere, such as in this definition of `square`:

```
extern int square();
```

An external function declaration can refer to a function defined in another C source file or to a function defined later in the same source file (that is, a "forward reference"). In the following example, this is used to implement mutually recursive functions `f` and `g`:

```
extern int f();
...
int g() { ... f(); ...}
int f() { ... g(); ...}
```

The same declaration style can also be used for static functions:

```
static int f();
...
static int g() { ... f(); ...}
static int f() { ... g(); ...}
```

Some C compilers may not permit this kind of forward reference to static functions. Sometimes they compromise by allowing the first declaration to use the storage specifier `extern`, changing the storage class to `static` when the definition is seen:

```
extern int f();  /* not really extern, see below... */
...
static int g() { ... f(); ...}
static int f() { ... g(); ...}  /* now, make f static */
```

This programming idiom is misleading at best. ANSI C requires that the first declaration of a function (in fact, of any identifier) specify whether it will be external or static. This permits one-pass compilation of C programs in those cases in which an implementation must treat static and external functions differently. ANSI C does not explicitly disallow the "extern-then-static" style, but it does not define how an implementation should treat it.

The only operation that can be applied to an expression of function type is to convert it to a function pointer or to call it. For example, the line

```
extern int f(), (*fp)(), (*apf[])(double);
```

declares external identifiers `f`, `fp`, and `apf` to have types "function returning `int`," "pointer to function returning `int`," and "array of pointers to functions taking a `double` parameter and returning `int`," respectively. The declaration of `apf` includes an ANSI C prototype for the function. These identifiers can be used in function call expressions by writing

```
int i,j,k;
i = f(14);
i = (*fp)(j, k);
i = (*apf[j])(k);
```

When a function with no visible prototype is called, certain standard conversions are applied to the actual arguments, but no attempt is made to check the type or number of arguments with the type or number of formal arguments to the function, if known. Arguments to functions with visible prototypes are converted to the indicated parameter type; in the above example, the integer argument `k` to the function designated by `*apf[j]` will be converted to type `double`.

In ANSI C and some other implementations, an expression of type "pointer to function" can be used in a function call without an explicit dereferencing; in that case, the call `(*fp)(j,k)` above can be written as `fp(j,k)`.

An expression of type "function returning…" that is not used in a function call, as the argument of the address operator, `&`, or as the argument of the `sizeof` operator is immediately converted to the type "pointer to function returning…." The only expressions that can yield a value of type "function returning T" are the name of such a function and an indirection expression consisting of the unary indirection operator, `*`, applied to an expression of type "pointer to function returning…." For example, the following program assigns the same pointer value to `fp1` and `fp2`:

```
extern int f();
int (*fp1)(), (*fp2)();
fp1 = f;   /* implicit conversion to pointer */
fp2 = &f;  /* explicit manufacture of a pointer */
```

(Not performing the conversion when the function is the argument of `sizeof` ensures that the `sizeof` expression will be illegal and not just result in the size of a pointer.)

All the information needed to invoke a function is assumed to be encapsulated in an object of type "pointer to function returning…." Although a pointer to a function is often assumed to be the address of the function's code in memory, on some computers a function pointer actually points to a block of information needed to invoke the function. Such representation issues are normally invisible to the C programmer and need concern only the compiler implementor.

References   function argument conversions 6.3.5; function call 7.4.3; function declarator 4.5.4; function definition 9.1; function prototype 9.2; indirection operator * 7.5.7; `sizeof` operator 7.5.2; usual unary conversions 6.3.3

5.9 THE VOID TYPE

The type `void` is a recent addition to C. It has no values and no operations and is used mainly as the return type of a function, signifying that the function returns no value:

void-type-specifier :
> void

For example:

```
extern void write_line();
...
write_line();
```

The void type may also be used in a cast expression when it is desired to explicitly discard a value. For example:

```
extern int write_line2(); /* returns error indication */
...
(void) write_line2(...);    /* don't check for error */
```

Casting the return value to void indicates clearly that the programmer knows that write_line2 returns a value but chooses to ignore it.

ANSI C introduces the type "void *", or pointer to void, to represent a "universal" data pointer. Traditionally C programmers have used char * for this purpose.

References   casts 7.5.1; discarded expressions 7.13; void * 5.3.2

5.10 TYPEDEF NAMES

When a declaration is written whose "storage class" is typedef, the type definition facility is invoked.

typedef-name :
> *identifier*

An identifier enclosed in any declarator of the declaration is defined to be a name for a type (a "typedef name"); the type is what would have been given the identifier if the declaration were a normal variable declaration. For example, in the declaration

```
typedef int *ptr, (*func)();
```

the name ptr is defined to be the type "pointer to int" and the name func is defined to be the type "pointer to function returning int."

Once a name has been declared as a type, it may appear anywhere a type specifier is permitted. This allows the use of mnemonic abbreviations for complicated types. For example, after writing the above type definitions, we can write

```
ptr link, *indirect_link;
func my_routine, my_vector[10];
```

in which case `link` has type "pointer to `int`," `indirect_link` has type "pointer to pointer to `int`," `my_routine` has type "pointer to function returning `int`," and `my_vector` has type "10-element array of pointers to functions returning `int`."

Typedef names should not be mixed with other type specifiers. Some implementations permit the following; ANSI C explicitly forbids it:

```
typedef long int bigint;
unsigned bigint x; /* probably illegal */
```

Declarations with the `typedef` storage specifier do not introduce new types; the names are always considered to be synonyms for types that could be specified in other ways. For instance, after the declaration

```
typedef struct S { int a; int b; } s1type, s2type;
```

the type specifiers `s1type`, `s2type`, and `struct S` can be used interchangeably to refer to the same type.

C implementations may wish to preserve the type distinctions internally so that debuggers and other associated tools can refer to types by the names used by the programmer.

References   type compatibility 5.11

5.10.1 Typedef Names for Function Types

A function type may be given a `typedef` name. For example, `DblFunc` may be established as a synonym for "function returning `double`" with this declaration:

```
typedef double DblFunc();
```

Once declared, `DblFunc` can be used to declare pointers to the function type, arrays of the function type, and so forth, using the normal rules for composing declarators:

```
extern DblFunc *f_ptr, *f_array[];
```

Abiding by the normal rules of type declarations, the programmer must not declare illegal types, such as an array of functions:

```
extern DblFunc f_array[10]; /* illegal! */
```

Perhaps surprisingly, `DblFunc` cannot be used to declare or define functions: functions must not inherit their "function-ness" from `typedef` names. For example, the following definition of `fabs` is rejected because it seems to define a function returning another function:

```
DblFunc fabs(x)
    double x;
{
    if (x<0.0) return -x; else return x;
}
```

It is not possible to get around this problem by omitting the parentheses after `fabs`, because that is where the parameter must be listed. The function definition must be written in the usual way, as if `DblFunc` did not exist:

```
double fabs(x)
    double x;
{
    if (x<0.0) return -x; else return x;
}
```

In ANSI C, `typedef` names can include function prototype information, including parameter names:

```
typedef double DFuncType( double x );
typedef double (*FuncPtr)( int, float );
```

In this example, `DFuncType` is a function type and `FuncPtr` is a function pointer type.

References   function declarators 4.5; function definitions 9.1; function prototypes 9.2

5.10.2 Redefining Typedef Names

The language specifies that `typedef` names may be redefined in inner blocks in the same fashion as ordinary identifiers:

```
typedef int T;
T foo;
...
{
    float T;
    T = 1.0;
    ...
}
```

(One restriction is that the redeclaration cannot omit the type specifiers on the assumption that the type will default to `int`.) However, some compilers have been known to have problems with such redeclarations, probably because of the pressure `typedef` names put on the C language grammar. We now turn to this problem.

References   scope of names 4.2.1

5.10.3 Implementation Note

Allowing ordinary identifiers to be type specifiers makes the C grammar context sensitive, and hence not LALR(1). To see this, consider the program line

```
A ( *B ) ;
```

If `A` has been defined as a `typedef` name, then the line is a declaration of a variable B to be of type "pointer to A." (The parentheses surrounding "`*B`" are ignored.) If `A` is not a type name, then the line is a call of the function A with the single parameter `*B`. This ambiguity cannot be resolved grammatically.

C compilers based on the UNIX parser-generator YACC—such as the Portable C Compiler—handle this problem by feeding information acquired during semantic analysis back to lexical analysis. C compilers must do some `typedef` analysis during lexical analysis.

5.11 TYPE COMPATIBILITY

Two types in C are *compatible* if they are either the same type or are "close enough" to be considered the same for many purposes. The notion of compatible types was introduced by ANSI C, but for the most part it captures in a more formal way the rules that are used in traditional C. Some additional rules are necessary to handle ANSI C features such as function prototypes and type qualifiers. For two types to be compatible, they either must be the same type, or must be pointers, functions, or arrays with certain properties. The specific rules are discussed in the following sections.

Associated with every two compatible types is a *composite type*, which is the common type that arises out of the two compatible types. This is similar to the way in which the usual binary conversions take two integral types and combine them to yield a common result type for some arithmetic operators. The composite type produced by two compatible types is described along with the rules for type compatibility.

References   array types 5.4; function prototypes 9.2; function types 5.8; pointer types 5.3; structure types 5.6; type qualifiers 4.4.3; union types 5.7; usual binary conversions 6.3

5.11.1 Identical Types

Two arithmetic types can be compatible only if they are the same type. If a type can be written using different combinations of type specifiers, all the alternate forms are the same type. That is, the types `short` and `short int` are the same, but the types `unsigned`, `int`, and `short` are all different. The type `signed int` is the same as `int` (and equivalently for `short` and `long`), except when they are used as the types of bit fields. The types `char`, `signed char`, and `unsigned char` are always different.

Any two types that are the same are compatible and their composite type is the same type. In ANSI C, the presence of any type qualifiers changes the type: type `const int` is not the same as —nor is compatible with—type `int`.

Consider, for example, the following declarations:

```
char * p, *q;
struct {int a, b;} x,y;
struct S {int a,b;} u;
typedef struct S TS;
struct S w;
```

After these declarations, the following groups of types are the same:

- The types of p and q are the same.
- The types of x and y are the same, but neither is the same as the type of u.
- The types TS and struct S are the same;
- The types of u and w are the same.

Names declared as types in `typedef` definitions are synonyms for types, not new types. Thus, in the following example, the type `my_int` is the same as type `int`, and the type `my_function` is the same as the type "`float * ()`":

```
typedef int my_int;
typedef float *my_function();
```

In the more complicated example

```
struct S { int a, b; } x;
typedef struct S t1, t2;
struct S w;
t1 y;
t2 z;
```

the variables w, x, y, and z all have the same type.

References   integer types 5.1; pointer types 5.3; structure types 5.6; `typedef` names 5.10

5.11.2 Enumeration Compatibility

Each enumerated type definition gives rise to a new integral type. ANSI C requires each enumerated type to be compatible with the implementation-defined integer type that represents it. The compatible integer type may be different for different enumerations in the same program. The composite type is the enumerated type. No two different enumerated types defined in the same source file are compatible. For example, in the following declarations, the types of E1 and E2 are not compatible, but the types of E1 and E3 are compatible because they are the same type.

```
enum e {a,b} E1;
enum {c,d} E2;
enum e E3;
```

Because enumerated types are generally treated as integer types, values of different enumerated types can be mixed freely regardless of type compatibility. The effect of the compatibility rule is that ANSI C will reject the second function declaration below because the argument type in the prototype does not agree with the first declaration:

```
extern int f( enum {a,b} x);
extern int f( enum {b,c} x);
```

Non-ANSI conforming implementations may treat enumerated types more strictly and not provide compatibility with integer types, or may treat them as fully compatible with int and with each other. Observing ANSI C rules provides maximum portability.

References   enumerated types 5.5

5.11.3 Array Compatibility

Two (similarly qualified) array types are compatible if their element types are compatible. If both types specify sizes, the sizes must be the same. However, if only one array type specifies a size—or if neither do—the two types are still compatible. For example, consider these declarations:

```
int a[];
int b[5];
int c[10];
const int d[10];
```

The type of a is compatible with the type of b and with the type of c, but the types of b and c are not compatible, because they specify different array bounds. The types of c and d are not compatible, because the element types, int and const int, are not compatible.

The composite type of two compatible array types is the array type with the composite element type. If either original type specifies a size, the composite type has that size also. Thus, the composite type of the types of a and b above is int [5].

References   array types 5.4, type qualifiers 4.4.3

5.11.4 Function Compatibility

For two function types to be compatible, they must specify compatible return types. If both types are specified in traditional (non-prototype) form, that is all that is required. The composite type is a (traditional-form) function type with the composite return type.

For two function types both declared in prototype form to be compatible, the following conditions must hold:

1. The function return types must be compatible.
2. The number of parameters and the use of the ellipsis must agree.
3. The corresponding parameters must have compatible types.

It is not necessary that any parameter names agree. The composite type is a function type whose parameters have the composite parameter type, with the same use of the ellipsis, and with the composite return type.

If only one of the two function types is in prototype form, then for the two types to be compatible the following conditions must hold:

1. The return types must be compatible.
2. The prototype must not include the ellipsis terminator.
3. Each parameter type T in the prototype must be compatible with the type resulting from applying the usual argument conversions to T.

The composite type is the prototype-form function type with the composite return value.

   References   function prototypes 9.2; function types 5.8

5.11.5 Structure and Union Compatibility

Each occurrence of a type specifier that is a structure type definition or union type definition introduces a new structure or union type that is neither the same as nor compatible with any other such type in the same source file.

A type specifier that is a structure, union, or enumerated type *reference* is the same type introduced in the corresponding *definition*. The type tag is used to associate the reference with the definition, and in that sense the tag may be thought of as the name of the type. Thus, the types of x, y, and u below are all different, but the types of u and v are the same:

```
struct { int a; int b; } x;
struct { int a; int b; } y;
struct S { int a; int b; } u;
struct S v;
```

   References   enumerations 5.5; structures 5.6; unions 5.7

5.11.6 Pointer Compatibility

Two (similarly qualified) pointer types are compatible if they point to compatible types. The composite type for two compatible pointer types is the (similarly qualified) pointer to the composite type.

5.11.7 Compatibility across Source Files

Although structure, union, and enumerated type definitions give rise to new (non-compatible) types, a loophole must be created to allow references across separately compiled source files within the same program. For example, suppose a header file contains these declarations:

```
struct S {int a,b;};
extern struct S x;
```

When two source files in a program both import this header file, the intent is that the two files reference the same variable, x, which has the single type struct S. However, each file theoretically contains a definition of a different structure type that just happens to be named struct S in each instance. Unless the two declarations of x have compatible types, ANSI C states that the run-time behavior of the program is undefined, and therefore the following rules must be introduced:

1. Two structures or unions defined in separate source files are compatible if they declare the same members in the same order and each corresponding member has a compatible type (including the width of bit fields).
2. Two enumerations defined in separate source files are compatible if they contain the same enumeration constants (in any order), each with the same value.

In these cases, the composite type is the type in the current source file.

References   enumerated types 5.5; structure types 5.6; union types 5.7

5.12 TYPE NAMES AND ABSTRACT DECLARATORS

There are two situations in C programming when it is necessary to write the name of a type without declaring an object of that type: when writing cast expressions and when applying the sizeof operator to a type. In these cases, one uses a type name built from an abstract declarator. (Don't confuse "type name" with "typedef name" described in section 5.10.)

type-name :
        declaration-specifiers abstract-declarator$_{opt}$

abstract-declarator :
        pointer
        pointer$_{opt}$ direct-abstract-declarator

pointer:
        * *type-qualifier-list$_{opt}$*
        * *type-qualifier-list$_{opt}$ pointer*

type-qualifier-list :   (ANSI C)
        type-qualifier
        type-qualifer-list type qualifier

direct-abstract-declarator :
  (*abstract-declarator*)
  direct-abstract-declarator$_{opt}$ [*constant-expression$_{opt}$*]
  direct-abstract-declarator$_{opt}$ (*parameter-type-list$_{opt}$*)

An abstract declarator resembles a regular declarator in which the enclosed identifier has been replaced by the empty string. Thus, a type name looks like a declaration from which the enclosed identifier has been omitted. In the syntax, the *declaration-specifiers* must not include storage class specifiers. The *parameter-type-list* is permitted only in ANSI C, where it is used for a prototype-form type declaration.

The precedences of the alternatives of the abstract declarator are the same as in the case of normal declarators. Some examples of type names are shown in the table below.

Examples of type names

Type name	Translation
`int`	type `int`
`float *`	pointer to `float`
`char (*)(int)`	pointer to function taking an `int` parameter and returning `char`
`unsigned *[4]`	array of 4 pointers to `unsigned`
`int (*(*)()) ()`	pointer to function returning pointer to function returning `int`

Type names always appear within the parentheses that form part of the syntax of the cast or `sizeof` operator. If the type specifier in the type name is a structure, union, or enumerated type definition, then most implementations will not define any included type tag. For example, assume that `struct S` is not defined when the following two statements are encountered:

```
i = sizeof( struct S {int a,b;}); /* OK, but strange */
j = sizeof( struct S ); /* Probably illegal because
                           struct S is still not defined. */
```

A good C implementation should issue a warning on the first line.

In ANSI C, function declarators in type names may have prototype information.

References casts 7.5.1; function prototypes 9.2; `sizeof` operator 7.5.2

5.13 EXERCISES

1. What C type would you choose to represent the following sets of values? Assume your main priority is portability across different compilers and computers, and your secondary priority is to minimize space consumption.
 (a) a 5-digit U. S. Postal Service zip code
 (b) a phone number consisting of a 3-digit area code and a 7-digit local number
 (c) the values 0 and 1

    (d) the values −1, 0, and 1

    (e) either an alphabetic character or the value −1

    (f) the balance in a bank account, in dollars and cents, up to 9,999,999.99

2.   Some popular computers support an extended character set that includes the normal ASCII characters as well as additional characters whose values are in the range 128 through 255. Assume that type `char` is represented in 8 bits. The `is_up_arrow` function below is supposed to return "true" if the input character represents the up-arrow key and "false" otherwise. Will this function be portable across different C compilers, assuming that the definition of UP_ARROW_KEY is given the proper value for the target computer? If not, rewrite it so that it is.

```
#define UP_ARROW_KEY   0x85
...
int is_up_arrow(c)
  char c;
{
  return c == UP_ARROW_KEY;
}
```

3.   If `vp` has type `void *` and `cp` has type `char *`, which of the following assignment statements are legal in ANSI C?

    (a) vp = cp;   (c) *vp = *cp;

    (b) cp = vp;   (d) *cp = *vp;

4.   If `iv` has type `int [3]`, and `im` has type `int [4][5]`, rewrite the following expressions without using the subscript operator.

    (a) iv[i]

    (b) im[i][j]

5.   What integer value is returned by the function `f` below? Is the cast to type `int` in the `return` statement necessary?

```
enum birds {wren, robin=12, blue_jay};
int f()
{
  return (int) blue_jay;
}
```

6.   Below is the definition of a structured type and a variable of that type. Write a series of statements that assign a legal value to every component of the structure. If two components of the structure overlap, assign to only one of the overlapping components.

```
struct S {
  int i;
  struct T {
    unsigned s: 1;
    unsigned e: 7;
    unsigned m: 24;
  } F;
  union U {
    double d;
    char a[6];
    int * p;
  } U;
} x;
```

7. Make two sketches of the structure defined in the previous problem, using the same format as in sections 5.6.5 and 5.7.3. Assume that the underlying computer is byte-addressed using 8 bits for type `char`, 32 bits for pointers and type `int`, and 64 bits for type `double`. In the first sketch, assume a big endian computer with bit fields packed right to left within 32-bit words; in the second, assume a little endian with bit fields packed right to left within words. In both cases, assume the compiler packs bit fields as tightly as possible.

8. Write a `typedef` definition of the type "function returning pointer to integer." Write a declaration of a variable that holds a pointer to such a function and write an actual function of that type, using the `typedef` definition where possible.

6

Conversions and Representations

Most programming languages are designed to hide from the programmer the details of the language's implementation on a particular computer. For the most part, the C programmer need not be aware of these details, either, although a major attraction of C is that it allows the programmer to go below the abstract language level and expose the underlying representation of programs and data. With this freedom comes a certain amount of risk: some C programmers inadvertently descend below the abstract programming level and build into their programs nonportable assumptions about data representations.

This chapter has three purposes. First, it discusses some characteristics of data and program representations, indicating how the choice of representations can affect a C program. Second, it discusses in some detail the conversion of values of one type to another, emphasizing the characteristics of C that are portable across implementations. Finally, it presents the "usual conversion rules" of C, which are the conversions that happen automatically when expressions are evaluated.

6.1 REPRESENTATIONS

This section discusses the representation of programs and data and how the choice of representations can affect C programs and C implementations.

6.1.1 Storage Units and Data Sizes

All data objects in C are represented at run time in the computer's memory in an integral number of abstract *storage units*, or *bytes*. Each storage unit is in turn made up of some fixed number of *bits*, each of which can assume either of two values, denoted 0 and 1.

By definition, the *size* of a data object is the number of storage units (bytes) occupied by that data object. A storage unit is taken to be the amount of storage occupied by one character; the size of an object of type `char` is therefore 1.

Because all data objects of a given type occupy the same amount of storage, we can also refer to the size of a *type* as the number of storage units occupied by an object of that type. The `sizeof` operator may be used to determine the size of a data object or type. We say that a type is "longer" or "larger" than another type if its size is greater. Similarly we say that a type is "shorter" or "smaller" than another type if its size is less. ANSI C requires certain minimum sizes for the integer and floating-point types and provides implementation-defined header files `limits.h` and `float.h` that define the sizes.

The following program determines the sizes of the principal C data types:

```
#include <stdio.h>
int main()
{
    printf("\tType sizes:\n");
    printf("char\tshort\tint\tlong\tfloat\tdouble\n");
    printf("%3d\t%3d\t%3d\t%3d\t%3d\t%3d\n",
            sizeof(char), sizeof(short), sizeof(int),
            sizeof(long), sizeof(float), sizeof(double) );
}
```

References   character types 5.1.3; `float.h` 5.2; `limits.h` 5.1.1; minimum integer sizes 5.1.1; `sizeof` operator 7.5.2; `stdio.h` standard I/O ch. 15

6.1.2 Byte Ordering

The addressing structure of a computer determines how storage pieces of various sizes are named by pointers. The addressing model most natural for C is one in which each character (byte) in the computer's memory can be individually addressed. Computers using this model are called "byte-addressable" computers. The address of a larger piece of storage—one used to hold an integer or a floating-point number, for example—is typically the same as the address of the first character in the larger unit. (The "first" character is the one with the lowest address.)

Even within this simple model, computers differ in their storage "byte order"; that is, they differ in which byte of storage they consider to be the "first" one in a larger piece. In "right-to-left" or "little endian" architectures, which include the DEC VAX computers and the Intel 80x86 microprocessors, the address of a 32-bit integer is also the address of the low-order byte of the integer. In "left-to-right" or "big endian" architectures, which include the Motorola 680x0 microprocessor family and the Zilog Z8000, the address of a 32-bit integer is the address of the high-order byte of the integer. These different conventions are pictured in the figure below, which shows the addresses of the individual bytes making up the integer $0x01020304$. In both cases, the address of the whole integer is A, and each byte holds two hexadecimal digits of data.

Big Endian,
left to right

01	02	03	04
A	A+1	A+2	A+3

Little Endian,
right to left

01	02	03	04
A+3	A+2	A+1	A

The DEC PDP-11 is an example of a computer that falls in between these two models. Although basically a 16-bit little endian, when referencing 32-bit integers the two 16-bit words are organized in big endian fashion:

Middle Endian
(PDP-11)

01	02	03	04
A+1	A	A+3	A+2

Components of a structure type are allocated in the order of increasing addresses, that is, either left to right or right to left depending on the byte order of the computer. Because bit fields are also packed following the byte order, it is natural to number the bits in a piece of storage following the same convention. Thus, in a left-to-right computer the most significant (leftmost) bit of a 32-bit integer would be bit number 0 and the least significant bit would be bit number 31. In right-to-left computers the least significant (rightmost) bit would be bit 0, and so forth.

Programs that assume a particular byte order will not be portable. For example, here is a program that determines a computer's byte ordering by using a union in a nonportable fashion. The union has the same size as an object of type `long` and is initialized so that the low-order byte of the union contains a 1 and all other bytes contain zeroes. In right-to-left architectures, the character component, `Char`, of the union will be overlaid on the low-order byte of the long component, `Long`, whereas in left-to-right architectures `Char` will be overlaid on the high-order byte of `Long`:

```
#include <stdio.h>
union { long Long; char Char[sizeof(long)]; } u;
int main()
{
    u.Long = 1;
    if (u.Char[0] == 1)
        printf("Addressing is right-to-left\n");
    else if (u.Char[sizeof(long)-1] == 1)
        printf("Addressing is left-to-right\n");
    else printf("Addressing is strange\n");
    return 0;
}
```

6.1.3 Alignment Restrictions

Some computers allow data objects to reside in storage at any address, regardless of the data's type. Others impose *alignment restrictions* on certain data types, requiring that objects of those types occupy only certain addresses. It is not unusual on a byte-addressed computer, for example, to require that 32-bit (4-byte) integers be located on addresses that are a multiple of four. In this case we say that the "alignment modulus" of those integers is four. Failing to obey the alignment restrictions can result either in a run-time error or in unexpected program behavior. Even when there are no alignment restrictions per se, there may be a performance penalty for using data on unaligned addresses, and therefore a C implementation may align data purely for efficiency.

The C programmer is not normally aware of alignment restrictions, because the compiler takes care to place data on the appropriate address boundaries. However, C does give the programmer the ability to violate alignment restrictions by casting pointers to different types.

In general, if the alignment requirement for a type S is at least as stringent as that for a type D (that is, the alignment modulus for S is no smaller than the alignment modulus for D), then converting a "pointer to type S" to a "pointer to type D" is safe. "Safe" here means that the resulting pointer to type D will work as expected if used to fetch or store an object of type D, and that a subsequent conversion back to the original pointer type will recover the original pointer. A corollary to this is that any data pointer can be converted to type `char *` and back safely. Functions such as `malloc` (section 16.1), which return pointers destined to be cast to various types, always return pointers of type `char *` (`void *` in ANSI C) aligned suitably for an object of any type.

If the alignment requirement for a type S is less stringent than that for type D, then the conversion from a "pointer to type S" to a "pointer to type D" could result in either of two kinds of unexpected behavior. First, an attempt to use the resulting pointer to fetch or store an object of type D may cause an error, halting the program. Second, the hardware or implementation may "adjust" the destination pointer to be legal, usually by forcing it back to the nearest previous legal address. A subsequent conversion back to the original pointer type may not recover the original pointer.

References   byte ordering 6.1.2; malloc function 16.1; pointer types 5.3

6.1.4 Pointer Sizes

There is no requirement in C that any of the integral types be large enough to represent a pointer, although C programmers often assume that type `long` is large enough, which it is on most computers.

In many C implementations it happens that pointers have the same size as type `int`. Because `int` is also the default type specifier, some programmers are careless with pointer/integer conversions. In particular, they may omit the return type when declaring or defining functions returning pointers, knowing the type will default to `int`, which is "good enough" because of C's standard conversion rules. This has proved to be a frequent source of portability problems.

Although function pointers are usually no larger than the widest data pointers (i.e., `char *` or `void *`), this is not always the case, as discussed in section 6.1.5. Programmers should not use data pointers to hold pointers to functions. Use a function pointer type that specifies the correct return type, such as `double (*) ()`. ANSI C specifically states that conversions between function and data pointers have undefined behavior. ANSI C does *not* guarantee that a function pointer can be safely converted to or from type `void *`.

References function types 5.8; pointer conversions 6.2.7; pointer types 5.3; sizes of types 6.1.1

6.1.5 Effects of Addressing Models

This section describes some ways in which a computer's memory design can impact the C programmer and implementor.

Memory models Some computers are designed in such a way that the choice of a representation for pointers involves a time-space tradeoff that may not be appropriate for all programs. For example, IBM PC's and other computers based on the Intel 8086 family of microprocessors can make use of both 16-bit and 32-bit addresses. The smaller addresses (those within a single *segment*) are more efficient in time and space, but limit the amount of memory that can be referenced to 64K bytes. Small programs want faster execution, but large programs rapidly exceed the limits of 16-bit addresses and require access to multiple segments.

To accommodate the needs of different programs, most C compilers for these computers allow the programmer to specify a *memory model* to use for a given C program. (The model is specified by an option to the C compiler.) The memory model chosen establishes the time-space tradeoff used in the program. The following table shows the memory models supported by the Microsoft C compiler and the Intel iC–86 compiler.

Memory models on IBM PC and compatibles

Memory model name	Data pointer size	Function pointer size	Characteristics
small	16 bits	16 bits	code and data areas each limited to a single 64K-byte segment, for a total program size of 128K bytes
medium	16	32	data area limited to a single 64K-byte segment; code can occupy many segments
compact	32	16	code limited to a single 64K segment; data can occupy many segments[1]
large	32	32	both code and data can occupy many segments[1]

[1] Stack data (automatic variables and parameters) are restricted to a single 64K segment.

There are several points to note here. In all the memory models, code and data are kept in separate memory segments with their own address space. Therefore, it is possible for a data pointer and a function pointer to contain the same value even though one points to an object and the other to a function. A C programmer unfamiliar with segmented architectures might suppose that a data pointer and function pointer could contain the same value only if both were null pointers, and might incorrectly try to abbreviate a test:

```
char *cp;
int (*fp)();
...
/* See if cp and fp are both null */
if ((int)cp == (int)fp) ...  /* Incorrect!! */
```

In the compact and medium memory models, data pointers and function pointers have different sizes. Some care should be used with null pointer constant, NULL (section 5.3.2), which is typically defined as a null data pointer. Simple uses of NULL in expressions involving function pointers will be properly converted, but passing NULL as a function pointer argument may not work correctly in the absence of a prototype. In the following example, the behavior of function f is undefined when using the compact or medium memory models because the data pointer passed as an argument is not the same size as the function pointer that is expected:

```
extern int f();
...
f(NULL);     /* This is NOT OK! */
...
int f(p)
  int (*fp)();
{ ... }
```

This problem can be mostly eliminated by the careful use of function prototypes in ANSI C, which will cause arguments to be correctly converted. The programmer must use similar care with library functions.

Explicit control over pointer sizes   An alternative to using a specific memory model for an entire program (or an addition to it) is to specify whether "near" or "far" pointers are to be used for specific functions or data objects. In this way, a programmer can avoid across-the-board performance penalties, although the program will be less portable and probably harder to maintain. Several C compilers for segmented architectures define new keywords near and far that can be used in declarations of variables and pointers. Syntactically, they can appear where ANSI C type qualifiers appear (though, of course, the language no longer conforms to ANSI C). For example:

```
char near near_char, *cp;
int far (*fp)(), big_array[30000]
```

The intent is that `far` pointers will occupy 32 bits while `near` pointers will use 16 bits. Functions or data objects declared `far` can be placed in remote segments by the implementation, whereas `near` ones must be grouped in the "root" segment. Programmers using these language extensions must be very careful when passing the pointers to functions not declared with prototypes.

Array addressing   Regardless of whether a computer uses a segmented addressing scheme or not, some computers are designed in a way that makes accessing elements of an array more efficient if the array size is small—typically, not bigger than 64K bytes. To use larger arrays, the programmer must supply a special compiler option or must designate the large arrays in some way. In Microsoft C, there is both a "huge" memory model and a `huge` keyword that can be applied to array objects and pointers. Huge pointers are only 32 bits wide, but the compiler understands that subscripting arrays marked "huge" require special (and less efficient) instructions.

Very difficult computers   Although C has been implemented efficiently on many computers, a few computers represent data and addresses in forms that are very awkward for C implementations. A major problem can occur when the computer's natural word size is not a multiple of its natural byte size. Suppose—this is a real example—our computer has a 36-bit word and represents characters in 7 bits; each word can hold five characters with one bit remaining unused. All noncharacter data types occupy one or more full words. This memory structure will be very difficult for a C implementor, because C programming relies upon the ability to map any data structure onto an array of characters. That is, to copy an object of type T at address A it should be sufficient to copy `sizeof`(T) characters beginning at A. The only alternative for the implementor on this computer would be to represent characters using some nonstandard number of bits (for example, 9 or 36) so that they fit tightly into a word. This representation could have a significant performance penalty.

A similar problem occurs on "word-addressed" computers—such as the supercomputers manufactured by Cray Research, Inc.—whose basic addressable storage unit is larger than a single character. On these computers, there may or may not be a special kind of address, a "byte pointer," that can represent characters within a word. Assuming there is such a byte pointer, it may very well be larger than a pointer to objects of noncharacter types, or—as is the case of the Cray computers—may use certain bits in the pointer that are ignored and normally set to zero in other kinds of pointers. A C implementor must decide whether to pay the increased overhead of representing all pointers as byte pointers or whether to use the larger format only for objects of type `char *` (and, in ANSI C, `void *`). The latter decision will force C programmers to be more careful about pointer conversions.

References   array types 5.4; character types 5.1.3; function argument conversions 6.3.5; function prototypes 9.2; pointer types 5.3; storage units 6.1.1

6.2 CONVERSIONS

The C language provides for values of one type to be converted to values of other types under several circumstances:

- A cast expression may be used to explicitly convert a value to another type.
- An operand may be implicitly converted to another type in preparation for performing some arithmetic or logical operation.
- An object of one type may be assigned to a location (lvalue) of another type, causing an implicit type conversion.
- An actual argument to a function may be implicitly converted to another type prior to the function call.
- A return value from a function may be implicitly converted to another type prior to the function return.

There are restrictions as to what types a given object may be converted. Furthermore, the set of conversions that are possible on assignment, for instance, is not the same as the set of conversions that are possible with type casts.

In the following sections we will discuss the set of possible conversions and then discuss which of these conversions are actually performed in each of the circumstances listed above.

6.2.1 Representation Changes

The representation of a data object is the particular pattern of bits in the storage area that holds the object; this pattern distinguishes the value of the object from all other possible values of that type.

A conversion of a value from one type to another may or may not involve a representation change. For instance, whenever the two types have different sizes, a representation change has to be made. When integers are converted to a floating-point representation, a representation change is made even if the integer and floating-point type have the same sizes. However, when a value of type `int` is converted to type `unsigned int`, a representation change may not be necessary.

Some representation changes are very simple, involving merely discarding of excess bits or padding with extra 0 bits. Other changes may be very complicated, such as conversions between integer and floating-point representations. For each of the conversions discussed in the following sections, we describe the possible representation changes that may be required.

6.2.2 Trivial Conversions

It is always possible to convert a value from a type to another type that is the same as (or compatible with) the first type. See section 5.11 for a discussion of when types are the same or compatible. No representation change needs to occur in this case.

Most implementations will refuse to convert structure or union types to themselves, because no conversions to structure or union types are normally permitted.

6.2.3 Conversions to Integer Types

Arithmetic types and pointer types may be converted to integers.

From integer types The general rule for converting from one integer type to another is that the mathematical value of the result should equal the original mathematical value if that is possible. For example, if an unsigned integer has the value 15 and this value is to be converted to a signed type, the resulting signed value should be 15 also.

If it is not possible to represent the original value of an object of the new type, then there are two cases. If the result type is a signed type, then the conversion is considered to have overflowed and the result value is technically not defined. If the result type is an unsigned type, then the result must be that unique value of the result type that is equal (congruent) mod 2^n to the original value, where n is equal to the number of bits used in the representation of the result type. If signed integers are represented using two's complement notation, then no change of representation is necessary when converting between signed and unsigned integers of the same size. On the other hand, if signed integers are represented in some other way, such as with one's-complement or sign-magnitude representation, then a change of representation will be necessary.

When an unsigned integer is converted to a signed integer of the same size, the conversion is considered to overflow if the original value is too large to represent exactly in the signed representation (that is, if the high-order bit of the unsigned number is 1). However, many programmers and many programs depend on the conversion being performed quietly and with no change of representation to produce a negative number.

If the destination type is longer than the source type, then the only case in which the source value will not be representable in the result type is when a negative signed value is converted to a longer, unsigned type. In that case, the conversion must necessarily behave as if the source value were first converted to a longer signed type of the same size as the destination type, and then converted to the destination type. For example, since the constant expression -1 has type `int`:

```
((unsigned long) -1) == ((unsigned long) ((long) -1)))
```

If the destination type is shorter than the source type, and both the original type and the destination type are unsigned, the conversion can be effected simply by discarding excess high-order bits from the original value; the bit pattern of the result representation will be equal to the n low-order bits of the original representation. This same rule of discarding works for converting signed integers in two's-complement form to a shorter unsigned type. The discarding rule is also one of several acceptable methods for converting signed or unsigned integers to a shorter signed type when signed integers are in two's-complement form. Note that this rule will not preserve the sign of the value in case of overflow, but the action on overflow is not defined anyway. When signed integers are not represented in two's-complement form, the conversions are necessarily more complicated.   While the C language does not require the two's-complement representation for signed integers, it certainly favors that representation, and implementations should use it whenever feasible.

From floating-point types   The conversion of a floating-point value to an integral value should produce a result that is (if possible) equal in value to the value of the old object. If the floating-point value has a nonzero fractional part, that fraction should be discarded; that is, conversion normally involves truncation of the floating-point value.

The behavior of the conversion is undefined if the floating-point value cannot be represented even approximately in the new type—for example, if its magnitude is much too large, or if a negative floating-point value is converted to an unsigned integer type. The handling of overflow and underflow is left to the discretion of the implementor.

From pointer types   When the source value is a pointer, the pointer is treated as if it were an unsigned integer of a size equal to the size of the pointer.   Then the unsigned integer is converted to the destination type using the rules listed above.   If null pointers are not represented as the value 0, then they must be explicitly converted to 0 when converting the null pointer to an integer.

C programmers have traditionally assumed that pointers could be converted to type `long` and back without loss of information.   Although this is almost always true, it is not required by the language definition.   (It is definitely wrong to assume that type `int` is large enough to hold a pointer.)   Some computers may have pointer representations that are longer than the largest integer type.   Programmers needing a "generic" data pointer type should use `char *` in traditional C and `void *` in ANSI C instead of `long`.

References   character types 5.1.3; floating-point types 5.2; integer types 5.1; overflow 7.2.2; pointer types 5.3; unsigned types 5.1.2; void * type 5.3.1

6.2.4 Conversions to Floating-point Types

Only arithmetic types may be converted to floating-point types.

When converting from `float` to `double` or from `double` to `long double` the result should have the same value as the original value.   This may be viewed as a restriction on the choice of representations for the floating-point types.

When converting from `double` to `float` or from `long double` to `double`, such that the original value is within the range of values representable in the new type, the result should be one of the two floating-point values closest to the original value. Whether the original value is rounded up or down is implementation-dependent.

If the original value is outside the range of values representable in the destination type—as when the magnitude of a `double` number is too large or too small for the representation of `float`—the resulting value is undefined, as is the overflow or underflow behavior of the program.

When converting to floating-point types from integer types, if the integer value is exactly representable in the floating-point type then the result is the equivalent floating-point value. If the integer value is not exactly representable but is within the range of values representable in the floating-point type, then one of the two closest floating-point values should be chosen as the result. If the integer value is outside the range of values representable in the floating-point type, the result is undefined.

References   floating types 5.2; integer types 5.1; overflow 7.2.2

6.2.5 Conversions to Structure and Union Types

No conversions between different structure types or union types are permitted.

References   structure types 5.6; union types 5.7

6.2.6 Conversions to Enumeration Types

The rules are the same as for conversions to integral types. Some permissible conversions, such as between enumeration and floating-point types, may be symptoms of a poor programming style.

References   enumeration types 5.5

6.2.7 Conversions to Pointer Types

In general, pointers and integers may be converted to pointer types. There are special circumstances under which an array or a function will be converted to a pointer.

A null pointer of any type may be converted to any other pointer type, and it will still be recognized as a null pointer. There may be a representation change in the conversion.

A value of type "pointer to S" may be converted to type "pointer to D" for any types S and D. However, the behavior of the resulting pointer may be affected by representation changes or any alignment restrictions in the implementation. In ANSI C, object pointers may be converted to function pointers or vice versa only through an intermediate integer.

The integer constant 0 (or `0L`) may always be converted to a pointer type. The conversion may or may not involve a representation change, regardless of the relative sizes of `int` and the pointer type. The result of such a conversion is a "null pointer" that is different from any legal pointer to a data object. Null pointers of different pointer types may have different internal representations in some implementations.

Integers other than the constant 0 may be converted to pointer type, but the result is nonportable. The intent is that the pointer be considered an unsigned integer (of the same size as the pointer) and the standard integer conversions then be applied to take the source type to the destination type.

An expression of type "array of T" is converted to a value of type "pointer to T" by substituting a pointer to the first element of the array. This occurs as part of the usual unary conversions (section 6.3.3).

An expression of type "function returning *T*" (i.e., a function designator) is converted to a value of type "pointer to function returning *T*" by substituting a pointer to the function. This occurs as part of the usual unary conversions (section 6.3.3).

References   alignment restrictions 6.1.3; array types 5.4; function calls 7.4.3; function designator 7.1; integer types 5.1; pointer types 5.3; `sizeof` operator 7.5.2; usual unary conversions 6.3.3

6.2.8 Conversions to Array and Function Types

No conversions to array or function types are possible. In particular, it is not permissible to convert between array types or between function types:

```
extern int f();
double d;
d = (( double () )f) (); /* illegal */
d = (double) f();        /* OK */
d = (*(double (*)()) f)();
    /* legal, but will have unexpected results */
```

In the last example, the address of f is converted to a pointer to a function returning type `double`; that pointer is then dereferenced and the function called. This is legal, but the resulting value stored in d will probably be garbage unless f was really defined (contrary to the external declaration above) to return a value of type `double`.

6.2.9 Conversions to the Void Type

Any value may be converted to type `void`. Of course, the result of such a conversion cannot be used for anything. Such a conversion may occur only in a context where an expression value will be discarded, such as in an expression statement.

References   discarded expressions 7.13; expression statements 8.2; `void` type 5.9

6.3 THE USUAL CONVERSIONS

6.3.1 The Casting Conversions

Any of the conversions discussed earlier in this chapter may be explicitly performed with a type cast without error. The table on the next page summarizes the permissible casts. Note that ANSI C does not permit a function pointer to be cast directly to an object pointer, or vice versa, although a conversion via a suitable integer type would be possible. This restriction reflects the possibility that object and function pointers could have significantly different representations.

The presence or absence of type qualifiers does not affect the allowability of the casting conversions, and some conversions could be used to circumvent the qualifiers. The allowable assignment conversions are more restrictive.

ANSI C guarantees that an object pointer converted to `void *` and back to the original type will retain its original value. This is likely to be true for conversions through `char *` in other C implementations.

References   assignment conversions 6.3.2; casts 7.5.1; type qualifiers 4.4.3; `void *` 5.3

Permitted casting conversions

Destination (cast) type	Permitted source types
any integer type	(a) any integer type
	(b) any floating-point type
	(c) pointer to Q, for any Q
a floating-point type	any arithmetic type
pointer to (object) T, or	(a) any integer type
(`void *`)	(b) (`void *`)
	(c) pointer to (object) Q, for any Q
	(d) pointer to (function) Q, for any Q[1]
pointer to (function) T	(a) any integer type
	(b) pointer to (function) Q, for any Q
	(c) pointer to (object) Q, for any Q[1]
structure or union	none; not a permitted cast
array of T or	none; not a permitted cast
function returning T	
void	any type

[1] Not permitted in ANSI C.

6.3.2 The Assignment Conversions

In a simple assignment expression, the types of the expressions on the left and right sides of the assignment operator should be the same. If they are not, an attempt will be made to convert the value on the right side of the assignment to the type on the left side. The conversions that are legal—a subset of the casting conversions— are listed in the table on the following page. Unless otherwise indicated, the presence of ANSI type qualifiers do not affect the allowability of the conversion, although a `const`-qualified lvalue cannot be used on the left side of the assignment.

Attempting any other conversion without an explicit cast will be rejected by ANSI-conforming implementations, but traditional C compilers almost always permit the assignment of mixed pointer types and often permit any types that would be allowed in a casting conversion.

The rules governing pointer assignment impose conditions on type qualifiers because the assignment could be used to circumvent the qualification.

References   assignment operator 7.9.1; casting conversions 6.3.1; compatible types 5.11

Allowable assignment conversions (ANSI)

Left side type	Permitted right side types
any arithmetic type	any arithmetic type
a structure or union type[1]	a compatible structure or union type
`(void *)`[2]	(a) the constant 0 (b) pointer to (object) T_1[3] (c) `(void *)`
pointer to (object) T_1[2,3]	(a) the constant 0 (b) pointer to T_2, where T_1 and T_2 are compatible (c) `(void *)`
pointer to (function) F_1[2]	(a) the constant 0 (b) pointer to F_2, where F_1 and F_2 are compatible

[1] Some older C compilers do not support assigning structures or unions.
[2] The referenced type on the left must have all the qualifiers of the referenced type on the right.
[3] T_1 may be an incomplete type if the other pointer has type `void *`. (ANSI C)

6.3.3 The Usual Unary Conversions

The usual unary conversions determine whether and how a single operand is converted before an operation is performed. Their purpose is to reduce the large number of arithmetic types to a smaller number that must be handled by the operators. The conversions are applied automatically to operands of the unary !, −, ~, and * operators, and to each of the operands of the binary << and >> operators. These conversions are listed in the table below for both ANSI and traditional C (which differ slightly); an operand of any type not listed in the table is unchanged under these conversions.

Usual unary conversions

Original operand type	ANSI C conversion	Traditional conversion
`char` or `short`	`int`	`int`
`unsigned char` or `unsigned short`	`int` or `unsigned int`[1]	`unsigned int`
`float`	`float`	`double`
array of T[2]	pointer to T	pointer to T
function returning T[2]	pointer to function returning T	pointer to function returning T

[1] If type `int` cannot represent all values of the original type without overflow, the converted type will be `unsigned int`.
[2] This conversion is sometimes suppressed; see section 6.2.7 for the exceptions.

The ANSI conversions differ from traditional implementations in two ways. First, the promotion from `float` to `double` is no longer mandated in expressions. This allows an implementation to use faster but less precise single-precision floating-point operations. Some older implementations include an optional compilation mode that has the same effect.

The second difference is in the promotion of the shorter integral types. ANSI C adopted the "value-preserving" rules used by some C compilers in preference to the "unsigned preserving" rules used by other compilers. The programmer should be cautious of these conversions, since the signedness of the result of the promotion is implementation-dependent and can affect the meaning of the surrounding expression. For example, if S is a variable of type `unsigned short` in ANSI C and its value is 1, then the expression `(-S)` has type `int` and value -1 if `sizeof(short)` is less than `sizeof(int)`, but the same expression has type `unsigned` and a large positive value if `sizeof(short)` is equal to `sizeof(int)` This is because in the first instance S is promoted to type `int` prior to the application of the unary minus operator, whereas in the second case S is promoted to type `unsigned`.

An lvalue of array type is converted to a pointer to the first element of the array except when:

1.   the array is an argument to the `sizeof` or address (`&`) operators
2.   a character string literal is used to initialize a character array
3.   a wide string literal is used to initialize an array of type `wchar_t`

For example:

```
char a[] =  abcd ;   /* No conversion */
char *b =  abcd ;    /* Array converted to pointer */
int i = sizeof(a);   /* No conversion; size of whole array */
b = a + 1;            /* Array converted to pointer. */
```

A function designator is converted to a pointer to the function unless the designator is the operand of the `sizeof` or address (`&`) operators. (If it is the operand of `sizeof`, it is also illegal.) For example:

```
extern int f();
int (*fp)();
int i;
fp = f;          /* OK, f is converted to &f */
fp = &f;         /* OK, implicit conversion suppressed */
i = sizeof(fp)   /* OK, result is the size of the pointer */
i = sizeof(f)    /* Illegal */
```

References   bitwise negation operator ~ 7.5.5; function calls 7.4.3; function designator 7.1; indirection operator * 7.5.7; initializers 4.6; logical negation operator ! 7.5.4; lvalue 7.1; shift operators << and >> 7.6.3; sizeof 7.5.2; unary minus operator - 7.5.3; wide strings 2.7.4

6.3.4 The Usual Binary Conversions

When two values must be operated upon in combination, they are first converted according to the usual binary conversions to a single common type, which is also typically the type of the result. The conversions are applied to the operands of most binary operators and to the second and third operands in a conditional expression.

An operator that performs the usual binary conversions on its two operands first performs the usual unary conversions on each of the operands independently, to widen short values and to convert arrays and functions to pointers. Afterward, if either operand is not of an arithmetic type, no further conversions are performed. Otherwise, the first applicable conversion from the following table is performed on both operands.

Usual binary conversions

Type of one operand	Type of the other operand	ANSI C conversion	Traditional conversion
`long double`	any	`long double`	not applicable
`double`	any	`double`	`double`
`float`	any	`float`	`double`
`unsigned long`	any	`unsigned long`	`unsigned long`
`long`	`unsigned`	`long` or `unsigned long`[1]	`unsigned long`
`long`	`int`[2]	`long`	`long`
`unsigned`	`int` or `unsigned`[2]	`unsigned`	`unsigned`
`int`	`int`[2]	`int`	`int`

[1] Type `long` is used if and only if it can represent all values of type `unsigned`.
[2] This is the only remaining possibility for the other operand type.

The ANSI rules differ from traditional rules when a `long` operand and an `unsigned` operand come together. Since some non-ANSI compilers use the ANSI rules, here is a small program that determines which conversion style is in effect:

```
unsigned int UI = -1;
long int LI = 0;
int main()
{
    if (UI < LI) printf("long+unsigned==long\n");
    else printf("long+unsigned==unsigned\n");
    return 0;
}
```

6.3.5 The Function Argument Conversions

When an expression appears as an argument in a function call that is not governed by an ANSI C prototype (or when it appears as an argument in the variable part of a prototype argument list), the value of the expression is converted before being passed to the function. The function argument conversions are the same as the usual unary conversions, except that arguments of type `float` are always promoted to type `double`, whereas in ANSI C and some other implementations the promotion to `float` is not mandatory in expressions. None of the standard C library routines are prepared to accept arguments of type `float`, because they all expect the automatic conversion to `double` to occur.

> **References**   function calls 7.4.3; prototypes 9.2; usual unary conversions 6.3.3

6.3.6 Other Function Conversions

The declared types of the formal parameters of a function, and the type of its return value, are subject to certain adjustments that parallel the function argument conversions. They are discussed in section 9.4.

6.4 EXERCISES

1. The following table lists pairs of source and destination types to be used in casting conversions. Which of the conversions are allowable in ANSI C? Which in traditional C? (For traditional C, replace `void` with `char`.)

	Destination type	Source type
(a)	`char`	`int`
(b)	`char *`	`int *`
(c)	`int (*f)()`	`int *`
(d)	`double *`	`int`
(e)	`void *`	`int (*f)()`
(f)	`int *`	`t *` (where: `typedef int t`)

2. In the table in exercise 1, which pairs are allowable assignment conversions in ANSI C? Which in traditional C? (The destination type is the left-side type; the source type is the right-side type.)

3. What is the resulting type when the usual binary conversions of traditional C are applied to the following pairs of types? In which cases is the result different under ANSI C?
   - (a) `char` and `unsigned`
   - (b) `unsigned` and `long`
   - (c) `float` and `double`
   - (d) `char` and `long double`
   - (e) `int []` and `int *`
   - (f) `short ()` and `short ()`

4. Is it allowable to have a C implementation in which type `char` can represent values ranging from −2,147,483,648 through 2,147,483,647? If so, what would be `sizeof(char)` under that implementation? What would be the smallest and largest ranges of type `int`?

5. What relationship must hold between `sizeof(long double)` and `sizeof(int)`?

6.   Suppose computers A and B are both byte-addressable and have a word size of 32 bits (four bytes), but computer A is a "big endian" and B is a "little endian." The integer 128 is stored in a word of computer A and is then transferred to a word in computer B by moving the first byte of the word in A to the first byte of the word in B, etc. What is the integer value stored in the word of computer B when the transfer is complete? If A were the "little endian" and B the "big endian," what would be the result?

7

Expressions

C has an unusually rich set of operators that provide access to most of the operations provided by the underlying hardware. This chapter presents the syntax of expressions and describes the function of each of the operators.

7.1 OBJECTS, LVALUES, AND DESIGNATORS

An *object* is a region of memory that can be examined and stored into. An *lvalue* (pronounced "ell-value") is an expression that refers to an object in such a way that the object may be examined or altered. Only an lvalue expression may be used on the left-hand side of an assignment. An expression that is not an lvalue is sometimes called an *rvalue* (pronounced "are-value") because it can be used only on the right-hand side of an assignment. An lvalue can have an incomplete array type, but not void.

As ANSI C uses the term, an "lvalue" does not necessarily permit modification of the object it designates. This is true if the lvalue has an array type, an incomplete type, a const-qualified type, or if it has a structure or union type one of whose members (recursively applied to nested structures and unions) has a const-qualified type. The term *modifiable lvalue* is used to emphasize that the lvalue does permit modification of the designated object.

A *function designator* is a value of function type. It is neither an object nor an lvalue. The name of a function is a function designator, as is the result of dereferencing a function pointer. Functions and objects are often treated differently in C, and we try to be careful to distinguish between "function types" and "object types," "lvalues" and "function designators," and "function pointers" and "object pointers." The phrase "lvalue designating an object" is redundant, but we will use it when appropriate to emphasize the exclusion of function designators.

The C expressions that can be lvalues are listed in the table below, along with any special conditions that must apply for the expression to be an lvalue. No other form of expression can produce an lvalue, and none of the listed expressions can be lvalues if their type is "array of...." Expressions that cannot be lvalues include: array names, functions, enumeration constants, assignment expressions, casts, and function calls.

Non-array expressions that can be values

Expression	Additional requirements
name	*name* must be a variable
e [*k*]	none
(*e*)	*e* must be an lvalue
e.*name*	*e* must be an lvalue
e->*name*	none
*e	none

The operators listed in the table below require certain operands to be lvalues.

Operators requiring lvalue operands

Operator	Requirement
& (unary)	operand must be an lvalue
++ --	operand must be an lvalue (postfix and prefix forms)
= += -= *= /= %= <<= >>= &= ^= |=	left operand must be an lvalue

References   address operator 7.5.6; assignment expressions 7.9; cast expression 7.5.1; component selection 7.4.2; decrement expression 7.4.4, 7.5.8; enumerations 5.5; function calls 7.4.3; increment expression 7.4.4, 7.5.8; indirection expression 7.5.7; literals 2.7, 7.3.2; names 7.3.1; subscripting 7.4.1

7.2 EXPRESSIONS AND PRECEDENCE

The grammar for expressions presented in this chapter completely specifies the precedence of operators in C. To summarize the information, Table 7–1 contains a concise list of the C operators in order from the highest to the lowest precedence, along with their associativity.

7.2.1 Precedence and Associativity of Operators

Each expression operator in C has a precedence level and a rule of associativity. Where parentheses do not explicitly indicate the grouping of operands with operators, the operands are grouped with the operator having higher precedence. If two operators have the same precedence, the operand is grouped with the left or right operator according to

Table 7–1: C operators in order of precedence

Tokens	Operator	Class	Precedence	Associates
names, literals	simple tokens	primary	17	n/a
a[k]	subscripting	postfix	17	left
f(...)	function call	postfix	17	left
.	direct selection	postfix	17	left
->	indirect selection	postfix	17	left
++ --	increment, decrement	postfix	16	left
++ --	increment, decrement	prefix	15	right
sizeof	size	unary	15	right
~	bitwise not	unary	15	right
!	logical not	unary	15	right
- +	arithmetic negation, plus	unary	15	right
&	address of	unary	15	right
*	indirection	unary	15	right
(*type name*)	casts	unary	14	right
* / %	multiplicative	binary	13	left
+ -	additive	binary	12	left
<< >>	left and right shift	binary	11	left
< > <= >=	relational	binary	10	left
== !=	equality/inequality	binary	9	left
&	bitwise and	binary	8	left
^	bitwise xor	binary	7	left
|	bitwise or	binary	6	left
&&	logical and	binary	5	left
||	logical or	binary	4	left
? :	conditional	ternary	3	right
= += -= *= /= %= <<= >>= &= ^= |=	assignment	binary	2	right
,	sequential evaluation	binary	1	left

whether the operators are left-associative or right-associative. All operators having the same precedence level always have the same associativity. The following table shows examples of the precedence and associativity rules.

Examples of precedence and associativity

Original expression	Equivalent expression	Reason for equivalence
a*b+c	(a*b)+c	* has higher precedence than +
a+=b!=c	a+=(b!=c)	+= and != are right-associative
a-b+c	(a-b)+c	− and + are left-associative
sizeof(int)*p	(sizeof(int))*p	sizeof has higher precedence than cast
*p->q	*(p->q)	-> has higher precedence than *

To summarize the associativity rules, all of the binary and ternary operators are left-associative except for the conditional and assignment operators, which are right-associative. The unary and postfix operators are sometimes described as being right-associative, but this is needed only to express the idea that an expression such as `*x++` is interpreted as `*(x++)` rather than as `(*x)++`. We prefer simply to state that the postfix operators have higher precedence than the (prefix) unary operators.

References   assignment operators 7.9; binary operators 7.6; concatenation of strings 2.7.4; conditional operator 7.8; postfix operators 7.4.4; unary + 7.5.3

7.2.2 Overflow and Other Arithmetic Exceptions

For certain operations in C such as addition and multiplication, it may be that the true mathematical result of the operation cannot be represented as a value of the expected result type (as determined by the usual conversion rules). This condition is called overflow or, in some cases, underflow.

In general, the C language does not specify the consequences of overflow. One possibility is that an incorrect value (of the correct type) is produced. Another possibility is that program execution is terminated. A third possibility is that some sort of machine-dependent trap or exception occurs that may be detected by the program in some implementation-dependent manner.

For certain operations, the C language explicitly specifies that the effects are unpredictable for certain operand values or (more stringently) that a value is always produced but the value is unpredictable for certain operand values. If the right-hand operand of the division operator, `/`, or the remainder operator, `%`, is zero, then the effects are unpredictable. If the right-hand operand of a shift operator `<<` or `>>` is too large or negative, then an unpredictable value is produced.

Traditionally, all implementations of C have ignored the question of signed integer overflow, in the sense that the result is whatever value is produced by the machine instruction used to implement the operation. (Many computers that use a two's-complement representation for signed integers handle overflow of addition and subtraction simply by producing the low-order bits of the true two's-complement result. No doubt many existing C programs depend on this fact, but such code is technically not portable.) Floating-point overflow and underflow are usually handled in whatever convenient way is supported by the machine; if the machine architecture provides more than one way to handle exceptional floating-point conditions, a library function may be provided to give the C programmer access to such options.

For unsigned integers the C language is quite specific on the question of overflow: every operation on unsigned integers always produces a result value that is congruent mod 2^n to the true mathematical result of the operation (where n is the number of bits used to represent the unsigned result). This amounts to computing the correct n low-order bits of the true result (of the true two's-complement result if the true result is negative, as when subtracting a big unsigned integer from a small one).

As an example, suppose that objects of type unsigned are represented using 16 bits; then subtracting the unsigned value 7 from the unsigned value 4 would produce the unsigned value 65533; that is, $2^{16}-3$, because this value is congruent mod 2^{16} to the true mathematical result -3.

An important consequence of this rule is that operations on unsigned integers are guaranteed to be completely portable between two implementations that use representations having the same number of bits. Any implementation can easily simulate the unsigned arithmetic of another implementation using some smaller number of bits.

References   division operator / 7.6.1; floating-point types 5.2; remainder operator % 7.6.1; shift operators << and >> 7.6.3; signed types 5.1.1; unsigned types 5.1.2

7.3 PRIMARY EXPRESSIONS

There are three kinds of primary expressions: names (identifiers), literal constants, and parenthesized expressions:

> *primary-expression :*
> > *name*
> > *literal*
> > *parenthesized-expression*

Function calls, subscript expressions, and component selection expressions were traditionally listed as primary expressions in C, but we have included them in the next section with the postfix expressions.

7.3.1 Names

The value of a name depends on its type. The type of a name is determined by the declaration of that name (if any), as discussed in chapter 4.

The name of a variable declared to be of arithmetic, pointer, enumeration, structure, or union type evaluates to an object of that type; the name is an lvalue expression.

An enumeration constant evaluates to the associated integer value; it is not an lvalue. In the example below, the four color names are enumeration constants. The switch statement (described in section 8.7) selects one of four statements to execute based on the value of the parameter color:

```
typedef enum { red, blue, green } colortype;

colortype next_color(color)
    colortype color;
{
    switch (color) {
        case red    : return blue;
        case blue   : return green;
        case green  : return red;
    }
}
```

The name of an array evaluates to that array; it is not an lvalue. In contexts where the result is subject to the usual conversions, the array value is immediately converted to a pointer to the first object in the array. This occurs in all contexts except as the argument to the `sizeof` operator, in which case the size of the array is returned, rather than the size of a pointer:

```
extern void PrintMatrix();
int Matrix[10][10], total_length, row_length;

total_length = sizeof Matrix;
row_length = sizeof Matrix[0];
PrintMatrix(Matrix); /* pointer to first
                        element is passed */
```

The name of a function evaluates to that function; it is not an lvalue. In contexts where the result is subject to the usual conversions, the function value is immediately converted to a pointer to the function. This occurs in all contexts but two: as the argument to the `sizeof` operator, where a function is illegal, and as the function in a function call expression, in which case the function itself is desired, and not a pointer to it. The following example shows a function name used as an argument to another function:

```
extern void PlotFunction(double (*f)(),double x0,double x1);

double fn(x)
    double x;
{
    return x*x - x;
}

int main()
{
    PlotFunction(fn, 0.01, 100.0); /* fn becomes a pointer */
    ...
}
```

It is not possible for a name, as an expression, to refer to a label, `typedef` name, structure component name, union component name, structure tag, union tag, or enumeration tag. Names used for those purposes reside in name spaces separate from the names that can be referred to by a name in an expression. Some of these names may be referred to within expressions by means of special constructs. For example, structure and union component names may be referred to using the . or `->` operators, and `typedef` names may be used in casts and as an argument to the `sizeof` operator.

References   array types 5.4; casts 7.5.1; enumeration types 5.5; function calls 7.4.3; function types 5.8; lvalue 7.1; name space 4.2; selection operators .   and `->` 7.4.2; `sizeof` operator 7.5.2; typedef names 5.10; usual unary conversions 6.3.3

7.3.2 Literals

A literal (lexical constant) is a numeric constant, and when evaluated as an expression yields that constant as its value. A literal expression is never an lvalue. See section 2.7 for a discussion of literals and their types and values.

7.3.3 Parenthesized Expressions

A parenthesized expression consists of a left parenthesis, any expression, and then a right parenthesis:

> *parenthesized-expression* :
>   (*expression*)

The type of a parenthesized expression is identical to the type of the enclosed expression; no conversions are performed. The value of a parenthesized expression is the value of the enclosed expression, and will be an lvalue if and only if the enclosed expression is an lvalue.

The purpose of the parenthesized expression is simply to delimit the enclosed expression for grouping purposes, either to defeat the default precedence of operators or to make code more readable. For example:

```
x1 = (-b + discriminant)/(2.0 * a)
```

Parentheses do not necessarily force a particular evaluation order. See section 7.12.

> **References**   lvalue 7.1

7.4 POSTFIX EXPRESSIONS

There are six kinds of postfix expressions: subscripting expressions, two forms of component selection (direct and indirect), function calls, and postfix increment and decrement expressions.

> *postfix-expression* :
>   *primary-expression*
>   *subscript-expression*
>   *component-selection-expression*
>   *function-call*
>   *postincrement-expression*
>   *postdecrement-expression*

Function calls, subscript expressions, and component selection expressions were traditionally listed as primary expressions, but their syntax is more closely related to the postfix expressions.

7.4.1 Subscripting Expressions

A subscripting expression consists of a postfix expression, a left bracket, an arbitrary expression, and a right bracket. This construction is used for array subscripting, where the postfix expression (commonly an array name) evaluates to a pointer to the beginning of the array and the other expression to an integer offset:

> *subscript-expression :*
>   *postfix-expression* [*expression*]

In C, the expression $e_1[e_2]$ is by definition precisely equivalent to the expression $*((e_1)+(e_2))$. The usual binary conversions are applied to the two operands, and the result is always an lvalue. The indirection (*) operator must have a pointer as its operand, and the only way that the result of the + operator can be a pointer is for one operand to be a pointer and the other an integer, and therefore it follows that for $e_1[e_2]$ one operand must be a pointer and the other an integer. Conventionally, e_1 is the name of an array and e_2 is an integer expression, but e_1 could alternatively be a pointer or the order of the operands could be reversed:

```
char buffer[100], *bptr = buffer;
int i = 99;
...
buffer[0] = '\0';        /* subscripting an array */
bptr[i-1] = bptr[0];     /* subscripting a pointer */
i[bptr]   = '\0';        /* unconventional subscripting */
```

A consequence of the definition of subscripting is that arrays use 0-origin indexing. In the example above, the first element allocated for the 100-element array buffer is referred to as buffer[0], and the last element as buffer[99]. The names buffer and bptr both point to the same place, namely buffer[0], the first element of the buffer array, and they can be used in identical ways within subscripting expressions. However, bptr is a variable (an lvalue), and thus can be made to point to some other place:

```
bptr = &buffer[6];
```

after which the expression bptr[-4] refers to the same place as the expression buffer[2]. (This illustrates the fact that negative subscripts make sense in certain circumstances.) An assignment can also make bptr point to no place at all:

```
bptr = NULL; /* Store a null pointer into bptr. */
```

On the other hand, the array name buffer is not an lvalue and cannot be modified; considered as a pointer, it always points to the same fixed place.

Multidimensional array references are formed by composing subscripting operators. The following code stores 1.0 in the diagonal elements of a 10-by-10 array, `matrix`, and stores 0.0 in the other elements:

```
int matrix[10][10];
...
for (i = 0; i < 10; i++)
    for (j = 0; j < 10; j++)
        matrix[i][j] = ((i == j) ? 1.0 : 0.0);
```

It is poor programming style to use a comma expression within the subscripting brackets, because it might mislead a reader familiar with other programming languages to think that it means subscripting of a multidimensional array. For example, the expression

```
commands[k=n+1, 2*k]
```

might appear to be a reference to an element of a two-dimensional array named `commands` with subscript expressions `k=n+1` and `2*k`, whereas its actual interpretation in C is as a reference to a one-dimensional array named `commands` with subscript `2*k` after `k` has been assigned `n+1`. If a comma expression is really needed (and it is hard for us to think of a plausible example), enclose it in parentheses to indicate that it is something unusual:

```
commands[(k=n+1, 2*k)]
```

It is possible to use pointers and casts to refer to a multidimensional array as if it were a one-dimensional array. This may be desirable for reasons of efficiency. It must be kept in mind that arrays in C are stored in row-major order. Here is an example of such trickery:

```
#define SIZE 10
double matrix[SIZE][SIZE];
int i;
/*
    Set up an identity matrix. Tricky but fast.
    Treats matrix as a one-dimensional array of
    length SIZE*SIZE. Clears it, then sets diagonal.
*/
for (i = 0; i < SIZE*SIZE; i++)
    ((double *) matrix)[i] = 0.0;
for (i = 0; i < SIZE*SIZE; i += (SIZE + 1))
    ((double *) matrix)[i] = 1.0;
```

References   addition operator + 7.6.2; array types 5.4; comma expressions 7.10; indirection operator * 7.5.7; integral types 5.1; lvalue 7.1; pointer types 5.3

7.4.2 Component Selection

Component selection operators are used to access fields (components) of structure and union types:

> *component-selection-expression* :
> > *direct-component-selection*
> > *indirect-component-selection*
>
> *direct-component-selection* :
> > *postfix-expression* . *name*
>
> *indirect-component-selection* :
> > *postfix-expression* -> *name*

A direct component selection expression consists of a postfix expression, a period (.), and a name. The postfix expression must be of a structure or union type, and the name must be the name of a component of that type. The result of the expression is the named member of the structure or union.

The result of the direct component selection expression is an lvalue if the expression before the period is an lvalue and if the selected component is not an array. The first condition is true for all structure and union values except those returned by a function. The following example illustrates this; f is a function that returns a structure:

```
struct S {int a,b;} x;
extern struct S f();
int i;
...
x = f();        /* OK */
i = f().a;      /* OK */
f().a = i;      /* Illegal; f() is not an lvalue */
```

(Note that some pre-ANSI implementations do not allow functions to return structures at all, and some that do will reject the expression f().a, although it is legal.)

In ANSI C, if the expression before the period has a qualified structure or union type, the result has the so-qualified type of the named component. For example, the assignment below is illegal because x.a has type "const int", the const having been inherited from x:

```
const struct {int a,b;} x;
...
x.a = 5;  /* Illegal */
```

An indirect component selection expression consists of a postfix expression, the operator ->, and a name. The value of the postfix expression must be a pointer to a structure or union type, and the name must be the name of a component of that structure or union type. The result is the named member of the union or structure and is an lvalue

unless the member is an array. The expression *e->name* is by definition precisely
equivalent to the expression (*e) .*name*. In the following example, both components of
structure Point are set to 0.0 in a roundabout fashion to demonstrate this equivalence:

```
struct {float x, y; } Point, *Point_Ptr;
...
Point.x = 0.0;        /* Sets x to 0.0 */
Point_Ptr = &Point;
Point_Ptr->y = 0.0; /* Sets y to 0.0 */
```

In ANSI C, if the expression before the -> operator is a pointer to a qualified
structure or union type, the result has the so-qualified type of the named component.
    ANSI C permits the null pointer to be used on the left of the indirect selection
operator; applying the address operator & to the result yields the offset in bytes of a
component within the structure. For example:

```
#define OFFSET(type,field)  \
    ((size_t)(char *)&((type *)0)->field)
```

References   address operator & 7.5.6; indirection operator * 7.5.7; lvalue 7.1; size_t 13.1;
structure types 5.6; type qualifiers 4.4.3; union types 5.7

7.4.3 Function Calls

A function call consists of a postfix expression (the function expression), a left parenthesis, a possibly empty sequence of expressions (the argument expressions) separated by
commas, and then a right parenthesis:

function-call :
> *postfix-expression* (*expression-list$_{opt}$*)

expression-list :
> *assignment-expression*
> *expression-list* , *assignment-expression*

The type of the function expression, after the usual unary conversions, must be
"pointer to function returning *T*" for some type *T*. The result of the function call has type
T and is never an lvalue. If *T* is void, then the function call produces no result and may
not be used in a context that requires the call to yield a result. *T* may not be an array type.
    In pre-ANSI compilers, the function expression is required to have type "function
returning T," and therefore function pointers have to be explicitly dereferenced. That is,
if fp is a function pointer, the function to which it points can be called only by writing
(*fp) (...). An exception is sometimes made if fp is a formal parameter; you can
write fp (...) in that case.
    To perform the function call, the function and argument expressions are first
evaluated; the order of evaluation is not specified.

Next, if the function call is governed by an ANSI C prototype (section 9.2), then the values of the argument expressions are converted to the types of the corresponding formal parameters as specified in the prototype. If such conversions are not possible, the call is in error. If the function has a variable number of arguments, then the extra arguments are converted according to the usual argument conversions (section 6.3.5) and no further checks on the extra arguments are made.

If the function call is not governed by a prototype, the argument expressions are only converted according to the usual argument conversions and no further checks are required of the compiler. This is because, lacking a prototype, the compiler may not have any information about the formal parameters of external functions.

After the actual arguments have been evaluated and converted, they are copied into the formal parameters of the called function; thus, all arguments are passed by value. Within the called function the names of formal parameters are lvalues, but assigning to a formal parameter changes only the copied value in the formal parameter and has no effect on any actual argument that may happen to be an lvalue. For example, consider the following function, `square`, which returns the square of its argument:

```
double square(y)
    double y;
{
    y = y*y;
    return y;
}
```

Suppose x is a variable of type `double` with value 4.0, and we perform the function call `square(x)`. The function will return the value 16.0, but the value of x will remain 4.0. The assignment to y within square changes only a copy of the actual argument.

Called functions can change the caller's data only if the data is independently visible to the function (say, in a global variable) or if the caller passes a pointer to the data as an argument to the function. When a pointer is passed, the pointer itself is copied but the object pointed to is not copied. Therefore, changes made indirectly through the pointer can be seen by the caller. For example, the function `swap` below exchanges the values of two integer objects when pointers to those objects are supplied as parameters:

```
void swap( xp, yp )
    int *xp, *yp;
{
    int t = *xp;
    *xp = *yp;
    *yp = t;
}
```

If a is an integer array all of whose elements are 0, and i is an integer variable with the value 4, then after the call `swap(&a[i],&i)`, i will have the value 0 and `a[4]` will have the value 4.

Formal and actual arguments of array types are always converted to pointers by C. Therefore, changes to an array formal parameter in a function will affect the actual argument, although it might not seem obvious that this is so. Consider the function f, below, which has an array parameter:

```
void f(a);
   int a[10];
{
   a[4] = 12;   /* changes caller's array */
}
```

If vec is an integer array, then calling f(vec) will set vec[4] to 12.

If a function whose return type is not void is called in a context where the value of the function would be discarded, the compiler may issue a warning to that effect. The intent to discard the result of the function call may be made explicit by using a cast, as in this call to strcat:

```
(void) strcat(word, suffix);
```

Comma expressions may be arguments to functions if they are enclosed in parentheses so that their parts are not interpreted as separate arguments. We can't think of a plausible reason for doing this, but here is an implausible example:

```
int main()
{
   int i, j;
   f( (i=1, i), (j=1, j)); /* legal, but strange */
   ...
}
```

References   agreement of argument and parameters 9.6; comma operator 7.10; discarded expressions 7.13; function types 5.8; function prototypes 9.2; indirection operator * 7.5.7; lvalue 7.1; pointer types 5.3; strcat 13.1; usual argument conversions 6.3.5; void type 5.9

7.4.4 Postfix Increment and Decrement Operators

The postfix operators ++ and -- are respectively used to increment and decrement their operands while producing the original value as a result. They are side-effect-producing operators:

postincrement-expression :
            postfix-expression ++

postdecrement-expression :
            postfix-expression --

The operand of both operators must be a modifiable lvalue and may be of any scalar type. The constant 1 is added to the operand in the case of ++ or subtracted from the operand in the case of --, modifying the operand. The result is the old value of the operand, before it was incremented or decremented. The result is not an lvalue. The usual binary conversions are performed on the operand and the constant 1 before the addition or subtraction is performed, and the usual assignment conversions are performed when storing the modified value back into the operand. The type of result is that of the lvalue operand before conversion. For example, if i and j are integer variables, the statement i=j--; may be rewritten as the two statements

```
i = j;
j = j-1;
```

These operations may produce unpredictable effects if overflow occurs and the operand is a signed integer or floating-point number. The result of incrementing the largest representable value of an unsigned type is 0, and the result of decrementing the value 0 of an unsigned integer type is the largest representable value of that type.

If the operand is a pointer, say of type "pointer to T" for some type T, the effect of ++ is to move the pointer forward beyond the object pointed to, as if to move the pointer to the next element within an array of objects of type T. [On a byte-addressed computer, this means advancing the pointer by sizeof(T) bytes.] Similarly, the effect of -- is to move the pointer backward as if to the previous element within an array of objects of type T. In both cases the value of the expression is the pointer before modification. It is very common to use the postfix increment operator when scanning the elements of an array or string, as in this example of counting the number of characters in a string:

```
int strlen(cp)
    char *cp;
{
    int count = 0;
    while (*cp++) count++;
    return count;
}
```

References   addition 7.6.2; array types 5.4; assignment conversions 6.3.2; floating-point types 5.2; integer types 5.1; lvalue 7.1; overflow 7.2.2; pointer types 5.3; scalar types ch. 5; signed types 5.1.1; subtraction 7.6.2; unsigned types 5.1.2; usual binary conversions 6.3.4

7.5 UNARY EXPRESSIONS

There are several kinds of unary expressions, discussed in the following sections:

unary-expression :
>   *postfix-expression*
>   *cast-expression*
>   *sizeof-expression*
>   *unary-minus-expression*
>   *unary-plus-expression*
>   *logical-negation-expression*
>   *bitwise-negation-expression*
>   *address-expression*
>   *indirection-expression*
>   *preincrement-expression*
>   *predecrement-expression*

The unary operators have precedence lower than the postfix expressions but higher than all binary and ternary operators. For example, the expression `*x++` is interpreted as `*(x++)`, not as `(*x)++`.

References   binary expressions 7.6; postfix expressions 7.4; precedence 7.2.1; unary plus operator 7.5.3

7.5.1 Casts

A cast expression consists of a left parenthesis, a type name, a right parenthesis, and an operand expression:

cast-expression :
>   (*type-name*)   *unary-expression*

The cast causes the operand value to be converted to the type named within the parentheses. Any permissible conversion (section 6.3.1) may be invoked by a cast expression. The result is not an lvalue:

```
extern char *alloc();
struct S *p;
p = (struct S *) alloc(sizeof(struct S));
```

Some implementations of C incorrectly ignore certain casts whose only effect is to make a value "narrower" than normal. For example, suppose that type `unsigned short` is represented in 16 bits and type `unsigned` is represented in 32 bits. Then the value of the expression

```
(unsigned)(unsigned short)0xFFFFFF
```

ought to be `0xFFFF`, because the cast (`unsigned short`) should cause truncation of the value `0xFFFFFF` to 16 bits, and then the cast (`unsigned`) should widen that value back to 32 bits. Deficient compilers fail to implement this truncation effect and generate code that passes the value `0xFFFFFF` through unchanged. Similarly, for the expression

```
(double)(float)3.1415926535897932384
```

deficient compilers do not produce code to reduce the precision of the approximation to π to that of a float, but pass through the double-precision value unchanged. For maximum portability using non-ANSI compilers, programmers should truncate values by storing them into variables or performing explicit masking operations (such as with the binary bitwise AND operator &) rather than relying on narrowing casts.

    References   bitwise AND operator 7.6.6; type conversions ch. 6; type names 5.12

7.5.2 Sizeof Operator

The sizeof operator is used to obtain the size of a type or data object:

> *sizeof-expression :*
>   sizeof (*type-name*)
>   sizeof *unary-expression*

The sizeof expression has two forms: the operator sizeof followed by a parenthesized type name, or the operator sizeof followed by an operand expression. The result is a constant integer value and is never an lvalue. In ANSI C the result of sizeof has the unsigned integer type size_t defined in the header file stddef.h. Traditional C implementations often use int or long as the result type. Following the C precedence rules, sizeof(long)-2 is interpreted as (sizeof(long))-2 rather than as sizeof((long)(-2)).

Applying the sizeof operator to a parenthesized type name yields the size of an object of the specified type, that is, the amount of memory (measured in storage units) that would be occupied by an object of that type, including any internal or trailing padding. By definition, sizeof applied to any of the character types yields 1. The type name may not name an incomplete array type (one with no explicit length), a function type, or the type void.

Applying the sizeof operator to an expression yields the same result as if it had been applied to the name of the type of the expression. The sizeof operator does not of itself cause any of the usual conversions to be applied to the expression in determining its type; this allows sizeof to be used to obtain the total size of an array, without the array name being converted to a pointer. However, if the expression contains operators that do perform usual conversions, then those conversions are considered when determining the type. The operand of sizeof may not have an incomplete array type or function type, except that if the sizeof operator is applied to the name of a formal parameter declared to have array or function type, then the value returned is the size of the pointer type obtained by the normal rules for converting formal parameters of those types. In ANSI C the operand of sizeof may not be an lvalue that designates a bit field in a structure or union object, but some non-ANSI implementations allow this and return the size of the declared type of the component (ignoring the bit-field designation).

Here are some examples of the application of sizeof. Assume that objects of type short occupy 2 bytes and objects of type int occupy 4 bytes.

Examples of sizeof

Expression	Value
`sizeof(char)`	1
`sizeof(int)`	4
`short s;… sizeof(s)`	2
`short s;… sizeof(s+0)`	4 (result of + has type int)
`short sa[10];… sizeof(sa)`	20
`extern int ia[]; … sizeof(ia)`	*illegal* (type is incomplete)

When `sizeof` is applied to an expression, the expression is analyzed at compile time to determine its type, but the expression itself is not evaluated. This means that any side effects that might be produced by execution of the expression will not take place. For example, execution of the expression

```
sizeof(j++)
```

will not increment `j`. A similar rule applies to type names; while it is legal to write

```
sizeof(struct S {int a,b;})
```

the type definition appearing as the `sizeof` operand does not create a new type in ANSI C. (Some non-ANSI implementations might do so.)

References   array types 5.4; function types 5.8; `size_t` 11.1; storage units 6.1.1; type names 5.12; unsigned types 5.1.2; usual binary conversions 6.3.4; void type 5.9

7.5.3 Unary Minus and Plus

The unary minus operator computes the arithmetic negation of its operand. The unary plus operator (introduced with ANSI C) simply yields the value of its operand:

unary-minus-expression :
      − *unary-expression*

unary-plus-expression :   (ANSI C)
      + *unary-expression*

The operands to both operators may be of any arithmetic type and the usual unary conversions are performed. The result has the promoted type and is not an lvalue.

The unary minus expression "$-e$" is a shorthand notation for "$0 - (e)$"; the two expressions perform the same computation. This computation may produce unpredictable effects if the operand is a signed integer or floating-point number and overflow occurs. For an unsigned integer operand k, the result is always unsigned and equal to $2^n - k$, where n is the number of bits used to represent the result. Because the result is unsigned, it can never be negative. This may seem strange, but note, however, that $(-x)+x$ is equal to 0 for any unsigned integer x. (This identity also holds for any signed integer x for which $-x$ is well defined.)

The unary plus expression "$+e$" is a shorthand notation for "$0 + (e)$"; the two expressions perform the same computation. The operator was added in ANSI C for symmetry with unary minus; it has no other purpose.

References   floating-point types 5.2; integer types 5.1; lvalue 7.1; overflow 7.2.2; subtraction operator – 7.6.2; unsigned types 5.1.2; usual unary conversions 6.3.3

7.5.4 Logical Negation

The unary operator ! computes the logical negation of its operand. The operand may be of any scalar type:

> *logical-negation-expression* :
>   ! *unary-expression*

The usual unary conversions are performed on the operand. The result of the ! operator is of type `int`; the result is 1 if the operand is zero (null in the case of pointers, 0.0 in the case of floating-point values) and 0 if the operand is not zero (or null or 0.0). The result is not an lvalue. The expression `!(x)` is identical in meaning to `(x)==0`:

```
/* Assume that assertion_failure accepts a string
   and reports it as a message to the user. */
#define assert(x,s) if (!(x)) assertion_failure(s)
...
assert(num_cases > 0, "No test cases.");
average = total_points/num_cases;
...
```

References   equality operator == 7.6.5; floating-point types 5.2; integer types 5.1; lvalue 7.1; pointer types 5.3; scalar types ch. 5; usual unary conversions 6.3.3

7.5.5 Bitwise Negation

The unary operator ~ computes the bitwise negation (NOT) of its operand:

> *bitwise-negation-expression* :
>   ~ *unary-expression*

The usual unary conversions are performed on the operand, which may be of any integral type. Every bit in the binary representation of ~e is the inverse of what it was in the (converted) operand e. The result is not an lvalue. For example, if `i` is a 16-bit integer with the value `0xF0F0` (binary: 1111000011110000), then `~i` has the value `0x0F0F` (binary 0000111100001111).

Because different implementations may use different representations for signed integers, the result of applying the bitwise NOT operator ~ to signed operands may not be portable. We recommend using ~ only on unsigned operands for portable code. For an unsigned operand *e*, ~*e* has the value UINT_MAX-*e* if the converted type of *e* is unsigned, or ULONG_MAX-*e* if the converted type of *e* is unsigned long. The values UINT_MAX and ULONG_MAX are defined in the ANSI C header file limits.h.

References   integer types 5.1; limits.h 5.1.1; lvalue 7.1; signed types 5.1.1; unsigned types 5.1.2; usual unary conversions 6.3.3

7.5.6 Address Operator

The unary operator & returns a pointer to its operand:

> *address-expression* :
>   & *unary-expression*

The operand of & must be either a function designator or an lvalue designating an object. If it is an lvalue, the object cannot be declared with storage class register or be a bit field. If the type of the operand for & is "*T*," then the type of the result is "pointer to *T*." The usual conversions are *not* applied to the operand of the & operator, and its result is never an lvalue.

The address operator applied to a function designator yields a pointer to the function. Since a function designator is converted to a pointer under the usual conversion rules, the & operator is seldom needed for functions. In fact, some pre-ANSI C implementations may not allow it. Here is an example:

```
extern int f();
int (*fp)();
...
fp = &f;    /* OK; & yields a pointer to f */
fp = f;     /* OK; usual conversions yield a pointer  to f */
```

A function pointer generated by the address operator is valid throughout the execution of the C program. An object pointer generated by the address operator is valid as long as the object's storage remains allocated. If the operand of & is an lvalue designating a variable with static extent, the pointer is valid throughout program execution. If the operand designates an automatic variable, the pointer is valid as long as the block containing the declaration of the variable is active.

The effect of the address operator in ANSI C differs from its effect in traditional C in one respect. In ANSI C, the address operator applied to an lvalue of type "array of *T*" yields a value of type "pointer to array of T," whereas many pre-ANSI compilers treat &a the same as a, that is, as a pointer to the first element of a. These two interpretations are inconsistent with each other, but the ANSI rule is more consistent with the interpretation of &. For example, in the ANSI C program fragment below, all the assignments to p are equivalent and all the assignments to i are equivalent:

```
int a[10],*p,i;
...
p = &a[0];
p = a;
p = *&a;
i = a[0];
i = *a;
i = **&a;
```

References   array type 5.4; function designator 7.1; function type 5.8; lvalue 7.1; pointer type 5.3; `register` storage class 4.3

7.5.7 Indirection

The unary operator * performs indirection through a pointer. The & and * operators are each the inverse of the other: if x is a variable, the expression *&x is the same as x.

> *indirection-expression* :
>   * *unary-expression*

The operand must be a pointer; if its type is "pointer to T," for some possibly qualified type T, then the type of the result is simply "T" (with the same qualifications). If the pointer points to an object, then the result is an lvalue referring to the object. If the pointer points to a function, then the result is a function designator. For example:

```
int i,*p;
const int *pc;
...
p = &i;   /* p now points to variable i */
*p = 10;  /* sets value of i to 10 */
*pc = 10; /* illegal, *pc has type 'const int' */
```

The usual unary conversions are performed on the operand to the indirection operator. The only relevant conversions are from arrays and function designators to pointers. Therefore, if f is a function designator, the expressions *&f and *f are equivalent; in the latter case f is converted to &f by the usual conversions.

The effect of applying the * operator to invalid or null pointers is undefined.

References   array types 5.4; function designators 7.1; function types 5.8; lvalue 7.1; pointer types 5.3; usual unary conversions 6.3.3

7.5.8 Prefix Increment and Decrement Operators

The unary operators ++ and -- are respectively used to increment and decrement their operands while producing the modified values of the operands as a result. These are side-effect-producing operations. (There are also postfix forms of these operators.)

preincrement-expression :
              ++ *unary-expression*

predecrement-expression :
              -- *unary-expression*

The operands of both operators must be modifiable lvalues and may be of any scalar type. The constant 1 is added to the operand in the case of ++ and subtracted from the operand in the case of --. In both cases the result is stored back in the lvalue and the result is the new value of the operand. The result is not an lvalue. The usual binary conversions are performed on the operand and the constant 1 before the addition or subtraction is performed, and the usual assignment conversions are performed when storing the new value back into the operand. The type of the result is that of the lvalue operand before conversion.

If the operand is a pointer, say of type "pointer to *T*" for some type *T*, then the effect of ++ is to move the pointer forward beyond the object pointed to, as if to move the pointer to the next object within an array of objects of type *T*. [On a byte-addressed computer, this means advancing the pointer by sizeof(*T*) bytes.] The effect of -- is to move the pointer back to the previous element within an array of objects of type *T*.

As an example of using these operators, the strrev function below copies into its second argument a reversed copy of its first argument:

```
int strrev(s1, s2)
   char *s1, *s2;
{
   char *p = s1;
   while (*p++); /* Locate end of first string. */
   --p;          /* Overshot: back up to the null. */
   /* Now copy the characters in reverse order. */
   while (p > s1)
       *s2++ = *--p;
   *s2 = '\0';  /* Terminate the result string. */
}
```

These operations may produce unpredictable effects if overflow occurs and the operand is a signed integer or floating-point number. The result of incrementing the largest representable value of an unsigned type is 0. The result of decrementing the value 0 of an unsigned integer type is the largest representable value of that type.

The expression ++*e* is identical in meaning to *e*+=1, and --*e* is identical to *e*-=1. When the value produced by the increment and decrement operators is not used, the prefix and postfix forms have the same effect; that is, the statement *e*++; is identical to ++*e*;, and *e*--; is identical to --*e*;.

References   addition 7.6.2; array types 5.4; assignment conversions 6.3.2; compound assignment 7.9.2; expression statements 8.2; floating-point types 5.2; integer types 5.1; lvalue 7.1; overflow 7.2.2; pointer types 5.3; postfix increment and decrement expressions 7.4.4; scalar types ch. 5; signed types 5.1.1; subtraction 7.6.2; unsigned types 5.1.2; usual binary conversions 6.3.4

7.6 BINARY OPERATOR EXPRESSIONS

A binary operator expression consists of two expressions separated by a binary operator. The kinds of binary expressions and their operand types are listed in order of decreasing precedence in the following table. All the operators are left-associative (see Table 7–1).

Binary operator expressions

Expression kind	Operators	Operands	Result
multiplicative-expression	* /	arithmetic	arithmetic
	%	integer	integer
additive-expression	+	arithmetic	arithmetic
		pointer and integer	pointer
	−	arithmetic	arithmetic
		pointer − integer	pointer
		pointer − pointer	integer
shift-expression	<< >>	integer	integer
relational-expression	< <= >= >	arithmetic or pointer	0 or 1
equality-expression	== !=	arithmetic or pointer	0 or 1
bitwise-and-expression	&	integer	integer
bitwise-xor-expression	^	integer	integer
bitwise-or-expression	|	integer	integer

For each of the binary operators described in this section, both operands are fully evaluated (but in no particular order) before the operation is performed.

> **References**   order of evaluation 7.12; precedence 7.2.1

7.6.1 Multiplicative Operators

The three multiplicative operators, * (multiplication), / (division), and % (remainder), have the same precedence and are left-associative:

multiplicative-expression :
        unary-expression
        multiplicative-expression mult-op unary-expression

mult-op : one of
        * / %

> **References**   precedence 7.2.1

Multiplication   The binary operator * indicates multiplication. Each operand may be of any arithmetic type. The usual binary conversions are performed on the operands, and the type of the result is that of the converted operands. The result is not an lvalue. For integral operands, integer multiplication is performed; for floating-point operands, floating-point multiplication is performed.

The multiplication operator may produce unpredictable effects if overflow occurs and the operands (after conversion) are signed integers or floating-point numbers. If the operands are unsigned integers, the result is congruent mod 2^n to the true mathematical result of the operation (where n is the number of bits used to represent the unsigned result).

References arithmetic types ch. 5; floating types 5.2; integer types 5.1; lvalue 7.1; order of evaluation 7.12; overflow 7.2.2; signed types 5.1.1; unsigned types 5.1.2; usual binary conversions 6.3.4

Division The binary operator / indicates division. Each operand may be of any arithmetic type. The usual binary conversions are performed on the operands, and the type of the result is that of the converted operands. The result is not an lvalue.

For floating-point operands, floating-point division is performed.

For integral operands, if the mathematical quotient of the operands is not an exact integer, then the result will be one of the two integers closest to the mathematical quotient of the operands. Of those two integers, the one closer to 0 must be chosen if both operands are positive (that is, division of positive integers is truncating division). Note that this completely specifies the behavior of division for unsigned operands. If either operand is negative, then the choice is left to the discretion of the implementor. For maximum portability, programs should therefore avoid depending on the behavior of the division operator when applied to negative integral operands.

The division operator may produce unpredictable effects if overflow occurs and the operands (after conversion) are signed integers or floating-point numbers. Note that overflow can occur for signed integers represented in two's-complement form if the most negative representable integer is divided by −1; the mathematical result is a positive integer that cannot be represented. Overflow cannot occur if the operands are unsigned integers.

The consequences of division by zero, whether integer or floating-point, are machine-dependent.

References arithmetic types ch. 5; floating types 5.2; integer types 5.1; lvalue 7.1; overflow 7.2.2; signed types 5.1.1; unsigned types 5.1.2; usual binary conversions 6.3.4

Remainder The binary operator % computes the remainder when the first operand is divided by the second. Each operand may be of any integral type. The usual binary conversions are performed on the operands, and the type of the result is that of the converted operands. The result is not an lvalue. The library functions div, ldiv, and fmod also compute remainders of integers and floating-point values.

It is always true that (a/b)*b + a%b is equal to a if b is not 0, so the behavior of the remainder operation is coupled to that of integer division. When both operands are positive, the remainder operation will always be equivalent to the mathematical "mod" operation. Note that this completely specifies the behavior of the remainder operation for unsigned operands. If either operand is negative, the behavior will be machine-dependent in a manner corresponding to the machine dependence of integer division. For maximum portability, programs should therefore avoid depending on the behavior of the remainder operator when applied to negative integral operands.

In the following example, gcd computes the greatest common divisor by Euclid's algorithm. The result is the largest integer that evenly divides x and y:

```
unsigned gcd(x, y)
    unsigned x, y;
{
    while ( y != 0 ) {
        unsigned temp = y;
        y = x % y;
        x = temp;
    }
    return x;
}
```

The remainder operator may produce unpredictable effects if performing division on the two operands would produce overflow. Note that overflow can occur for signed integers represented in two's-complement form if the most negative representable integer is divided by -1; the mathematical result of the division is a positive integer that cannot be represented, and therefore the results are unpredictable, even though the remainder itself (zero) is representable. Overflow cannot occur if the operands are unsigned integers.

The consequences of taking a remainder with a second operand of zero are implementation-dependent.

References   div, ldiv 17.1; fmod 17.3; integer types 5.1; lvalue 7.1; overflow 7.2.2; signed types 5.1.1; unsigned types 5.1.2; usual binary conversions 6.3.4

7.6.2 Additive Operators

The two additive operators, + (addition) and − (subtraction), have the same precedence and are left-associative:

additive-expression :
    multiplicative-expression
    additive-expression add-op multiplicative-expression

add-op : one of
    + −

References   precedence 7.2.1

Addition   The binary operator + indicates addition. The usual binary conversions are performed on the operands. The operands may both be arithmetic, or one may be an object pointer and the other an integer. No other operand types are allowed. The result is not an lvalue.

When the operands are arithmetic, the type of the result is that of the converted operands. For integral operands, integer addition is performed; for floating-point operands, floating-point addition is performed.

When adding a pointer p and an integer k, it is assumed that the object that p points to lies within an array of such objects or is one beyond the last object in the array, and the result is a pointer to that object within (or just after) the presumed array that lies k objects away from the one p points to. For example, $p+1$ points to the object just after the one p points to, and $p+(-1)$ points to the object just before. If the pointers p or $p+k$ do not lie within (or just after) the array, then the behavior is undefined. It is illegal for p to be a function pointer or to have type `void *`.

As a more concrete example, suppose we are on a computer that is byte-addressable and on which the type `int` is allocated 4 bytes. Let `a` be an array of 10 integers that begins at address `0x100000`. Let `ip` be a pointer to an integer, and assign to it the address of the first element of array `a`. Finally, let `i` be an integer variable currently holding the value 6. We now have the following situation:

```
int *ip, i, a[10];
ip = &a[0];
i = 6;
```

What is the value of `ip+i`? Because integers are 4 bytes long, the expression `ip+i` becomes

```
0x100000 + 4*6
```

or `0x100018` (24_{10} is 18_{16}).

The addition operator may produce unpredictable effects if overflow occurs and the operands (after conversion) are signed integers or floating-point numbers, or if either operand is a pointer. If the operands are both unsigned integers, then the result is congruent mod 2^n to the true mathematical result of the operation (where n is the number of bits used to represent the unsigned result).

References   array types 5.4; floating-point types 5.2; integer types 5.1; lvalue 7.1; order of evaluation 7.12; overflow 7.2.2; pointer representations 5.3.2; pointer types 5.3; scalar types ch. 5; signed types 5.1.1; unsigned types 5.1.2; usual binary conversions 6.3.4

Subtraction   The binary operator − indicates subtraction. The usual binary conversions are performed on the operands. The operands may both be arithmetic or may both be pointers to compatible object types (ignoring any type qualifiers), or the left operand may a pointer and the other an integer. No other operand types are permitted. The result is not an lvalue.

If the operands are both arithmetic, the type of the result is that of the converted operands. For integral operands, integer subtraction is performed; for floating-point operands, floating-point subtraction is performed. Note that the result of subtracting one unsigned integer from another is always unsigned and therefore cannot be negative.

However, unsigned numbers always obey such identities as `(a+(b-a))==b` and `(a-(a-b))==b`.

Subtraction of an integer from a pointer is analogous to addition of an integer to a pointer. When subtracting an integer k from a pointer p, it is assumed that the object that p points to lies within an array of such objects or is one past the last object, and the result is a pointer to that object within (or just after) the presumed array that lies $-k$ objects away from the one p points to. For example, $p-1$ points to the object just before the one p points to, and $p-(-1)$ points to the object just after. If the pointers p or $p-k$ lie outside the array, then the behavior is undefined. It is illegal for p to be a function pointer or of type `void *`.

Given two pointers p and q of the same type, the difference $p-q$ is an integer k such that adding k to q yields p. The type of the difference may be either `int` or `long`, depending on the implementation. (In ANSI C the type of the difference is the signed integer type `ptrdiff_t`, defined in `stddef.h`.) The result is well defined and portable only if the two pointers point to objects in the same array or point to one past the last object of the array. The difference k is the difference in the subscripts of the two objects pointed to. If the pointers p or $p-q$ lie outside the array, the behavior is undefined. It is illegal for either p or q to be a function pointer or to be of type `void *`.

The subtraction operator may produce unpredictable effects if overflow occurs and the operands (after conversion) are signed integers or floating-point numbers, or if either operand is a pointer. If the operands are both unsigned integers, the result is congruent mod 2^n to the true mathematical result of the operation (where n is the number of bits used to represent the unsigned result).

References   array types 5.4; floating-point types 5.2; integer types 5.1; lvalue 7.1; overflow 7.2.2; pointer representations 5.3.2; pointer types 5.3; `ptrdiff_t` 11.1; scalar types ch. 5; signed types 5.1.1; type compatibility 5.11; type qualifiers 4.4.3; unsigned types 5.1.2; usual binary conversions 6.3.4

7.6.3 Shift Operators

The binary operator `<<` indicates shifting to the left and the binary operator `>>` indicates shifting to the right. Both have the same precedence and are left-associative:

> *shift-expression* :
> > *additive-expression*
> > *shift-expression shift-op additive-expression*
>
> *shift-op* : one of
> > `<<  >>`

Each operand must be of integral type. The usual unary conversions are performed separately on each operand (the usual binary conversions are not used), and the type of the result is that of the converted left operand. The result is not an lvalue.

The first operand is a quantity to be shifted, and the second operand specifies the number of bit positions by which the first operand is to be shifted. The direction of the shift operation is controlled by the operator used . The operator $<<$ shifts the value of the left operand to the left, excess bits shifted off to the left are discarded, and 0-bits are shifted in from the right. The operator $>>$ shifts the value of the left operand to the right; excess bits shifted off to the right are discarded. The bits shifted in from the left for $>>$ depend on the type of the converted left operand: if it is unsigned (or signed and nonnegative), then 0-bits are shifted in from the left; but if it is signed, then at the implementor's option either 0-bits or copies of the leftmost bit of the left operand are shifted in from the left. For this reason, the result of applying the shift operators $<<$ and $>>$ to signed operands is not portable.

Table 7–2 on the next page shows how unsigned shift operations may be used to compute the greatest common divisor of two integers by the binary algorithm. This method is more complicated than the Euclidean algorithm, but it may be faster because in some implementations of C the remainder operation is slow, especially for unsigned operands.

The result value is undefined if the value of the right operand is negative, so specifying a negative shift distance does not (necessarily) cause $<<$ to shift to the right or $>>$ to shift to the left. The result value is also undefined if the value of the right operand is greater than or equal to the width (in bit positions) of the value of the converted left operand. Note, however, that the right operand may be 0, in which case no shift occurs and the result value is identical to the value of the converted left operand.

The two shift operators have the same precedence and are left-associative. One can exploit this fact to write expressions that are visually pleasing but semantically confusing:

```
b << 4 >> 8
```

If b is a 16-bit quantity, this expression extracts the middle 8 bits. As always, it is better to use parentheses when there is any possibility of confusion:

```
(b << 4) >> 8
```

References   integer types 5.1; lvalue 7.1; precedence 7.2.1; signed types 5.1.1; unsigned types 5.1.2; usual unary conversions 6.3.3

7.6.4 Relational Operators

The binary operators $<$, $<=$, $>$, and $>=$ are used to compare their operands:

> *relational-expression* :
> > *shift-expression*
> > *relational-expression   relational-op   shift-expression*

> *relational-op* : one of
> > $<$ $<=$ $>$ $>=$

Table 7–2: Computing the greatest common divisor

```
unsigned binary_gcd(x, y)
    unsigned x, y;
{
    unsigned temp;
    unsigned common_power_of_two = 0;
    /* Special cases: if either argument is zero,
       then return the other one. */
    if (x == 0) return y;
    if (y == 0) return x;
    /* Determine the largest power of two that
       divides both x and y. */
    while (((x | y) & 1) == 0) {
        x = x >> 1; /* One could write "x >>= 1;" */
        y = y >> 1;
        ++common_power_of_two;
    }
    while ((x & 1) == 0)
        x = x >> 1;
    while (y) {
        /* At this point x is guaranteed odd,
           and y is nonzero. */
        while ((y & 1) == 0)   y = y >> 1;
        /* At this point both x and y are odd. */
        temp = y;
        if (x > y)    y = x - y;
        else y = y - x;
        x = temp;
        /* Now x has the old value of y; y was odd, so
           now x is odd.  Now y is even, because it
           was computed as the difference of two odd
           numbers; therefore it will be right-shifted
           at least once on the next iteration. */
    }
    return (x << common_power_of_two);
}
```

The usual binary conversions are performed on the operands. The operands may both be of arithmetic types, or may both be pointers to compatible types, or may both be pointers to compatible incomplete types. The presence of any type qualifiers on the pointer types does not affect the comparison. The result is always of type int and has the value 0 or 1. The result is not an lvalue.

The operator < tests for the relationship "is less than"; the operator <= tests "is less than or equal to"; the operator > tests "is greater than"; and the operator >= tests "is greater than or equal to." The result is 1 if the stated relationship holds for the particular operand values and 0 if the stated relationship does not hold.

For integral operands, integer comparison is performed (signed or unsigned as appropriate). For floating-point operands, floating-point comparison is performed. For pointer operands, the result depends on the relative locations within the address space of the two objects pointed to; the result is defined only if the objects pointed to lie within the same array or structure, in which case "greater than" means "having a higher index" for arrays or "declared later in the list of components" for structures. As a special case for arrays, the pointer to the object one beyond the end of the array is well defined and compares greater than all pointers to objects strictly within the array. All pointers to members of the same union argument compare equal.

The binary relational operators all have the same precedence and are left-associative. It is therefore permitted to write an expression such as $3<x<7$. This does not have the meaning it has in usual mathematical notation, however; by left-associativity it is interpreted as $(3<x)<7$. Because the result of $(3<x)$ is 0 or 1, either of which is less than 7, the result of $3<x<7$ is always 1. One can express the meaning of the usual mathematical notation by using a logical AND operator, as in $3<x$ && $x<7$.

The programmer should exercise care when using relational operators on mixed types. A particularly confusing case is this expression:

```
-1 < (unsigned) 0
```

One might think that this expression would always produce 1 (true), because −1 is less than 0. However, the usual binary conversions cause the value −1 to be converted to a (large) unsigned value before the comparison, and such an unsigned value cannot be less than 0. Therefore, the expression always produces 0 (false).

Some implementations permit relational comparisons between pointers and integers, which is disallowed by the language. The implementations may treat the comparisons as signed or unsigned.

References   arithmetic types ch. 5; array types 5.4; bitwise AND operator & 7.6.6; compatible types 5.11; floating-point types 5.2; incomplete types 5.4, 5.6.1; integer types 5.1; logical AND operator && 7.7; lvalue 7.1; pointer types 5.3; precedence 7.2.1; signed types 5.1.1; type qualifiers 4.4.3; unsigned types 5.1.2; usual binary conversions 6.3.4

7.6.5 Equality Operators

The binary operators == and ! = are used to compare their operands for equality:

equality-expression :
        relational-expression
        equality-expression equality-op relational-expression

equality-op : one of
        ==   ! =

Several kinds of operands are permitted:

1. Both operands may be arithmetic types.
2. Both operands may be pointers to compatible types, or both may be `void *` types.
3. One operand may be a pointer to an object or to an incomplete type and the other may have type `void *`. The first operand will be converted to the `void *` type.
4. One of the operands may be a pointer and the other a null pointer constant (the integer constant 0).

In the case of pointer operands, the presence or absence of type qualifiers on the type pointed to does not affect whether the comparison is allowed or the result of the comparison. The usual binary conversions are performed on the arithmetic operands. The result is always of type `int` and has the value 0 or 1. The result is not an lvalue.

For integral operands, integer comparison is performed. For floating-point operands, floating-point comparison is performed. Pointer operands compare equal if and only if one of the following conditions is met:

1. Both pointers point to the same object or function.
2. Both pointers are null pointers.
3. Both pointers point one past the last element of the same array object.

The operator `==` tests for the relationship "is equal to"; `!=` tests "is not equal to." The result is 1 if the stated relationship holds for the particular operand values and 0 if the stated relationship does not hold.

Structures or unions cannot be compared for equality, even though assignment of these types is allowed. The gaps in structures and unions caused by alignment restrictions could contain arbitrary values, and compensating for this would impose an unacceptable overhead on the equality comparison or on all operations that modified structure and union types.

The binary equality operators both have the same precedence (but lower precedence than `<`, `<=`, `>`, and `>=`) and are left-associative. It is therefore permitted to write an expression such as `x==y==7`. This does not have the meaning it has in usual mathematical notation, however; by left-associativity it is interpreted as `(x==y)==7`. Because the result of `(x==y)` is 0 or 1, neither of which is equal to 7, the result of `x==y==7` is always 0. One must express the meaning of the usual mathematical notation by using a logical AND operator, as in `x==y && y==7`.

There is a bitwise XOR operator as well as bitwise AND and OR operators, but there is no logical XOR operator to go along with the logical AND and OR operators. The `!=` operator serves the purpose of a logical XOR operator: One may write `a<b != c<d` for an expression that yields 1 if exactly one of `a<b` and `c<d` yields 1, and 0 otherwise. If either of the operands might have a value other than 0 or 1, then the unary `!` operator can be applied to both operands: `!x != !y` yields 1 if exactly one of `x` and `y` is nonzero, and yields 0 otherwise. In a similar manner, `==` serves as a logical equivalence (EQV) operator.

A common C programming error is to write the `=` operator (assignment) where the `==` operator (comparison) was intended. Several other programming languages use `=` for equality comparison. As a matter of style, if it is necessary to use an assignment expression in a context that will test the value of the expression against zero, it is best to write "! = 0" explicitly to make the intent clear. For example, it is unclear whether the following loop is correct or whether it contains a typographical error:

```
while (x = next_item()) {   /* Should this be "x==next_item()" ?? */
   ...
}
```

If the original form was correct, then the intent can be made clear in this manner:

```
while ((x = next_item()) != 0) {
   ...
}
```

References   alignment restrictions 5.6.4, 6.1.3; bitwise operators 7.6.6; compatible types 5.11; logical operators 7.5.4, 7.7; lvalue 7.1; null pointer 5.3.2; pointer types 5.3; precedence 7.2.1; assignment operator = 7.9.1; type qualifiers 4.4.3; usual binary conversions 6.3.4; void * 5.3.1

7.6.6 Bitwise Operators

The binary operators &, ^, and | designate the bitwise AND, XOR, and OR functions. Individually, they are left-associative; together, their different precedences determine the expression evaluation order. Their operands must be integral and are subject to the usual binary conversions. The type of the result is that of the converted operands; the result is not an lvalue:

> *bitwise-or-expression* :
> > *bitwise-xor-expression*
> > *bitwise-or-expression* | *bitwise-xor-expression*
>
> *bitwise-xor-expression* :
> > *bitwise-and-expression*
> > *bitwise-xor-expression* ^ *bitwise-and-expression*
>
> *bitwise-and-expression* :
> > *equality-expression*
> > *bitwise-and-expression* & *equality-expression*

Each bit of the result of these operators is equal to a boolean function of the two corresponding bits of the two (converted) operands:

- The & (AND) function yields a 1-bit if both arguments are 1-bits, and otherwise a 0-bit.
- The ^ (XOR) function yields a 1-bit if one argument is a 1-bit and the other is a 0-bit, and yields a 0-bit if both arguments are 1-bits or both are 0-bits.

• The | (OR) function yields a 1-bit if either argument is a 1-bit, and otherwise a 0-bit.

This behavior is summarized in the following table.

Results of the bitwise operators

a	b	a&b	a^b	a|b
0	0	0	0	0
0	1	0	1	1
1	0	0	1	1
1	1	1	0	1

Each of the bitwise operators is commutative and associative, and the compiler is permitted to rearrange an expression containing the operators subject to the restrictions discussed in section 7.12.

For portable code we recommend using the bitwise operators only on unsigned operands. Signed operands will cause no problems among the majority of computers that use the two's-complement representation for signed integers, but they may cause failures on other computers.

Programmers should be careful not to accidentally use the bitwise operators & and | in place of the logical AND and OR operators, && and ||. The bitwise operators give the same result as the corresponding logical operators only if the arguments have no side effects and are known to be boolean (0 or 1). For example, if a is 2 and b is 4, then a&b is 0 (false) whereas a&&b is 1 (true). Also, the bitwise operators always evaluate both their operands, whereas the logical operators do not evaluate their right-hand operand if the value of the left operand is sufficient to determine the final result of the expression.

References   integer types 5.1; logical operators && and || 7.7; lvalue 7.1; order of evaluation 7.12; relational operators 7.6.4; signed types 5.1.1; unsigned types 5.1.2; usual binary conversions 6.3.4

7.7 LOGICAL OPERATOR EXPRESSIONS

A logical operator expression consists of two expressions separated by one of the logical operators && and ||. These operators are sometimes "conditional AND" and "conditional OR" in other languages because their second operand is not evaluated at all if the value of the first operand provides sufficient information to determine the result of the expression:

> *logical-or-expression* :
> > *logical-and-expression*
> > *logical-or-expression* || *logical-and-expression*

logical-and-expression :
       bitwise-or-expression
       logical-and-expression `&&` *bitwise-or-expression*

The logical operators accept operands of any scalar type. There is no connection between the types of the two operands; each is independently subject to the usual unary conversions. The type of the result is always `int`; the result has the value 0 or 1 and is not an lvalue.

AND   The left operand of `&&` is fully evaluated first. If the left operand is equal to zero (in the sense of the `==` operator), then the right operand is not evaluated and the result value is 0. If the left operand is not equal to zero, then the right operand is evaluated; if the right operand is equal to zero, then the result value is 0 and otherwise is 1. The expression $r=a\&\&b$ is therefore equivalent to

```
if  ((a)==0)  r=0;
else {
    if  ((b)==0)  r=0;
    else r=1;
}
```

OR   The left operand of `||` is fully evaluated first. If the value of the left operand is not equal to zero (in the sense of the `==` operator), then the right operand is not evaluated and the result value is 1. If the left operand is equal to zero, then the right operand is evaluated; if the right operand is not equal to zero, then the result value is 1 and otherwise is 0. The expression $r=a||b$ is therefore equivalent to

```
if  ((a)!=0)  r = 1;
else {
    if  ((b)!=0)  r=1;
    else r=0;
}
```

Examples of the logical operators are shown in the table below.

Examples of logical operators

a	b	a && b	Is b evaluated?	a || b	Is b evaluated?
1	0	0	yes	1	no
0	34.5	0	no	1	yes
1	"Hello\n"	1	yes	1	no
'\0'	0	0	no	0	yes
&x	y=2	1	yes	1	no

Both of the logical operators are described as being syntactically left-associative, though this doesn't matter much to the programmer, because the operators happen to be fully associative semantically and no other operators have the same levels of precedence. The operator && has higher precedence than | |, although it often makes programs more readable to use parentheses liberally around logical expressions.

References bitwise operators & and | 7.6.6; equality operators == and ! = 7.6.5; lvalue 7.1; pointer types 5.3; precedence 7.2.1; scalar types ch. 5; usual unary conversions 6.3.3

7.8 CONDITIONAL EXPRESSIONS

The ? and : operators introduce a conditional expression, which has lower precedence than the binary expressions and differs from them in being right-associative:

> *conditional-expression :*
>> *logical-or-expression*
>> *logical-or-expression* ? *expression* : *conditional-expression*

A conditional expression consists of three subexpressions, with the first and second operands separated by a question mark and the second and third operands separated by a colon. The first operand must be of a scalar type. The second and third operands can be of various types and they are subject to the usual unary conversions—if they are evaluated at all. The type of the result depends on the types of the second and third operands. In traditional C, the second and third operands can have the types given in the following table, with the indicated result type for the entire conditional expression.

Conditional expression operands (traditional)

One operand type	The other operand type	Result Type
arithmetic	arithmetic	type after usual binary conversions
structure or union[1]	the same structure or union	the structure or union type
pointer	the same pointer type, or 0	the pointer type

[1] These operand types may not be permitted in some compilers.

ANSI C is more complicated. The permissible operand types and the result type are shown in the table on the following page.

The execution of the conditional expression proceeds as follows:

1. The first operand is fully evaluated and tested against zero, in the sense of the == operator.
2. If the first operand is not equal to zero, then the second operand is evaluated and its value, converted to the result type, becomes the value of the conditional expression. The third operand is not evaluated.

Conditional expression operands (ANSI C)

One operand type	The other operand type	Result type
arithmetic	arithmetic	type after usual binary conversions
structure or union	compatible structure or union	the structure or union type
void	void	void
pointer to qualified or unqualified version of type T	pointer to qualified or unqualified version of type T', if types T and T' are compatible	composite pointer type[1]
pointer to type T[2]	qualified or unqualified void *	void *[1]
any pointer type	null pointer constant	the pointer type[1]

[1] The type pointed to by the result has all the qualifiers of the types pointed to by both operands.
[2] T must be an object or incomplete type.

3. If the first operand is equal to zero, then the third operand is evaluated and its value, converted to the result type, becomes the value of the conditional expression. The second operand is not evaluated.

Thus, the expression $r=a?b:c$ is equivalent to

```
if (a != 0) r = b;
else r = c;
```

Conditional expressions are right-associative with respect to their first and third operands, so that

```
a ? b : c ? d : e ? f : g
```

is interpreted as

```
a ? b : (c ? d : (e ? f : g))
```

Here is one example where this might be useful—the `signum` function, which returns 1, −1, or 0 depending on whether its argument is positive, negative, or zero:

```
int signum(x)
    int x;
{
    return (x > 0) ? 1 : (x < 0) ? -1 : 0;
}
```

Anything more complicated than this is probably better done with one or more if statements. As a matter of style, it is a good idea to enclose the first operand of a conditional expression in parentheses, but this is not required.

References arithmetic types ch. 5; array types 5.4; floating-point types 5.2; integer types 5.1; lvalue 7.1; pointer types 5.3; precedence 7.2.1; scalar types ch. 5; signed types 5.1.1; structure types 5.6; union types 5.7; unsigned types 5.1.2; usual binary conversions 6.3.4; usual unary conversions 6.3.3; void type 5.9

7.9 ASSIGNMENT EXPRESSIONS

Assignment expressions consist of two expressions separated by an assignment operator; they are right-associative. The operator = is called the simple assignment operator; all the others are compound assignment operators:

> *assignment-expression* :
>> *conditional-expression*
>> *unary-expression assignment-op assignment-expression*

> *assignment-op* : one of
>> =   +=   -=   *=   /=   %=
>> <<=   >>=   &=   ^= |=

Assignment operators are all of the same level of precedence and are right-associative (all other operators in C that take two operands are left-associative). For example, the expression x*=y=z is treated as x*=(y=z), not as (x*=y)=z; similarly, the expression x=y*=z is treated as x=(y*=z), not as (x=y)*=z. The right-associativity of assignment operators allows multiple assignment expressions to have the "obvious" interpretation. That is, the expression a=b=d+7 is interpreted as a=(b=(d+7)), and therefore assigns the value of d+7 to b and then to a.

Every assignment operator requires a modifiable lvalue as its left operand and modifies that lvalue by storing a new value into it; the operators are distinguished by how they compute the new value to be stored. The result of an assignment expression is never an lvalue.

References modifiable lvalue 7.1; precedence 7.2.1

7.9.1 Simple Assignment

The single equal sign, =, indicates simple assignment. The value of the right operand is converted to the type of the left operand and is stored into that operand. The permitted operand types are given in the following table.

Assignment operands

Left operand type	Right operand type
arithmetic	arithmetic
structure or union	compatible structure or union
pointer to T	pointer to T', where T and T' are compatible
void *	pointer to T[1]
pointer to T[1]	void *
any pointer	null pointer constant

[1] ANSI C: T must be an object or incomplete type.

The original definition of C did not permit the assignment of structures and unions; a few older compilers may still have this restriction.

In ANSI C, there are additional restrictions on the operands having to do with type qualifiers. First, the left operand must not have a `const`-qualified type. In addition:

1. If the operands are arithmetic, they can be qualified or unqualified. (Of course, the left operand can never be `const`-qualified.)
2. If the operands are structures or unions, they must be qualified or unqualified versions of compatible types. This means, for example, that their members must be identically qualified.
3. If the operands are both object or function pointers, they must be qualified or unqualified versions of pointers to compatible types, and the type pointed to by the left operand must have all the qualifiers of the type pointed to by the right operand. This prevents a `const int *` pointer from being assigned to an `int *` pointer, after which the constant integer could be modified.
4. If one operand is a qualified or unqualified version of `void *`, the other must be a pointer to an object or incomplete type. The type pointed to by the left operand must have all the qualifiers of the type pointed to by the right operand. The reason is the same as for the previous case.

The type of the result of the assignment operator is equal to the (unconverted and unqualified) type of the left operand. The result is the value stored into the left operand. The result is not an lvalue. When the two operands are of arithmetic types, the usual assignment conversions are used to convert the right operand to the type of the left operand before assignment.

The simple assignment operator cannot be used to copy the entire contents of one array into another. The name of an array is not an lvalue and so cannot appear on the left-hand side of an assignment. Also, the name of an array appearing on the right-hand side of an assignment is converted (by the usual conversions) to be a pointer to the first element, and so the assignment would copy the pointer, not the contents of the array. The = operator can, therefore, be used to copy the address of an array into a pointer variable:

```
int a[20], *p;
...
p = a;
```

In this example, `a` is an array of integers and `p` is of type "pointer to integer." The assignment causes `p` to point to (the first element of) the array `a`.

It is possible to get the effect of copying an entire array by embedding the array within a structure or union, because simple assignment can copy an entire structure or union:

```
struct matrix {double contents[10][10]; };
struct matrix a, b;
...
{
    /* Clear the diagonal elements. */
    for (j = 0; j < 10; j++)
        b.contents[j][j] = 0;
    /* Copy whole 10x10 array from b to a. */
    a = b;
}
```

The implementation of the simple assignment operator assumes that the right-hand value and the left-hand object do not overlap in memory (unless they exactly overlap, as in the assignment `X=X`). If overlap does occur, the behavior of the assignment is undefined.

References   arithmetic types 5.1–2; array types 5.4; usual assignment conversions 6.3.2; lvalue 7.1; null pointer 5.3.2; pointer types 5.3; structure types 5.6; type compatibility 5.11; union types 5.7

7.9.2 Compound Assignment

The compound assignment operators may be informally understood by taking the expression "*a op= b*" to be equivalent to "*a = a op b*," with the proviso that the expression *a* is evaluated only once. The permitted types of the operands depend on the operator being used. The possibilities are listed in the table at the top of the next page.

More precisely, the left and right operands of *op=* are evaluated, and the left operand must be a modifiable lvalue. The operation indicated by the operator *op* is then applied to the two operand values, includeing any "usual conversions" performed by the operator. The resulting value is then stored into the object designated by the left operand, after performing the usual assignment conversions.

For the compound assignment operators, as for the simple assignment operator, the type of the result is equal to the (unconverted) type of the left operand. The result is the value stored into the left operand, and is not an lvalue.

Operand types for compound assignment expressions

Assignment operator	Left operand	Right operand
*= /=	arithmetic	arithmetic
%=	integer	integer
+= -=	arithmetic	arithmetic
+= -=	pointer	integer
<<= >>=	integer	integer
&=	integer	integer
^=	integer	integer
|=	integer	integer

In the earliest versions of C, the compound assignment operators were written in the reverse form, with the equal sign preceding the operation. This led to syntactic ambiguities; x=-1 could be interpreted as either x=(-1) or x=-(1). The newer form eliminates these difficulties. Some C compilers continue to support the older forms for the sake of compatibility, and will mistake x=-1 as x=-(1) unless a blank appears between the equal and minus signs.

References   arithmetic types ch. 5; assignment conversions 6.3.2; floating-point types 5.2; integer types 5.1; pointer types 5.3; signed types 5.1.1; unsigned types 5.1.2; usual binary conversions 6.3.4; usual unary conversions 6.3.3

7.10 SEQUENTIAL EXPRESSIONS

A comma expression consists of two expressions separated by a comma. The comma operator is described here as being syntactically left-associative, though this doesn't matter much to the programmer, because the operator happens to be fully associative semantically. Note that the *comma-expression* is at the top of the C expression syntax tree:

> *comma-expression* :
> > *assignment-expression*
> > *comma-expression* , *assignment-expression*
>
> *expression* :
> > *comma-expression*

The left operand of the comma operator is fully evaluated first. It need not produce any value; if it does produce a value, that value is discarded. The right operand is then evaluated. The type and value of the result of the comma expression are equal to the type and value of the right operand, after the usual unary conversions. The result is not an lvalue. Thus, the statement "r=(a,b,...,c);" (notice that the parentheses are required) is equivalent to "a;b;... r=c;". The difference is that the comma operator may be used in expression contexts, such as in loop control expressions. For example, in the for statement the comma operator allows several assignment expressions to be combined into a single expression for the purpose of initializing or stepping several variables in a single loop:

```
for( x=0, y=N; x<N && y>0; x++, y--) ...
```

The comma operator is associative, and so one may write a single expression consisting of any number of expressions separated by commas; the subexpressions will be evaluated in order, and the value of the last one will become the value of the entire expression.

The overuse of the comma operator can be confusing, and in certain places it conflicts with other uses of the comma. For example, the expression

```
f(a, b=5,2*b, c)
```

is always treated as a call to the function f with four arguments. Any comma operators in the argument list must be surrounded by parentheses:

```
f(a, (b=5,2*b), c)
```

Other contexts where the comma operator may not be used without parentheses include field-length expressions in structure and union declarator lists, enumeration value expressions in enumeration declarator lists, and initialization expressions in declarations and initializers. The comma is also used as a separator in preprocessor macro calls.

While the comma operator guarantees that its operands will be evaluated in left-to-right order, other uses of the comma character do not make this guarantee. For example, the argument expressions in a function invocation need not be evaluated left to right.

References   discarded expressions 7.13; enumeration types 5.5; for statement 8.6.3; function calls 7.4.3; initializers 4.6; lvalue 7.1; macro calls 3.3; structure types 5.6; union types 5.7

7.11 CONSTANT EXPRESSIONS

In several contexts the C language permits an expression to be written that must evaluate to a constant at compile time. Each context imposes slightly different restrictions on what forms of expression are permitted. It is useful to consider three classes of constant expressions:

1. *preprocessor constant expressions*, which are used as the tested value in the #if preprocessor control statement
2. *integral constant expressions*, which are used for array bounds, the length of a bit field in a structure, explicit enumerator values, and the values in case labels in switch statements
3. *initializer constant expressions*, which are used as the initializers for static and external variables, or for automatic variables of aggregate types

No constant expression may contain assignment, increment, decrement, function call, or comma expressions unless they are contained within the operand of a `sizeof` operator. Otherwise any literal or operator can appear, subject to the additional restrictions discussed in the following sections for each expression class. These restrictions are imposed by ANSI; other compilers may have somewhat looser requirements in individual cases.

7.11.1 Preprocessor Constant Expressions

Preprocessor constant expressions must be evaluated at compile time, and are subject to some relatively strict constraints. Such expressions must have integral type, and can involve only integer constants, character constants, and the special `defined` operator. All arithmetic is to be done using types `long` or `unsigned long`, as appropriate to the signedness of the operands, which frees the preprocessor from having to deal with several sizes of integer types.

Preprocessor expressions must not perform any environmental inquiries. Casts are not permitted, nor is the `sizeof` operator. That is, the expressions remain insulated from implementation details on the target computer. For example, this code incorrectly attempts to see if type `int` on the target computer is larger than 16 bits:

```
#if 1<<16
/* Target computer integer has more than 16 bits */
...
#endif
```

In actuality, the code may only be testing the representation of type `long` on the *host* computer.

The preprocessor must recognize escape sequences in character constants, but is allowed to use either the source or target character sets in converting character constants to integers. This means that the expressions `'\n'` or `'z'-'a'` might have different values in a preprocessor expression than they would appearing in, say, an `if` statement. Programmers using cross-compilers in which the host and target character sets are different should beware of this license.

After macro expansion, if the preprocessor constant expression contains any remaining identifiers they are each replaced by the constant 0. This is probably a bad rule, because the presence of such identifiers is almost certainly a programming error. A better way to test whether a name is defined in the preprocessor is to use the `defined` operator or the `#ifdef` and `#ifndef` commands.

Compilers are free to accept additional forms of preprocessor constant expressions, but programs making use of these extensions are not portable.

References   cast expressions 7.5.1; character constants 2.7.3; character sets 2.1; `defined` operator 3.5.5; enumeration constants 5.5; escape characters 2.7.5; `#ifdef` and `#ifndef` 3.5.3; `sizeof` operator 7.5.2

7.11.2 Integral Constant Expressions

An integral constant expression is used for array bounds, the length of a bit field in a structure, explicit enumerator values, and the values in `case` labels in `switch` statements. An integral constant expression must have an integral type and can include integer constants, character constants, and enumeration constants. The `sizeof` operator can be used and can have any operand. Cast expressions may be used, but only to convert arithmetic types to integer types (unless they are part of the operand to `sizeof`). A floating-point constant is permitted only if it is the immediate operand of a cast or is part of the operand of `sizeof`.

Constant expressions not appearing in preprocessor commands should be evaluated the same as they would be on the target computer, including the values of character constants.

Compilers are free to accept additional forms of integral constant expressions, including more general floating-point expressions that are converted to an integer type, but programs making use of these extensions are not portable. Some pre-ANSI compilers do not permit casts of any kind in constant expressions. Programmers concerned with portability to these compilers might be wise to avoid casts in constant expressions.

References   bit fields 5.6.5; cast expressions 7.5.1; enumeration types 5.5; floating-point constants 2.7.2; `sizeof` operator 7.5.2; switch statement 8.7

7.11.3 Initializer Constant Expressions

The constant expression in an initializer can include arithmetic constant expressions and address constant expressions.

Arithmetic constant expressions include the integral constant expressions, but can also include floating-point constants generally (not just those cast to integers or in `sizeof`), and casts to any arithmetic type (including the floating-point types). If a floating-point expression is evaluated at compile time in a constant expression, the implementation may use a representation that provides more precision or a greater range than the target environment. Therefore, the value of a floating-point expression may be slightly different at compile time than it would be if evaluated during program execution. This rule reflects the difficulty of exactly simulating a foreign floating-point implementation. Other than this case, the expressions should be evaluated just as they would be on the target computer.

An address constant expression can be the null pointer constant [for example, `(void *)0`] or the address of a static or external object or function, or the address of a static or external object plus or minus an integer constant expression. In forming addresses, the address (`&`), indirection (`*`), subscript (`[ ]`), and component selection (`.` and `->`) operators may be used, but no attempt must be made to access the value of any object. Casts to pointer types may also be used. Examples of address constant expressions are shown below in the initializers for `p` and `pf`:

```
static int a[10];
static struct { float f1, f2 } s;
extern int f();
int i = 3;
...
int *p[] = { &i, a, &a[0], (char *)&a[0]+sizeof(a), &s.f2 }}
int (*pf)() = &f;
```

Compilers are free to accept additional forms of initializer constant expressions, such as more complicated addressing expressions involving several addresses, but programs making use of these extensions are not portable.

ANSI C states that an implementation is free to perform initializations at run time, and so could avoid floating-point arithmetic. However, it might be difficult to do this initialization before executing any code that accesses the initialized variable.

References   address operator & 7.5.6; array types 5.4; initializers 4.6; `sizeof` operator 7.5.2; structure types 5.6

7.12 ORDER OF EVALUATION

In general, the compiler can rearrange the order in which an expression is evaluated. The rearrangement may consist of evaluating only the arguments of a function call, or the two operands of a binary operator, in some particular order other than the obvious left-to-right order. The binary operators +, *, &, ^, and | are assumed to be completely associative and commutative, and a compiler is permitted to exploit this assumption. The compiler is free, for example, to evaluate (a+b)+(c+d) as if it were written (a+d)+(b+c) (assuming all variables have the same arithmetic type).

The assumption of commutativity and associativity is always true for &, ^, and | on unsigned operands. It may not be true for &, ^, and | on signed operands, because of potential problems with certain signed representations. It may not be true for * and +, because of the possibility that the order indicated by the expression as written might avoid overflow but another order might not. Nevertheless, the compiler is allowed to exploit the assumption. In such situations the programmer must use assignments to temporary variables to force a particular evaluation order:

```
int temp1, temp2;
...
/* Compute q=(a+b)+(c+d), exactly that way. */
temp1 = a+b;
temp2 = c+d;
q = temp1 + temp2;
```

Any rearrangement of expressions involving these operators must not alter the implicit type conversions of the operands. In the example below, the two expressions are not equivalent and the compiler is not free to substitute one for the other, despite the fact that one is obtained from the other "merely by rearranging the additions":

```
(1.0 + -3) + (unsigned) 1;  /* Result is -1.0 */
1.0 + (-3 + (unsigned) 1);  /* Result is large */
```

The first assignment is straightforward and produces the expected result. The second produces a large result, because the usual binary conversions cause the signed value -3 to be converted to a large unsigned value 2^n-3, where n is the number of bits used to represent an unsigned integer. This is then added to the unsigned value 1, the result converted to floating-point representation and added to 1.0, resulting in the value 2^n-3 in a floating-point representation. Now, this result may or may not be what the programmer intended, but the compiler must not confuse the issue further by capriciously rearranging the additions.

When evaluating the actual arguments in a function call, the order in which the arguments and the function expression are evaluated is not specified; but the program should behave as if it chose one argument, evaluated it fully, then chose another argument, evaluated it fully, and so on, until all arguments were evaluated. (A similar restriction holds for each operand to a binary expression operator.) Consider this example:

```
char *x[10], **p=x;
...
if ( strcmp(*p++, *p++) == 0 ) printf("Same.");
```

The variable x is an array of pointers to characters and is to be regarded as an array of strings. The variable p is a pointer to a pointer to a character and is to be regarded as a pointer to a string. The purpose of the if statement is to determine whether the string pointed to by p (call it s1) and the next string after that one (call it s2) are equal (and, in passing, to step the pointer p beyond those two strings in the array). It is, of course, bad programming style to have two side effects on the same variable in the same expression, because the order of the side effects is not defined; but this all-too-clever programmer has reasoned that the order of the side effects doesn't matter, because the two strings in question may be given to strcmp in either order.

In ANSI C, if a single object is modifed more than once between successive sequence points, the result is undefined. A *sequence point* is a point in the program's execution sequence at which all previous side effects of execution are to have taken place and at which no subsequent side effects will have occurred. Sequence points occur:

- at the end of a full expression; that is, an initializer, an expression statement, the expression in a return statement, and the control expressions in a conditional, iterative, or switch statement (including each expression in a for statement)
- after the first operand of a &&, ||, ?:, or comma operator
- after the evaluation of the arguments and function expression in a function call

According to this rule, the value of the expression ++i*++i is undefined, as is the strcmp example above.

References   addition operator + 7.6.2; binary operators 7.6; bitwise AND operator & 7.6.6; bitwise OR operator | 7.6.8; bitwise XOR operator ^ 7.6.7; comma operator 7.10; conditional expression ? : 7.8; conditional statement 8.5; expression statement 8.2; function calls 7.4.3; initializers 4.6; iterative statements 8.6; logical and && and or || 7.7; multiplication operator * 7.6.1; return statement 8.9; strcmp function 13.2; usual binary conversions 6.3.4

7.13 DISCARDED VALUES

There are three contexts in which an expression can appear but its value is not used:

1. an expression statement
2. the first operand of a comma expression
3. the initialization and incrementation expressions in a for statement

In these contexts we say that the expression's value is discarded.

When the value of an expression without side effects is discarded, the compiler may presume that an error has been made and issue a warning. Side-effect-producing operations include assignment and function calls. For example:

```
extern void f();
f(x);   /* These expressions do not */
i++;    /* justify any warning about */
a = b;  /* discarded values.  */
```

The compiler may issue a warning message if the main operator of a discarded expression has no side effect. For example, these statements, though legal, may elicit warning messages:

```
extern int g();
g(x); /* The call to g may have side effects
         but it also returns a value that is
         discarded. */
x + 7; /* Addition has no defined
          side effects. */
x + (a *= 2);
        /* The expression has a side effect,
           but the last operation to be
           performed, "+", does not, and its
           value is discarded. */
```

The programmer may avoid warnings about discarded values by using a cast to type void to indicate that the value is purposely being discarded:

```
extern int g();
(void) g(x);    /* The returned value is
                   purposely discarded. */
(void)(x + 7); /* This is pretty silly, but
                   presumably the programmer
                   has a purpose. */
```

C compilers typically do not issue warnings when the value of a function call is discarded, because traditionally functions that returned no result had to be declared of type "function returning `int`." Although ANSI C gives compilers more information, vendors try to be compatible with old code.

If a compiler determines that the main operator of a discarded expression has no side effect, it may choose not to generate code for that operator (whereupon its operands become discarded values and may be recursively subjected to the same treatment).

References   assignments 7.9; casts 7.5.1; comma operator 7.10; for statement 8.6.3; function calls 7.4.3; expressions statements 8.2; void type 5.9

7.14 OPTIMIZATION OF MEMORY ACCESSES

As a general rule, a compiler is free to generate any code equivalent in computational behavior to the program as written. The compiler is explicitly granted certain freedoms to rearrange code, as described in section 7.12. It may also generate no code for an expression when the expression has no side effects and its value is discarded, as described in section 7.13.

Some compilers may also reorganize the code in such a way that it does not always refer to memory as many times, or in the same order, as specified in the program. For example, if a certain array element is referred to more than once, the compiler may cleverly arrange to fetch it only once to gain speed; in effect, it might rewrite this code:

```
int x,a[10];
...
x = a[j] * a[j] * a[j];   /* Cube the table entry. */
```

causing it to be executed as if it had been written like this:

```
int x,a[10];
register int temp;
...
temp = a[j];
x = temp * temp * temp;   /* Cube the table entry. */
```

For most applications, including nearly all portable applications, such optimization techniques are a very good thing, because the speed of a program may be improved by a factor of two or better without altering its effective computational behavior.

However, this may be a problem when writing interrupt handlers and certain other machine-dependent programs in C. In this case, the programmer should use the ANSI C type qualifier `volatile` to control some memory accesses.

References   `volatile` 4.4.5

7.15 EXERCISES

1. Which of the following expressions are legal in traditional C? For the ones that are legal, what type does the expression have? Assume that `f` is of type `float`, `i` is of type `int`, `ip` is of type `char *`, and `ip` is of type `int *`.

    (a) `cp+0x23`   (f) `f==0`
    (b) `i+f`   (g) `!ip`
    (c) `++f`   (h) `cp && cp`
    (d) `ip[i]`   (i) `f%2`
    (e) `cp?i:f`   (j) `f+=i`

2. Assume `p1` and `p2` have type `char *`. Rewrite the following two statements without using the increment or decrement operators.

    (a) `*++p1=*++p2;`
    (b) `*p1--=*p2--;`

3. A "bit mask" is an integer consisting of a specified sequence of binary zeroes and ones. Write macros that produce the following bit masks. If the macro arguments are constants, the result should also be a constant. You can assume a two's complement representation for integers but your macros should not depend on how many bits are in an integer or whether the computer is a "big endian" or "little endian."

    (a) `low_zeroes(n)`, a word in which the low-order *n* bits are zeroes and all other bits are ones.
    (b) `low_ones(n)`, a word whose low-order *n* bits are ones and all other bits are zeroes.
    (c) `mid_zeroes(width,offset)`, a word whose low-order *offset* bits are ones, whose next higher *width* bits are zeroes, and all other bits are ones.
    (d) `mid_ones(width,offset)`, a word whose low-order *offset* bits are zeroes, whose next higher *width* bits are ones, and all other bits are zeroes

4. Is `j++==++j` a legal expression? What about `j++&&++j`? If `j` begins with the value 0, what is the result of each of the expressions?

5. The following table lists pairs of types of the left- and right-hand sides of a simple assignment expression. Which of the combinations are allowable in ANSI C?

	Left-side type	*Right-side type*
(a)	`short`	`signed short`
(b)	`char *`	`const char *`
(c)	`int (*)[5]`	`int (*)[]`
(d)	`short`	`const short`
(e)	`int (*)()`	`signed (*)(int x, float d)`
(f)	`int *`	`t *` (where: `typedef int t`)

6. If the variable `x` has the type `struct{int f;}` and the variable `y` has a separately defined type `struct{int f;}` can you legally write `x=y` in ANSI C?

8

Statements

The C language provides the usual assortment of statements found in most algebraic programming languages, including conditional statements, loops, and the ubiquitous "goto." We describe each of the statements in turn after some general comments about the syntax of statements:

statement :
  expression-statement
  labeled-statement
  compound-statement
  conditional-statement
  iterative-statement
  switch-statement
  break-statement
  continue-statement
  return-statement
  goto-statement
  null-statement

conditional-statement :
  if-statement
  if-else-statement

iterative-statement :
  do-statement
  while-statement
  for-statement

8.1 GENERAL SYNTACTIC RULES FOR STATEMENTS

Although C statements will be familiar to programmers used to ALGOL-like languages, there are a few syntactic differences that are often the cause of confusion and errors.

As in Pascal or Ada, semicolons typically appear between consecutive statements in C. However, in C the semicolon is not a statement separator, but rather simply a part of the syntax of certain statements. The only C statement that does not require a terminating semicolon is the compound statement (or block), which is delimited by braces (`{ }`) instead of the more usual `begin` and `end` keywords:

```
a = b;
{ b = c;  d = e;  }
x = y;
```

Another rule for C statements is that "control" expressions appearing in conditional and iterative statements must be enclosed in parentheses. There is no special keyword following control expressions, such as "then," "loop," or "do;"; the remainder of the statement immediately follows the expression:

```
if (a<b)  x=y;
while (n<10)  n++;
```

Finally, the assignment statement in other languages is an assignment *expression* in C. It can appear as part of more complicated expressions, or can be followed by a semicolon allowing it to stand by itself:

```
if ((x=y)>3)  a=b;
```

References   assignment expression 7.9; compound statement 8.4; conditional statements 8.5; iterative statements 8.6

8.2 EXPRESSION STATEMENTS

Any expression can be treated as a statement by writing the expression followed by a semicolon:

expression-statement :
        expression ;

The statement is executed by evaluating the expression and then discarding the resulting value, if any.
An expression statement is useful only if evaluation of the expression involves a side effect, such as assigning a value to a variable or performing input or output. Usually the expression is an assignment, an increment or decrement operation, or a function call. Here are some examples of expression statements:

```
speed = distance / time;   /* assign a quotient */
 ++event_count;            /* Add 1 to event_count.   */
printf("Again?");          /* Call the function printf. */
pattern &= mask;           /* Mask out some bits of the pattern. */
(x<y) ? ++x : ++y;         /* Increment the smaller of x and y. */
```

The last example, though legal, might be written more clearly with an if statement:

```
if (x < y) ++x; else ++y;
```

The compiler is not obligated to evaluate an expression, or a portion of an expression, that has no side effects and whose result is discarded. (See section 7.13.)

References   assignment expressions 7.9; discarded expressions 7.13; expressions ch. 7; function call 7.4.3; increment expressions 7.5.8, 7.4.4

8.3 LABELED STATEMENTS

A label can be used to mark any statement so that control may be transferred to the statement by a goto or switch statement. There are three kinds of labels. A named label may appear on any statement and is used in conjunction with the goto statement. A case label or default label may appear only on a statement within the body of a switch statement:

> *labeled-statement* :
> > *label* : *statement*

> *label* :
> > *named-label*
> > *case-label*
> > *default-label*

A label cannot appear by itself but must always be attached to a statement. If it is desired to place a label by itself, for example at the end of a compound statement, it may be attached to a null statement.

Named labels are discussed further in the description of the goto statement. The case and default labels are discussed with the switch statement.

References   goto statement 8.10; null statement 8.11; switch statement 8.7

8.4 COMPOUND STATEMENTS

A compound statement—also called a block—consists of a (possibly empty) sequence of declarations followed by a (possibly empty) sequence of statements, all enclosed in braces:

> *compound-statement* :
> > { *declaration-list$_{opt}$*   *statement-list$_{opt}$* }

> *declaration-list* :
> > *declaration*
> > *declaration   declaration-list*

> *statement-list* :
> > *statement*
> > *statement-list statement*

A compound statement may appear anywhere a statement does. When the compound statement has no declarations, it just represents a group of statements. When the compound statement has declarations, it brings into existence a new scope. If there are declarations, they must come before any statements.

A compound statement is normally executed by first processing all the declarations one at a time, in sequence, and then executing all the statements one at a time, in sequence. Execution ceases when the last statement has been executed or when control is transferred out of the compound statement through execution of a `goto`, `return`, `continue`, or `break` statement.

It is also possible to jump to a labeled statement within a compound statement by using a `goto` or `switch` statement outside the compound statement. When that happens, storage is allocated for any `auto` or `register` variables declared in the compound statement, but no initialization expressions for those variables are evaluated and no initialization occurs. Execution then begins at the statement to which control was transferred and continues in sequence until the last statement has been executed or until control is transferred out of the compound statement through execution of a `goto`, `return`, `continue`, or `break` statement.

An unlabeled compound statement used as the body of a `switch` statement cannot be executed normally but only through transfer of control to labeled statements within it. Therefore, initializations of auto and register variables in such a compound statement never occur and their presence is *a priori* an error.

References   auto storage class 4.3; break and continue statements 8.8; declarations ch. 4; goto statement 8.10; register storage class 4.3; return statement 8.9; scope 4.2.1

8.4.1 Declarations within Compound Statements

Each identifier declared at the beginning of a compound statement has a scope that extends from its declaration point to the end of the block. It is visible throughout that scope except when hidden by a declaration of the same identifier in an inner block.

An identifier declared at the beginning of a compound statement without a storage class specifier is assumed to have storage class `extern` if identifier has a function type, and is assumed to have storage class `auto` in all other cases. It is illegal for an identifier of function type to have any storage class except `extern` when it is declared at the beginning of a block.

If a variable or function is declared in a compound statement with storage class `extern`, then no storage is allocated and no initialization expression is permitted. The declaration refers to an external variable or function defined elsewhere, either in the same source file or a different source file.

If a variable is declared in a compound statement with storage class `auto` or `register`, then it is effectively reallocated every time the compound statement is entered and deallocated when the compound statement is exited. If there is an initialization expression for the variable, then the expression is reevaluated and the variable reinitialized every time the compound statement is entered normally. (The initialization expression is not evaluated and the variable is not initialized when control is passed to a statement within the compound statement via a `goto` or `switch` statement from outside.) If there is no initialization expression for the variable, then the value of the variable is initially undefined every time the compound statement is executed; the value of the variable does not carry over from one execution of the compound statement to the next.

    If a variable is declared in a compound statement with storage class `static`, then it is effectively allocated once, prior to program execution, just like any other static variable. If there is an initialization expression for the variable, then the expression is evaluated only once, prior to program execution, and the variable retains its value from one execution of the compound statement to the next.

References   `auto` storage class 4.3; `extern` storage class 4.3; `goto` statement 8.10; initial values 4.2.8; initializers 4.6; `register` storage class 4.3; scope 4.2.1; `static` storage class 4.3; `switch` statement 8.7; visibility 4.2.2

8.4.2 Use of Compound Statements

Compound statements without declarations are particularly useful as parts of other control statements, so that more than one statement can be executed conditionally or in a loop:

```
if (error_seen) {
    ++error_count;
    print_error_message();
}
```

    With declarations, compound statements can also introduce additional variables with reduced visibility. This often helps to make a program clearer by restricting the area over which a variable is accessible:

```
if (first_time) {
    /* Clear the array. */
    int i;
    for (i = 0; i < 10; i++)
        a[i] = 0;
    /* Reset first-time flag. */
    first_time = 0;
}
```

    C permits unrestricted jumps into compound statements, but we think this is bad programming style. In fact, none of the languages Ada, ALGOL 60, Modula-2, Pascal, or PL/I permit jumps into blocks. The particular danger in C is not having initializations occur. For example, the following code fragment is unlikely to work if the statement labeled `L:` is the target of a jump from outside the compound statement, because the variable `sum` will not be initialized. Furthermore, it is not possible to tell if any such jump does occur without examining the entire body of the enclosing function:

```
      {
              extern int a[100];
              int i, sum = 0;
              ...
         L:
              for (i = 0; i < 100; i++)
                  sum += a[i];
              ...
      }
```

References   declarations ch. 4; goto statement 8.10; labeled statement 8.3

8.5 CONDITIONAL STATEMENTS

There are two forms of conditional statement: with or without an `else` clause. Note that C, unlike other programming languages such as Pascal, does not use the keyword "then" as part of the syntax of its `if` statement:

> *conditional-statement* :
>> *if-statement*
>> *if-else-statement*
>
> *if-statement* :
>> `if` (*expression*)   *statement*
>
> *if-else-statement* :
>> `if` (*expression*)   *statement*   `else`   *statement*

For each form of `if` statement the expression within parentheses is first evaluated. If this value is nonzero (section 8.1), then the statement immediately following the parentheses is executed. If the value of the control expression is zero and there is an `else` clause, then the statement following the keyword `else` is executed instead; but if the value of the control expression is zero and there is no `else` clause, then execution continues immediately with the statement following the conditional statement.

References   control expression 8.1

8.5.1 Multiway Conditional Statements

A multiway decision can be expressed as a cascaded series of `if-else` statements, where each `if` statement but the last has another `if` statement in its `else` clause. Such a series looks like this:

```
if (expression₁)
    statement₁
else if (expression₂)
    statement₂
else if (expression₃)
    statement₃
    ...
else
    statementₙ
```

Here is an example of a three-way decision: the function `signum` returns −1 if its argument is less than zero, 1 if its argument is greater than zero, and otherwise 0:

```
int signum(x)
    int x;
{
    if (x > 0) return 1;
    else if (x < 0) return -1;
    else return 0;
}
```

Compare this with the version of `signum` that uses conditional expressions shown in section 7.8.

The `switch` statement handles the specific kind of multiway decision where the value of an expression is to be compared against a fixed set of constants.

References   `switch` statement 8.7

8.5.2 The Dangling Else Problem

An ambiguity arises because a conditional statement may contain another conditional statement. In some situations it may not be apparent to which of several conditional statements an `else` might belong. Consider this example, which is indented in a misleading fashion:

```
if ((k >= 0) && (k < TABLE_SIZE))
    if (table[k] >= 0)
        printf("Entry %d is %d\n", k, table[k]);
else printf("Error: index %d out of range.\n",k);
```

Inspection of the code might lead one to assume that whoever wrote this code intended the `else` part to be an alternative to the outer `if` statement: the error message should be printed when the test

```
(k >= 0) && (k < TABLE_SIZE)
```

is false.

However, if we change the wording of the last error message to

```
else printf("Error: entry %d is negative.\n", k);
```

then one might assume that the programmer intended the `else` part to be executed when the test `table[k]>=0` is false.

The C language does not require the compiler to interpret the meanings of error messages and make assumptions about the programmer's intentions. Instead, the ambiguity is resolved in an arbitrary but customary way: an else part is always assumed to belong to the innermost `if` statement possible. From this rule we see that the second interpretation of the code fragment above will work as intended, while the first will not. The first fragment can be made to work as intended by introducing a compound statement:

```
if (k >= 0 && k < TABLE_SIZE) {
    if (table[k] >= 0)
        printf("Entry %d is %d\n", k, table[k]);
}
else printf("Error: index %d out of range.\n", k);
```

To reduce confusion, the second interpretation could also use a compound statement:

```
if (k >= 0 && k < TABLE_SIZE) {
    if (table[k] >= 0)
        printf("Entry %d is %d\n", k, table[k]);
    else printf("Error: entry %d is negative.\n",k);
}
```

Confusion can be eliminated entirely if braces are always used to surround statements controlled by an `if` statement. However, this conservative rule can clutter a program with unnecessary braces. It seems to us that a good stylistic compromise between confusion and clutter is to use braces with an `if` statement whenever the statement controlled by the `if` is anything but an expression or null statement.

References   compound statement 8.4; expression statement 8.2; null statement 8.11

8.6 ITERATIVE STATEMENTS

Three kinds of iterative statements are provided in C:

iterative-statement :
        while-statement
        do-statement
        for-statement

The `while` statement tests an exit condition before each execution of a statement. The `do` statement tests an exit condition after each execution of a statement. The `for` statement provides a special syntax that is convenient for initializing and updating one or more control variables as well as testing an exit condition. The statement embedded within an iteration statement is sometimes called the body of the iterative statement.

8.6.1 While Statement

Unlike other programming languages such as Pascal, C does not use the keyword "do" as part of the syntax of its `while` statement:

> *while-statement* :
> > `while` (*expression*) *statement*

The `while` statement is executed by first evaluating the control expression. If the result is true (not zero), then the statement is executed. The entire process is then repeated, alternately evaluating the expression and then, if the value is true, executing the statement. The value of the expression can change from time to time because of side effects in the statement or in the expression itself.

The execution of the `while` statement is complete when the control expression evaluates to false (zero), or when control is transferred out of the body of the `while` statement by a `return`, `goto`, or `break` statement. Also, the `continue` statement can modify the execution of a `while` statement.

The following function uses a `while` loop to raise an integer `base` to the power specified by the nonnegative integer `exponent` (with no checking for overflow). The method used is that of repeated squaring of the base and decoding of the exponent in binary notation to determine when to multiply the base into the result. To see why this works, note that the `while` loop maintains the invariant condition that the correct answer is `result` times `base` raised to the `exponent` power. When eventually `exponent` is 0, this condition degenerates to simply stating that `result` has the correct value:

```
int pow(base,exponent)
   int base,exponent;
{
   int result = 1;
   while (exponent > 0) {
      if ( exponent % 2 )
         result *= base;
      base *= base;
      exponent /= 2;
   }
   return result;
}
```

A while loop may usefully have a null statement for its body:

```
while ( *char_pointer++ );
```

The character pointer is advanced along by the ++ operator until a null character is found, and it is left pointing to the character after the null. This is a compact idiom for locating the end of a string. (Notice that the test expression depends on the fact that the postfix operator ++ has higher precedence than the indirection operator *. The test expression is interpreted as * (char_pointer++), not as (*char_pointer) ++, which would increment the character pointed to by char_pointer.)

A variation on this idea uses two pointers to copy a character string from one place to another:

```
while ( *dest_pointer++ = *source_pointer++ );
```

Characters are copied until the terminating null character is found (and also copied). Of course, in writing this the programmer should have reason to believe that the destination area will be large enough to contain all the characters to be copied.

References   break and continue statements 8.8; control expression 8.1; goto statement 8.10; null statement 8.11; return statement 8.9

8.6.2 Do Statement

The do statement differs from the while statement in that the do statement always executes the body at least once, whereas the while statement may never execute its body at all:

do-statement :
              do *statement* while (*expression*) ;

The do statement is executed by first executing the embedded statement. Then the control expression is evaluated; if the value is true (not zero), then the entire process is repeated, alternately executing the statement, evaluating the control expression, and then, if the value is true, repeating the process.

The execution of the do statement is complete when the control expression evaluates to zero or when control is transferred out of the body of the do statement by a return, goto, or break statement. Also, the continue statement can modify the execution of a do statement.

The C do statement is similar in function to the "repeat-until" statement in Pascal. The C do statement is unusual in that it terminates execution when the control expression is false, whereas a Pascal repeat-until statement terminates if its control expression is true. C is more consistent in this regard: all iteration constructs in C (while, do, and for) terminate when the control expression is false.

As an example of the use of the do statement, consider this program fragment that reads and processes characters, halting after a newline character has been processed:

```
int ch;
do
    process( ch = getchar());
while (ch != '\n');
```

The same effect could have been obtained by moving the computations into the control expression of a `while` statement, but the intent would be less clear:

```
int ch;
while( ch = getchar(ch),
        process(ch),
        ch != '\n' ) /*empty*/ ;
```

It is possible to write a `do` statement whose body is a null statement:

```
do ; while (expression );
```

It is cumbersome to do so, however, because such a `do` statement is identical in meaning to a more conventional `while` statement whose body is a null statement:

```
while ( expression );
```

References   `break` and `continue` statements 8.8; control expression 8.1; `goto` statement 8.10; null statement 8.11; `return` statement 8.9; `while` statement 8.6.1

8.6.3 For Statement

C's `for` statement is considerably more general than the "increment and test" statements found in most other languages. After explaining the execution of the `for` statement, we give several examples of how it can be used:

for-statement :
>   for *for-expressions statement*

for-expressions :
>   (*expression*_{opt} ; *expression*_{opt} ; *expression*_{opt})

A `for` statement consists of the keyword `for`, followed by three expressions separated by semicolons and enclosed in parentheses, followed by a statement. Each of the three expressions within the parentheses is optional and may be independently omitted, but the two semicolons separating them and the parentheses surrounding them are mandatory.

Typically, the first expression is used to initialize a loop variable, the second tests whether the loop should continue or terminate, and the third updates the loop variable (for example, by incrementing it). However, in principle the expressions may be used to perform any computation that is useful within the framework of the `for` control structure.

The for statement is executed as follows:

1. If present, the first expression is evaluated and the value is discarded.
2. If present, the second expression is evaluated like a control expression. If the result is zero, then execution of the `for` statement is complete. Otherwise (if the value is not zero or if the second expression was omitted), proceed to step 3.
3. The body of the `for` statement is executed.
4. If present, the third expression is evaluated and the value is discarded.
5. Return to step 2.

The execution of a `for` statement is terminated when the second (control) expression evaluates to zero or when control is transferred outside the `for` statement by a `return`, `goto`, or `break` statement. The execution of a `continue` statement within the body of the for statement has the effect of causing a jump to step 4 above.

Stated another way, a `for` loop of the form

> `for` (*expression₁*; *expression₂*; *expression₃*) *statement*

is similar (except for the action of the `continue` statement) to

> *expression₁;*
> `while` (*expression₂*) {
>   *statement*
>   *expression₃;*
> }

where if *expression₁* or *expression₃* is not present in the `for` statement, then it is simply omitted in the expansion also, and if *expression₂* is not present in the `for` statement, then the constant `1` is used for it in the expansion (and so the `while` loop never terminates due to the control expression becoming zero).

References   `break` and `continue` statements 8.8; control expression 8.1; discarded expressions 7.13; `goto` statement 8.10; `return` statement 8.9; `while` statement 8.6.1

8.6.4 Using the For Statement

The common way in C to write a loop that "never terminates" (sometimes known as a "do forever" loop) is as a `for` loop with no expressions:

> `for` (`;;`) *statement*

Of course, the loop can still be terminated by a `break`, `goto`, or `return` statement within the body. One can write a "do forever" loop in other ways, such as

```
while  (1)  statement
```

Typically, the first expression in a `for` statement is used to initialize a variable, the second expression to test the variable in some way, and the third to modify the variable toward some goal. For example, to print the integers from 0 to 9 and their squares, one might write

```
for (j = 0; j < 10;  j++)
    printf("%d %d\n",  j,  j*j);
```

Here the first expression initializes `j`; the second expression tests whether it has reached 10 yet (if it has, the loop is terminated); and the third expression increments `j`.

The `pow` function used above to illustrate the `while` statement can be rewritten using a `for` statement:

```
int pow(base,exponent)
    int base,  exponent;
{
    int result = 1;
    for (; exponent > 0; exponent /= 2) {
        if ( exponent % 2 )
            result *= base;
        base *= base;
    }
    return result;
}
```

This form stresses the fact that the loop is controlled by the variable `exponent` as it progresses toward 0 by repeated divisions by 2. Note that the loop variable `exponent` still had to be declared outside the `for` statement. The `for` statement itself does not include the declaration of any variables. A common programming error is to forget to declare a variable such as `i` or `j` used in a `for` statement, only to discover that some other variable named `i` or `j` elsewhere in the program is inadvertently modified by the loop.

The `for` statement need not be used only for counting over integer values. Here is an example of scanning down a linked chain of structures, where the loop variable is a pointer:

```
struct intlist {
    struct intlist *link;
    int data;
};
```

```
void print_duplicates(p)
    struct intlist *p;
{
    for (; p; p = p->link) {
        struct intlist *q;
        for (q = p->link; q; q = q->link)
            if (q->data == p->data) {
                printf("Duplicate data %d", p->data);
                break;
            }
    }
}
```

The structure `intlist` is used to implement a linked list of records, each record
containing some data. Given such a linked list, the function `print_duplicates`
prints the data for every redundant record in the list. The first `for` statement uses the
formal parameter p as its loop variable—it scans down the given list. The loop terminates when a null pointer is encountered. For every record, all the records following it
are examined by the inner `for` statement, which scans a pointer q along the list in the
same fashion.

As another example of nested `for` loops, here is a simple sorting routine that uses
the insertion sort algorithm. Insertion sort is a simple and efficient sorting method for
small arrays (for n less than, say, 20) or for arrays that are already almost sorted. It is not
a good method for very large unordered arrays, because in the worst case the time to
perform the sort is proportional to the square of the number of items to be sorted:

```
void insertsort(v, n)
    int v[], n;
{
    register int i, j, temp
    for (i = 1; i < n; i++) {
        temp = v[i];
        for (j = i-1; j >= 0 && v[j] > temp; j--)
            v[j+1] = v[j];
        v[j+1] = temp;
    }
}
```

The outer `for` loop counts i up from 1 (inclusive) to n (exclusive). At each step,
elements v[0] through v[i-1] have already been sorted, and elements v[i] through
v[n-1] remain to be sorted. The inner loop counts j down from i-1, moving
elements of the array up one at a time, until the right place to insert v[i] has been
found. (That is why this is called "insertion sort.") Notice that the termination test for
the inner loop uses the && operator. This prevents the array reference v[j] from being
executed when j is less than 0.

A simple modification to insertion sort can make it astonishingly more efficient by wrapping a third loop around the first two! The following sort routine, using the shell sort algorithm, is similar to one called `shell` that appeared as an example in Kernighan and Ritchie's *The C Programming Language.* The original `shell` routine was a good example of the use of three different nested `for` loops in a practical setting. However, we have modified it here in four ways, two of them suggested by Knuth and Sedgewick (see the Preface), to make it faster:

```
void shellsort(v, n)
    register int v[], n;
{
    register int gap, i, j, temp;
    gap = 1;
    do (gap = 3*gap + 1); while (gap <= n);
    for (gap /= 3; gap > 0; gap /= 3)
        for (i = gap; i < n; i++) {
            temp = v[i];
            for (j=i-gap; (j>=0)&&(v[j]>temp); j-=gap)
                v[j+gap] = v[j];
            v[j+gap] = temp;
        }
}
```

References   pointer types 5.3; `register` storage class 4.3; selection operator `->` 7.4.2; structure types 5.6; `void` type 5.9

8.6.5 Multiple Control Variables

Sometimes it is convenient to have more than one variable controlling a `for` loop. In this connection the comma operator is especially useful, because it can be used to group several assignment expressions into a single expression:

```
/* Returns 1 if the two string arguments
   are equal, 0 otherwise. */
int string_equal(s1, s2)
    char s1[], s2[];
{
    char *p1, *p2;
    for (p1=s1, p2=s2; *p1 && *p2; p1++, p2++)
        if (*p1 != *p2) return 0;
    return *p1 == *p2;
}
```

The example function `string_equal` accepts two strings and returns 1 if they are equal and 0 otherwise. The `for` statement is used to scan two pointer variables in parallel down the two strings. The expression `p1++, p2++` causes each of the two pointers to be advanced to the next character. If the strings are found to differ at some position, the return statement is used to terminate execution of the entire function and return 0. (This is probably a little faster than using `break` to terminate the loop and letting the following `return` redo the comparison.) If a null character is found in either string, as determined by the expression `*p1 && *p2`, then the loop is terminated normally, whereupon the second `return` statement determines whether or not both strings ended with a null character in the same place. (The function would still work correctly if the expression `*p1` were used instead of `*p1 && *p2`. It would also be a bit faster, though not as pleasantly symmetrical.)

References   `break` and `continue` statements 8.8; comma operator 7.10; pointer types 5.3; selection operator `->` 7.4.2; structure types 5.6

8.7 SWITCH STATEMENTS

The `switch` statement is a multiway branch based on the value of a control expression. In use, it is similar to the "case" statement in Pascal or Ada, but it is implemented more like the FORTRAN "computed goto" statement:

switch-statement :
            `switch` (*expression*) *statement*

case-label :
            `case` *constant-expression*

default-label :
            `default`

The control expression that follows the keyword `switch` must have an integral type and is subject to the usual unary conversions. The expression following the keyword `case` must be an integral constant expression (section 7.11.2). The statement embedded within a `switch` statement is sometimes called the body of the `switch` statement; it is usually a compound statement but need not be.

A `case` label or `default` label is said to belong to the innermost `switch` statement that contains it. Any statement within the body of a `switch` statement—or the body itself—may be labeled with a `case` label or a `default` label. In fact, the same statement may be labeled with several `case` labels and a `default` label. A `case` label or `default` label is not permitted to appear other than within the body of a `switch` statement, and no two `case` labels belonging to the same `switch` statement may have constant expressions with the same value. At most one `default` label may belong to any one `switch` statement.

A `switch` statement is executed as follows:

1. The control expression is evaluated.
2. If the value of the control expression is equal to that of the constant expression in some `case` label belonging to the `switch` statement, then program control

is transferred to the point indicated by that `case` label as if by a `goto` statement.

3. If the value of the control expression is not equal to any `case` label, but there is a `default` label that belongs to the `switch` statement, then program control is transferred to the point indicated by that `default` label.

4. If the value of the control expression is not equal to any `case` label and there is no `default` label, no statement of the body of the `switch` statement is executed; program control is transferred to whatever follows the `switch` statement.

When comparing the control expression and the `case` expressions, the `case` expressions are converted to the type of the control expression (after the usual unary conversions).

When control is transferred to a `case` or `default` label, execution continues through successive statements, ignoring any additional `case` or `default` labels that are encountered, until the end of the `switch` statement is reached or until control is transferred out of the `switch` statement by a `goto`, `return`, `break`, or `continue` statement.

Although ANSI C allows the control expression to be of any integer type, some older compilers do not permit it to be of type `long` or `unsigned long`. ANSI C also permits an implementation to limit the number of separate `case` labels in a `switch` statement to 257 (that is, more than enough to handle all values of type `char`).

References   `break` and `continue` statements 8.8; constant expressions 7.11; `goto` statement 8.10; integer types 5.1; labeled statement 8.3; `return` statement 8.9

8.7.1 Use of Switch Statements

The usual style in which the `switch` statement is used calls for the body to be a compound statement, statements within which are labeled by `case` and `default` labels. It should be noted that `case` and `default` labels do not themselves alter the flow of program control; execution proceeds unimpeded by such labels. The `break` statement can be used within the body of a `switch` statement to terminate its execution.

As an example, consider this program fragment:

```
switch (x) {
    case 1: printf("*");
    case 2: printf("**");
    case 3: printf("***");
    case 4: printf("****");
}
```

If the value of x is 2, then nine asterisks will be printed. The reason for this is that the `switch` statement transfers control to the `case` label with the expression 2. The call to `printf` with argument `"**"` is executed; next the call to `printf` with argument `"***"` is executed; and finally the call to `printf` with argument `"****"` is executed.

If it is desired to terminate execution of the `switch` body after a single call to `printf` in each case, then the `break` statement should be used:

```
switch (x) {
    case 1: printf("*");
            break;
    case 2: printf("**");
            break;
    case 3: printf("***");
            break;
    case 4: printf("****");
            break;
}
```

While the last `break` statement in this example is logically unnecessary, it is a good thing to put in as a matter of style. It will help to prevent program errors in the event that a fifth `case` is later added to the `switch` statement.

We recommend sticking to this simple rule of style for `switch` statements: the body should always be a compound statement, and all labels belonging to the `switch` statement should appear on "top-level" statements within that compound statement. (The same stylistic guidelines apply as for `goto` statements.) Furthermore, every `case` (or `default`) label but the first should be preceded by one of two things: either a `break` statement that terminates the code for the previous `case` or a comment noting that the previous code is intended to drop in:

```
...
case fatal:
    printf("Fatal ");
    /* Drops through. */
case error:
    printf("Error");
    ++error_count;
    break;
...
```

While this is considered good style, the language definition itself does not require that the body be a compound statement, or that `case` and `default` labels appear only at the "top level" of the compound statement, or that `case` and `default` labels appear in any particular order or on different statements. Here is an example of how the best intentions can lead to chaos. The intent was to implement this simple program fragment as efficiently as possible:

```
if (prime(x)) process_prime(x);
else process_composite(x);
```

The function `prime` returns 1 if its argument is a prime number and 0 if the argument is a composite number. Program measurements indicated that most of the calls to `prime` were being made with small integers, so to avoid the overhead of calls to `prime` the code was changed to use a `switch` statement to detect the small integers, leaving the `default` label to handle larger numbers. By steadily compressing the code, the following statement was produced:

```
switch (x)
    default:
    if (prime(x))
        case 2: case 3: case 5: case 7:
            process_prime(x);
    else
        case 4: case 6: case 8: case 9: case 10:
            process_composite(x);
```

This is, frankly, the most bizarre `switch` statement we have ever seen that still has pretenses to being purposeful. Not only is it unstructured and difficult to understand, but good compilers can generate code from a well-structured `switch` statement that is as efficient as from the above statement.

8.8 BREAK AND CONTINUE STATEMENTS

The `break` and `continue` statements are used to alter the flow of control inside loops and—in the case of `break`—in `switch` statements. It is stylistically better to use these statements than to use the `goto` statement to accomplish the same purpose:

break-statement :
         `break;`

continue-statement :
         `continue;`

Execution of a `break` statement causes execution of the smallest enclosing `while, do, for,` or `switch` statement to be terminated. Program control is immediately transferred to the point just beyond the terminated statement. It is an error for a `break` statement to appear where there is no enclosing iterative or `switch` statement.

Execution of a `continue` statement causes execution of the body of the smallest enclosing `while, do,` or `for` statement to be terminated. Program control is immediately transferred to the end of the body, and the execution of the affected iterative statement continues from that point with a reevaluation of the loop test (or the increment expression, in the case of the `for` statement). It is an error for a `continue` statement to appear where there is no enclosing iterative statement.

The `continue` statement, unlike the `break` statement, has no interaction whatever with `switch` statements. A `continue` statement may appear within a `switch` statement, but it will affect only the smallest enclosing iterative statement, not the `switch` statement.

The `break` and `continue` statements can be explained in terms of the `goto` statement. Consider the statements affected by a `break` or `continue` statement:

> `while` (*expression*) *statement*
>
> `do` *statement* `while` (*expression*);
>
> `for` (*expression₁*; *expression₂*; *expression₃*) *statement*
>
> `switch` (*expression*) *statement*

Imagine that all such statements were to be rewritten in this manner:

> `{ while` (*expression*) `{`*statement* `C:;} B:;}`
>
> `{ do {`*statement* `C:;} while` (*expression*)`; B:;}`
>
> `{ for` (*expression₁*; *expression₂*; *expression₃*) `{`*statement* `C:;} B:;}`
>
> `{ switch` (*expression*) *statement* `B:;  }`

where in each case B and C are labels that appear nowhere else in the enclosing function. Then any occurrence of a `break` statement within the body of any of these statements is equivalent to "goto B;" and any occurrence of a continue statement within the body of any of these statements (except `switch`) is equivalent to "goto C;". This assumes that the loop bodies do not contain yet another loop containing the `break` or `continue`.

References   do statement 8.6.2; `for` statement 8.6.3; `goto` statement 8.10; `switch` statement 8.7; `while` statement 8.6.1

8.8.1 Examples

The `break` statement is frequently used in two very important contexts: to terminate the processing of a particular case within a `switch` statement, and to terminate a loop prematurely. The first use is illustrated in conjunction with `switch` in section 8.7. The second use is illustrated by this example of filling an array with input characters, stopping when the array is full or when the input is exhausted.:

```
#include <stdio.h>
static char array[100];
int i, c;
...
for (i = 0; i < 100; i++) {
    c = getchar();
    if (c == EOF) break;    /* Quit if end-of-file. */
    array[i] = c;
}
/* Now "i" has the actual number of characters read. */
```

Note how `break` is used to handle the abnormal case. It is generally better style to handle the normal case in the loop test itself.

Here is an example of the use of a `break` statement within a "do forever" loop. The idea is to find the smallest element in the array `a` (whose length is `N`) as efficiently as possible. It is assumed that the array may be modified temporarily.

```
int temp = a[0];
register int smallest = a[0];
register int *ptr = &a[N];   /* starts just beyond end of a */
...
for (;;) {
    while (*--ptr > smallest) ;
    if (ptr == &a[0]) break;
    a[0] = smallest = *ptr;
}
a[0] = temp;
```

The point is that most of the work is done by a very tight `while` loop, which scans the pointer `ptr` backward through the array, skipping elements that are larger than the smallest one found so far. (If the elements are in a random order, then once a reasonably small element has been found, most elements will be larger than that and so will be skipped.) The `while` loop cannot fall off the front of the array, because the smallest element so far is also stored in the first array element. When the `while` loop is done, if the scan has reached the front of the array, then the `break` statement terminates the outer loop. Otherwise `smallest` and `a[0]` are updated and the `while` loop is entered again. At the end of the computation, element `a[0]` is restored to its original value.

Compare the code above with a simpler, more obvious approach:

```
register int smallest = a[0];
register int j;
...
for (j = 1; j < n; ++j)
  if (a[j] < smallest)
      smallest = a[j];
```

This version is certainly easier to understand. However, on every iteration of the loop an explicit check (`j<n`) must be made for falling off the end of the array, as opposed to the implicit check made by the more clever code. Under certain circumstances where efficiency is paramount, the more complicated code may be justified; otherwise, the simpler, clearer loop should be used.

8.9 RETURN STATEMENTS

A `return` statement is used to terminate the current function, perhaps returning a value:

> *return-statement* :
>> return *expression*_{opt} ;

Execution of a return statement causes execution of the current function to be terminated; program control is transferred to the caller of the function at the point immediately following the call.

If no expression appears in the return statement, then no value is returned from the function; this is always permitted, even if the function has a declared return type other than void. If the function is called from a context requiring a value, then the program's behavior is undefined. If program control reaches the end of a function body without encountering a return statement, then the effect is as if a return statement with no expression were executed.

If an expression appears in the return statement, then it is converted as if by assignment to the return type of the function in which the statement appears. The return statement is illegal if the conversion is not possible, or if the function was declared with return type void. The rules governing the agreement of the actual value returned with the declared return value in the function definition are discussed in section 9.8.

References   discarded values 7.13; function call 7.4.3; function definition 9.1

8.10 GOTO STATEMENTS

A goto statement may be used to transfer control to any statement within a function:

> *goto-statement* :
>> goto *identifier* ;

> *named-label* :
>> *identifier*

The identifier following the keyword goto must be the same as a named label on some statement within the current function. Execution of the goto statement causes an immediate transfer of program control to the point in the function indicated by the label; the statement labeled by the indicated name is executed next.

References   labeled statement 8.3

8.10.1 Using the goto Statement

C permits a goto statement to transfer control to any other statement within a function, but certain kinds of branching can result in confusing programs, and the branching may hinder compiler optimizations.

The following rules should result in a more clear use of the goto:

1. Do not branch into the "then" or "else" arm of an if statement from outside the if statement.
2. Do not branch from the "then" arm to the "else" arm or back.

3. Do not branch into the body of a `switch` or iteration statement from outside the statement.

4. Do not branch into a compound statement from outside the statement.

Such branches should be avoided not only when using the `goto` statement, but also when placing `case` and `default` labels in a `switch` statement (which, in effect, executes a `goto` statement to get to the appropriate `case` label). Branching into the middle of a compound statement from outside it can be especially confusing, because such a branch bypasses the initialization of any variables declared at the top of the compound statement.

It is good programming style to use the `break`, `continue`, and `return` statements in preference to `goto` whenever possible.

Finally, the programmer wanting to produce a C program that executes as rapidly as possible should remember that the presence of any label—whether explicit, named labels or implicit labels required by `break` and `continue`—may inhibit compiler optimizations and therefore may slow down the C program.

References   `break` and `continue` statements 8.8; control expression 8.1; `if` statement 8.5; labeled statement 8.3; `return` statement 8.9; `switch` statement 8.7

8.11 NULL STATEMENTS

The null statement consists simply of a semicolon:

null-statement :
      `;`

The null statement is useful primarily in two situations. First, a null body is often desired for an iterative statement (`while`, `do`, or `for`). For example, the following loop needs no body because the control expression does all the work:

```
char *p;
...
while ( *p++ ); /* find the end of the string */
```

The second case is where a label is desired just before the right brace that terminates a compound statement. A label cannot simply precede the right brace, but must always be attached to a statement.   For example:

```
if (e) {
    ...
    goto L; /* terminate this arm of the 'if' */
    ...
    L:;}
else ...
```

References   `do` and `for` statements 8.6.2; labeled statement 8.3; `while` statement 8.6.1

8.12 EXERCISES

1.   Rewrite the following statements without using `for`, `while`, or `do` statements or the
     increment operator.
     (a) `for(n=A;n<B;n++) sum+=n;`
     (b) `while(a<b) a++;`
     (c) `do sum+=*p; while (++p < q);`

2.   What is the value of `j` at the end of the following program fragment?

```
{
    int j=1;
    goto L;
    {
        static int i = 3;
    L:
        j = i;
    }
}
```

3.   What is the value of `sum` after the following program fragment is executed?

```
int i, sum = 0;
for(i=0;i<10;i++) {
    switch(i) {
    case 0:
    case 1:
    case 3:
    case 5:
        sum++;
    default:
        continue;
    case 4:
        break;
    }
    break;
}
```

9

Functions

This chapter discusses the use of functions in the C language and provides more details for declaring and defining functions, for specifying formal parameters and return types, and for calling functions. Some information on functions appears previously in this book: function declarators are described in section 4.5.4 and function types and declarations are discussed in section 5.8.

The description of functions has become more complicated since the original definition of C. ANSI C has introduced a new way of declaring functions using function *prototypes* that specify more information about a function's parameters. The operation of a function call when a prototype has appeared is different from its operation without a prototype. Although the prototype and non-prototype forms are individually easy to understand, there are complicated rules for deciding what should happen when these two forms are mixed for the same function. We do not encourage programmers to mix the two forms, but as older C programs are converted to ANSI C there will be instances in which ANSI-conforming code will have to coexist with non-ANSI-conforming code or libraries. Users of non-ANSI-conforming implementations must, of course, use only the non-prototype forms.

The presence of a function prototype is determined by the syntax of a function declarator (section 4.5.4). Briefly, in traditional C (or in ANSI C when a prototype is *not* used):

- Function arguments undergo automatic promotions (the usual argument conversions) before a call.
- No checking of the type or number of arguments occurs.
- Any function can potentially take a variable number of arguments.

In contrast to this, when the ANSI C prototypes *are* used:

237

- Function arguments are converted, as if by assignment, to the declared types of the formal parameters.
- The number and types of the arguments must match the declared types, or else the program is in error.
- Functions taking a variable number of arguments are designated explicitly, and the unspecified arguments undergo the usual argument conversions

The following sections discuss both prototype-form and non-prototype-form function declarations.

9.1 FUNCTION DEFINITIONS

A function definition introduces a new function and provides the following information:

1. the type of the value returned by the function, if any
2. the type and number of the formal parameters
3. the visibility of the function outside the file in which it is defined
4. the code that is to be executed when the function is called

The syntax for a function definition is shown below. Function definitions can appear only at the top level of a C source file, or *translation unit*.

translation-unit :
      top-level-declaration
      translation-unit   top-level-declaration

top-level-declaration :
      declaration
      function-definition

function-definition :
      function-specifier   compound-statement

function-specifier :
      declaration-specifiers$_{opt}$ declarator   declaration-list$_{opt}$

declaration-list :
      declaration
      declaration-list   declaration

The syntax for other top-level declarations was discussed in chapter 4. Unlike other top-level declarations, a function definition need not include any storage class specifiers, type specifiers, or type qualifiers; there is no syntactic ambiguity in that case, and the single type specifier int will be assumed.

Within a *function-specifier*, the declarator must contain a *function-declarator* that specifies the function identifier immediately before the left parenthesis. The syntax of a function declarator was shown in section 4.5.4 and is repeated below for convenience:

function-declarator :
        direct-declarator (*parameter-type-list*)   (ANSI C)
        direct-declarator (*identifier-list$_{opt}$*)

parameter-type-list :
        parameter-list
        parameter-list , . . .

parameter-list :
        parameter-declaration
        parameter-list , *parameter-declaration*

parameter-declaration :
        declaration-specifiers declarator
        declaration-specifiers abstract-declarator$_{opt}$

identifier-list :
        identifier
        identifier-list , *identifier*

If the function declarator that names the defined function includes a *parameter-type-list*, the function definition is said to be in prototype form; otherwise it is in non-prototype, or traditional, form. In prototype form the parameter names and types are listed in the declarator. In traditional form, the parameter names are listed in the declarator and the types are specified (in any order) in the *declaration-list$_{opt}$* following the declarator. If any parameter is not declared, its type defaults to `int`. For example:

```
int f(int i, int j) { … }      /* prototype form */
int f(i,j) int i,j; { … }      /* traditional form */
int f(i,j) int j; int i; { … } /* traditional form */
```

There are several constraints on the form of the *function-specifier*. The identifier declared in a function definition must have a function type, as indicated by the declarator portion of the definition. That is, the declarator must contain a *function-declarator* that specifies the function identifier immediately before the left parenthesis. It is not allowed for the identifier to inherit its "functionness" from a typedef name.

The function return type cannot be an array or function type.

The declarator must specify the function's parameter names. If the declarator is in prototype form, the *parameter-declarations* must include a *declarator* as opposed to an *abstract-declarator*. If the declarator is not in prototype form, it must include *identifier-list* unless the function takes no arguments . To avoid an ambiguity between an identifier list and a parameter type list, it is illegal to have a parameter name that is the same as a visible typedef name. (This restriction is usually not present in older compilers.)

The only storage class specifier allowed in a parameter declaration is `register`.

The *declaration-list$_{opt}$* is permitted only with non-prototype definitions and can include only declarations of parameter identifiers. Some pre-ANSI compilers will permit additional declarations, but the meaning of such declarations is problematic and they are better placed in the function body.

To illustrate these rules, the following are legal function definitions:

`void f()` `{…}`	f is a function taking no parameters and returning no value

`int g(x,y)`
`    int x,y;`
`{…}`
	g is a function taking two integer parameters and returning an integer result

`int (*f(int x))[]` `{…}`	f is a function taking an integer parameter and returning a pointer to an array of integers (prototype form)

The following are not legal function definitions for the reasons given. Assume the typedef name T was declared as "`typedef int T();`".

`int (*q)() {…}`	q is a pointer, not a function
`T r {…}`	r cannot inherit "functionness" from a typedef name
`T s()   {…}`	declares s as a function returning a function
`void t(int, double)` `{…}`	t's parameter names do not appear in the declarator

`void u(int x, y)`
`    int y;`
`{…}`
	parameter declarations are only partially in prototype form

The only storage class specifiers that may appear in a function definition are `extern` and `static`. `extern` signifies that the function can be referenced from other files; that is, the function name is exported to the linker. The specifier `static` signifies that the function cannot be referenced from other files; that is, the name is not exported to the linker. If no storage class appears in a function definition, `extern` is assumed. In any case, the function is always visible from the definition point to the end of the file. In particular, it is visible within the body of the function itself.

References   declarators 4.5; `extern` storage class 4.3; function declarations 5.8; initialized declaration 4.1; `static` storage class 4.3; type specifiers 4.4

9.2 FUNCTION PROTOTYPES

A function prototype is a function declaration written in the prototype syntax (the *parameter-type-list*), or a function definition written in that syntax. Like a traditional function declaration, a function prototype declares the return type of a function. Unlike a traditional function declaration, a function prototype also declares the number and type of the function's formal parameters.

There are three basic kinds of prototypes depending on whether a function has no parameters, a fixed number of parameters, or a variable number of parameters:

1. A function that has no parameters must have a parameter type list consisting of the single type specifier `void`. For example:

    ```
    extern int random_generator(void);
    static void do_nothing(void) {return;}
    ```

2. A function that has a fixed number of parameters indicates the types of those parameters in the parameter type list. If the prototype appears in a function declaration, parameter names may be included or not, as desired. (We think they help in documenting the function.) Parameter names must appear in function definitions. For example:

    ```
    double square(double x) { return x*x; }
    extern char *strncpy(char *, char *, int);
    ```

3. A function that has a variable number of parameters or parameters of varying types indicates the types of any fixed parameters as above and follows them by the notation ", . . ." (which is composed of four tokens: a comma and three periods):

    ```
    extern int fprintf( FILE *file, char *format,… );
    ```

    There must be at least one fixed parameter, or else the parameter list cannot be referenced using the standard library facilities from `stdarg.h` (section 11.4).

Prototypes may be used in any function declarator, including those used to form more complicated types. For example, the ANSI C declaration of `signal` (section 19.6) is

```
void (*signal(int sig,void (*func)(int sig)))(int sig);
```

This declares `signal` to be a function that takes takes two arguments: `sig`, an integer, and `func`, a pointer to a `void` function of a single integer argument, `sig`. `signal` returns a pointer of the same type as its second parameter, i.e., a pointer to a `void` function taking a single integer argument. A clearer way to write the declaration of `signal` is

```
typedef void sig_handler(int sig);
sig_handler *signal(int sig, sig_handler *func);
```

However, when actually defining a signal handler function, the `sig_handler` typedef name cannot be used according to the rules for function definitions. Instead, the type must be repeated:

```
void new_signal_handler(int sig) {…}
```

It is possible to use prototypes for some declarators and not for others in the same declaration. If we were to declare `signal2` as

```
typedef void sig_handler2();   /* not a prototype */
sig_handler2 *signal2(int sig, sig_handler2 *func);
```

then we would lose the prototype for the `sig_handler2` function, although `signal2` still has the prototype form.

References   function declarator 4.5.4; function declarations 5.8; function definitions 9.1; `void` type 5.9

9.2.1 When Is a Prototype Present?

In order to predict how a function call will be performed, it is important that the programmer know whether or not the function (or function type) being called is governed by a prototype. A function call is governed by a prototype when:

1. a declaration for the function (or type) is visible, and the declaration is in prototype form, or
2. the function definition is visible and that definition is in prototype form

Note that the visibility of *any* prototype for the function is all that is required; there may be other non-prototype declarations or definitions visible.

If there are two or more prototype declarations of the same function or function type, or a prototype declaration and a prototype definition, then in all the prototypes:

- the function return types must be compatible,
- the number of parameters and the use of the ellipsis must agree, and
- the corresponding parameters must have compatible types.

These are just the rules for compatibility of function types. If these conditions are met, the function is governed by the common prototype. If the conditions are not met, the compiler will reject the program. The names of the formal parameters, if present in the two prototypes, need not agree, but it is always good style to be sure they do.

References   compatible types 5.11

9.2.2 Mixing Prototype and Non-Prototype Declarations

Although mixing prototype declarations and non-prototype declarations for the same function is not recommended, ANSI C does specify conditions under which the two kinds of declarations are compatible.

The behavior of a function call is undefined if the call supplies arguments that do not "match" the function definition. In traditional C, the programmer assumes all responsibility for making sure the call matches the definition; the language helps by converting arguments and parameters to a smaller and perhaps more manageable set of types. In ANSI C, through the use of prototype declarations, the compiler can check at the call site that the arguments match the prototype.

Depending on where function declarations appear, it is possible that some function calls will be governed by prototype declarations, some by traditional declarations, and some by the actual function definition. The calls and definition may be in a single source file or many files. Whenever some calls are not governed by a prototype, the programmer must assume the additional responsibility in being sure that the arguments in those calls match the function definition.

When prototype and non-prototype declarations appear, ANSI C sets forth compatibility rules that are necessary (but may not be sufficient) to ensure that the calls are compatible. If these rules are not satisfied, and the declarations appear in the same source file, the compiler will reject the C program. If the declarations appear in different source files, the compiler cannot warn the programmer that executing the program is likely to have unpredictable results.

The compatibility rules can be summarized by saying that the prototype declaration must specify explicitly the argument types that would be passed to a non-prototype function under the implicit argument conversion rules. There are two sets of rules: some "looser" rules that apply when the non-prototype form is a function (or type) declaration (i.e., with no parameter information specified), and a "tighter" set that applies when the non-prototype form is an actual function definition (possibly with parameters).

A function type declared in prototype form is compatible with a function type declaration whose argument list is empty (i.e., which is not a prototype) if:

1. the return types are compatible,
2. the prototype does not include the ellipsis terminator, and
3. each parameter type T in the prototype is compatible with the type resulting from applying the usual argument conversions to T.

In general, there are many different prototypes that are individually compatible with a non-prototype declaration. For example, suppose the non-prototype declaration

```
extern int f();
```

appeared somewhere in a C program. Table 9–1 shows some compatible and incompatible prototype declarations.

Calls under control of two declarations will match if the calls not governed by the prototype in fact supply arguments that, after the usual argument conversions, match the prototype.

A function type declared in prototype form is compatible with a non-prototype function definition if:

Table 9–1: Examples of prototypes for a traditional function declaration

Prototype	Compatible with int f()?	Reason
`extern double f(void);`	no	the parameter list is OK, but the return types are not compatible
`extern int f(int, float);`	no	`float` is not compatible with `double`
`extern int f(double x);`	yes	parameter type does not change upon conversion
`extern int f(int i, ...);`	no	the prototype must not contain ellipses
`extern int f(float *);`	yes	the argument is a pointer that is not converted

1. the return types are compatible,
2. the prototype does not include the ellipsis terminator,
3. the number of parameters in the prototype and the function definition is the same, and
4. the type of the ith parameter in the prototype is compatible with the type resulting from applying the usual argument conversions to the ith parameter in the definition.

These conditions are more stringent and actually check that the prototype matches the parameter specifications in the definition. In general, there is only one prototype that matches a non-prototype function definition; this prototype is sometimes referred to as the function's *Miranda prototype*, since it is "appointed" to a function definition that otherwise would not have one. For example, suppose the following definition appeared in a C program:

```
int f(x,y)
    float x;
    int y;
{...}
```

Table 9–2 lists some compatible and incompatible prototype declarations for this function definition.

Under ANSI C, functions taking a variable number of arguments must be governed by prototypes. This means that any existing functions that take a variable number of arguments (e.g., `printf`) must be rewritten to have a prototype before they are compiled by an ANSI C implementation.

References compatible types 5.11; `printf` 15.11

Table 9–2: Examples of prototypes for a traditional function definition

Prototype	Compat-ible?	Reason
`extern double` `    f(double x, int y);`	no	the parameter list is OK, but the return types are not compatible
`extern int f(float, int);`	no	the first parameter must have type `double`
`extern int` `    f(float, int, ...);`	no	the prototype must not contain ellipses
`extern int` `    f(double a, int b);`	yes	this is the only compatible prototype; the parameter names do not matter

9.2.3 Using Prototypes Wisely

Argument checking with prototypes is not foolproof. In a C program divided into many source files, the compiler cannot check that all calls to a function are governed by a prototype, that all the prototypes for the same function are compatible, or that all the prototypes match the function definition.

However, if the programmer follows some simple rules, the loopholes can be eliminated for all practical purposes:

1. Every external function should have a single prototype declaration in a header file. By having a single prototype, the possibility of incompatible prototypes for the same function is eliminated.
2. Every source file that has in it a call to the function should include the header file with the prototype. This ensures that all calls to the function will be governed by the same prototype and allows the compiler to check the arguments at the call sites.
3. The source file containing the definition of the function should also include the header file. This allows the compiler to check that the prototype and the declaration match, and, by transitivity, that all calls match the definition.

It is not necessary that the function definition be in prototype form.

The use of static functions should follow similar rules. Be sure a prototype-form declaration of the static function appears before any calls to the function and before the function's definition.

9.2.4 Prototypes and Calling Conventions

This section will be primarily useful to compiler implementors, although it may give other programmers some insight into the rules for function prototypes.

One advantage to function prototypes is that they can permit a compiler to generate more efficient calling sequences for some functions. For example, under traditional C rules, even if a function were defined to take a parameter of type `float`, the compiler had no choice but convert arguments to type `double`, call the function, and then convert the arguments back to `float`. In ANSI C, if the compiler sees a function call governed by the prototype

```
extern int f(float);
```

then the compiler is free to *not* convert the argument to type `double`, assuming it makes the corresponding assumption on the other side when it implements the definition of `f`:

```
int f(float x) {…}
```

The subtle point here is that the compiler does not have to remain compatible with calls that are not governed by a prototype in this case, because no non-prototype declarations (or definition) of `f` could possibly be compatible with the indicated prototype. Hence, ANSI C does not define what should happen if a call to `f` is made without the prototype visible. The compiler is even free to pass the argument in a register even if the non-prototype convention is to pass all arguments on a stack.

On the other hand, if a prototype declaration *could* be a Miranda prototype for a function declared or defined in the traditional way, then the compiler must use a compatible calling convention. That is, a call to a function `g` governed by either of the following declarations would have to be implemented in a compatible way:

```
extern short g();
extern short g(int,double);   /* Could be g's Miranda */
```

Stated another way, if a compiler for ANSI C sees the function call

```
process( a, b, c, d );
```

where no prototype is visible and where the types of the actual arguments are

```
short a;
struct {int a,b;} b;
float *c;
float d;
```

then the function call must be implemented the same as if this prototype were in effect:

```
int process(int, struct {int a,b;}, float *, double);
```

This rule does not actually establish a prototype that might affect later calls. Should a second call on `process` appear later in the program or in another source file, at which time the arguments to `process` are three values of type `double`, then that second call must be implemented as if the prototype were

```
int process( double, double, double );
```

even though the two calls will probably be incompatible at execution time.

To summarize the rules, a compiler is allowed to *depend* upon *all* calls to a function being governed by a prototype only if it sees a call of the function that is governed by a prototype and that prototype

1. includes an argument type that is not compatible with the usual argument conversions (`char`, `short`, their unsigned variants, or `float`), or
2. includes ellipses, indicating a variable argument list.

Since the conversions of `char` and `short` to `int` have minimal cost on most computers, the first rule is useful mainly with arguments of type `float`.

The second rule indicates that the compiler's standard calling convention need not support variable argument lists, as it must in traditional C. For example, an ANSI compiler could elect in its standard convention to use registers for the first four (fixed) argument words to any function, with the remainder of the arguments passed on the stack. This convention would probably not be appropriate in traditional C, because some functions taking variable arguments depend on all the arguments being passed contiguously on the stack. Any traditional C functions that take a variable number of arguments (e.g., `printf`) must be rewritten to have a prototype before they are compiled by an ANSI C implementation.

The storage class `register` is ignored when it appears in a prototype declaration. This means that `register` cannot be used to alter the calling convention of the function; it can only be used as a hint within the function body.

9.3 FORMAL PARAMETER DECLARATIONS

In function definitions, formal parameters are declared either in the prototype syntax allowed in ANSI C or in the traditional syntax.

The only storage class specifier that may be present in a parameter declaration is `register`, which is a hint to the compiler that the parameter will be used heavily and might better be stored in a register after the function has begun executing. The normal restrictions as to what types of parameters may be marked register apply (see section 4.3).

In ANSI C, formal parameters have the same scope as identifiers declared at the top level of the function body, and therefore they cannot be hidden or redeclared by declarations in the body. Some current C implementations allow such a redeclaration, which is almost invariably a programming error:

```
int f(x)
   int x;
{
   double x;   /* hides parameter!? */
   ...
}
```

In ANSI C, a parameter may be declared to be of any type except `void`. However, if a parameter is declared to have a type "function returning T" it is implicitly rewritten to have type "pointer to function returning T," and if a parameter is declared to have type "array of T" it is rewritten to have type "pointer to T." (The array type in the parameter declaration can be incomplete.) This adjustment is made regardless of whether a prototype or traditional definition is used. The programmer need not be aware of this change of parameter types in most cases, since the parameters can be used within the function as if they had the declared type. For example, suppose the function `FUNC` were defined as

```
void FUNC(int f(void), int (*g)(void), int h[], int *j)
{
   int i;
   i = f();   /* OK */
   i = g();   /* OK */
   i = h[3];  /* OK */
   i = j[3];  /* OK */
   ...
}
```

Suppose moreover that the following call were made to FUNC:

```
extern int a(void), b[20];
...
FUNC( a, a, b, b );
```

Then within `FUNC` the expression `f` would be equivalent to `g`, and `h` would be equivalent to `j`.

In most pre-ANSI implementations, parameters with array types are similarly converted, but some implementations reject declarations of parameters of type "function returning T," requiring instead that they be explicitly declared as "pointer to function returning T." For compatibility with these implementations, the programmer should declare the pointers explicitly.

A formal parameter is treated just like a local variable of the specified (or rewritten) type into which is copied the value of the corresponding argument passed to the function. The parameter can be assigned to, but the assignment only changes the local argument value, not the argument in the calling function. Parameter names declared to have function or array types are lvalues due to the rewriting rules, even though identifiers with those types are not normally lvalues.

It is permissible in current implementations (not in ANSI C) to include typedef, structure, union, or enumeration type declarations in the parameter declaration section. For example:

```
int process_record(r);
    struct { int a; int b; } *r;
{
    ...
}
```

It is generally bad programming style to do this. If the declarations involve the parameters, the declarations should be moved outside the function where the caller can also see them. If the declarations do not involve the parameters, they should be moved into the function body.

References   enumeration types 5.5; function declarator 4.5.4; function prototype 9.2; incomplete types 5.4; register storage class 4.3; storage class specifiers 4.3; structure types 5.6; typedef 5.10; union types 5.7; void type 5.9

9.4 ADJUSTMENTS TO PARAMETER TYPES

In traditional C—and in ANSI C when a prototype is not present—certain conversions (promotions) of the values of function arguments must be made. These conversions, which are designed to simplify and regularize function arguments, are called the usual argument conversions and are listed in section 6.3.5. Expecting these argument conversions by the caller, C functions arrange for the promoted argument values to be converted to the declared parameter types before the function body is executed. For example, if a function F was declared to take a parameter, x, of type short, and a call to F specified a value of type short, then the call would be implemented as if the following sequence of events occurred:

1. The caller widens the argument of type short to become a value of type int.
2. The value of type int is passed to F.
3. F narrows the int value to type short.
4. F stores value of type short is stored in the parameter x.

Fortunately, the conversions that occur have very little, if any, overhead—at least for integers. The argument types affected by the conversions include char, short, unsigned char, unsigned short, and float.

In ANSI C, when a function call is governed by a prototype, arguments are first converted to the type of the corresponding formal parameter. The C implementation is then permitted to perform the usual argument conversions before passing the argument, but it need not do so. Those arguments corresponding to the variable argument list specified by ", . . ." in the function prototype always undergo the usual argument conversions.

Programmers should be aware that some pre-ANSI compilers fail to perform the required narrowing operations upon entry to a function. For example, consider the following function, which has a parameter of type `char`:

```
int pass_through(c)
    char c;
{
    return c;
}
```

Some compilers will implement this function as if it were defined with an `int` parameter:

```
int pass_through(c)
    int c;
{
    return c;
}
```

A consequence of this incorrect implementation is that the argument value is not narrowed to type `char`. That is, `pass_through(0x1001)` would return the value `0x1001` instead of `1`. The correct implementation of the function would resemble this:

```
int pass_through(anonymous)
    int anonymous;
{
    char c = anonymous;
    return c;
}
```

References   array types 5.4; floating-point types 5.2; function argument conversions 6.3.5; function definition 9.1; function prototypes 9.2; function types 5.8; integer types 5.1; lvalue 7.1; pointer types 5.3

9.5 PARAMETER-PASSING CONVENTIONS

C provides only call-by-value parameter passing. This means that the values of the actual parameters are conceptually copied into a storage area local to the called function. It is possible to use a formal parameter name as the left side of an assignment, for instance, but in that case only the local copy of the parameter is altered.

If the programmer wants the called function to alter its actual parameters, the addresses of the parameters must be passed explicitly. For example, function `swap` below will not work correctly, because x and y are passed by value:

```
void swap(x, y)
/* swap: exchange the values of x and y */
/* Incorrect version! */
    int x, y;
{
    int temp;
    temp = x; x = y; y = temp;
}
...
swap(a, b); /* Fails to swap a and b. */
```

A correct implementation of the function requires that addresses of the arguments be passed:

```
void swap(x, y)
/* swap - exchange the values of *x and *y */
/* correct version */
    int *x, *y;
{
    int temp;
    temp = *x; *x = *y; *y = temp;
}
...
swap(&a, &b); /* Swaps contents of a and b. */
```

The local storage area for parameters is usually implemented on a pushdown stack. However, the order of pushing parameters on the stack is not specified by the language, nor does the language prevent the compiler from passing parameters in registers. It is legal to apply the address operator & to a formal parameter name (unless it was declared with storage class register), thereby implying that the parameter in question would have to be in addressable storage when the address was taken. (Note that the address of a formal parameter is the address of the copy of the actual parameter, not the address of the actual parameter itself.)

When writing functions that take a variable number of arguments, programmers should use the `varargs` or `stdargs` facilities in the standard library for maximum portability.

References   address operator & 7.5.6; function prototype 9.2; `register` storage class 4.3; `varargs` facility 11.4

9.6 AGREEMENT OF PARAMETERS

Most modern programming languages such as Pascal and Ada check the agreement of formal and actual parameters to functions; that is, both the number of arguments and the types of the individual arguments must agree. This checking is also performed in ANSI C when a function is declared with a prototype.

In the example below, the call to the function `sqrt` is not governed by a prototype; therefore, the C compiler is not required to warn the programmer that the actual parameter to `sqrt` is of type `long`, whereas the formal parameter is declared to have type `double`. (In fact, if the call and definition were in different source files, then the compiler would be unable to do so.) The function will simply return an incorrect value:

```
double sqrt( x )        /* not a prototype */
    double x;
{
    ...
}


long hypotenuse(x,y)
    long x,y;
{
    return sqrt(x*x + y*y);
}
```

When a call is governed by a prototype in ANSI C, the actual arguments are converted to the corresponding formal parameter type. Only if this conversion is impossible, or if the number of arguments does not agree with the number of formal parameters, will the C compiler reject the program. Therefore, by adding a prototype to the definition of `sqrt` above, the example will work correctly: the `long` argument will be converted to `double` without the programmer's knowledge:

```
double sqrt( double x )    /* prototype */
{
    ...
}

long hypotenuse(x,y)
    long x,y;
{
    return sqrt(x*x + y*y);
}
```

As a matter of good programming style, we recommend using explicit casts to convert arguments to the expected parameter type except when that conversion is just duplicating the usual argument conversions. That is, we would write the return statement in the example above like this:

```
return  sqrt( (double) (x*x + y*y) );
```

Some C functions, such as `fprintf`, are written to take arguments that vary in number and type. In traditional C, the `varargs` library facility has evolved to provide a fairly reliable way of writing such functions, although the usage is not portable, since different implementations have slightly different forms of `varargs`. In ANSI C a similar library mechanism, stdargs, was created to provide portability and reliability. Functions using stdargs must be declared with a prototype that uses the ellipses notation, ", . . .", before any call, thus giving the compiler an opportunity to prepare a suitable calling mechanism.

References   conversion of actual parameters 9.4; function argument conversions 6.3.5; function prototypes 9.2; fprintf 15.11

9.7 FUNCTION RETURN TYPES

A function may be defined to return a value of any type except "array of T" or "function returning T." These two cases must be handled by returning pointers to the array or function. There is no automatic rewriting of the return type, as there is for formal parameters.

The value returned by the function is specified by an expression in the return statement that causes the function to terminate. The rules governing the expression are discussed in section 9.8.

The value returned by a function is not an lvalue (the return is "by value"), and therefore a function call cannot appear as the outermost expression on the left side of an assignment operator:

```
f() = x;    /* Illegal */
*f() = x;   /* OK if f returns a pointer of suitable type */
f().a = x;  /* OK if f returns a structure of suitable type */
```

References   array types 5.4; function calls 7.4.3; function parameters 9.4; function types 5.8; lvalue 7.1; pointer types 5.3; void type 5.9

9.8 AGREEMENT OF RETURN TYPES

If a function has a declared return type T that is not void, then the type of any expression appearing in a return statement must be convertible to type T by assignment, and that conversion in fact happens on return in both ANSI and traditional C. For instance, in a function with declared return type int, the statement

```
return 23.1;
```

is equivalent to

```
return (int) 23.1;
```

which is the same as

```
return 23;
```

If a function has a declared return type of void, it is an error to supply an expression in any return statement in the function. It is also an error to call the function in a context that requires a value. With older compilers that do not implement void, it is the custom to omit the type specifier on those functions that return no value:

```
process_something()
{
    ...
}
```

However, it is also possible to define your own void type to improve readability (see section 4.4.1).

Whether a function has a void or nonvoid return type, ANSI and traditional C permit a return statement with no expression, that is, simply "return;". This rule is to provide backward compatibility with compilers that do not implement void. When a function has a nonvoid return type, and a return statement with no arguments is executed, then the value actually returned is unpredictable and it is therefore unwise to call the function in a context that requires a value. We recommend that this form of return be used only when the function is declared to have return type void.

References adjustments to formal parameters 9.4; default type specifiers 4.4.1; lvalue 7.1; return statement 8.9; void type 5.9

9.9 MAIN PROGRAMS

By convention all C programs must define a single external function named main. That function will become the entry point of the program, that is, the first function executed when the program is started. Information about parameters usually supplied to main and its return value is given in the library chapters, section 20.1.

References main 20.1

9.10 EXERCISES

1. Which of the following declarations serve as ANSI C prototypes?
    (a) short f(void);
    (b) int f();
    (c) double f(...);
    (d) int f(i,j);
    (e) int *f(float);
    (f) int f(i) int i; {…}

2. Declarations and definitions of functions are shown below. Which pairs are compatible in ANSI C?

	Declaration	*Definition*
(a)	`extern int f(short x);`	`int f(x) short x; {…}`
(b)	`extern int f();`	`int f(short x) {…}`
(c)	`extern f(short x);`	`int f(short int y) {…}`
(d)	`extern void f(int x);`	`void f(int x,...) {…}`
(e)	`extern f();`	`int f(x,y) short x,y; {…}`
(f)	`extern f();`	`f(void) {…}`

3. Declarations and invocations of functions are shown below. In each case, indicate if the invocation is legal in ANSI C and, if so, what conversions will be applied to each actual parameter. Assume s has type `short` and ld has type `long double`.

	Declaration	Invocation
(a)	`extern int f(int *x);`	`f(&s)`
(b)	`extern int f();`	`f(s,ld)`
(c)	`extern f(short x);`	`f(ld)`
(d)	`extern void f(short,...);`	`f(s,s,ld)`
(e)	`int f(x) short x; {…}`	`f(s)`
(f)	`int f(x) short x; {…};`	`f(ld)`

4. In the following program fragment, is the invocation of P governed by a prototype? Why?
   ```
   extern void P(void);
   …
   int Q()
   {
      extern P();
      P();
      …
   }
   ```

5. If the declared return type of a function is `short`, which of the following types of expressions appearing in a `return` statement would be allowable and would produce a predictable value at the call site?
   - (a) `int`
   - (b) `long double`
   - (c) `void` (e.g., the invocation of a function returning `void`)
   - (d) `char *`

10

Introduction to the Libraries

Many facilities that are used in C programs are part of the "standard libraries" that are written for use by C programs. These facilities include operations on characters and strings, input and output operations, mathematical functions, date and time conversions, and dynamic storage allocation.

Each of these facilities belongs to a particular library. The correct way to use a facility is to have a preprocessor #include command that references the proper library declarations. For example, in order to use the trigonometric function cos in a program, the C programmer should put the command

```
#include <math.h>
```

at the start of the program, thus declaring cos for subsequent use. Unfortunately, implementations of traditional C do not declare all the facilities in standard header files; some must be declared explicitly by the programmer.

The word *facility* has been used in order to evade the question of whether an operation is implemented as a function or a macro. We will often refer to the operations as "functions," but the implementor is usually free to provide an equivalent macro. A facility implemented as a macro should evaluate every argument expression exactly once, just as a function would. In some cases the implementation choice is important: if an operation is defined as a macro, it can be removed with #undef; if it is a function, the function's address can be passed to another function.

ANSI C is the first description of C to explicitly include a large standard library that is independent of the host operating system. Older implementations of C provide different sets of facilities, although the libraries originally provided with UNIX have been a model for many implementations. In the following chapters, we will describe not only the facilities included in ANSI C, but also the facilities in common use that duplicate facilities in ANSI C and other facilities in common use that are fairly portable across many systems.

10.1 ANSI C FACILITIES

The ANSI C language includes a portable run-time library that includes most of the features commonly used in traditional C. Tables 10–1 through 10–3 list the library facilities in ANSI C and give the section numbers of discussions in subsequent chapters.

Library facilities and header files in ANSI C are special in many ways, mostly to protect the integrity of implementations:

1. Library names are in principle reserved. Programmers may not define external objects whose names duplicate the names of the standard library. All names beginning with an underscore are also reserved to implementations.
2. Library header files or file names may be "built in" to the implementation, although they still must be included for their names to become visible.
3. Programmers may include library header files in any order, any number of times. (This may not be true in traditional C implementations.)

The last requirement is a convenience for programmers, but may force an implementation to use some careful mechanisms to avoid duplicate declarations, such as this:

```
/* Header stddef.h */
#ifndef _STDDEF
#define _STDDEF 1
typedef int ptrdiff_t;   /* Don't try to redeclare */
...
#endif
```

ANSI C requires that most "function-like" library facilities really be implemented as functions, so that the programmer can pass their address, say, to another function. However, to allow for more efficiency, the header files may hide the function name with an equivalent macro. Here is a hypothetical declaration of a function nonzero that returns 1 if its argument is nonzero and otherwise returns 0:

```
extern int nonzero( int x );       /* Functional form */
#define nonzero(x) ((int)(x)?1:0)  /* Macro form */
```

Note that the cast to int is necessary in the macro to simulate the action of a function call in the scope of a prototype. A programmer requiring the functional form would have to include an explicit #undef command to hide any macros:

```
#ifdef nonzero
#undef nonzero
#endif
```

The library functions are mostly written to take arguments whose types are un-changed under the usual argument conversions. This allows them to be called without the help of a prototype for compatibility with existing implementations. Compatibility cannot be reliably preserved for functions like `fprintf` and `fscanf` that take a variable number of arguments, because ANSI C requires such functions to be called in the scope of a prototype.

References   fprintf 15.11; fscanf 15.8; function prototypes 9.2; `#undef` 3.3.5

10.2 LIBRARY DESCRIPTIONS

The facilities are divided into groups according to their general purpose. Each facility is described by giving the appropriate header file (if there is one), a typical function or macro declaration of the facility, and a longer prose description. The declarations are given in two forms: the ANSI C form and the traditional C form. For example, here is the declaration of the `perror` facility:

ANSI C facilities	Traditional and alternate facilities
`#include <stdio.h>`	`#include <stdio.h>`
`void perror(const char *s)`	`void perror(char * s)`

Both forms are written in ANSI C prototype notation for readability, although traditional C implementations would not permit that style of declaration. In some cases the ANSI and traditional forms differ only subtly; in other cases, facilities may be present in ANSI C and not in traditional C, or vice versa. The accompanying prose descriptions should help to clarify the situation. The grouping of facilities in ANSI C does not always follow the divisions used in this book. Tables 10–1 through 10–3 list the standard facilities as organized in ANSI C.

Table 10–1: ANSI C library facilities (1 of 3)

Common definitions (stddef.h)

NULL (11.1)	ptrdiff_t (11.1)	wchar_t (11.1)
offsetof (11.1)	size_t (11.1)	

Built-in facilities

__DATE__ (11.3)	__LINE__ (11.3)	__TIME__ (11.3)
__FILE__ (11.3)	__STDC__ (11.3)	

Errors (errno.h)

EDOM (11.2)	ERANGE (11.2)	errno (11.2)

Diagnostics (assert.h)

assert (19.1)	NDEBUG (19.1)

Character handling (ctype.h)

isalnum (12.1)	islower (12.5)	isupper (12.5)
isalpha (12.1)	isprint (12.4)	isxdigit (12.3)
iscntrl (12.1)	ispunct (12.4)	tolower (12.9)
isdigit (12.3)	isspace (12.6)	toupper (12.9)
isgraph (12.4)		

Localization (locale.h)

LC_ALL (11.5)	LC_NUMERIC (11.5)	localeconv (11.6)
LC_COLLATE (11.5)	LC_TIME (11.5)	NULL (11.1)
LC_CTYPE (11.5)	struct lconv (11.6)	setlocale (11.5)
LC_MONETARY (11.5)		

Mathematics (math.h)

HUGE_VAL (17)	cosh (17.10)	modf (17.5)
acos (17.9)	sinh (17.10)	pow (17.6)
asin (17.9)	tanh (17.10)	sqrt (17.6)
atan (17.9)	exp (17.4)	ceil (17.3)
atan2 (17.9)	frexp (17.5)	fabs (17.2)
cos (17.8)	ldexp (17.5)	floor (17.3)
sin (17.8)	log (17.4)	fmod (17.3)
tan (17.8)	log10 (17.4)	

Non-local jumps (setjmp.h)

jmpbuf (19.4)	setjmp (19.4)	longjmp (19.4)

Table 10–2: ANSI C library facilities (2 of 3)

Signal handling (`signal.h`)

`sig_atomic_t` (19.6)	`SIGABRT` (19.6)	`SIGSEGV` (19.6)
`SIG_DFL` (19.6)	`SIGFPE` (19.6)	`SIGTERM` (19.6)
`SIG_ERR` (19.6)	`SIGILL` (19.6)	`signal` (19.6)
`SIG_IGN` (19.6)	`SIGINT` (19.6)	`raise` (19.6)

Variable arguments (`stdarg.h`)

`va_list` (11.4)	`va_arg` (11.4)	`va_end` (11.4)
`va_start` (11.4)		

Input/output (`stdio.h`)

`_IOFBF` (15.3)	`rename` (15.15)	`fputc` (15.9)
`_IOLBF` (15.3)	`tmpfile` (15.16)	`fputs` (15.10)
`_IONBF` (15.3)	`tmpnam` (15.14)	`getc` (15.6)
`BUFSIZ` (15.3)	`fclose` (15.2)	`getchar` (15.6)
`EOF` (15.1)	`fflush` (15.2)	`gets` (15.7)
`FILE` (15)	`fopen` (15.2)	`putc` (15.9)
`FILENAME_MAX` (15.2)	`freopen` (15.2)	`putchar` (15.9)
`FOPEN_MAX` (15.2)	`setbuf` (15.3)	`puts` (15.10)
`fpos_t` (15.5)	`setvbuf` (15.3)	`ungetc` (15.6)
`L_tmpnam` (15.14)	`fprintf` (15.11)	`fread` (15.13)
`NULL` (11.1)	`fscanf` (15.8)	`fwrite` (15.13)
`SEEK_CUR` (15.5)	`printf` (15.11)	`fgetpos` (15.5)
`SEEK_END` (15.5)	`scanf` (15.8)	`fseek` (15.5)
`SEK_SET` (15.5)	`sprintf` (15.11)	`fsetpos` (15.5)
`size_t` (11.1)	`sscanf` (15.8)	`ftell` (15.5)
`stderr` (15.4)	`vfprintf` (15.12)	`rewind` (15.5)
`stdin` (15.4)	`vprintf` (15.12)	`clearerr` (15.14)
`stdout` (15.4)	`vsprintf` (15.12)	`feof` (15.14)
`TMP_MAX` (15.16)	`fgetc` (15.6)	`ferror` (15.14)
`remove` (15.15)	`fgets` (15.7)	`perror` (11.2)

Table 10–3: ANSI C library facilities (3 of 3)

General utilities (`stdlib.h`)

EXIT_FAILURE (19.3)	strtol (13.8)	system (19.2)
EXIT_SUCCESS (19.3)	strtoul (13.8)	bsearch (20.5)
MB_CUR_MAX (11.7)	rand (17.7)	qsort (20.6)
NULL (11.1)	srand (17.7)	abs (17.1)
RAND_MAX (17.7)	calloc (16.1)	div (17.1)
div_t (17.1)	free (16.2)	labs (17.1)
ldiv_t (17.1)	malloc (16.1)	ldiv (17.1)
size_t (11.1)	realloc (16.3)	mblen (11.7)
wchar_t (11.1)	abort (19.3)	mbtowc (11.7)
atof (13.9)	atexit (19.5)	wctomb (11.7)
atoi (13.9)	exit (19.3)	mbstowcs (11.8)
atol (13.9)	getenv (20.4)	wcstombs (11.8)
strtod (13.8)		

String handling (`string.h`)

NULL (11.1)	memcmp (14.2)	strpbrk (13.6)
size_t (11.1)	strcmp (13.2)	strrchr (13.5)
memcpy (14.3)	strcoll (13.10)	strspn (13.6)
memmove (14.3)	strncmp (13.2)	strstr (13.7)
strcpy (13.3)	strxfrm (13.10)	strtok (13.7)
strncpy (13.3)	memchr (14.1)	memset (14.4)
strcat (13.1)	strchr (13.5)	strerror (11.2)
strncat (13.1)	strcspn (13.6)	strlen (13.4)

Date and time (`time.h`)

CLOCKS_PER_SEC (18.1)	struct tm (18.4)	asctime (18.3)
NULL (11.1)	clock (18.1)	ctime (18.3)
clock_t (18.1)	difftime (18.5)	gmtime (18.4)
time_t (18.2)	mktime (18.4)	localtime (18.4)
size_t (11.1)	time (18.2)	strftime (18.6)

11

Standard Language Additions

Chapter summary

Name	Section	Name	Section	Name	Section
__DATE__	11.3	NULL	11.1	stdarg	11.4
errno	11.2	offsetof	11.1	strerror	11.2
__FILE__	11.3	perror	11.2	vararg	11.4
__LINE__	11.3	ptrdiff_t	11.1	wctomb	11.7
localeconv	11.6	setlocale	11.5	wchar_t	11.1
mblen	11.7	size_t	11.1	wcstombs	11.8
mbtowc	11.7	__STDC__	11.3		
mbstowcs	11.8	__TIME__	11.3		

The facilities of this section are closely tied to the C language. They provide some standard definitions and parameterizations that help make C programs more portable.

11.1 NULL, PTRDIFF_T, SIZE_T, OFFSETOF, WCHAR_T

ANSI C facilities	Traditional and alternate facilities
`#include <stddef.h>`	`#include <stdio.h>`
`#define NULL …`	`#define NULL 0`
`typedef … ptrdiff_t;`	
`typedef … size_t;`	
`#define offsetof(`	
`    type,  member-designator  ) …`	
`typedef … wchar_t;`	

The value of the macro NULL is the traditional null pointer constant. Many implementations define it to be simply the integer constant 0. In ANSI C the macro is defined in many header files for convenience. In traditional C NULL is often found in `stdio.h`.

Three type definitions are supplied here in ANSI C. The type `ptrdiff_t` is an implementation-defined signed integral type that is the type of the result of subtracting two pointers; existing implementations use `int` or `long` for this type. The type `size_t` is the unsigned integral type of the result of the `sizeof` operator—probably `unsigned long`; pre-ANSI implementations often use the (signed) type `int` for this purpose. Type `wchar_t` (the "wide character" type) is an integral type that can represent all distinct values for any extended character set in the supported locales. Like NULL, the three type definitions appear in several header files in ANSI C.

The macro `offsetof` expands to an integral constant expression (of type `size_t`) that is the offset in bytes of member *member-designator* within structure type *type*. If the member is a bit field, the result is unpredictable. If `offsetof` is not defined in a non-ANSI implementation, it is often possible to define it as follows:

```
#define offsetof(type,memb)  ((size_t)&((type *)0)->memb)
```

If the implementation does not permit the use of the null pointer constant in this fashion, it may be possible to compute the offset by using a predefined, non-null pointer and subtracting the member's address from the structure's base address.

For example, at the end of the following program fragment the value of `diff` will be 1 and the values of `size` and `offset` will be equal. [For a byte-addressed computer on which `sizeof(int)` is 4, `size` and `offset` will both be equal to 4.]

```
#include <stdlib.h>
#include <stddef.h>
struct s {int a; int b; } x;
size_t size, offset;
ptrdiff_t diff;
…
diff = &x.b - &x.a;
size = sizeof(x.a);
offset = offsetof(struct s,b);
```

References conversion of integers to pointers 6.2.7; null pointers 5.3.2; pointer types 5.3; sizeof operator 7.5.2; subtraction of pointers 7.6.2; wide characters 2.7.3

11.2 ERRNO, STRERROR, PERROR

ANSI C facilities	Traditional and alternate facilities

`#include <errno.h>`
`extern int errno;`
or `#define errno …`
`#define EDOM …`
`#define ERANGE …`
	`#include <errno.h>`
	`extern int errno;`
	`#define EDOM …`
	`#define ERANGE …`

`#include <stdio.h>` `void perror(const char *s)`	`#include <stdio.h>` `void perror(char * s)`

`#include <string.h>`
`char *strerror(int errnum)`
	`#include <stdio.h>`
	`extern int sys_nerr;`
	`extern char *sys_errlist[];`

The external variable errno is used to hold implementation-defined error codes from library routines, traditionally defined in the header file errno.h. All error codes are positive integers, and library routines should never clear errno. Therefore, the typical way of using errno is to clear it before calling a library function and check it afterward:

```
errno = 0;
x = sqrt(y);
if (errno) {
    printf("?sqrt failed, code %d\n", errno);
    x = 0;
}
```

In ANSI C errno need not be a variable; it can be a macro that expands to any modifiable lvalue, such as a dereferenced pointer returned by a function:

```
extern int *_errno();
#define errno (*_errno())
```

The function strerror returns a pointer to an error message string whose contents are implementation-defined; the string is not modifiable and may be overwritten by a subsequent call to the strerror function.

The function perror prints the following sequence on the standard error output stream: the argument string s, a colon, a space, a short message concerning the error whose error code is currently in errno, and a newline. For example, the sqrt example in section 11.1 could be rewritten to use perror:

```
#include <math.h>
#include <errno.h>
errno = 0;
x = sqrt(y);
if (errno) {
    perror("sqrt failed");
    x = 0;
}
```

The error messages corresponding to values of errno may also be stored in a vector of string pointers, sys_errlist, which can be indexed by the value in errno. The variable sys_nerr contains the maximum integer that can be used to index sys_errlist; this should be checked to ensure that errno does not contain a nonstandard error number.

C implementations generally define a standard list of error codes that can be stored in errno. Traditional implementations define them in a central place, such as the header file errno.h; others may define them in the individual library header files. Two standard error codes are

EDOM	An argument was not in the domain accepted by a mathematical function. An example of this is giving a negative argument to the log function.
ERANGE	The result of a mathematical function is out of range; the function has a well-defined mathematical result but cannot be represented because of the limitations of the floating-point format. An example of this is trying to use the pow function to raise a large number to a very large power.

11.3 __DATE__, __FILE__, __LINE__, __TIME__, __STDC__

ANSI C facilities	Traditional and alternate facilities
#define __DATE__ ...	#define __FILE__ ...
#define __FILE__ ...	#define __LINE__ ...
#define __LINE__ ...	
#define __TIME__ ...	
#define __STDC__ ...	

These identifiers are special macros built into implementations of ANSI C; some existing implementations also define them, especially __FILE__ and __LINE__. These macros cannot be redefined or undefined, and no header file is needed to define them. The values of __DATE__ and __TIME__ should remain constant throughout the translation unit.

__DATE__ is a string constant representing the date of translation of the source file in the form "Mmm dd yyyy", e.g., "Jan 1 1990". __FILE__ is a string constant representing the name of the source file. __LINE__ is a decimal integer constant representing the current line number in the source file. __TIME__ is a string constant representing the time of day at which translation occurred in the form "hh:mm:ss", e.g., "14:02:30". __STDC__ should be defined (with a nonzero value) only by implementations that conform to ANSI C. For example:

```
printf("This file was named %s\n", __FILE__);
#ifdef __STDC__
printf("It was compiled on %s at %s\n", __DATE__,__TIME__);
#endif
```

11.4 VARARG, STDARG

ANSI C facilities	Traditional and alternate facilities

`#include <stdarg.h>`	`#include <varargs.h>`
	`#define va_alist …`
	`#define va_dcl …`

`typedef … va_list;`	`typedef … va_list;`

`void va_start(`
`    va_list ap,`
`  type LastFixedParm);`
	`void va_start(`
	`    va_list ap );`

`type va_arg( va_list ap, type);`	`type va_arg( va_list ap, type);`
`void va_end(va_list ap);`	`void va_end(va_list ap);`

The varargs (or stdargs) facility gives programmers a portable way to access variable argument lists, as is needed in functions such as fprintf (implicitly) and vfprintf (explicitly).

C originally placed no restrictions on the way arguments were passed to functions, and programmers consequently made nonportable assumptions based on the behavior of one computer system. Eventually the varargs facility arose under UNIX to promote portability, and ANSI C adopts a similar facility under the name stdarg. The usage of stdarg differs from vararg because ANSI C allows a fixed number of parameters to precede the variable part of an argument list, whereas previous implementations force the entire argument list to be treated as variable.

The meanings of the defined macros, functions, and types are listed below. This facility is very stylized, making very few assumptions about the implementation:

va_alist   This macro replaces the parameter list in the definition of a func-
                tion taking a variable number of arguments; not used in ANSI C.

va_dcl   In traditional C, this macro replaces the parameter declarations in the function definition. It should not be followed by a semicolon, to allow for it to be empty. The macro is not used in ANSI C.

va_list   This type is used to declare a local state variable, uniformly called ap in this exposition, which is used to traverse the parameters.

va_start   This macro initializes the state variable ap, and must be called before any calls to va_arg or va_end. In traditional C, va_start sets the internal pointer in ap to point to the first argument passed to the function; in ANSI C, va_start takes an additional parameter—the last fixed parameter name—and sets the internal pointer in ap to point to the first variable argument passed to the function.

va_arg   This macro returns the value of the next parameter in the argument list and advances the internal argument pointer (in ap) to the next argument (if any). The type of the next argument (after the usual argument conversions) must be specified (as *type*) so that va_arg can compute its size on the stack. The first call to va_arg after calling va_start will return the value of the first variable parameter.

va_end   This function or macro should be called after all the arguments have been read with va_arg. It performs any necessary cleanup operations on ap and va_alist.

As an example, the following "traditional C" function, printargs, takes a variable number of arguments of different types and prints their values on the standard output. The first argument to printargs is an array of integers that indicates the number and types of the following arguments. The array is terminated by a zero element. The meanings of the integers are given in file printargs.h:

```
#define INTARG 1
#define DBLARG 2
...
```

The printargs function itself is shown in table 11–1. The corresponding example for ANSI C is shown in table 11–2; the only differences are in the function argument list and in the call to va_start. In either case, the function can be tested with the following program:

```
#include "printargs.h"
int arg_types[] = { INTARG, DBLARG, INTARG, DBLARG, 0 };
int main()
{
    printargs( &arg_types[0], 1, 2.0, 3, 4.0 );
    return 0;
}
```

Table 11–1: Using a variable argument list in traditional C

```
#include <stdio.h>
#include <varargs.h>
#include "printargs.h"
void printargs( va_alist )
    va_dcl
{   va_list ap;
    int argtype, *argtypep;
    va_start(ap);
    argtypep = va_arg(ap, int *);
    while ( (argtype = *argtypep++) != 0 ) {
        switch (argtype) {
        case INTARG:
            printf("int: %d\n", va_arg(ap, int) ); break;
        case DBLARG:
            printf("double: %f\n", va_arg(ap, double) ); break;
            /* … */
        }
    }
    va_end(ap);
    return; }
```

Table 11–2: Using a variable argument list in ANSI C

```
#include <stdio.h>
#include <stdarg.h>
#include "printargs.h"
void printargs( int *argtypep, … )
{   va_list ap;
    int argtype;
    va_start(ap, argtypep);
    while ( (argtype = *argtypep++) != 0 ) {
        switch (argtype) {
        case INTARG:
            printf("int: %d\n", va_arg(ap, int) ); break;
        case DBLARG:
            printf("double: %f\n", va_arg(ap, double) ); break;
        /* … */
        }
    }
    va_end(ap);
    return; }
```

References printf 15.11; vfprintf 15.12

11.5 *SETLOCALE*

ANSI C facilities	Traditional and alternate facilities

`#include <locale.h>`
`#define LC_ALL …`
`#define LC_COLLATE …`
`#define LC_CTYPE …`
`#define LC_MONETARY …`
`#define LC_NUMERIC …`
`#define LC_TIME …`
`char *setlocale(`
`    int category,`
`    const char *locale);`	

The ANSI C language was designed for an international community whose members have different alphabets and different conventions for formatting numbers, monetary quantities, dates, and time. The language standard allows implementations to adjust the behavior of the run-time library accordingly, while still permitting reasonable portability across national boundaries.

The set of conventions for nationality, culture, and language is termed the *locale*. The locale affects such things as the format of decimal and monetary quantities, the alphabet and collation sequence (as for the character-handling facilities in chapter 14), and the format of date and time values. The "current locale" can be changed at run time by choosing from an implementation-defined set of locales. The ANSI C standard predefines only the "C" locale, which specifies a minimal environment consistent with the original definition of C.

The `setlocale` function is used to change locale-specific features of the run-time library. The first argument, `category`, is a code that specifies the behavior to be changed. The permitted values for `category` include the values of the macros in the following table, possibly augmented by additional implementation-defined categories spelled beginning with the letters `LC_`.

Predefined setlocale categories

Name	Behavior affected
`LC_ALL`	all behavior
`LC_COLLATE`	behavior of `strcoll` and `strxfrm` facilities
`LC_CTYPE`	character handling functions (Chapter 14)
`LC_MONETARY`	monetary information returned by `localeconv`
`LC_NUMERIC`	decimal-point and non-monetary information returned by `localeconv`
`LC_TIME`	behavior of `strftime` facility

The second argument, `locale`, is an implementation-defined string that names the locale whose conventions are to be used for the behavior designated by `category`. The only predefined values for `locale` are `"C"` for the standard C locale, and the empty string, `""`, which by convention means an implementation-defined native locale. The run-time library always uses the C locale until it is explicitly changed with `setlocale`.

If the `locale` argument to `setlocale` is a null pointer, the function does not change the locale but instead returns a pointer to a string that is the name of the current locale for the indicated category. This name is such that if `setlocale` were to be later called using the same value for `category` and the returned string as the value for `locale`, the effect would be to change the behavior to the one that was in effect when `setlocale` was called with the null `locale`. For example, a programmer who was about to change locale-specific behavior might first call `setlocale` with arguments `LC_AL` and `NULL` to get a value for the current locale that could later be used to restore the previous locale-specific behavior. The string returned must not be altered, and may be overwritten by subsequent calls to `setlocale`.

If the `locale` argument to `setlocale` is not null, `setlocale` changes the current locale and returns a string that names the new locale. A null pointer is returned if `setlocale` cannot honor the request for any reason.   The string returned must not be altered, and may be overwritten by subsequent calls to `setlocale`.

For example, the function `original_locale` below returns a description of the current locale so that it can be later restored if necessary. There is no fixed maximum length for the string returned by `setlocale`, so space for it must be dynamically allocated:

```c
#include <locale.h>
#include <string.h>
#include <stdlib.h>

char *original_locale(void)
{
    /* Return a copy of the current locale's description. */
    char *temp, *copy;
    temp = setlocale(LC_ALL, NULL);
    if (temp == NULL) return NULL;   /* setlocale() failed */
    copy = (char *)malloc(strlen(temp)+1);
    if (copy == NULL) return NULL;   /* malloc() failed */
    strcpy(copy,temp);
    return copy;
}
```

The following code uses `original_locale` to change and then restore the locale:

```c
#include <locale.h>
extern char *original_locale(void);
char *saved_locale;
...
saved_locale = original_locale();
setlocale(LC_ALL,"");            /* Change to native locale */
setlocale(LC_ALL,saved_locale);/* Restore former locale   */
```

References   malloc 16.1; localeconv 11.6; strcoll 13.10; strcpy 13.3; strftime
18.6; strlen 13.4; strxfrm 13.10

11.6 LOCALECONV

ANSI C facilities	Traditional and alternate facilities

```#include <locale.h>```
```struct lconv {…};```
```struct lconv *localeconv(void);```	

The localeconv function is used to obtain information about the conventions for
formatting numeric and monetary quantities in the current locale. This allows a
programmer to implement application-specific conversion and formatting routines with
some portability across locales, and avoids the necessity of adding locale-specific
conversion facilities to ANSI C. The localeconv function returns a pointer to an
object of type struct lconv, whose components must include at least those in
Table 11–3. The returned structure must not be altered by the programmer, and it may be
overwritten by a subsequent call to localeconv. In struct lconv, string
components whose value is the empty string and character components whose value is
CHAR_MAX should be interpreted as "don't know."

For example, the following function uses localeconv to print a floating-point
number with the correct decimal point character:

```
#include <locale.h>
#include <stdio.h>
…
void P(int int_part, int fract_part, int fract_digits)
{
    struct lconv *lconv;
    char *pt;
    lconv = localeconv();
    if (!(pt = lconv->decimal_point))
        pt = ".";
    printf("%d%s%0*d\n",
        int_part, pt, fract_digits, fract_part);
}
```

Other contents of struct lconv are discussed below.

Digit groupings   The grouping and mon_grouping components of struct
lconv are sequences of integer values of type char. Although they are described as
strings, the string is just a way to encode a sequence of small integers. Each integer in the
sequence specifies the number of digits in a group. The first integer corresponds to the
first group to the left of the decimal point; the second integer corresponds to the next

Table 11–3: lconv struct components

Type	Name	Use	Value in C locale
char *	decimal_point	Decimal point character (non-monetary)	"."
char *	thousands_sep	Non-monetary digit group separator character(s)	""
char *	grouping	Non-monetary digit groupings (see below)	""
char *	int_curr_symbol	The three-character international currency symbol, plus the character used to separate the international symbol from the monetary quantity	""
char *	currency_symbol	The local currency symbol for the current locale	""
char *	mon_decimal_point	Decimal point character (monetary)	""
char *	mon_thousands_sep	Monetary digit group separator character(s)	""
char *	mon_grouping	Monetary digit groupings (see below)	""
char *	positive_sign	Sign character(s) for nonnegative monetary quantities	""
char *	negative_sign	Sign character(s) for negative monetary quantities	""
char	int_frac_digits	Digits shown to the right of the decimal point for international monetary amounts	CHAR_MAX
char	frac_digits	Digits shown to the right of the decimal point for other than international formats	CHAR_MAX
char	p_cs_precedes	1 if currency_symbol precedes non-negative monetary values; 0 if it follows	CHAR_MAX
char	p_sep_by_space	1 if currency_symbol is separated from nonnegative monetary values by a space; else 0	CHAR_MAX
char	n_cs_precedes	Like p_cs_precedes, for negative values	CHAR_MAX
char	n_sep_by_space	Like p_sep_by_space, for negative values	CHAR_MAX
char	p_sign_posn	The positioning of positive_sign for a nonnegative monetary quantity (plus its currency_symbol)	CHAR_MAX
char	n_sign_posn	The positioning of negative_sign for a negative monetary quantity (plus its currency_symbol)	CHAR_MAX

group moving leftward, etc. The integer 0 (the null character at the end of the string) means that the previous digit group is to be repeated; the integer CHAR_MAX means that no further grouping is to be performed. The conventional grouping by thousands would

be specified by `"\3"`—three digits in the first group, repeated for subsequent groups—
and the string `"\1\2\3\127"` would group 1234567890 as 1234 567 89 0
(`CHAR_MAX` is assumed to be 127).

Sign positions   The `p_sign_posn` and `n_sign_posn` components of
`struct lconv` determine where `positive_sign` and `negative_sign`
(respectively) are placed. The possible values and their meaning are

0	Parentheses surround the number (including currency_symbol).
1	The sign string precedes the number (including currency_symbol).
2	The sign string follows the number (including currency_symbol).
3	The sign string immediately precedes the currency_symbol.
4	The sign string immediately follows the currency_symbol.

Some complete examples of monetary formatting are shown in tables 11–4 and 11–5,
which were taken from the ANSI C standard. Table 11–4 shows typical monetary
formatting in four countries. Table 11–5 shows the values of the components
of `struct lconv` that would specify the formatting illustrated in table 11–4.

Table 11–4: Examples of formatted monetary quantities

Country	Positive	Negative	International
Italy	L.1.234	-L.1.234	ITL.1.234
Netherlands	F 1.234,56	F -1.234,56	NLG 1.234,56
Norway	kr1.234,56	kr1.234,56-	NOK 1.234,56
Switzerland	SFrs.1,234.56	SFrs.1,234.56C	CHF 1,234.56

Table 11–5: Examples of struct lconv contents

Component	Italy	Netherlands	Norway	Switzerland
int_curr_symbol	"ITL."	"NLG "	"NOK "	"CHF "
currency_symbol	"L."	"F"	"kr"	"SFrs."
mon_decimal_point	""	","	","	"."
mon_thousands_sep	"."	"."	"."	","
mon_grouping	"\3"	"\3"	"\3"	"\3"
positive_sign	""	""	""	""
negative_sign	"-"	"-"	"-"	"C"
int_frac_digits	0	2	2	2
frac_digits	0	2	2	2
p_cs_precedes	1	1	1	1
p_sep_by_space	0	1	0	0
n_cs_precedes	1	1	1	1
n_sep_by_space	0	1	0	0
p_sign_posn	1	1	1	1
n_sign_posn	1	4	2	2

11.7 MBLEN, MBTOWC, WCTOMB

ANSI C facilities	Traditional and alternate facilities
| ```
#include <stdlib.h>
typedef … wchar_t;
#define MB_CUR_MAX …
int mblen(
    const char *s,
    size_t n)
int mbtowc(
    wchar_t *pwc,
    const char *s,
    size_t n);
int wctomb(
    char *s,
    wchar_t wchar);
``` | |

The ANSI C language has been extended to handle locale-specific character sets ("extended character sets") that are too large for each character to be represented within a single object of type char (a byte). For such character sets, ANSI C provides both an internal and an external representation scheme. Internally, an extended character code is assumed to fit in a "wide character," an object of the implementation-defined integral type wchar_t. Strings of extended characters can be represented as objects of type wchar_t[]. Externally, a single wide character is assumed to map into a sequence of normal characters—the "multibyte character" corresponding to the wide character. The maximum number of bytes used in representing a multibyte character in the current locale is given by the (non-constant) expression MB_CUR_MAX. Individual multibyte characters are not typically terminated by a null character.

No particular representation for wide or multibyte characters is mandated or excluded, but the single null character, '\0', must act as a terminator in both normal and multibyte character sequences. Multibyte encodings may be state-dependent, employing "shift characters" to alter the meaning of subsequent characters; the functions in this section individually retain state information from the multibyte character they last processed. Changing the LC_CTYPE category of the locale (section 11.5) may change the character encodings and leave the shift state indeterminate. The value of MB_CUR_MAX will include enough space for shift characters.

The mblen function returns the number of bytes that make up the single multibyte character pointed to by s, which is not more than n characters long. The value −1 is returned if s does not point to a legal multibyte character. If s is a null pointer, mblen returns a nonzero value if the locale-specific encoding of multibyte characters is state-dependent; as a side effect, such a call resets any internal state to a predefined "initial" condition.

The mbtowc ("multibyte to wide character") function converts a multibyte character to a wide character. The argument s points to the beginning of a multibyte character, which is not more than n characters long. The function converts the character
```

to its wide representation, storing the result in the object designated by pwc if pwc is not a null pointer. The function returns the number of characters that made up the multibyte character, or −1 if the character was not valid. If s is a null pointer, mbtowc returns a nonzero value if the locale-specific encoding of multibyte characters is state-dependent; as a side effect, such a call resets any internal state to a predefined "initial" condition.

The wctomb ("*wide character to multibyte*") function converts the wide character wchar to multibyte representation and stores the result in the character array designed by s, which should be at least MB_CUR_MAX characters long. A null character is not appended. The number of characters stored at s is returned if wchar is a valid character encoding; otherwise −1 is returned. If s is a null pointer, wctomb returns a nonzero value if the locale-specific encoding of multibyte characters is state-dependent; as a side effect, such a call resets any internal state to a predefined "initial" condition.

The following example shows an implementation of the library function mbstowcs (section 11.8) using the mbtowc function:

```
#include <stdlib.h>
size_t mbstowcs(wchar_t *pwcs, const char *pmbs, size_t n)
{
    size_t i = 0; /* index into output array */

    (void) mbtowc(NULL,NULL,0);   /* Set initial shift state */
    while (*pmbs && i < n) {
        int len = mbtowc(&pwcs[i++],pmbs,MB_CUR_MAX);
        if (len == -1)
            return (size_t) -1;
        pmbs += len;    /* to next input multibyte character */
    }
    return i;
}
```

References   multibyte characters 2.1.5

11.8 MBSTOWCS, WCSTOMBS

ANSI C facilities	Traditional and alternate facilities
```#include <stdlib.h>``` ```size_t mbstowcs(``` ``` wchar_t *pwcs,``` ``` const char *s,``` ``` size_t n);``` ```size_t wcstombs(``` ``` char *s,``` ``` const wchar_t *pwcs,``` ``` size_t n);```	

The function `mbstowcs` converts a sequence of multibyte characters in the null-terminated string `s` to a corresponding sequence of wide characters, storing the result in the array designated by `pwcs`. The multibyte string `s` must begin in the initial shift state. No more than `n` elements of the output wide character array will be modified.

The function `wcstombs` converts a sequence of wide characters beginning with the value designated by `pwcs` to a sequence of multibyte characters, storing the result in the character array designated by `s`. The sequence of wide characters is terminated by a character with value 0. The multibyte character sequence will begin in the initial shift state. No more than `n` bytes in the output multibyte string `s` will be modified.

If no invalid source characters are encountered, both functions return the number of elements of the destination array modified (not including any terminating zero element); otherwise, `(size_t)(-1)` is returned. The functions will store a terminating null value at the end of the converted sequence if there is room for it, but no more than `n` elements of the destination will be modified. If the value returned by either function is equal to `n`, the converted sequence will not be terminated with a zero value and may not represent all elements of the source string.

For example, the following statements read in a multibyte character string (`mbs`), convert it to a wide character string (`wcs`), and then convert it back to a multibyte character string (`mbs2`). We consider it to be an error if the conversion functions completely fill the destination arrays because then the converted strings will not be null-terminated:

```
#include <stdlib.h>
#include <stdio.h>
#define MAX_WCS 100
#define MAX_MBS (100*MB_CUR_MAX)
wchar_t wcs[MAX_WCS+1];
char mbs[MAX_MBS], mbs2[MAX_MBS];
size_t len_wcs, len_mbs;

/* Read in multibyte string; check for error */
if (!fgets(mbs,MAX_MBS,stdin))
    abort();
/* Convert to wide character string; check for error */
len_wcs = mbstowcs(wcs,mbs,MAX_WCS);
if (len_wcs == MAX_WCS || len_wcs == (size_t)-1)
    abort();
/* Convert back to multibyte string; check for error */
len_mbs = wcstombs(mbs2,wcs,MAX_MBS);
if (len_mbs == MAX_MBS || len_mbs == (size_t)-1)
    abort();
```

12

Character Processing

The facilities for handling characters are of two kinds: classification and conversion. Every character classification facility has a name beginning with "is" and returns a value of type int that is nonzero (true) if the argument is in the specified class and zero (false) if not. Every character conversion facility has a name beginning with "to" and returns a value of type int representing a character or EOF. The ANSI C standard warns that more conversion and classification facilities may be added to the library following this naming convention. All of the facilities described here are declared by the library header file ctype.h.

The negative value EOF is conventionally used as a value that is not a "real character." For example, fgetc (section 15.6) returns EOF when at end-of-file, because there is no "real character" to be read. It must be remembered, however, that the type char may be signed in some implementations, and so EOF is not necessarily distinguishable from a "real character" if nonstandard character values appear. (Standard character values are always nonnegative, even if the type char is signed.) All of the facilities described here operate properly on all values representable as type char or type unsigned char, and also on the value EOF, but are undefined for all other integer values, unless the individual description states otherwise.

The formulation of these facilities in ANSI C takes into account the possibility that several locales will be supported, and in general tries to make as few assumptions as possible about character encodings or concepts such as "letter." The traditional C version of these functions is roughly equivalent to the ANSI C formulation for the "C" locale, except that any ASCII-dependencies (such as `isascii` and `toascii`) are also removed.

A warning: Some non-ANSI implementations of C let the type `char` be signed and also support a type `unsigned char`, yet the character-handling facilities fail to operate properly on all values representable by type `unsigned char`. In some cases the facilities even fail to operate properly on all values representable by type `char`, but handle only "standard" character values and EOF.

12.1 ISALNUM, ISALPHA, ISASCII, ISCNTRL

ANSI C facilities	Traditional and alternate facilities
`#include <ctype.h>`	`#include <ctype.h>`
`int isalnum(int c);`	`int isalnum(char c);`
`int isalpha(int c);`	`int isalpha(char c);`
	`int isascii(int c);`
`int iscntrl(int c);`	`int iscntrl(char c);`

The `isalnum` function returns a nonzero value if `c` is the code for an alphanumeric character; that is, one of the following in the C locale:

```
0 1 2 3 4 5 6 7 8 9
A B C D E F G H I J K L M N O P Q R S T U V W X Y Z
a b c d e f g h i j k l m n o p q r s t u v w x y z
```

Otherwise, the returned value is zero. This function is by definition equivalent to

```
isalpha(c) || isdigit(c)
```

The `isalpha` function returns a nonzero value if `c` is the code for an alphabetic character; that is, one of the following for the C locale:

```
A B C D E F G H I J K L M N O P Q R S T U V W X Y Z
a b c d e f g h i j k l m n o p q r s t u v w x y z
```

Otherwise the returned value is zero. In any locale, this function is true whenever `islower(c)` or `isupper(c)` is true, and it is false whenever `iscntrl(c)`, `isdigit(c)`, `ispunct(c)`, or `isspace(c)` is true, but otherwise it is implementation-defined.

The function `isascii` returns a nonzero value if the value of `c` is between 0 and `0177` (the range of the standard 128-character ASCII character set). Otherwise `isascii` returns zero. Unlike most of of the character classification functions in traditional C, isascii operates properly on any value of type int. Because of its non-generality, isascii is not supplied in ANSI C.

The function iscntrl returns a nonzero value if c is the code for a "control character." If the standard 128-character ASCII set is in use, the control characters are those with codes 000 through 037, and also code 0177. The isprint function (section 12.4) is the complementary function, at least for standard ASCII implementations.

Example   The function is_id below returns TRUE if the argument string s is a legal C identifier; otherwise it returns FALSE. The current locale must be C for this function to work correctly.

```
#include <ctype.h>
int is_id(s)
    const char *s;
{
    char ch;
    /* Check first character */
    if ((ch = *s++) == '\0')
        return FALSE;     /* s is empty */
    if (!(isalpha(ch) || ch == '_'))
        return FALSE;    /* 1st character not letter or _ */
    /* Check remaining characters */
    while ((ch = *s++) != '\0') {
        if (!(isalnum(ch) || ch == '_'))
            return FALSE; /* char not letter, digit, or _ */
    }
    return TRUE;
}
```

12.2 ISCSYM, ISCSYMF

ANSI C facilities	Traditional and alternate facilities
	`#include <ctype.h>`
	`int iscsym(char c);`
	`int iscsymf(char c);`

The iscsym function returns a nonzero value if c is the code for a character that may appear in a C identifier. iscsymf returns a nonzero value if c is the code for a character that may additionally appear as the first character of an identifier.

The iscsymf function will accept at least the 52 upper and lowercase letters, and the underscore character. iscsym will additionally accept at least 10 ten decimal digits. Other characters may be accepted by these functions as well, depending on the implementation. These functions are not found in ANSI C.

12.3 ISDIGIT, ISODIGIT, ISXDIGIT

ANSI C facilities	Traditional and alternate facilities

`#include <ctype.h>`
`int isdigit(int c);`
`int isxdigit(int c)`
	`#include <ctype.h>`
	`int isdigit(char c);`
	`int isxdigit(char c);`
	`int isodigit(char c);`

The `isdigit` tests if c is the code for one of the 10 decimal digits. The `isodigit` function tests if c is the code for one of the 8 octal digits. The `isxdigit` function tests if c is the code for one of the 22 hexadecimal digits; that is, one of the following:

```
0 1 2 3 4 5 6 7 8 9 A B C D E F a b c d e f
```

12.4 ISGRAPH, ISPRINT, ISPUNCT

ANSI C facilities	Traditional and alternate facilities

`#include <ctype.h>`
`int isgraph(int c);`
`int isprint(int c);`
`int ispunct(int c);`
	`#include <ctype.h>`
	`int isgraph(char c);`
	`int isprint(char c);`
	`int ispunct(char c);`

The `isprint` function tests if c is the code for a "printing character"; that is, any character that is not a control character. A space is always considered to be a printing character. The `isgraph` function tests if c is the code for a "graphic character"; that is, any printing character other than space. The `isprint` and `isgraph` functions differ only in how they handle the space character; `isprint` is the opposite of `iscntrl` in most implementations, but this need not be so for every locale in ANSI C.

If the standard 128-character ASCII set is in use, the printing characters are those with codes 040 through 0176; that is, space plus the following:

```
! " # $ % & ' ( ) * + , - . / 0 1 2 3 4 5 6 7 8 9 : ; < = > ?
@ A B C D E F G H I J K L M N O P Q R S T U V W X Y Z [ \ ] ^ _
` a b c d e f g h i j k l m n o p q r s t u v w x y z { | } ~
```

The graphic characters are the same but space is omitted.

The function `ispunct` returns a nonzero value if c is the code for a "punctuation character"; that is, a printing character that is neither a space nor any character for which `isalnum` returns true. If the standard 128-character ASCII character set is in use, the punctuation characters are space plus the following:

```
! " # $ % & ' ( ) * + , - . / : ; < = > ? @ [ \ ] ^ _ ` { | } ~
```

12.5 ISLOWER, ISUPPER

ANSI C facilities	Traditional and alternate facilities
`#include <ctype.h>`	`#include <ctype.h>`
`int islower(int c);`	`int islower(char c);`
`int isupper(int c);`	`int isupper(char c);`

In the C locale, the `islower` function tests if c is one of the 26 lowercase letters, and the `isupper` function tests if c is one of the 26 uppercase letters. In other locales, additional characters may be included. If any of `iscntrl`, `isdigit`, `ispunct`, or `isspace` return true for a character, then `islower` and `isupper` must return false for the character.

12.6 ISSPACE, ISWHITE

ANSI C facilities	Traditional and alternate facilities
`#include <ctype.h>`	`#include <ctype.h>`
`int isspace(int c);`	`int isspace(char c);`
	`int iswhite(char c);`

The `isspace` function tests if c is the code for a whitespace character. In the C locale, `isspace` returns true for only the tab (`'\t'`), carriage return (`'\r'`), newline (`'\n'`), vertical tab (`'\v'`), form feed (`'\f'`), and space (`' '`) characters. Many other library facilities use `isspace` as the definition of whitespace. Some implementations of C provide not this exact function but a variant called `iswhite`.

12.7 TOASCII

ANSI C facilities	Traditional and alternate facilities
	`#include <ctype.h>`
	`int toascii(int c);`

The `toascii` function accepts any integer value and reduces it to the range of valid ASCII characters (codes 0 through 0177) by discarding all but the low-order seven bits of the value. If the argument is already a valid ASCII code, then the result is equal to the argument. This facility is not present in ANSI C.

12.8 TOINT

ANSI C facilities	Traditional and alternate facilities
	`#include <ctype.h>` `int toint(char c);`

The `toint` function returns the "weight" of a hexadecimal digit: 0 through 9 for the characters `'0'` through `'9'`, respectively, and 10 through 15 for the letters `'a'` through `'f'` (or `'A'` through `'F'`), respectively. The function's behavior if the argument is not a hexadecimal digit is implementation-defined. This facility is not present in ANSI C, but is easily implemented:

```
int toint( int c )
{
    if (c >= '0' && c <= '9') return c - '0';
    if (c >= 'A' && c <= 'F') return c - 'A' + 10;
    if (c >= 'a' && c <= 'f') return c - 'a' + 10;
    /* c is not a hexadecimal digit */
    return 0;
}
```

12.9 TOLOWER, TOUPPER

ANSI C facilities	Traditional and alternate facilities

`#include <ctype.h>`
`int tolower(int c);`
`int toupper(int c);`
	`#include <ctype.h>`
	`int tolower(char c);`
	`int toupper(char c);`
	`#define _tolower(c) ...`
	`#define _toupper(c) ...`

If `c` is an uppercase letter, then `tolower` returns the corresponding lowercase letter. If `c` is a lowercase letter, then `toupper` returns the corresponding uppercase letter. In all other cases, the argument is returned unchanged.

In some locales, there may be uppercase letters without corresponding lowercase letters, or vice versa; in these cases, the functions return their arguments unchanged.

When using non-ANSI implementations, you should be wary of the value returned by `tolower` when its argument is not an uppercase letter, and of the value returned by `toupper` when its argument is not a lowercase letter. Many non-ANSI implementations work correctly only when the argument is a letter of the proper case.

Implementations that allow more general arguments to `tolower` and `toupper` may provide faster versions of these— `_tolower` and `_toupper`—which require the more restrictive arguments and which are correspondingly faster.

Example   If the version of `tolower` in your C library is not well behaved for arbitrary arguments, the function `safe_tolower` below acts like `tolower` but is safe for all arguments. It is difficult to write `safe_tolower` as a macro because the argument is evaluated twice (by `isupper` and by `tolower`):

```
#include <ctype.h>
int safe_tolower(c)
    int c;
{
    if (isupper(c))
        return tolower(c);
    else
        return c;
}
```

13

String Processing

Chapter summary

Name	Section	Name	Section	Name	Section
atof	13.9	strlen	13.4	strspn	13.6
atoi	13.9	strncat	13.1	strstr	13.7
atol	13.9	strncmp	13.2	strtod	13.8
strcat	13.1	strncpy	13.3	strtok	13.7
strchr	13.5	strpbrk	13.6	strtol	13.8
strcoll	13.10	strpos	13.5	strtoul	13.8
strcmp	13.2	strrchr	13.5	strxfrm	13.10
strcpy	13.3	strrpbrk	13.6		
strcspn	13.6	strrpos	13.5		

By convention, strings in C are terminated by a null character (`'\0'`). The compiler automatically supplies an extra null character after all string constants, but it is up to the programmer to make sure that strings created in character arrays end with a null character. All of the string-handling facilities described here assume that strings are terminated by a null character.

All the characters in a string, not counting the terminating null character, are together called the contents of the string. An empty string contains no characters and is represented by a pointer to a null character. Note that this is not the same as a null character pointer (NULL), which is a pointer that points to no character at all.

When characters are transferred to a destination string, often no test is made for overflow of the destination. It is up to the programmer to make sure that the destination area in memory is large enough to contain the result string, including the terminating null character.

Most of the facilities described here are declared by the library header file `string.h`; some ANSI C conversion facilities are provided by `stdlib.h`. In ANSI

C, string parameters that are not modified are generally declared to have type `const char *` instead of `char *`; integer arguments or return values that represent string lengths have type `size_t` instead of `int`.

Other string facilities are provided by the memory functions (chapter 14), `sprintf` (section 15.11), and `sscanf` (section 15.8).

13.1 STRCAT, STRNCAT

ANSI C facilities	Traditional and alternate facilities

`#include <string.h>`
`char *strcat(`
`   char *dest,`
`   const char *src);`
`char *strncat(`
`   char *dest,`
`   const char *src, size_t n);`
	`#include <string.h>`
	`char *strcat(`
	`   char *dest,`
	`   char *src);`
	`char *strncat(`
	`   char *dest,`
	`   char *src, int n);`

The function `strcat` appends the contents of the string `src` to the end of the string `dest`. The value of `dest` is returned. The null character that terminates `dest` (and perhaps other characters following it in memory) is overwritten with characters from `src` and a new terminating null character. Characters are copied from `src` until a null character is encountered in `src`. The memory area beginning with `dest` is assumed to be large enough to hold both strings.

Example   The following statements append three strings to D; at the end, D contains the string `"All for one."`:

```
#include <string.h>
char D[20];
...
D[0] = '\0';   /* Set string to empty */
strcat(D,"All ");
strcat(D,"for ");
strcat(D,"one.");
```

The `strncat` function appends up to n characters from the contents of `src` to the end of `dest`. If the null character that terminates `src` is encountered before n characters have been copied, then the null character is copied but no more. If no null character appears among the first n characters of `src`, then the first n characters are copied and then a null character is supplied to terminate the destination string; that is, n+1 characters in all are written. If the value of n is zero or negative, then calling `strncat` has no effect.

The behavior of both functions is undefined if the strings overlap in memory.

13.2 STRCMP, STRNCMP

ANSI C facilities	Traditional and alternate facilities
| ```
#include <string.h>
int strcmp(
    const char *s1,
    const char *s2);
int strncmp(
    const char *s1,
    const char *s2, size_t n);
``` | ```
#include <string.h>
int strcmp(
    char *s1,
    char *s2);
int strncmp(
    char *s1,
    char *s2, int n);
``` |

The function strcmp lexicographically compares the contents of the null-terminated string s1 with the contents of the null-terminated string s2. It returns a value of type int that is less than zero if s1 is less than s2; equal to zero if s1 is equal to s2; and greater than zero if s1 is greater than s2. Therefore, to check only if two strings are equal the programmer negates the return value from strcmp:

```
if (!strcmp(s1,s2)) printf("Strings are equal\n");
else printf("Strings are not equal\n");
```

Two strings are equal if their contents are identical. String s1 is lexicographically less than string s2 under either of two circumstances:

1. The contents of the strings are equal up to some character position, and at that first differing character position the character value from s1 is less than the character value from s2.
2. The string s1 is shorter than the string s2, and the contents of s1 are identical to those of s2 up to length of s1.

The function strncmp is like strcmp except that it compares up to n characters of the null-terminated string s1 with up to n characters of the null-terminated string s2. In comparing the strings, the entire string is used if it contains fewer than n characters, and otherwise the string is treated as if it were n characters long. If the value of n is zero or negative, then both strings are treated as empty and therefore equal, and zero is returned.

The function memcmp (section 14.2) provides similar functionality to strcmp. The strcoll function (section 13.10) provides locale-specific comparison facilities.

13.3 STRCPY, STRNCPY

ANSI C facilities	Traditional and alternate facilities

`#include <string.h>`
`char *strcpy(`
`    char *dest,`
`    const char *src);`
`char *strncpy(`
`    char *dest,`
`    const char *src,`
`    size_t n);`
	`#include <string.h>`
	`char *strcpy(`
	`    char *dest,`
	`    char *src);`
	`char *strncpy(`
	`    char *dest,`
	`    char *src,`
	`    int n);`

The function `strcpy` copies the contents of the string `src` to the string `dest`, overwriting the old contents of `dest`. The entire contents of `src` are copied, plus the terminating null character, even if `src` is longer than `dest`. The argument `dest` is returned.

Example   The `strcat` function (section 13.1) can be implemented with the `strcpy` and `strlen` (section 13.4) functions as follows:

```
#include <string.h>
char *strcat(dest,src)
    char *dest;
    const char *src;
{
    char *s = dest + strlen(dest);
    strcpy(s,src);
    return dest;
}
```

The function `strncpy` copies exactly n characters to `dest`. It first copies up to n characters from `src`. If there are fewer than n characters in `src` before the terminating null character, then null characters are written into `dest` as padding until exactly n characters have been written. If there are n or more characters in `src`, then only n characters are copied, and so only a truncated copy of `src` is transferred to `dest`. It follows that the copy in `dest` is terminated with a null by `strncpy` only if the length of `src` (not counting the terminating null) is less than n. If the value of n is zero or negative, then calling strncpy function has no effect.

The functions `memcpy` and `memccpy` (section 14.3) provide similar functionality to `strcpy`. The results of both `strcpy` and `strncpy` are unpredictable if the two string arguments overlap in memory; the function `memmove` (section 14.3) is provided in ANSI C for cases in which overlap may occur.

13.4 STRLEN

ANSI C facilities	Traditional and alternate facilities
`#include <string.h>` `size_t strlen(const char *s)`	`#include <string.h>` `int strlen( char *s )`

The function `strlen` returns the number of characters in `s` preceding the terminating null character. An empty string has a null character as its first character and therefore its length is zero. In some implementations of C this function is called `lenstr`.

13.5 STRCHR, STRPOS, STRRCHR, STRRPOS

ANSI C facilities	Traditional and alternate facilities

`#include <string.h>`
`char *strchr(`
`   const char *s, int c);`
`char *strrchr(`
`   const char *s, int c);`
	`#include <string.h>`
	`char *strchr(`
	`   char *s, char c);`
	`char *strrchr(`
	`   char *s, char c);`
	`int strpos(`
	`   char *s, char c);`
	`int strrpos(`
	`   char *s, char c);`

The functions in this section all search for a single character `c` within a null-terminated string `s`.

The function `strchr` searches the string `s` for the first occurrence of the character `c`. If the character `c` is found in the string, a pointer to the first occurrence is returned. If the character is not found, a null pointer is returned.

The function `strrchr` is like `strchr` except that it returns a pointer to the last occurrence of the character `c`. If the character is not found, a null pointer is returned.

The function `strpos` is like `strchr` except that the position of the first occurrence of `c` is returned, where the first character of `s` is considered to be at position 0. If the character is not found, the value −1 is returned. The function `strrpos` is like `strrchr` except that the position of the last occurrence of `c` is returned. Neither `strpos` nor `strrpos` are provided by ANSI C.

These functions consider the terminating null character to be a part of `s` for the purposes of the search, so searching for a null character will always succeed and result in a pointer to (or the position of) the terminating null character.

The function `memchr` (section 14.1) provides similar functionality to `strchr`. In some implementations of C `strchr` and `strrchr` are called `index` and `rindex`, respectively. Some implementations of C provide the function `scnstr`, which is a variant of `strpos`.

Example   The function `how_many` below uses `strchr` to count the number of times a specified character appears in a string. The parameter `s` is repeatedly updated to point to the portion of the string just after the last-found character:

```
int how_many(char *s, int c)
{
    int n = 0;
    while(s) {
        s = strchr(s,c);
        if (s) n++,s++;
    }
    return n;
}
```

13.6 STRSPN, STRCSPN, STRPBRK, STRRPBRK

ANSI C facilities	Traditional and alternate facilities

`#include <string.h>`
`size_t strspn(`
`   const char *s,`
`   const char *set);`
`size_t strcspn(`
`   const char *s,`
`   const char *set);`
`char *strpbrk(`
`   const char *s,`
`   const char *set);`
	`#include <string.h>`
	`int strspn(`
	`   char *s,`
	`   char *set);`
	`int strcspn(`
	`   char *s,`
	`   char *set);`
	`char *strpbrk(`
	`   char *s,`
	`   char *set);`
	`char *strrpbrk(`
	`   char *s,`
	`   char *set);`

The functions in this section all search a null-terminated string `s` for occurrences of characters specified by whether or not they are included in a second null-terminated string set. The second argument is regarded as a set of characters; the order of the characters, or whether there are duplications, does not matter.

The function `strspn` searches the string `s` for the first occurrence of a character that is not included in the string `set`, skipping over ("spanning") characters that are in set. The value returned is the length of the longest initial segment of `s` that consists of characters found in `set`. If every character of `s` appears in `set`, then the total length of `s` (not counting the terminating null character) is returned. If `set` is an empty string, then the first character of `s` will not be found in it, and so zero will be returned.

The function `strcspn` is like `strspn` except that it searches `s` for the first occurrence of a character that is included in the character set set, skipping over characters that are not in `set`.

The function `strpbrk` is like `strcspn` except that it returns a pointer to the first character found from `set` rather than the number of characters skipped over. If no characters from `set` are found, a null pointer is returned.

The function `strrpbrk` is like `strpbrk` except that it returns a pointer to the last character from set found within s. If no character within s occurs in `set`, then a null pointer is returned. This function is not provided by ANSI C.

In some implementations, `strspn` and `strcspn` are called `notstr` and `instr`.

Example   The function `is_id` determines if the input string is a legal C identifier. `strspn` is used to see if all the string's characters are letters, digits, or the underscore character. If so, a final test is made to be sure the first character is not a digit. Compare this solution with the one given in section 12.1:

```
#include <string.h>
int is_id(char *s)
{
    static char *id_chars =
            "abcdefghijklmnopqrstuvwxyz"
            "ABCDEFGHIJKLMNOPQRSTUVWXYZ"
            "0123456789_";
    if (s == NULL) return FALSE;
    if (strspn(s,id_chars) != strlen(s)) return FALSE;
    return isalpha(*s) || *s == '_';
}
```

13.7 STRSTR, STRTOK

ANSI C facilities	Traditional and alternate facilities

`#include <string.h>`
`char *strtok(`
`   char *str,`
`   const char *set);`
`char *strstr(`
`   const char *src,`
`   const char *sub );`
	`#include <string.h>`
	`char *strtok(`
	`   char *str,`
	`   char *set);`

The function `strstr` is new in ANSI C. It locates the first occurrence of the string `sub` in the string `src` and returns a pointer to the beginning of the first occurrence. If `sub` does not occur in `src`, a null pointer is returned.

The function `strtok` may be used to separate a string `str` into tokens separated by characters from the string `set`. A call is made on `strtok` for each token, possibly changing the value of `set` in successive calls. The first call includes the string `str`; subsequent calls pass a null pointer as the first argument, directing `strtok` to continue from the end of the previous token.

More precisely, if `str` is not null then `strtok` first skips over all characters in `str` that are also in `set`. If all the characters of `str` occur in `set` then `strtok` returns a null pointer and an internal state pointer is set to a null pointer. Otherwise, the internal state pointer is set to point to the first character of `str` not in `set` and execution continues as if `str` had been null.

If `str` is null and the internal state pointer is null, then `strtok` returns a null pointer and the internal state pointer is unchanged. If `str` is null but the internal state pointer is not null, then the function searches beginning at the internal state pointer for the first character contained in `set`. If such a character is found, the character is overwritten with `'\0'`, `strtok` returns the value of the internal state pointer, and the internal state pointer is adjusted to point to the character immediately following inserted null character. If no such character is found, `strtok` returns the value of the internal state pointer and the internal state pointer is set to null.

Library facilities in ANSI C are not permitted to alter the internal state of `strtok` in any way that the programmer could detect. That is, the programmer does not have to worry about a library function using `strtok` and thereby interfering with the programmer's own use of the function.

Example   The following program reads lines from the standard input and uses `strtok` to break the lines into "words"—sequences of characters separated by spaces, commas, periods, quotation marks, and/or question marks. The words are printed on the standard output:

```
#include <stdio.h>
#include <string.h>
#define LINELENGTH 80
#define SEPCHARS " .,?\"\n"
int main()
{
    char line[LINELENGTH];
    char *word;

    while(TRUE) {
        printf("\nNext line?  (empty line to quit)\n");
        fgets(line,LINELENGTH,stdin);
        if (strlen(line) <= 1) break;       /* exit program */
        printf("That line contains these words:\n");
        word = strtok(line,SEPCHARS);    /* find first word */
        while (word != NULL) {
            printf("\"%s\"\n",word);
            word = strtok(NULL,SEPCHARS);  /* find next word */
        }
    }
}
```

Here is a sample execution of the program:

```
Next line?   (empty line to quit)
"My goodness," she said, "Is that right?"
That line contains these words:
"My"
"goodness"
"she"
"said"
"Is"
"that"
"right"

Next line?   (empty line to quit)
```

13.8 STRTOD, STRTOL, STRTOUL

ANSI C facilities	Traditional and alternate facilities
`#include <stdlib.h>`	
`double strtod(`	`double strtod(`
`   const char *str,`	`   char *str,`
`   char **ptr );`	`   char **ptr );`
`long strtol(`	`long strtol(`
`   const char *str,`	`   char *str,`
`   char **ptr,`	`   char **ptr,`
`   int base );`	`   int base );`
`unsigned long strtoul(`	
`   const char *str,`	
`   char **ptr,`	
`   int base );`	

The string-to-number conversion functions `strtod` and `strtol` originated in System V UNIX and were adopted by ANSI for C. The `strtoul` function was invented by the ANSI for completeness. In each case, `str` points to the string to be converted and `ptr` (if not null) is set by the functions to point to the first character in `str` immediately following the converted part of the string. If `str` begins with whitespace characters (as defined by the `isspace` function), they are skipped. In general, these functions provide more control over conversions than, say, the corresponding facilities of `sscanf`. Note that the functions are defined in the ANSI C header `stdlib.h`, not `string.h`.

The function `strtod` expects the number to be converted to consist of

1. an optional plus or minus sign,
2. a sequence of decimal digits possibly containing a single decimal point, and
3. an optional exponent part, consisting of the letter e or E, an optional sign, and a sequence of decimal digits.

The longest sequence of characters matching this model is converted to a floating-point number of type `double`, which is returned. The model differs from C's own floating-point constant syntax in that an optional − or + may appear, no decimal point is needed, the decimal point may not be a period (based on locale), and no floating suffix (`f`, `F`, `l`, or `L`) may appear.

If no conversion is possible because the string does not match the expected number model (or is empty), zero is returned, `*ptr` (if `ptr` is not null) is set to the value of `str`, and `errno` is set to ERANGE. If the number converted would cause overflow, HUGE_VAL (with the correct sign) is returned; if the number converted would cause underflow, zero is returned. In either case, `errno` is set to ERANGE. (According to this definition, an illegal number is indistinguishable from one that causes underflow, except perhaps by the value set in `*ptr`. Some non-ANSI implementations may set `errno` to EDOM when the string does not match the number model.)

The functions `strtol` and `strtoul` convert the initial portion of the argument string to an integer of type `long int` or `unsigned long int`, respectively. The expected format of the number—which changes with the value of `base`, the expected radix—is the same in both cases, including an optional − or + sign. No integer suffix (`l`, `L`, `u`, or `U`) may appear for either function.

If `base` is zero, the number (after the optional sign) should have the format of a *decimal-constant*, *octal-constant*, or *hexadecimal-constant*. The number's radix is deduced from its format. If the value of `base` is between 2 and 36, inclusive, the number must consist of a nonzero sequence of letters and digits representing an integer in the specified base. The letters a through z (or A through Z) represent the values 10 through 36, respectively. Only those letters representing values less than `base` are permitted. As a special case, if `base` is 16 then the number may begin with 0x or 0X, which is ignored.

If no conversion can be performed, the functions return zero, `*ptr` (if `ptr` is not null) is set to the value of `str`, and `errno` is set to ERANGE. If the number to be converted would cause an overflow, then `strtol` returns LONG_MAX or LONG_MIN (depending on the sign of the result) and `strtoul` returns ULONG_MAX ; `errno` is set to ERANGE.

References *decimal-constant* 2.7; `errno` 11.2; *floating-constant* 2.7; *hexadecimal-constant* 2.7; HUGE_VAL 19; *integer-constant* 2.7; `isspace` function 12.6; LONG_MAX, LONG_MIN, ULONG_MAX 5.1.1; *octal-constant* 2.7; *type-marker* 2.7

13.9 ATOF, ATOI, ATOL

ANSI C facilities	Traditional and alternate facilities
`#include <stdlib.h>`	
`double atof( const char *str );`	`double atof( char *str );`
`int   atoi( const char *str );`	`int   atoi( char *str );`
`long  atol( const char *str );`	`long  atol( char *str );`

These functions, which convert strings to numbers, are found in many UNIX implementations. In ANSI C they are present for compatibility, but the functions `strtod`, `strtol`, and `strtoul` are preferred. If they are unable to convert the input string, their behavior is undefined. Except for their behavior on error, the new functions may be defined in terms of the more general ones:

```
#include <stdlib.h>

double atof(char *str)
{
    return strtod(str, (char **)NULL);
}

int atoi(char *str)
{
    return (int) strtol(str, (char **) NULL, 10);
}

long atol(char * str)
{
    return strtol(str, (char **) NULL, 10);
}
```

Note that these functions are defined in the ANSI C header `stdlib.h`, not `string.h`.

13.10 STRCOLL, STRXFRM

ANSI C facilities	Traditional and alternate facilities

`#include <string.h>`
`int strcoll(`
`   const char *s1,`
`   const char *s2);`
`size_t strxfrm(`
`   char *dest,`
`   const char *src,`
`   size_t len);`	

The `strcoll` and `strxfrm` functions provide locale-specific string-sorting facilities. The `strcoll` function compares the strings `s1` and `s2` and returns an integer greater than, equal to, or less than zero depending on whether the string `s1` is greater than, equal to, or less than the string `s2`. The comparison is computed according to the locale-specific collating conventions (`LC_COLLATE` with `setlocale`, section 11.5). In contrast, the `strcmp` function (section 13.2) always compares two strings using the normal collating sequence of the target character set.

The `strxfrm` function transforms (in a way described below) the string `src` into a second string that is stored in the character array `dest`, which is assumed to be at least `len` characters long. The number of characters needed to store the string (excluding the terminating null character) is returned by `strxfrm`. Thus, if the value returned by `strxfrm` is greater than or equal to `len`, or if `src` and `dest` overlap in memory, the final contents of `dest` is undefined. Additionally, if `len` is 0 and `dest` is a null pointer, `strxfrm` simply computes and returns the length of the transformed string corresponding to `src`.

The `strxfrm` function transforms strings in such a way that the `strcmp` function can be used on the transformed strings to determine the correct sorting order. That is, if `s1` and `s2` are strings, and `t1` and `t2` are the transformed strings produced by `strxfrm` from `s1` and `s2`, then

> `strcmp(t1,t2)` is greater than zero if `strcoll(s1,s2)` is greater than zero
> `strcmp(t1,t2)` is equal to zero if `strcoll(s1,s2)` is equal to zero
> `strcmp(t1,t2)` is less than zero if `strcoll(s1,s2)` is less than zero

The functions `strcoll` and `strxfrm` have different performance tradeoffs. The `strcoll` function does not require the programmer to supply extra storage, but it may have to perform string transformations internally each time it is called. Using the `strxfrm` function may be more efficient when many comparisons must be done on the same set of strings.

Example   The function transform below uses `strxfrm` to create a transformed string corresponding to the argument s. Space for the string is dynamically allocated:

```
#include <string.h>
#include <stdlib.h>

char *transform( char *s )
   /* Return the result of applying strxfrm to s */
{
   char *dest;      /* Buffer to hold transformed string */
   size_t length;   /* Buffer length required */
   length = strxfrm(NULL,s,0) + 1;
   dest = (char *) malloc(length);
   (void) strxfrm(dest,s,length);
   return dest;
}
```

14

Memory Functions

Chapter summary

Name	Section	Name	Section	Name	Section
bcmp	14.2	memccpy	14.3	memcpy	14.3
bcpy	14.3	memchr	14.1	memmove	14.3
bzero	14.4	memcmp	14.2	memset	14.4

The facilities in this chapter give the C programmer efficient ways to copy, compare, and set blocks of memory. In ANSI C these functions are considered part of the string functions and are declared in the library header file string.h. In many other implementations they are declared in their own header file, memory.h.

Blocks of memory are designated by a pointer of type void * in ANSI C and char * in traditional C. In ANSI C, memory is interpreted as an array of objects of type unsigned char; in traditional C, this is not explicitly stated, and either char or unsigned char might be used.

14.1 MEMCHR

ANSI C facilities	Traditional and alternate facilities
#include <string.h> void *memchr(const void *ptr, int val, size t len);	#include <memory.h> char *memchr(char *ptr, int val, int len);

The function memchr searches for the value val (converted to type unsigned char) in each of the first len characters (also unsigned char) beginning at ptr. It returns a pointer to the first character containing `val`, if any, or returns a null pointer if no such character is found. See also `strchr` (section 13.5).

14.2 MEMCMP, BCMP

ANSI C facilities	Traditional and alternate facilities
| ```
#include <string.h>
int memcmp(
    const void *ptr1,
    const void *ptr2,
    size_t len );
``` | ```
#include <memory.h>
int memcmp(
    char *ptr1,
    char *ptr2,
    int len );
int bcmp(
    char *ptr1,
    char *ptr2,
    int len );
``` |

The function `memcmp` compares the first `len` characters beginning at `ptr1` with the first `len` character beginning at `ptr2`. If the first string of characters is lexicographically less than the second, `memcmp` returns a negative integer. If the first string of characters is lexicographically greater than the second, `memcmp` returns a positive integer. Otherwise `memcmp` returns 0.

The function `bcmp`, found in some implementations, also compares two strings of characters, but returns 0 if they are the same and nonzero otherwise. No comparison for less or greater is made. See also `strcmp` (section 13.2).

14.3 MEMCPY, MEMCCPY, MEMMOVE, BCPY

ANSI C facilities	Traditional and alternate facilities
| ```
#include <string.h>
char *memcpy(
    void *dest,
    const void *src,
    size_t len );
void * memmove(
    void *dest,
    const void *src,
    size_t len);
``` | ```
#include <memory.h>
char *memcpy(
    char *dest,
    char *src,
    int len );
char * memccpy(
    char *dest,
    char *src,
    int val,
    int len);
char *bcopy(
    char *src,
    char *dest,
    int len );
``` |

The functions `memcpy` and `memmove` (ANSI C) copy `len` characters from `src` to `dest` and return the value of `src`. The difference is that `memmove` will work correctly for overlapping memory regions; that is, `memmove` acts as if the source area were first copied to a separate temporary area and then copied back to the destination area. (In fact, no temporary areas are needed to implement `memmove`.) The behavior of `memcpy` is undefined when the source and destination overlap, although some versions of `memcpy` do implement the copy-to-temporary semantics. If both versions are available, the programmer should expect `memcpy` to be faster.

The function `memccpy`, found in some implementations, also copies `len` characters from `src` to `dest`, but it will stop immediately after copying a character whose value is `val`. When all `len` characters are copied `memccpy` returns a null pointer; otherwise it returns a pointer to the character following the copy of `val` in `dest`.

The function `bcopy`, found in some implementations, works like `memcpy` but the source and destination operands are reversed. See also `strcpy` (section 13.3).

14.4 MEMSET, BZERO

ANSI C facilities	Traditional and alternate facilities

`#include <string.h>`
`void *memset(`
`    void *ptr,`
`    int val,`
`    size_t len )`
	`#include <memory.h>`
	`char *memset(`
	`    char *ptr,`
	`    int val,`
	`    int len )`
	`void bzero(`
	`    char *ptr,`
	`    int len );`

The function `memset` copies the value `val` into each of `len` characters (type `unsigned char`) beginning at `ptr`. It returns the value of `ptr`.

The more restricted function `bzero` copies the value 0 into each of `len` characters beginning at `ptr`; it is found in some UNIX implementations.

15

Input/Output Facilities

Chapter summary

Name	Section	Name	Section	Name	Section
clearerr	15.14	fscanf	15.8	rewind	15.5
EOF	15.1	fseek	15.5	scanf	15.8
fclose	15.2	fsetpos	15.5	setbuf	15.3
feof	15.14	ftell	15.5	setvbuf	15.3
ferror	15.14	fwrite	15.13	sprintf	15.11
fflush	15.2	getc	15.6	sscanf	15.8
fgetc	15.6	getchar	15.6	stderr	15.4
fgetpos	15.5	gets	15.7	stdin	15.4
fgets	15.7	mktemp	15.16	stdout	15.4
FILE	15.1	perror	11.2	tmpfile	15.16
fopen	15.2	printf	15.11	tmpnam	15.16
fprintf	15.11	putc	15.9	ungetc	15.6
fputc	15.9	putchar	15.9	vfprintf	15.12
fputs	15.10	puts	15.10	vprintf	15.12
fread	15.13	remove	15.15	vsprintf	15.12
freopen	15.2	rename	15.15		

C has a very rich and useful set of I/O facilities based on the concept of a stream, which may be a file or some other source or consumer of data, including a terminal or other physical device. The data type FILE (defined in stdio.h along with the rest of the I/O facilities) holds information about a stream. A *file pointer*, an object of type FILE *, is created by calling fopen and is used as an argument to most of the I/O facilities described in this chapter.

Among the information included in a FILE object is the current position within the stream, pointers to any associated buffers, and indications whether an error or end-of-file has occurred. Streams are normally buffered unless they are associated with physical devices. The programmer has some control over buffering with the `setvbuf` facility, but in general streams can be implemented very efficiently and the programmer should not have to worry about performance.

There are two general forms of streams: text and binary. A text stream consists of a sequence of characters divided into lines; each line consists of zero or more characters followed by (and including) a newline character, `'\n'`. Text streams are portable when they consist only of complete lines made from characters from the standard character set. The hardware and software components underlying a particular C run-time library implementation may have different representations for text files (especially for the end-of-line indication) but the run-time library must map those representations into the standard one. ANSI C requires implementations to support text stream lines of at least 254 characters including the terminating newline.

Binary streams are sequences of data values of type `char`. Because any C data value may be mapped onto an array of values of type `char`, binary streams can transparently record internal data. Implementations do not have to distinguish between text and binary streams if it is more convenient not to.

When a C program begins execution, there are three text streams predefined and open: *standard input*, *standard output*, and *standard error*.

References `fopen` 15.2; `setvbuf` 15.3; standard character set 2.1

15.1 FILE, EOF

ANSI C facilities	Traditional and alternate facilities
`#include <stdio.h>`	`#include <stdio.h>`
`typedef … FILE …;`	`typedef … FILE …;`
`#define EOF (-n)`	`#define EOF (-1)`
`#define NULL …`	`#define NULL …`
`#define size_t`	

Type FILE is used throughout the standard I/O library to represent control information for a stream.

The value `EOF` is conventionally used as a value that signals *end-of-file*, that is, the exhaustion of input data. It has the value −1 in most traditional implementations, but ANSI C requires only that it be a negative integral constant expression. Because `EOF` is sometimes used to signal other problems, it is best to use the `feof` facility (section 15.14) to determine whether end-of-file has indeed been encountered when `EOF` is returned.

The type `size_t` and the null pointer constant `NULL` are defined in the header file `stdio.h` for convenience. In ANSI C they are also defined in `stddef.h`, although it does no harm to use both header file.

15.2 FOPEN, FCLOSE, FFLUSH, FREOPEN

ANSI C facilities	Traditional and alternate facilities
| ```
#include <stdio.h>
FILE *fopen(
    const char *filename,
    const char *mode);
int fclose(
    FILE *stream);
int fflush(
    FILE *stream);
FILE *freopen(
    const char *filename,
    const char *mode,
    FILE *stream);
#define FOPEN_MAX …
#define FILENAME_MAX …
``` | ```
#include <stdio.h>
FILE *fopen(
    char *filename,
    char *mode);
int fclose(
    FILE *stream);
int fflush(
    FILE *stream);
FILE *freopen(
    char *filename,
    char *mode,
    FILE *stream);
``` |

The function fopen takes as arguments a file name and a mode; each is specified as a character string. The file name is used in an implementation-specified manner to open or create a file and associate it with a stream. (The value of the macro FILENAME_MAX is the maximum length for a file name, or an "appropriate" length if there is no practical maximum.) A pointer of type FILE * is returned to identify the stream for other input/output operations. If any error is detected, fopen stores an error code into errno and returns a null pointer. The number of streams that may be open simultaneously is not specified; in ANSI C it is given by the value of the macro FOPEN_MAX, which must be at least eight (including the three predefined streams).

The function fclose closes an open stream in an appropriate and orderly fashion, including any necessary emptying of internal data buffers. The function fclose returns EOF if an error is detected; otherwise, it returns zero.

The function fflush empties any buffers associated with the output or update stream argument. The stream remains open. If any error is detected, fflush returns EOF; otherwise, it returns 0. fflush is typically used only in exceptional circumstances; fclose and exit normally take care of flushing output buffers.

The function freopen takes a file name, a mode, and an open stream. It first tries to close stream as if by a call to fclose, but any error while doing so is ignored. Then, filename and mode are used to open a new file as if by a call to fopen, except that the new stream is associated with stream rather than getting a new value of type FILE *. The function freopen returns stream if it is successful; otherwise (if the new open fails) a null pointer is returned. One of the main uses of freopen is to reassociate one of the standard input/output streams stdin, stdout, and stderr with another file.

The following values are permitted for the mode specification in the functions fopen and freopen.

Type specifications for fopen and freopen

Mode	Meaning
"r"	Open an existing file for input.
"w"	Create a new file, or truncate an existing one, for output.
"a"	Create a new file, or append to an existing one, for output.
"r+"	Open an existing file for update (both reading and writing), starting at the beginning of the file.
"w+"	Create a new file, or truncate an existing one, for update.
"a+"	Create a new file, or append to an existing one, for update.

When a file is opened for update (+ is present in the mode string), the resulting stream may be used for both input and output. However, an output operation may not be followed by an input operation without an intervening call to `fsetpos`, `fseek`, `rewind`, or `fflush`, and an input operation may not be followed by an output operation without an intervening call to `fsetpos`, `fseek`, `rewind`, or `fflush` or an input operation that encounters end-of-file. (These operations empty any internal buffers.)

ANSI C allows any of the types listed above to be followed by the character b to indicate a "binary" (as opposed to "text") stream is to be created. (The distinction under UNIX was blurred because both kinds of files are handled the same; other operating systems are not so lucky.) ANSI C also allows any of the "update" file types to assume binary mode; the b designator may appear before or after the + in the stream mode specification.

ANSI C also permits the mode string to contain other characters after the modes listed above. Implementations may use these additions to specify other attributes of streams, e.g.:

```
f = fopen("C:\work\dict.txt","r,access=lock");
```

The following table lists some properties of each of the stream modes.

Properties of fopen modes

Property	Mode					
	r	w	a	r+	w+	a+
Named file must already exist	yes	no	no	yes	no	no
Existing file's contents are lost	no	yes	no	no	yes	no
Read from stream permitted	yes	no	no	yes	yes	yes
Write to stream permitted	no	yes	yes	yes	yes	yes
Write permitted only at end of stream	no	no	yes	no	no	yes

Example   Here are some functions that open and close normal text files. They handle error conditions and print diagnostics as necessary, and their return values match those of `fopen` and `fclose`:

```
#include <errno.h>
#include <stdio.h>

FILE *open_input(char *filename)
    /* Open filename for input; return NULL if problem */
{
    FILE *f;
    errno = 0;
    f = fopen(filename,"r");   /* "w" for open_output */
    if (f == NULL) fprintf(stderr,
                    "Open of %s for input failed: %s\n",
                    filename, strerror(errno));
    return f;
}

int close_file(FILE *f)
    /* Close file f */
{
    int s  = 0;
    if (f == NULL) return 0; /* Ingore this case */
    errno = 0;
    s = fclose(f);
    if (s == EOF) perror("Close failed");
    return s;
}
```

References EOF 15.1; exit 19.3; stdin 15.4

15.3 SETBUF, SETVBUF

ANSI C facilities	Traditional and alternate facilities
`#include <stdio.h>`	`#include <stdio.h>`
`int setvbuf(`	`int setvbuf(`
`    FILE *stream,`	`    FILE *stream,`
`    char *buf,`	`    char *buf,`
`    int bufmode,`	`    int bufmode,`
`    size_t size );`	`    int size );`
`void setbuf(`	`void setbuf(`
`    FILE *stream,`	`    FILE *stream,`
`    char *buf );`	`    char *buf );`
`#define BUFSIZ …`	`#define BUFSIZ …`
`#define _IOFBF …`	`#define _IOFBF …`
`#define _IOLBF …`	`#define _IOLBF …`
`#define _IONBF …`	`#define _IONBF …`

These functions allow the programmer to control the buffering strategy for streams in those rare instances in which the default buffering is unsatisfactory. The functions must be called after a stream is opened and before any data are read or written.

The function `setvbuf` is the more general function, adopted from UNIX System V. The first argument is the stream being controlled; the second (if not null) is a character array to use in place of the automatically generated buffer; `bufmode` specifies the type of buffering, and `size` specifies the buffer size. The function returns zero if it is successful and nonzero if the arguments are improper or the request cannot be satisfied.

The macros `_IOFBF`, `_IOLBF`, and `IONBF` expand to values that can be used for `bufmode`. If `bufmode` is `_IOFBF`, the stream is fully buffered; if `bufmode` is `_IOLBF`, the buffer is flushed when a newline character is written or when the buffer is full; if `bufmode` is `_IONBF`, the stream is unbuffered. If buffering is requested and if `buf` is not a null pointer, then the array specified by `buf` should be `size` bytes long and will be used in place of the automatically generated buffers. The constant `BUFSIZ` is an "appropriate" value for the buffer size.

The function `setbuf` is a simplified form of `setvbuf`. The expression

```
setbuf(stream,buf)
```

is equivalent to the expression

```
((buf==NULL)  ?
(void)  setvbuf(stream,NULL,_IONBF,0)  :
(void)  setvbuf(stream,buf,_IOFBF,BUFSIZ))
```

References EOF 15.1; fopen 15.2; size_t 11.1

15.4 STDIN, STDOUT, STDERR

ANSI C facilities	Traditional and alternate facilities
`#include <stdio.h>`	`#include <stdio.h>`
`extern FILE *stderr;`	`extern FILE *stderr;`
`extern FILE *stdin;`	`extern FILE *stdin;`
`extern FILE *stdout;`	`extern FILE *stdout;`

The external variables `stdin`, `stdout`, and `stderr` are initialized prior to the start of an application program to certain standard text streams. `stdin` is initialized to an input stream that is the "normal input" to the program.; stdout to an output stream for the "normal output"; and `stderr` to an output stream for error messages and other unexpected output from the program. In an interactive environment, all three streams are typically associated with the terminal used to start the program. All streams except `stderr` are buffered.

UNIX systems in particular provide convenient ways to associate these standard streams with files or other programs when the application is launched, making them very powerful when used according to certain standard conventions.

15.5 FSEEK, FTELL, REWIND, FGETPOS, FSETPOS

ANSI C facilities	Traditional and alternate facilities
| ```
#include <stdio.h>
int fseek(
    FILE *stream,
    long int offset,
    int wherefrom);
long int ftell(FILE *stream);
void rewind(FILE *stream);
#define SEEK_SET 0
#define SEEK_CUR 1
#define SEEK_END 2
typedef … fpos_t …;
int fgetpos(
    FILE *stream,
    fpos_t *pos);
int fsetpos(
    FILE *stream,
    const fpos_t *pos);
``` | ```
#include <stdio.h>
int fseek(
    FILE *stream,
    long int offset,
    int wherefrom);
long int ftell(FILE *stream);
void rewind(FILE *stream);
``` |

The function fseek allows random access within a file. The first argument must be an open stream. The second two arguments specify a file position: offset is a signed integer specifying a number of characters, and wherefrom is a "seek code" indicating from what point in the file offset should be measured. The stream is positioned as requested and fseek returns zero if successful or a nonzero value if an error occurs. Any end-of-file indication is cleared and any effect of ungetc is undone. ANSI C defines the constants SEEK_SET, SEEK_CUR, and SEEK_END to represent the values of wherefrom; other implementations must use the integer values specified. The new position of the file is

- offset characters from the beginning if wherefrom is SEEK_SET (0);
- offset characters from the current position if wherefrom is SEEK_CUR (1); or
- offset characters from the end if wherefrom is SEEK_END (2).

If wherefrom is SEEK_END and offset is positive, then the file is extended the indicated amount from its end with unspecified contents.

The function fseek is usually applied to binary streams; this more limited set of calls is permitted (portably) for text streams:

```
fseek(stream,0L,SEEK_SET)        /* Position at beginning */
fseek(stream,0L,SEEK_CUR)        /* No effect */
fseek(stream,0L,SEEK_END)        /* Position at end */
fseek(stream,ftell-pos,SEEK_SET) /* Position at prev. location */
```

The value *ftell-pos* must be a value previously returned by `ftell` for `stream`. These limitations recognize that a position within a text file may not map directly onto the file's internal representation. For example, a position may require a record number and an offset within the record.

The function `ftell` takes a stream that is open for input or output and returns the position in the stream in the form of a value suitable for the second argument to `fseek`. Using `fseek` on a saved result of `ftell` will result in resetting the position of the stream to the place in the file at which `ftell` had been called. For binary files, the value returned will be the number of characters preceding the current file position. For text files, the value returned is implementation-defined (usable in `fseek`), but the value `0L` must be used to represent the beginning of the file. If `ftell` encounters an error, it returns `-1L` and sets `errno` to an implementation-defined value. Since `-1L` may also be a valid file position, `errno` must be checked to confirm the error. Conditions that can cause `ftell` to fail include an attempt to locate the position in a stream attached to a terminal, or an attempt to report a position that cannot be represented as an object of type `long int`.

The function `rewind` resets a stream to its beginning. By definition, the call `rewind(stream)` is equivalent to `fseek(stream,0L,SEEK_SET)`.

The functions `fgetpos` and `fsetpos` are new to ANSI C. They were added to handle files that are too large for their positions to be representable within an integer of type `long int` (for `ftell` and `fseek`). The `fgetpos` function stores the current file position in the object pointed to by `pos`; the `fsetpos` function sets the current file position according to the value in `*pos`, which must be a value returned earlier by `fgetpos` on the same stream. `fsetpos` undoes any effect of `ungetc`.

References ungetc 15.6

15.6 FGETC, GETC, GETCHAR, UNGETC

ANSI C facilities	Traditional and alternate facilities
`#include <stdio.h>`	`#include <stdio.h>`
`int fgetc(FILE *stream);`	`int fgetc(FILE *stream);`
`int getc(FILE *stream);`	`int getc(FILE *stream);`
`int getchar(void);`	`int getchar(void);`
`int ungetc(`	`int ungetc(`
`  int c,`	`  char c,`
`  FILE *stream);`	`  FILE *stream);`

The function `fgetc` takes as its argument an input stream. It reads the next character from the stream and returns it as a value of type `int`. Successive calls to `fgetc` will return successive characters from the input stream. If an error occurs or if the stream is at end-of-file, then `fgetc` returns EOF. The `feof` facility should be used in this case to determine whether end-of-file has really been reached.

The function getc is identical to fgetc, except that getc is usually implemented as a macro for efficiency. The argument expression should not have any side effects, because it may be evaluated more than once.

The function getchar reads the next character from the standard input stream stdin and returns it as a value of type int. The call getchar() is the same as the call getc(stdin). Like getc, getchar is often implemented as a macro.

The function ungetc causes the character c (converted to unsigned char) to be pushed back onto the specified input stream, so that it will be returned by the next call to fgetc, getc, or getchar on that stream. If several characters are pushed, they are returned in the reverse order of their pushing (that is, last character first). ungetc returns c when the character is successfully pushed back, EOF if the attempt fails.

One character of pushback is guaranteed provided the stream is buffered and at least one character has been read from the stream since the last fseek, fopen, or freopen operation on the stream. An attempt to push the value EOF back onto the stream as a character has no effect on the stream and returns EOF. A call to fsetpos, rewind, fseek, or freopen erases all memory of pushed-back characters from the stream, without affecting any external storage associated with the stream.

The function ungetc is useful for implementing input-scanning operations such as scanf. A program can "peek ahead" at the next input character by reading it and then putting it back if it is unsuitable.

References EOF 15.1; feof 15.14; fseek 15.5; fopen 15.2; freopen 15.2; scanf 15.8; stdin 15.4

15.7 FGETS, GETS

ANSI C facilities	Traditional and alternate facilities
`#include <stdio.h>`	`#include <stdio.h>`
`char *fgets(`	`char *fgets(`
`    char *s,`	`    char *s,`
`    int n,`	`    int n,`
`    FILE *stream);`	`    FILE *stream);`
`char *gets(`	`char *gets(`
`    char *s);`	`    char *s);`

The function fgets takes three arguments: a pointer s to the beginning of a character array, a count n, and an input stream. Characters are read from the input stream into s until

1. a newline is seen,
2. end-of-file is reached, or
3. n−1 characters have been read without encountering end-of-file or a newline character.

A terminating null character is then appended to the array after the characters read. If the input is terminated because a newline was seen, the newline character will be stored in the array just before the terminating null character. The argument s is returned upon successful completion.

If end-of-file is encountered before any characters have been read from the stream, then fgets returns a null pointer and the contents of the array s are unchanged. If an error occurs during the input operation, then fgets returns a null pointer and the contents of the array s are indeterminate. The feof facility (section 15.14) should be used to determine whether end-of-file has really been reached when NULL is returned.

The function gets reads characters from the standard input stream, stdin, into the character array s. However, unlike fputs, when the input is terminated by a newline character gets discards the newline and does not put into s. The use of gets can be dangerous because it is always possible for the input length to exceed the storage available in the character array. The function fgets is safer because no more than n characters will ever be placed in s.

References feof 15.14; stdin 15.4

15.8 FSCANF, SCANF, SSCANF

ANSI C facilities	Traditional and alternate facilities

```#include <stdio.h>```
```int fscanf(```
    ```FILE *stream,```
    ```const char *format,```
    ```...);```
```int scanf(```
    ```const char *format,```
    ```...);```
```int sscanf(```
    ```char *s,```
    ```const char *format,```
    ```...);```
	```#include <stdio.h>```
	```int fscanf(```
	    ```FILE *stream,```
	    ```char *format,```
	    ```...);```
	```int scanf(```
	    ```char *format,```
	    ```...);```
	```int sscanf(```
	    ```char *s,```
	    ```char *format,```
	    ```...);```

The function fscanf parses formatted input text, reading characters from the stream specified as the first argument and converting sequences of characters according to the control string format. Additional arguments may be required, depending on the contents of the control string. Each argument after the control string must be a pointer; converted values read from the input stream are stored into the objects designated to by the pointers.

The functions scanf and sscanf are like fscanf. In the case of scanf characters are read from the standard input stream stdin. In the case of sscanf characters are read from the string s. When sscanf attempts to read beyond the end of the string s it operates as fscanf and scanf do when end-of-file is reached.

The input operation may terminate prematurely because the input stream reaches end-of-file or because there is a conflict between the control string and a character read from the input stream. The value returned by these functions is the number of successful assignments performed before termination of the operation for either reason. If the input reaches end-of-file before any conflict or assignment is performed, then the functions return EOF. When a conflict occurs, the character causing the conflict remains unread and will be processed by the next input operation.

15.8.1 Control String

The control string is a picture of the expected form of the input. (In ANSI C, it is a multibyte character sequence beginning and ending in its initial shift state.) One may think of fscanf as performing a simple matching operation between the control string and the input stream. The contents of the control string may be divided into three categories:

1. *Whitespace characters.* A whitespace character in the control string causes whitespace characters to be read and discarded. The first input character encountered that is not a whitespace character remains as the next character to be read from the input stream. Note that if several consecutive whitespace characters appear in the control string, the effect is the same as if only one had appeared. Thus, any sequence of consecutive whitespace characters in the control string will match any sequence of consecutive whitespace characters, possibly of different length, from the input stream.

2. *Conversion specifications.* A conversion specification begins with a percent sign, %; the remainder of the syntax for conversion specifications is described in detail below. The number of characters read from the input stream depends on the conversion operation. As a rule of thumb, a conversion operation processes characters until: (a) end-of-file is reached, (b) a whitespace character or other inappropriate character is encountered, or (c) the number of characters read for the conversion operation equals the explicitly specified maximum field width. A conversion operation may cause an assignment to a location indicated by the next pointer argument to be used.

3. *Other characters.* Any (multibyte) character other than a whitespace character or a percent sign must match the next character of the input stream. If it does not match, a conflict has occurred; the fscanf operation is terminated, and the conflicting input character remains in the input stream to be read by the next input operation on that stream.

There should be exactly the right number of pointer arguments, each of exactly the right type, to satisfy the conversion specifications in the control string; otherwise, the results are undefined. If any conversion specification is malformed, the behavior is likewise undefined.

15.8.2 Conversion Specifications

A conversion specification begins with a percent sign, %. After the percent sign, the following conversion specification elements should appear in this order:

1. An optional *assignment suppression flag*, written as an asterisk ,*. If this is present for a conversion operation that normally performs an assignment, then characters are read and processed from the input stream in the usual way for that operation, but no assignment is performed and no pointer argument is consumed.

2. An optional *maximum field width*, expressed as an unsigned, positive decimal integer.

3. An optional *size specification*, expressed as the character h, meaning short, or as the character l (lowercase letter L), meaning long or double, or as the character L meaning long double. The letter h may be used with the d, i, n, u, o, or x operation to indicate assignment to a location of type short or unsigned short. The letter l may be used with the d, i, n, u, o, or x operation to indicate assignment to a location of type long or unsigned long. The letter l may be used with the e, f, or g operation to indicate assignment to a location of type double rather than type float. The letter L may be used with the e, f, or g operation to indicate assignment to a location of type long double.

4. A required *conversion operation*, expressed (with one exception) as a single character: c, d, e, f, g, i, n, o, p, s, u, x, %, or [. The exception is the [operation, which causes all following characters up to the next] to be part of the conversion specification.

The conversion specifications for fscanf are similar in syntax and meaning to those for fprintf. In a few cases it is possible to use the same format control string for both fscanf and fprintf. However, there are certain differences. The [conversion operation is peculiar to fscanf. On the other hand, fscanf does not admit any precision specification of the kind accepted by fprintf, nor any of the flag characters -, +, *space*, 0, and # that are accepted by fprintf. For fprintf, an explicitly specified field width is a minimum; for fscanf, it is a maximum. Whereas fprintf allows a field width to be specified by a computed argument, indicated by using an asterisk for the field width, fscanf uses the asterisk for another purpose, namely assignment suppression; this is perhaps the most glaring inconsistency of all. It is best to regard the control string syntax for fprintf and fscanf as being only vaguely similar; do not use the documentation for one as a guide to the other.

Except as noted, all conversion operations skip over any initial whitespace before conversion. This initial whitespace is not counted toward the maximum field width. None of the conversion operations normally skips over trailing whitespace characters as a matter of course. Trailing whitespace characters (such as the newline that terminates a line of input) will remain unread unless explicitly matched in the control string. (Doing this may be tricky because a whitespace character in the control string will attempt to match many whitespace character in the input, resulting in an attempt to read beyond a newline character.)

It is not possible to determine directly whether matches of literal character in the control string succeed or fail. It is also not possible to determine directly whether conversion operations involving suppressed assignments succeed or fail. The value returned by these functions reflects only the number of successful assignments performed.

The conversion operations are very complicated. A brief summary is presented in table 15–1; detailed explanations then follows.

Table 15–1: Input conversions (scanf, fscanf, sscanf)

Conversion letter	Size specifier	Argument type	Input format

d	*none*
	h
	l
		`int *`
		`short *`
		`long *`
			[-l+]dd...d

i	*none*
	h
	l
		`int *`
		`short *`
		`long *`
			[–l+][0x]dd...d[1]

u	*none*
	h
	l
		`unsigned *`
		`unsigned short *`
		`unsigned long *`
			[–l+]dd...d

o	*none*
	h
	l
		`unsigned *`
		`unsigned short *`
		`unsigned long *`
			[–l+]dd...d[2]

x	*none*
	h
	l
		`unsigned *`
		`unsigned short *`
		`unsigned long *`
			[–l+][0x]dd...d[3]

c	none	`char *`	a fixed-width sequence of characters
s	none	`char *`	a sequence of non-whitespace characters
p	none	`void **`	a sequence of characters such as output with %p in fprintf.

n	*none*
	h
	l
		`int *`
		`short *`
		`long *`
			none; the number of characters read is stored in the argument

f, e, g	*none* l L		any floating-point constant or decimal integer constant, optionally preceded by – or +
[	none	`char *`	a sequence of characters from a scanning set

[1] The base of the number is determined by the first digits in the same way as for C constants.

[2] The number is assumed to be octal.

[3] The number is assumed to be hexadecimal regardless of the presence of 0x.

The d conversion   Signed decimal conversion is performed. One argument is consumed; it should be of type `int *`, `short *`, or `long *` depending on the size specification.

The format of the number read is the same as expected for the input to the `strtol` function with the value 10 for the `base` argument; that is, a sequence of decimal digits optionally preceded by – or +. If the value expressed by the input is too large to be represented as a signed integer of the appropriate size, then the behavior is undefined.

The i conversion   Signed integer conversion is performed. One argument is consumed; it should be of type `int *`, `short *`, or `long *` depending on the size specification.

The format of the number read is the same as expected for the input to the `strtol` function with the value 0 for the `base` argument; that is, a C *integer-constant* without suffix and optionally preceded by – or +. If the value expressed by the input is too large to be represented as a signed integer of the appropriate size, then the behavior is undefined.

The u conversion   Unsigned decimal conversion is performed. One argument is consumed; it should be of type `unsigned *`, `unsigned short *`, or `unsigned long *` depending on the size specification.

The format of the number read is the same as expected for the input to the `strtol` function with the value 10 for the `base` argument; that is, a sequence of decimal digits optionally preceded by – or +. If the value expressed by the input is too large to be represented as an unsigned integer of the appropriate size, then the behavior is undefined.

The o conversion   Unsigned octal conversion is performed. One argument is consumed; it should be of type `unsigned *`, `unsigned short *`, or `unsigned long *` depending on the size specification.

The format of the number read is the same as expected for the input to the `strtol` function with the value 8 for the `base` argument; that is, a sequence of octal digits optionally preceded by – or +. If the value expressed by the input is too large to be represented as an unsigned integer of the appropriate size, then the behavior is undefined.

The x conversion   Unsigned hexadecimal conversion is performed. One argument is consumed; it should be of type `unsigned *`, `unsigned short *`, or `unsigned long *` depending on the size specification.

The format of the number read is the same as expected for the input to the `strtol` function with the value 8 for the `base` argument; that is, a sequence of hexadecimal digits optionally preceded by – or +. The operation accepts all of the characters `0123456789abcdefABCDEF` as valid hexadecimal digits. If the value expressed by the input is too large to be represented as an unsigned integer of the appropriate size, then the behavior is undefined.

Some C implementations accept the letter X as an equivalent conversion operation.

The c conversion   One or more characters are read. One pointer argument is consumed; it must be of type `char *`. The c conversion operation does not skip over initial whitespace characters.

If no field width is specified, then exactly one character is read unless the input stream is at end-of-file, in which case the conversion operation fails. The character value is assigned to the location indicated by the next pointer argument

If a field width is specified, then the pointer argument is assumed to point to the beginning of an array or characters, and the field width specifies the number of characters to be read; the conversion operation fails if end-of-file is encountered before that many characters have been read. The characters read are stored into successive locations of the array. No extra terminating null is appended to the characters that are read. The size specification is not relevant to the c conversion operation.

The s conversion   A string is read. One pointer argument is consumed; it must be of type char *. The s conversion operation does skip initial whitespace.

Characters are read until end-of-file is reached, until a whitespace character is seen (in which case that character remains unread), or (if a field width was specified) until the maximum number of characters has been read. If end-of-file is encountered before any non-whitespace character is seen, the conversion operation is considered to have failed.

The pointer argument is assumed to point to the beginning of an array of characters. The characters read are stored into successive locations of the array and an extra terminating null is appended to the stored characters. The size specification is not relevant to the s conversion operation. The s conversion operation can be dangerous if no maximum field width is specified because it is always possible for the input length to exceed the storage available in the character array.

The s operation with an explicit field width differs from the c operation with an explicit field width. The c operation does not skip over whitespace characters, and will read exactly as many characters as were specified unless end-of-file is encountered; the s operation skips over initial whitespace characters, will be terminated by a whitespace character after reading in some number of characters that are not whitespace, and will append a null character to the stored characters.

The f, e, and g conversions   Signed decimal floating-point conversion is performed. One pointer argument is consumed; it must be of type float *, double *, or long double *, depending on the size specification.

The format of the number read is the same as expected for the input to the strtod function; that is, a sequence of decimal digits optionally preceded by − or + and optionally containing a decimal point and signed exponent part. (An integer with no decimal point is acceptable.)

The characters read are interpreted as a floating-point number representation and converted to a floating-point number of the specified size. If no digits are read, or at least no digits are read before the letter e or E is seen, then the value is zero. If no digits are seen after the letter e or E, then the exponent part of the decimal representation is assumed to be zero. If the value expressed by the input is too large or too small to be represented as a floating-point number of the appropriate size, then the value HUGE_VAL is returned (with the proper sign) and the value ERANGE is stored in ERRNO. (In implementations that do not conform to ANSI C, the return value and setting of ERRNO are unpredictable.) If the value expressed by the input is not too large or too small but nevertheless cannot be represented exactly as a floating-point number of the appropriate size, then some form of rounding or truncation occurs.

The f, e, E, and g conversion operations are completely identical; any one of them will accept any style of floating-point representation. Some implementations may accept G and E as floating-point conversion letters.

The % conversion   A single percent sign is expected in the input. Because a percent sign is used to indicate the beginning of a conversion specification, it is necessary to write two of them in order to have one matched. No pointer argument is consumed. The assignment suppression flag, field width, and size specification are not relevant to the % conversion operation.

The [conversion   A string is read and one pointer argument of type char * is consumed. The [conversion operation does not skip over initial whitespace characters. The conversion specification indicates exactly what characters may be read as a part of the input field. The [must be followed in the control string by more characters, terminated by]. All the characters up to the] are part of the conversion specification. If the character immediately following the [is the circumflex ^, it has a special meaning as a negation flag; all other characters between the [and], including ^ if it does not immediately follow the initial [, are treated alike. The characters in the control string between the initial [and the terminating], other than the negation flag if it is present, are regarded as a set in the mathematical sense. Note that [may be in the set, but] cannot be. Moreover, ^ can be in the set only if a negation flag is present or if some other character precedes the ^; it is impossible to have a set consisting only of ^ without a negation flag.

Characters are read until end-of-file is reached, until a terminating character is seen (in which case that character remains unread), or (if a field width was specified) until the maximum number of characters has been read. If a negation flag is not present, then a character is a terminating character if it is not in the set; if a negation flag is present, then a character is a terminating character if it is in the set. Looking at the other side of the coin, if no negation flag is present then only characters in the set are read, but if a negation flag is present then only characters not in the set are read.

The pointer argument is assumed to point to the beginning of an array of characters. The characters read are stored into successive locations of the array unless the assignment suppression flag * is present in the conversion specification. If assignment is not suppressed then an extra terminating null is appended to the stored characters. Size specification is not relevant to the [conversion operation.

Like the s conversion, the [conversion operation can be dangerous if no maximum field width is specified because it is always possible for the input length to exceed the storage available in the character array.

References EOF 15.1; fprintf 15.11; stdin 15.4;

15.9 FPUTC, PUTC, PUTCHAR

ANSI C facilities	Traditional and alternate facilities

`#include <stdio.h>`
`int fputc(`
`    int c,`
`    FILE *stream);`
`int putc(`
`    int c,`
`    FILE *stream);`
`int putchar(int c);`
	`#include <stdio.h>`
	`int fputc(`
	`    char c,`
	`    FILE *stream);`
	`int putc(`
	`    char c,`
	`    FILE *stream);`
	`int putchar(char c);`

The function `fputc` takes as arguments a character value and an output stream. It writes the character to the stream and also returns the character as a value of type `int`. Successive calls to `fputc` will write the given characters successively to the output stream. If an error occurs, `fputc` returns EOF instead of the character that was to have been written.

The function `putc` operates like `fputc`, but it is usually implemented as a macro. The argument expressions must not have any side effects because they may be evaluated more than once.

The function `putchar` writes a character to the standard output stream `stdout`. Like `putc`, `putchar` is usually implemented as a macro and is quite efficient. The call `putchar(c)` is equivalent to `putc(c,stdout)`.

References EOF 15.1; stdout 15.4

15.10 FPUTS, PUTS

ANSI C facilities	Traditional and alternate facilities

`#include <stdio.h>`
`int fputs(`
`    const char *s,`
`    FILE *stream);`
`int puts(const char *s);`
	`#include <stdio.h>`
	`int fputs(`
	`    char *s,`
	`    FILE *stream);`
	`int puts(char *s);`

The function `fputs` takes as arguments a null-terminated string and an output stream. It writes to the stream all the characters of the string, not including the terminating null character. If an error occurs, `fputs` returns EOF; otherwise, it returns some other, nonnegative value.

The function `puts` is like `fputs` except:

1. The characters are always written to the stream `stdout`.
2. After the characters in `s` are written out, an additional newline character is written (regardless of whether `s` contained a newline character).

Several UNIX implementations of `fputs` have an error that causes the return value to be indeterminate if `s` is the empty string. Programmers might be alert for that boundary case.

References EOF 15.1; `fputc`, `putc`, `putchar` 15.9; `stdout` 15.4

15.11 FPRINTF, PRINTF, SPRINTF

ANSI C facilities	Traditional and alternate facilities

`#include <stdio.h>`
`int fprintf(`
`    FILE *stream,`
`    const char *format, ... );`
`int printf(`
`    const char *format, ...);`
`int sprintf(`
`    char *s,`
`    const char *format, ...);`
	`#include <stdio.h>`
	`int fprintf(`
	`    FILE *stream,`
	`    char *format, … );`
	`int printf(`
	`    char *format, …);`
	`int sprintf(`
	`    char *s,`
	`    char *format, …);`

The function `fprintf` performs output formatting, sending the output to the stream specified as the first argument. The second argument is a format control string. Additional arguments may be required, depending on the contents of the control string. A series of output characters is generated as directed by the control string; these characters are sent to the specified stream.

The functions `printf` and `sprintf` are related to `fprintf`. `printf` sends the characters to the standard output stream `stdout`, whereas `sprintf` causes the output characters to be stored into the string buffer `s`. In the case of `sprintf`, a final null character is output to `s` after all characters specified by the control string have been output. (It is the programmer's responsibility to ensure that the destination string area is large enough to contain the output generated by the formatting operation.)

The value returned by these functions is EOF if an error occurred during the output operation; otherwise, the result is some value other than EOF. In ANSI C and most current implementations the functions return the number of characters sent to the output stream if no error occurs. In the case of `sprintf`, the count does not include the terminating null character. (ANSI C allows these functions to return any negative value if an error occurs.)

References EOF 15.1; `scanf` 15.8; `stdout` 15.4;

15.11.1 Output Format

The control string is simply text to be copied verbatim, except that the string may contain conversion specifications. (In ANSI C, it is a multibyte character sequence beginning and ending in its initial shift state.) A conversion specification may call for the processing of some number of additional arguments, resulting in a formatted conversion operation that generates output characters not explicitly contained in the control string. There should be exactly the right number of arguments, each of exactly the right type, to satisfy the conversion specifications in the control string; otherwise, the results are unpredictable. If any conversion specification is malformed, then the effects are unpredictable. The conversion specifications for output are similar to those used for input by fscanf and related functions; the differences are discussed in section 15.8.2.

The sequence of characters output for a conversion specification may be conceptually divided into three elements: the *converted value* proper, which reflects the value of the converted argument; the *prefix*, which, if present, is typically +, −, or a space; and the *padding*, which is a sequence of spaces or zero digits added if necessary to increase the width of the output sequence to a specified minimum. The prefix always precedes the converted value. Depending on the conversion specification, the padding may precede the prefix, separate the prefix from the converted value, or follow the converted value. Examples are shown in the figure below; the enclosing boxes show the extent of the output governed by the conversion specification.

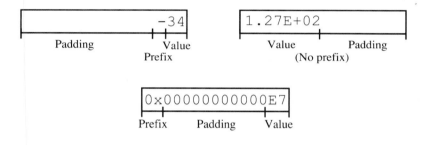

15.11.2 Conversion Specifications

A conversion specification begins with a percent sign, %, and has the following elements in order:

1. Zero or more *flag characters* (−, +, 0, #, or space), which modify the meaning of the conversion operation.
2. An optional *minimum field width*, expressed as an decimal integer constant.
3. An optional *precision specification*, expressed as a period optionally followed by a decimal integer.
4. An optional *size specification*, expressed as one of the letters l, L, or h.
5. The *conversion operation*, a single character from the set c, d, e, E, f, g, G, i, n, o, p, s, u, x, X, and %.

The conversion letter terminates the specification. The size specification letters L and h, and the conversion operations i, p, and n, are available in ANSI C but are rare elsewhere. The conversion specification "%-#012.4hd" is shown below broken into its constituent elements:

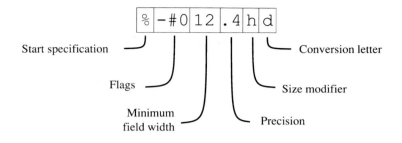

15.11.3 Conversion Flags

The optional flag characters modify the meaning of the main conversion operation:

–	Left-justify the value within the field width .
0	Use 0 for the pad character rather than space.
+	Always produce a sign, either + or –.
space	Always produce either the sign – or a space.
#	Use a variant of the main conversion operation.

The effects of the flag characters are described in more detail below.

The – flag If a minus-sign flag is present, then the converted value will be left-justified within the field; that is, any padding will be placed to the right of the converted value. If no minus sign is present, then the converted value will be right-justified within the field. This flag is relevant only when an explicit minimum field width is specified and the converted value is smaller than that minimum width; otherwise, the value will fill the field without padding.

The 0 flag If a 0 (zero) flag is present, then 0 will be used as the pad character if padding is to be placed to the left of the converted value. The 0 flag is relevant only when an explicit minimum field width is specified and the converted value is smaller than that minimum width. In integer conversions, this flag is superseded by the precision specification.

If no zero-digit flag is present, then a space will be used as the pad character. Space is always used as the pad character if padding is to be placed to the right of the converted value; that is, if the – flag character is present.

The + flag If a + flag is present, then the result of a signed conversion will always begin with a sign; that is, an explicit + will precede a converted positive value. (Negative values are always preceded by – regardless of whether a plus-sign flag is specified.) This flag is relevant only for the conversion operations d, e, E, f, g, G, and i.

The space flag   If a space flag is present and the first character in the converted value resulting from a signed conversion is not a sign (+ or −), then a space will be added before the converted value. The adding of this space on the left is independent of any padding that may be placed to the left or right under control of the − flag character. If both the space and + flags appear in a single conversion specification, the space flag is ignored because the + flag ensures that the converted value will always begin with a sign. This flag is relevant only for the conversion operations d, e, E, f, g, G, and i.

The # flag   If a # flag is present, then an alternate form of the main conversion operation is used. This flag is relevant only for the conversion operations e, E, f, g, G, i, o, x, and X. The modifications implied by the # flag are described in conjunction with the relevant conversion operations.

15.11.4 Minimum Field Width

An optional minimum field width, expressed as an decimal integer constant, may be specified. The constant must be a nonempty sequence of decimal digits that does not begin with a zero digit (which would be taken to be the 0 flag). If the converted value (including prefix) results in fewer characters than the specified field width, then pad characters are used to pad the value to the specified width. If the converted value results in more characters than the specified field width, then the field is expanded to accommodate it without padding.

The field width may also be specified by an asterisk, *, in which case an argument of type int is consumed and specifies the minimum field width. The result of specifying a negative width is unpredictable. For example, the following two calls to printf result in the same output:

```
int width, value;
...
printf("%5d", value);
width = 5;
printf("%*d", width, value);
```

15.11.5 Precision

An optional precision specification may be specified, expressed as a period followed by an optional decimal integer. The precision specification is used to control

1. the minimum number of digits to be printed for d, i, o, u, x, and X conversions
2. the number of digits to the right of the decimal point in e, E, and f conversions
3. the number of significant digits in the g and G conversions
4. the maximum number of characters to be written from a string in the s conversion

If the period appears but the integer is missing, then the integer is assumed to be zero, which usually has a different effect from omitting the entire precision specification.

The precision may also be specified by an asterisk following the period, in which case an argument of type int is consumed and specifies the precision. If both the field width and the precision are specified with asterisks, then the field width argument precedes the precision argument.

15.11.6 Size Specification

An optional size modifier, one of the letters l, L, or h, may precede some conversion operations. The letter l in conjunction with the conversion operations d, i, o, u, x, and X, indicates that the conversion argument has type long or unsigned long. In conjunction with the n conversion, it specifies that the argument has type long *.

The letter h in conjunction with the conversion operations d, i, o, u, x, and X, indicates that the conversion argument has type short or unsigned short. That is, although the argument would have been converted to int or unsigned by the argument promotions, it should be converted to short or unsigned short before conversion. In conjunction with the n conversion, the h modifier specifies that the argument has type short *. The h size modifier is available in ANSI C but is rare elsewhere.

The letter L in conjunction with the conversion operations e, E, f, F, g, and G, indicates that the argument has type long double. The L size modifier is available in ANSI C but is rare elsewhere.

15.11.7 Conversion Operations

The conversion operation is expressed as a single character: c, d, e, E, f, g, G, i, n, o, p, s, u, x, X, or %. The specified conversion determines the permitted flag and size specification characters, the expected argument type, and how the output looks. Table 15–2 summarizes the conversion operations. Each operation is then discussed individually.

The d and i conversions   Signed decimal conversion is performed. The argument should be of type int if no size modifier is used, type short if h is used, or type long if l is used. The i operator is present ANSI C for compatibility with fscanf; it is recognized on output for uniformity, where it is identical to the d operator.

The converted value consists of a sequence of decimal digits that represents the absolute value of the argument. This sequence is as short as possible but not shorter than the specified precision. The converted value will have leading zeros if necessary to satisfy the precision specification; these leading zeros are independent of any padding, which might also introduce leading zeros. If the precision is 1 (the default), then the converted value will not have a leading 0 unless the argument is 0, in which case a single 0 is output. If the precision is 0 and the argument is 0, then the converted value is empty (the null string).

Table 15–2: Output conversion specifications

Conver–sion	Defined flags – + # 0 space	Size modifier	Argument type	Def. prc[1]	Output
d, i[2]	– + 0 space	none	int	1	dd...d
		h	short		–dd...d
		l	long		+dd...d
u	– + 0 space	none	unsigned int	1	dd...d
		h	unsigned short		
		l	unsigned long		
o	– + # 0 space	none	unsigned int	1	oo...o
		h	unsigned short		0oo...o
		l	unsigned long		
x, X	– + # 0 space	none	unsigned int	1	hh...h
		h	unsigned short		0xhh...h
		l	unsigned long		0Xhh...h
f	– + # 0 space	none	double	6	d...d.d...d
		L	long double		–d...d.d...d
					+d...d.d...d
e, E	– + # 0 space	none	double	6	d.d...de+dd
		L	long double		–d.d...dE–dd
g, G	– + # 0 space	none	double	6	*like* e,E, *or* f
		L	long double		
c	–		none	int	1	c
s	–		none	char *	∞	cc...c
p[2]	*impl. defined*	none	void *	1	*impl. defined*
n[2]		none	int *	*n/a*	*none*
		h	short *		
		l	long *		
%		none	none	*n/a*	%

[1]   Default precision, if none is specified.
[2]   Available in ANSI C; may be rare elsewhere. i and d are equivalent on output.

     The prefix is computed as follows. If the argument is negative, the prefix is a minus sign. If the argument is nonnegative and the + flag is specified, then the prefix is a plus sign. If the argument is nonnegative, the space flag is specified, and the + flag is not specified, then the prefix is a space. Otherwise, the prefix is empty. The # flag is not relevant to the d and i conversions.

Examples of the d conversion

Sample format	Sample output Value = 45	Sample output Value = –45
%12d	45	-45
%012d	000000000045	-00000000045
% 012d	00000000045	-00000000045
%+12d	+45	-45
%+012d	+00000000045	-00000000045
%-12d	45	-45
%- 12d	45	-45
%-+12d	+45	-45
%12.4d	0045	-0045
%-12.4d	0045	-0045

The u conversion   Unsigned decimal conversion is performed. The argument should be of type unsigned if no size modifier is used, type unsigned short if h is used, or type unsigned long if l is used.

The converted value consists of a sequence of decimal digits that represents the value of the argument. This sequence is as short as possible but not shorter than the specified precision. The converted value will have leading zeros if necessary to satisfy the precision specification; these leading zeros are independent of any padding, which might also introduce leading zeros (see below). If the precision is 1 (the default), then the converted value will not have a leading 0 unless the argument is 0, in which case a single 0 is output. If the precision is 0 and the argument is 0, then the converted value is empty (the null string). The prefix is always empty. The +, *space*, and # flags are not relevant to the u conversion operation.

Examples of the u conversion

Sample format	Sample output Value = 45	Sample output Value = –45
%14u	45	4294967251
%014u	00000000000045	00004294967251
%#14u	45	4294967251
%#014u	00000000000045	00004294967251
%-14u	45	4294967251
%-#14u	45	4294967251
%14.4u	0045	4294967251
%-14.4u	0045	4294967251

The o Conversion   Unsigned octal conversion is performed. The argument should be of type unsigned if no size modifier is used, type unsigned short if h is used, or type unsigned long if l is used.

The converted value consists of a sequence of octal digits that represents the value of the argument. This sequence is as short as possible but not shorter than the specified precision. The converted value will have leading zeros if necessary to satisfy the precision specification; these leading zeros are independent of any padding, which might also introduce leading zeros. If the precision is 1 (the default), then the converted value will not have a leading 0 unless the argument is 0, in which case a single 0 is output. If the precision is 0 and the argument is 0, then the converted value is empty (the null string). If the # flag is present, then the prefix is 0. If the # flag is not present, then the prefix is empty. The + and *space* flags are not relevant to the o conversion operation.

Examples of the o conversion

Sample format	Sample output Value = 45	Sample output Value = –45
%14o	55	37777777723
%014o	00000000000055	00037777777723
%#14o	055	037777777723
%#014o	00000000000055	00037777777723
%-14o	55	37777777723
%-#14o	055	037777777723
%14.4o	0055	37777777723
%-#14.4o	00055	037777777723

The x and X conversions   Unsigned hexadecimal conversion is performed. The argument should be of type unsigned if no size modifier is used, type unsigned short if h is used, or type unsigned long if l is used.

Examples of the x and X conversions

Sample format	Sample output Value = 45	Sample output Value = –45
%12x	2d	fffffd3
%012x	00000000002d	0000fffffd3
%#12X	0X2D	0XFFFFFD3
%#012X	0X000000002D	0X00FFFFFD3
%-12x	2d	fffffd3
%-#12x	0x2d	0xfffffd3
%12.4x	002d	fffffd3
%-#12.4x	0x002d	fffffd3

The converted value consists of a sequence of decimal digits that represents the value of the argument. This sequence is as short as possible but not shorter than the specified precision. The x operation uses 0123456789abcdef as digits, whereas the X operation uses 0123456789ABCDEF. The converted value will have leading zeros if necessary to satisfy the precision specification; these leading zeros are independent of any padding, which might also introduce leading zeros (see below). If the precision is 1, then the converted value will not have a leading 0 unless the argument is 0, in which case a single 0 is output. If the precision is 0 and the argument is 0, then the converted value is empty (the null string). If no precision is specified, then a precision of 1 is assumed.

If the # flag is present, then the prefix is 0x (for the x operation) or 0X (for the X operation). If the # flag is not present, then the prefix is empty. The + and space flags are not relevant to the x conversion operation.

The c conversion   The argument is printed as a character. One argument is consumed, which should be of type `int` and is converted to type `unsigned char`. The converted value is the single character specified by the argument. The prefix is always empty. The +, *space*, and # flags, the precision specification, and the size specification are not relevant to the c conversion operation.

Examples of the c conversion

Sample format	Sample output Value = '*'
%12c	*
%012c	00000000000*
%-12c	*

The s conversion   The argument is printed as a string. One argument is consumed, which should be of type `char *`. If no precision specification is given, then the converted value is the sequence of characters in the string argument up to but not including the terminating null character. If a precision specification p is given, then the converted value is the first p characters of the string, or up to but not including the terminating null character, whichever is shorter. The prefix is always empty. The +, space, and # flags and the l (long size) specification are not relevant to the s conversion.

Examples of the s conversion

Sample format	Sample output Value = "zap"	Sample output Value = "longish"
%12s	zap	longish
%12.5s	zap	longi
%012s	000000000zap	00000longish
%-12s	zap	longish

The p conversion   The argument must have type `void *` and it is printed in an implementation-defined format. For most computers, this will probably be the same as the format produced by the o, x, or X conversions. This conversion operator is found in ANSI C but is otherwise not common.

The n conversion   The argument must have type `int *` if no size modifier is used, type `long *` if the l specifier is used, or type `short *` if the h specifier is used. Instead of outputing characters, this conversion operator causes the number of characters output so far to be written into the designated integer. This conversion operator is found in ANSI C but is otherwise not common.

The f conversion   Signed decimal floating-point conversion is performed. One argument is consumed, which should be of type `double` if no size modifier is used or type `long double` if L is used. If an argument of type `float` is supplied, it is converted to type `double` by the usual argument promotions, so it does work to use `%f` to print a number of type `float`.

The converted value consists of a sequence of decimal digits, possibly with an embedded decimal point, that represents the approximate absolute value of the argument. At least one digit appears before the decimal point. The precision specifies the number of digits to appear after the decimal point. If the precision is 0, then no digits appear after the decimal point; moreover, the decimal point itself also does not appear unless the # flag is present. If no precision is specified, then a precision of 6 is assumed.

If the floating-point value cannot be represented exactly in the number of digits produced, then the converted value should be the result of rounding the exact floating-point value to the number of decimal places produced. (Some C implementations do not perform correct rounding in all cases.)

The prefix is computed as follows. If the argument is negative, the prefix is a minus sign. If the argument is nonnegative and the + flag is specified, then the prefix is a plus sign. If the argument is nonnegative, the *space* flag is specified, and the + flag is not specified, then the prefix is a space. Otherwise, the prefix is empty.

Examples of the f conversion

Sample format	Sample output Value = 12.678	Sample output Value = −12.678
`%10.2f`	12.68	−12.68
`%010.2f`	000000012.68	−00000012.68
`% 010.2f`	00000012.68	−00000012.68
`%+10.2f`	+12.68	−12.68
`%+010.2f`	+00000012.68	−00000012.68
`%-10.2f`	12.68	−12.68
`%- 10.2f`	12.68	−12.68
`%-+10.4f`	+12.6780	−12.6780

The e and E conversions   Signed decimal floating-point conversion is performed. One argument is consumed, which should be of type `double` if no size specifier is used or type `long double` if L is used. An argument of type `float` is permitted, as for the f conversion. The e conversion is described; the E conversion differs only in that the letter E appears whenever e appears in the e conversion.

The converted value consists of a decimal digit, then possibly a decimal point and more decimal digits, then the letter e, then a plus sign or minus sign, then finally at least two more decimal digits. Unless the value is zero, the part before the letter e represents a value between 1.0 and 9.99…. The part after the letter e represents an exponent value as a signed decimal integer. The value of the first part, multiplied by 10 raised to the value of the second part, is approximately equal to the absolute value of the argument. The number of exponent digits is the same for all values and is the maximum number needed to represent the range of the implementation's floating-point types.

Examples of e and E conversions

Sample format	Sample output Value = 12.678	Sample output Value = −12.678
%10.2e	1.27e+01	-1.27e+01
%010.2e	00001.27e+01	-0001.27e+01
% 010.2e	0001.27e+01	-0001.27e+01
%+10.2E	+1.27E+01	-1.27E+01
%+010.2E	+0001.27E+01	-0001.27E+01
%-10.2e	1.27e+01	-1.27e+01
%- 10.2e	1.27e+01	-1.27e+01
%-+10.2e	+1.27e+01	-1.27e+01

The precision specifies the number of digits to appear after the decimal point; if not supplied, then 6 is assumed. If the precision is 0, then no digits appear after the decimal point; moreover, the decimal point itself also does not appear unless the # flag is present. If the floating-point value cannot be represented exactly in the number of digits produced, then the converted value is obtained by rounding the exact floating-point value. The prefix is computed as for the f conversion.

The g and G conversions   Signed decimal floating-point conversion is performed. One argument is consumed, which should be of type double if no size specifier is used, or type long double if L is used. An argument of type float is permitted, as for the f conversion. Only the g conversion operator is discussed below; the G operation is identical except that wherever g uses e conversion, G uses E conversion. If the specified precision is less than 1, then a precision of 1 is used. If no precision is specified, then a precision of 6 is assumed.

The g conversion begins the same as either the f or e conversions; which one is selected depends on the value to be converted. The ANSI C specification says that the e conversion is used only if the exponent resulting from the e conversion is less than −4 or greater than or equal to the specified precision. Some other implementations use the e conversion if the exponent is less than −3 or strictly greater than the specified precision.

The converted value (whether by f or e) is then further modified by stripping off trailing zeros to the right of the decimal point. If the result has no digits after the decimal point, then the decimal point also is removed. If the # flag is present, this stripping of zeros and the decimal point does not occur.

The prefix is computed as for the f and e conversions.

The % conversion   A single percent sign is printed. Because a percent sign is used to indicate the beginning of a conversion specification, it is necessary to write two of them in order to have one printed. No arguments are consumed and the prefix is empty.

ANSI C does not permit any flag characters, minimum width, precision, or size modifiers to be present; the complete conversion specification must be %%. However, other C implementations perform padding just as for any other conversion operation; for example, the conversion specification `%05%` prints `0000%` in these implementations. The `+`, *space*, and `#` flags, the precision specification, and the size specifications are never relevant to the `%` conversion operation.

15.12 VFPRINTF, VPRINTF, VSPRINTF

ANSI C facilities	Traditional and alternate facilities
`#include <stdarg.h>`	`#include <varargs.h>`
`#include <stdio.h>`	`#include <stdio.h>`
`int vfprintf(`	`int vfprintf(`
`    FILE *stream,`	`    FILE *stream,`
`    const char *format,`	`    char *format,`
`    va_list arg);`	`    va_list arg);`
`int vprintf(`	`int vprintf(`
`    const char *format,`	`    char *format,`
`    va_list arg);`	`    va_list arg);`
`int vsprintf(`	`int vsprintf(`
`    char *s,`	`    char *s,`
`    const char *format,`	`    char *format,`
`    char *arg);`	`    char *arg);`

The functions `vfprintf`, `vprintf`, and `vscanf` are the same as the functions `fprintf`, `printf`, and `sprintf`, respectively, except that the extra arguments are given as a variable argument list as defined by the `vararg` facility (section 11.4). They were adopted into ANSI C from System V UNIX. These functions are useful when the programmer wants to define his own variable-argument functions that use the formatted output facilities. The functions do not invoke the `va_end` facility.

As an example, suppose the programmer wanted to write a general function, `trace`, that printed the name of a function and its arguments. Any function to be traced would begin with a call to trace of the form:

```
trace(name,format,parm1,parm2,…,parmN)
```

where `name` is the name of the function being called and `format` is a format string suitable for printing the argument values `parm1`, `parm2`, ..., `parmN`. For example, here is what a function `f` would look like with a call to `trace`:

```
int f(x,y)
    int x;
    double y;
{
    trace("f","x=%d, y=%f", x, y);
    …
}
```

A possible implementation of trace is given below for traditional C:

```
#include <varargs.h>
#include <stdio.h>
extern global_trace_enabled;
void trace(va_alist)
    va_dcl
{
    va_list args;
    char *name;
    char *format;
    va_start(args);
    name = va_arg(args,char *);
    format = va_arg(args,char *);
    fprintf(stderr,"--> entering %s(", name);
    vfprintf(stderr, format, args);
    fprintf(stderr,")\n");
    va_end(args);
}
```

15.13 FREAD, FWRITE

ANSI C facilities	Traditional and alternate facilities

`#include <stdio.h>`
`size_t fread(`
    `void *ptr,`
    `size_t element_size,`
    `size_t count,`
    `FILE *stream);`
`size_t fwrite(`
    `void *ptr,`
    `size_t element_size,`
    `size_t count,`
    `FILE *stream);`
	`#include <stdio.h>`
	`int fread(`
	    `char *ptr,`
	    `unsigned element_size,`
	    `int count,`
	    `FILE *stream);`
	`int fwrite(`
	    `char *ptr,`
	    `unsigned element_size,`
	    `int count,`
	    `FILE *stream);`

The functions fread and fwrite perform input and output, respectively, to binary files. In both cases, stream is the input or output stream and ptr is a pointer to an array of count elements, each of which is element_size characters long.

The function fread reads up to count elements of the indicated size from the input stream into the specified array. The actual number of items read is returned by fread; it may be less than count if end-of-file is encountered. If an error is encountered, zero is returned. The feof or ferror facilities may be used to determine whether an error or an immediate end-of-file caused zero to be returned. If either count or element_size is zero, no data are transferred and zero is returned. As a simple example, the following program reads an input file containing objects of a structure type and prints the number of such objects read. The program depends on the exit function to close the input file:

```
/* Count the number of elements
    of type "struct S" in file "in.dat" */
#include <stdio.h>
static char *FileName = "in.dat";
struct S { int a,b; double d; char str[103]; };

main()
{
    struct S buffer;
    int items_read = 0;
    FILE *in_file = fopen(FileName,"r");
    if (in_file == NULL)
    { fprintf(stderr,"?Couldn't open %s\n",FileName);
      exit(1); }
    while (fread((char *) &buffer,
          sizeof(struct S), 1, in_file) == 1)
       items_read++;
    if (ferror(in_file))
       { fprintf(stderr,"?Read error, file %s record %d\n",
          FileName,items_read+1); exit(1); }
    printf("Finished; %d elements read\n",items_read);
    exit(0);
}
```

The function `fwrite` writes `count` elements of size `element_size` from the specified array. The actual number of items written is returned by `fwrite`; it will be the same as `count` unless an error occurs.

References `exit` 19.3; `feof`, `ferror` 15.14; `fseek`, `ftell` 15.5

15.14 FEOF, FERROR, CLEARERR

ANSI C facilities	Traditional and alternate facilities
`#include <stdio.h>`	`#include <stdio.h>`
	`int feof(FILE *stream);`
	`int ferror(FILE *stream);`
	`void clearerr(FILE *stream);`

The function `feof` takes takes as its argument an input stream. If end-of-file has been detected while reading from the input stream, then a nonzero value is returned; otherwise, zero is returned. Note that even if there are no more characters in the stream to be read, `feof` will not signal end-of-file unless and until an attempt is made to read "past" the last character. The function is normally used after an input operation has signaled a failure.

The function `ferror` returns the error status of a stream. If an error has occurred while reading from or writing to the stream, then `ferror` returns a nonzero value;

otherwise, zero is returned. Once an error has occurred for a given stream, repeated calls
to `ferror` will continue to report an error unless `clearerr` is used to explicitly reset
the error indication. Closing the stream, as with `fclose`, will also reset the error
indication.

The function `clearerr` resets any error and end-of-file indication on the specified
stream; subsequent calls on `ferror` will report that no error has occurred for that stream
unless and until another error occurs.

15.15 REMOVE, RENAME

ANSI C facilities	Traditional and alternate facilities

`#include <stdio.h>`
`int rename(`
`    const char *oldname,`
`    const char *newname);`
`int remove(char *filename);`
	`#include <stdio.h>`
	`int rename(`
	`    const char *oldname,`
	`    const char *newname);`

The `remove` function removes or deletes the named file; it returns zero if the operation
succeeds and a nonzero value if it does not. The string pointed to by filename is not
altered. Implementations may differ in the details of what "remove" or "delete" actually
mean, but it should not be possible for a program to open a file it has deleted. If the file
is open or if the file does not exist, then the action of `remove` is implementation-defined.
This function is not present in traditional C; instead, a UNIX-specific `unlink` function
is commonly provided.

The `rename` function changes the name of `oldname` to `newname`; it returns zero
if the operation succeeds and a nonzero value if it does not. The strings pointed to by
`oldname` and `newname` are not altered. If `oldname` names an open or nonexistent
file, or if `newname` names a file that already exists, then the action of `rename` is
implementation-defined.

15.16 TMPFILE, TMPNAM, MKTEMP

ANSI C facilities	Traditional and alternate facilities

`#include <stdio.h>`
`FILE *tmpfile(void);`
`char *tmpnam(char *buf);`
`#define L_tmpnam …`
`#define TMP_MAX …`
	`#include <stdio.h>`
	`FILE *tmpfile(void);`
	`char *tmpnam(char *buf);`
	`#define L_tmpnam …`
	`char *mktemp(char *buf);`

The function `tmpfile` creates a new file and opens it using `fopen` mode `"w+"`
(`"w+b"` in ANSI C). A file pointer for the new file is returned if the operation succeeds,
or a null pointer if it fails. The intent is that the new file be used only during the current
program's execution. The file is deleted when it is closed or upon program termination.

After writing data to the file, the programmer can use the `rewind` function to reposition the file at its beginning for reading.

The function `tmpnam` is used to create new file names that do not conflict with other file names currently in use; the programmer can then open a new file with that name using the full generality of `fopen`. The files so created are not "temporary"; they are not deleted automatically upon program termination. If `buf` is NULL, `tmpnam` returns a pointer to the new file name string; the string may be altered by subsequent calls to `tmpnam`. If `buf` is not NULL it must point to an array of not less than `L_tmpnam` characters; `tmpnam` will copy the new file name string into that array and return `buf`. If `tmpnam` fails, it returns a null pointer. ANSI C defines the value `TMP_MAX` to be the number of successive calls to `tmpnam` that will generate unique names; it must be at least 25.

The function `mktemp` is like `tmpnam` except that `buf` (the "template") must point to a string with six trailing X characters, which will be overwritten with other letters or digits to form a unique file name. The value `buf` is returned. Successive calls to `mktemp` should specify different templates to ensure unique names. UNIX implementations often substitute the program's process identification for XXXXXX. `mktemp` is not found in ANSI C.

An example of a common but poor programming practice in C is to write

```
ptr = fopen(mktemp("/tmp/abcXXXXXX"),"w+");
```

This idiom will fail if the string constant is not modifiable. The programmer also loses the ability to reference the file name string. It is better and no less efficient to write

```
char filename[]="/tmp/abcXXXXXX";
ptr = fopen(mktemp(filename),"w+");
```

16

Storage Allocation

Chapter summary

Name	Section	Name	Section	Name	Section
calloc	16.1	free	16.2	realloc	16.3
cfree	16.2	malloc	16.1	relalloc	16.3
clalloc	16.1	mlalloc	16.1		

The storage allocation facilities provide a simple form of heap memory management that allows a program to repeatedly request allocation of a "fresh" region of memory and perhaps later to deallocate such a region when it is no longer needed. Explicitly deallocated regions are recycled by the storage manager for satisfaction of further allocation requests.

When a region of memory is allocated in response to a request, a pointer to the region is returned to the caller. This pointer will be of type char * (void * in ANSI C) but is guaranteed to be properly aligned for any data type. The caller may then use a cast operator to convert this pointer to another pointer type.

In ANSI C the facilities described in this section are declared in the header file stdlib.h. In other C implementations there is typically no associated header file, and the programmer must declare the facilities.

16.1 MALLOC, CALLOC, MLALLOC, CLALLOC

ANSI C facilities	Traditional and alternate facilities

`#include <stdlib.h>`
`void *malloc(size_t size);`
`void *calloc(`
`    size_t elt_count,`
`    size_t elt_size);`
	`char *malloc(unsigned size);`
	`char *calloc(`
	`    unsigned elt_count,`
	`    unsigned elt_size);`
	`char *mlalloc(`
	`    unsigned long size);`
	`char *clalloc(`
	`    unsigned long elt_count,`
	`    unsigned long elt_size);`

The function `malloc` allocates a region of memory large enough to hold an object whose size (as measured by the `sizeof` operator) is `size`. A pointer to the first element of the region is returned. If it is impossible for some reason to perform the requested allocation, a null pointer is returned. If the requested size is 0, either a null pointer or an implementation-defined unique pointer is returned, at the implementation's discretion. The region of memory is not specially initialized in any way, and the caller must assume that it will contain garbage information.

The function `calloc` allocates a region of memory large enough to hold an array of `elt_count` elements, each of size `elt_size` (typically given by the `sizeof` operator). The region of memory is set to zero, and a pointer to the first element of the region is returned. If it is impossible for some reason to perform the requested allocation, or if `elt_count` or `elt_size` is zero, then the return value is the same as for `malloc`. Programmers should note that memory cleared in this fashion and then treated as a floating-point value may not be the same as 0.0.

The function `mlalloc` is just like `malloc`, except that its arguments are of type `unsigned long int` rather than `unsigned int`. In some C implementations it is possible to allocate memory regions so large that numbers of type `unsigned int` are not large enough to specify them. This function is not provided in ANSI C, because the use of type `size_t` for the parameter of `malloc` avoids the problem. Similarly, the function `clalloc` is just like `calloc`, except that its arguments are of type `unsigned long int` rather than unsigned int.

The caller of an allocation routine will typically cast the result pointer to an appropriate pointer type. In the following example, we assume that T is some object type that we wish to allocate dynamically; it might be a structure, array, or even a character:

```
T *NewObject()
{
    T *objptr = (T *) malloc(sizeof(T));
    if (objptr==NULL)
        printf("NewObject: ran out of memory!\n");
    return objptr;
}
```

16.2 FREE, CFREE

ANSI C facilities	Traditional and alternate facilities
`#include <stdlib.h>` `void free(void *ptr);`	`void free(char *ptr);` `void cfree(char *ptr);`

The function `free` deallocates a region of memory previously allocated by `malloc`, `mlalloc`, `realloc` (section 16.3), or `relalloc`. The argument to `free` must be a pointer that is equivalent (except for possible intermediate type casting) to a pointer previously returned by the allocation routine. (If the argument to `free` is a null pointer then no action should occur, but this is known to cause trouble in some C implementations.) Once a region of memory has been explicitly freed it must not be used for any other purpose.

The function `cfree` deallocates a region of memory previously allocated by `calloc` or `clalloc`. In ANSI C, `free` is used to deallocate storage returned by `calloc`.

16.3 REALLOC, RELALLOC

ANSI C facilities	Traditional and alternate facilities

`#include <stdlib.h>`
`void *realloc(`
   `void *ptr,`
   `size_t size);`
	`char *realloc(`
	   `char *ptr,`
	   `unsigned size);`
	`char *relalloc(`
	   `char *ptr,`
	   `unsigned long size);`

The function `realloc` takes a pointer to memory region previously allocated by one of the standard functions and changes its size while preserving its contents. If necessary, the contents are copied to a new memory region. A pointer to the (possibly new) memory region is returned. If the request cannot be satisfied, a null pointer is returned and the old region is not disturbed.

If the first argument to `realloc` is a null pointer, then the function behaves like `malloc` (section 16.1). If `ptr` is not null and size is zero, `realloc` returns a null pointer and the old region is deallocated. If the new size is smaller than the old size, then some of the old contents at the end of the old region will be discarded. If the new size is larger than the old size, then all of the old contents are preserved and new space is added at the end; the new space is not specially initialized in any way, and the caller must assume that it contains garbage information. Whenever `realloc` returns a pointer that is different from its first argument the programmer should assume that the old region of memory was deallocated and should not be used.

The function `relalloc` behaves like `relalloc` except that the `size` argument has type `unsigned long int` instead of `unsigned int`. This function is not present in ANSI C, in which the `size` argument to `realloc` has type `size_t`.

Below is shown a typical use of `realloc` to expand the dynamic array `samples`. (The elements of such an array must be referenced using subscript expressions; any pointers into the array could be invalidated by the call to `realloc`.)

```
#define SAMPLE_INCREMENT 100
int sample_limit = 0; /* Maximum size of current array */
int sample_count = 0; /* Number of elements now in array */
double *samples = NULL;

int AddSample( double new_sample )
    /* Add an element to the end of the array */
{
    if (sample_count == sample_limit) {
        sample_limit += SAMPLE_INCREMENT;
        samples = (double *)
            realloc((char *)samples,
                    sample_limit * sizeof(double));
        if (samples == NULL) {
            fprintf(stderr,"Out of memory\n");
            return 0;
        }
    }
    samples[sample_count++] = new_sample;
    return sample_count;
}
```

17

Mathematical Functions

Chapter summary

Name	Section	Name	Section	Name	Section
abs	17.1	fabs	17.2	modf	17.5
acos	17.9	floor	17.3	pow	17.6
asin	17.9	fmod	17.3	rand	17.7
atan	17.9	frexp	17.5	sin	17.8
atan2	17.9	HUGE_VAL	17.0	sinh	17.10
ceil	17.3	labs	17.1	sqrt	17.6
cos	17.8	ldexp	17.5	srand	17.7
cosh	17.10	ldiv	17.1	tan	17.8
div	17.1	log	17.4	tanh	17.10
exp	17.4	log10	17.4		

Most of the facilities described in this section are declared by the library header file math.h, although in ANSI C a few of the more common facilities are in stdlib.h. All of the operations on floating-point numbers are defined only for arguments of type double, because of the rule that all actual function arguments of type float are converted to type double before the call is performed. In ANSI C this convention is maintained for compatibility.

Two general kinds of errors are possible with the mathematical functions, although older C implementations may not handle them consistently. When an input argument lies outside the domain over which the function is defined, a *domain error* occurs. The variable errno (section 11.2) is set to the value EDOM and the function returns an implementation-defined value. Zero is the traditional error return value but some implementations may have better choices, such as special "not a number" values. (System V UNIX has a more elaborate mechanism, matherr.)

If the result of a function is too large in magnitude to be represented as a value of the function's return type, then a *range error* occurs. When this happens, `errno` should be set to the value `ERANGE` and the function should return the largest representable floating-point value with the same sign as the correct result. In ANSI C this is the value of the macro `HUGE_VAL`; in UNIX System V it is `HUGE`.

If the result of a function is too small in magnitude to be represented, then the function should return zero; whether `errno` is also set to `ERANGE` is left to the discretion of the implementation.

17.1 ABS, LABS, DIV, LDIV

ANSI C facilities	Traditional and alternate facilities
`#include <stdlib.h>`	`#include <math.h>`
`int abs(int x);`	`int abs(int x);`
`long labs(long int x);`	`long labs(long x);`
`typedef … div_t;`	
`typedef … ldiv_t;`	
`div_t div(int n,int d);`	
`ldiv_t ldiv(long n,long d);`	

The four functions in this section are integer arithmetic functions, defined in `stdlib.h` in ANSI C and in `math.h` in traditional C. The functions `abs`, `fabs` (section 17.2), and `labs` all return the absolute value of their arguments. The argument and the result are both of type `int` for `abs`, of type `double` for `fabs`, and of type `long int` for `labs`. The absolute value functions are so easy to implement that some compilers may treat them as built-in functions; this is permitted in ANSI C.

The functions `div` and `ldiv` are found in ANSI C but are otherwise not common in C implementations. They compute simultaneously the quotient and remainder of the division of n by d. The type `div_t` is a structure containing two components, `quot` and `rem` (in any order), both of type `int`. The type `ldiv_t` is also a structure with components `quot` and `rem`, both of type `long int`. The returned quotient `quot` has the same sign as `n/d`, and its magnitude is the largest integer not greater than `abs(n/d)`. The remainder `rem` is such that `quot*d+rem` equals n. The behavior of the functions when d is zero, or when `n/d` is not representable, is undefined (not necessarily a domain error) to allow for the most efficient implementation.

17.2 FABS

ANSI C facilities	Traditional and alternate facilities
`#include <math.h>`	`#include <math.h>`
`double fabs(double x)`	`double fabs(double x)`

The `fabs` function computes the absolute value. In ANSI C, it is defined in `math.h` rather than `stdlib.h`, where the other absolute value functions are defined.

17.3 CEIL, FLOOR, FMOD

ANSI C facilities	Traditional and alternate facilities
`#include <math.h>`	`#include <math.h>`
`double ceil(double x);`	`double ceil(double x);`
`double floor(double x);`	`double floor(double x);`
`double fmod(`	`double fmod(`
`    double x,`	`    double x,`
`    double y);`	`    double y);`

The function `ceil` returns the smallest floating-point number not less than x whose value is an exact mathematical integer. If the x is already an integer, it is returned. Similarly, `floor` returns the largest floating-point number not greater than x whose value is an exact mathematical integer.

The function `fmod` returns an approximation to the mathematical value f such that f has the same sign as x, the absolute value of f is less than the absolute value of y, and there exists an integer k such that $k*y+f$ equals x. If y is zero, an ANSI C conforming implementation may generate a domain error or may return 0; in some traditional C implementations, x is returned in this case. If the quotient x/y cannot be represented, the result is undefined.

The function `fmod` should not be confused with `modf` (section 17.5), a function that extracts the fractional and integer parts of a floating-point number.

17.4 EXP, LOG, LOG10

ANSI C facilities	Traditional and alternate facilities
`#include <math.h>`	`#include <math.h>`
`double exp(double x);`	`double exp(double x);`
`double log(double x);`	`double log(double x);`
`double log10(double x);`	`double log10(double x);`

The function `exp` computes the exponential function of x; that is, e^x, where e is the base of the natural logarithms. A range error can occur for large arguments.

The function `log` computes the natural logarithm function of x. If x is negative, a domain error occurs. If x is zero or close to zero, a range error may occur (toward minus infinity). Some traditional C implementations treat zero as a domain error, and some implementations name this function `ln`.

The function `log10` computes the base-10 logarithm function. The conditions causing domain and range errors are the same as for the function `log`.

17.5 FREXP, LDEXP, MODF

ANSI C facilities	Traditional and alternate facilities

`#include <math.h>`
`double frexp(`
`    double x,`
`    int *nptr);`
`double ldexp(`
`    double x,`
`    int n);`
`double modf(`
`    double x,`
`    double *nptr);`
	`#include <math.h>`
	`double frexp(`
	`    double x,`
	`    int *nptr);`
	`double ldexp(`
	`    double x,`
	`    int n);`
	`double modf(`
	`    double x,`
	`    double *nptr);`

The function `frexp` splits a floating-point number into a fraction f and an exponent n, such that either f is 0.0 or $0.5 \le |f| < 1.0$, and $f*2^n$ is equal to x. The fraction f is returned, and as a side effect the exponent n is stored into the place pointed to by `nptr`. If x is zero then both returned values will be zero.

The function `ldexp` is the inverse of `frexp`; it computes the value $x*2^n$. A range error may occur.

The function `modf` splits a floating-point number into a fractional part f and an integer part n, such that $|f| < 1.0$ and $f+n$ is equal to x. Both f and n will have the same sign as x. The fractional part f is returned, and as a side effect the integer part n is stored as a floating-point number into the object pointed to by `nptr`. The name `modf` is a misnomer; the value it computes is properly called a remainder.

The function `modf` should not be confused with `fmod` (section 17.3), a function that computes the remainder from dividing one floating-point number by another. Some UNIX implementations are reported to define `modf` differently; check your local library documentation.

17.6 POW, SQRT

ANSI C facilities	Traditional and alternate facilities

`#include <math.h>`
`double pow(`
`    double x,`
`    double y);`
`double sqrt(double x);`
	`#include <math.h>`
	`double pow(`
	`    double x,`
	`    double y);`
	`double sqrt(double x);`

The function `pow` computes x^y. When x is nonzero and y is zero, the result is 1.0. When x is zero and y is positive, the result is zero. Domain errors occur if x is negative and y is not an exact integer, or if x is zero and y is nonpositive. Range errors may also occur.

The function `sqrt` computes the nonnegative square root of `x`. A domain error occurs if `x` is negative. Implementations that support the concept of a negative floating-point zero may return that number as the square root of itself, while still recording a domain error.

17.7 RAND, SRAND

ANSI C facilities	Traditional and alternate facilities

`#include <stdlib.h>`
`int rand(void);`
`void srand(unsigned seed);`
`#define RAND_MAX …`
	`#include <math.h>`
	`int rand(void);`
	`void srand(int seed);`

Successive calls to `rand` return integer values in the range 0 to the largest representable positive value of type `int` (inclusive) that are the successive results of a pseudo-random-number generator. In ANSI C the facility is defined in `stdlib.h`, and the upper bound of the range of `rand` is given by RAND_MAX, which will be at least 32767.

The function `srand` may be used to initialize the pseudo-random-number generator that is used to generate successive values for calls to `rand`. After a call to `srand`, successive calls to `rand` will produce a certain series of pseudo-random numbers. If `srand` is called again with the same argument, then after that point successive calls to `rand` will produce the same series of pseudo-random numbers. Successive calls made to `rand` before `srand` is ever called in a user program will produce the same series of pseudo-random numbers that would be produced after `srand` is called with argument 1.

C library routines should not call `rand` or `srand` in a way that affects the programmer's observed sequence of pseudo-random numbers.

17.8 COS, SIN, TAN

ANSI C facilities	Traditional and alternate facilities

`#include <math.h>`
`double cos(double x);`
`double sin(double x);`
`double tan(double x);`
	`#include <math.h>`
	`double cos(double x);`
	`double sin(double x);`
	`double tan(double x);`

The function `cos` computes the trigonometric cosine function of `x`, which is taken to be in radians. No domain or range errors are possible, but the programmer should be aware that the result may have little significance for very large values of `x`.

The functions `sin` and `tan` similarly compute the trigonometric sine and tangent functions, respectively. A range error may occur in the `tan` function if the argument is close to an odd multiple of $\pi/2$. The same caution about large-magnitude arguments applies to `sin` and `tan`.

17.9 ACOS, ASIN, ATAN, ATAN2

ANSI C facilities	Traditional and alternate facilities
`#include <math.h>`	`#include <math.h>`
`double acos(double x);`	`double acos(double x);`
`double asin(double x);`	`double asin(double x);`
`double atan(double x);`	`double atan(double x);`
`double atan2(`	`double atan2(`
`    double y,`	`    double y,`
`    double x);`	`    double x);`

The function `acos` computes the principal value of the trigonometric arc cosine function of x. The result is in radians and lies between 0 and π. (The range of these functions is approximate, because of the effect of round-off errors.) A domain error occurs if the argument is less than -1.0 or greater than 1.0.

The function `asin` computes the principal value of the trigonometric arc sine function of x. The result is in radians and lies between $-\pi/2$ and $\pi/2$. A domain error occurs if the argument is less than -1.0 or greater than 1.0.

The function `atan` computes the principal value of the arc tangent function of x. The result is in radians and lies between $-\pi/2$ and $\pi/2$. No range or domain errors are possible. In some implementations of C this function is called `arctan`.

The function `atan2` computes the principal value of the trigonometric arc tangent function of the value y/x. The signs of the two arguments are taken into account to determine quadrant information. Viewed in terms of a Cartesian coordinate system, the result is the angle between the positive x-axis and a line drawn from the origin through the point (x, y). The result is in radians and lies between $-\pi$ and π. If x is zero the result is $\pi/2$ or $-\pi/2$, depending on whether y is positive or negative. A domain error occurs if both x and y are zero.

17.10 COSH, SINH, TANH

ANSI C facilities	Traditional and alternate facilities
`#include <math.h>`	`#include <math.h>`
`double cosh(double x);`	`double cosh(double x);`
`double sinh(double x);`	`double sinh(double x);`
`double tanh(double x);`	`double tanh(double x);`

The function `cosh` computes the hyperbolic cosine function of x. The function `sinh` computes the hyperbolic sine function of x. The function `tanh` computes the hyperbolic tangent function of x. A range error can occur if the absolute value of the argument to `sinh` or `cosh` is large.

18

Time and Date Functions

Chapter summary

Name	Section	Name	Section	Name	Section
`asctime`	18.3	`difftime`	18.5	`time`	18.2
`clock`	18.1	`gmtime`	18.4	`time_t`	18.2
`clock_t`	18.1	`localtime`	18.4	`times`	18.1
`CLOCKS_PER_SEC`	18.1	`mktime`	18.4	`tm` (struct)	18.4
`ctime`	18.3	`strftime`	18.6		

The facilities in this section give the C programmer ways to manipulate the (calendar) date and time and the process time—the amount of time used by the running program.

Calendar time is represented in two forms: a simple arithmetic value returned by the time function, and a "broken-down," structured form computed from the arithmetic value by the `gmtime` and `localtime` functions. Locale-specific formatting is provided by the ANSI C function `strftime`.

Process time is represented by an arithmetic value (usually integral) returned by the `clock` function.

18.1 CLOCK, CLOCK_T, CLOCKS_PER_SEC, TIMES

ANSI C facilities	Traditional and alternate facilities
`#include <time.h>`	`#include <sys/types.h>`
	`#include <sys/times.h>`
`typedef … clock_t;`	
`#define CLOCKS_PER_SEC …`	
`clock_t clock();`	`long clock(void);`
	`void times(tmsbuf)`
	`struct tms {…} tmsbuf;`

342

The `clock` function returns an approximation to the processor time used by the current process. The units in which the time is expressed vary with the implementation; microseconds are customary. Although in traditional C the return type of `clock` is long, the value returned is really of type `unsigned long`; the use of `long` predates the addition of `unsigned long` to the language. Unsigned arithmetic should always be used when computing with process times.

Programmers should be aware of "wrap-around" in the process time. For instance, if type `long` is represented in 32 bits and `clock` returns the time in microseconds, the time returned will "wrap around" to its starting value in about 36 minutes.

The ANSI C version of `clock` allows the implementor freedom to use any arithmetic type, `clock_t`, for the process time. The number of time units ("clock ticks") per second is defined by the macro CLOCKS_PER_SEC. If the processor time is not available, the value –1 (cast to be of type `clock_t`) will be returned.

Here is how the `clock` function can be used to time an ANSI C program:

```
#include <time.h>
clock_t start, finish, duration;
start = clock();
process();
finish = clock();
printf("process() took %f seconds to execute\n",
        ((double) (finish - start)) / CLOCKS_PER_SEC );
```

Note how the cast to type `double` allows `clock_t` and CLOCKS_PER_SEC to be either floating-point or integral.

The `times` function is found in Berkeley UNIX and in some non-UNIX systems instead of `clock`; it returns a structured value that reports various components of the process time, each typically measured in units of 1/60 seconds. A rough equivalent to the `clock` function can be written using `times`:

```
#include <sys/types.h>
#include <sys/times.h>
#define CLOCKS_PER_SEC 60
long clock()
{
    struct tms tmsbuf;
    times(tmsbuf);
    return (tmsbuf.tms_utime + tmsbuf.tms_stime);
}
```

There is a type, `time_t`, used in the above structure; it is a "process time" unit and therefore is not the same as the "calendar time" type `time_t` defined in conjunction with the `time` function.

References `time` 18.2; `time_t` 18.2

18.2 TIME, TIME_T

ANSI C facilities	Traditional and alternate facilities

`#include <time.h>`
`typedef ... time_t;`
`time_t time(time_t *tptr);`
	`long time(long *tptr);`

The function `time` returns the current calendar time encoded in an integer of type `long`. If the parameter `tptr` is not null, the return value is also stored at `*tptr`. If errors are encountered, the value −1 is returned, cast to the appropriate return type; in System V UNIX `errno` is also set to `EFAULT`. Although the traditional return type of `time` is `long`, the value returned is usually of type `unsigned long`. The ANSI C version of `time` allows the return type, `time_t`, to be any arithmetic type.

Typically, the value returned by time is passed to the function `asctime` or `ctime` to convert it to a readable form, or is passed to `localtime` or `gmtime` to convert it to a form that is more easily processed. Computing the interval between two calendar times can be done by the ANSI C function `difftime`; in other implementations the programmer must either work with the broken-down time from `gmtime` or depend on a customary representation of the time as the number of seconds since some arbitrary past date. (January 1, 1970 is popular.)

References `asctime` 18.3; `ctime` 18.3; `difftime` 18.5; `errno` 11.2; `gmtime` 18.4; `localtime` 18.4

18.3 ASCTIME, CTIME

ANSI C facilities	Traditional and alternate facilities

`#include <time.h>`
`char *asctime(`
`   const struct tm *ts);`
`char *ctime(`
`   const time_t *timptr);`
	`#include <sys/time.h>`
	`char *asctime(struct tm *ts);`
	
	`char *ctime(long *timptr);`

The `asctime` and `ctime` functions both return a pointer to a string that is a printable date and time of the form

```
Sat May 15 17:30:00 1982\n\0
```

The `asctime` function takes as its single argument a pointer to a structured calendar time; such a structure is produced by `localtime` or `gmtime` from the arithmetic time that is returned by `time`. The `ctime` function takes a pointer to the value returned by `time`, and therefore `ctime(tp)` is equivalent to `asctime(localtime(tp))`.

In most implementations the functions return a pointer to a static data area, and therefore the returned string should be printed or copied (with `strcpy`) before any subsequent call to either function. Here is an example of how to print the current date and time using `time` and `ctime`:

```
#include <time.h>
#include <stdio.h>
time_t now;
...
now = time(NULL);
printf("The current date and time is: %s",ctime(&now));
```

References `gmtime` 18.4; `localtime` 18.4; `strcpy` 13.3; `struct tm` 18.4; `time` 18.2

18.4 GMTIME, LOCALTIME, MKTIME

ANSI C facilities	Traditional and alternate facilities

`#include <time.h>`
`struct tm { ... };`
`struct tm *gmtime(`
`   const time_t *t);`
`struct tm *localtime(`
`   const time_t *t);`
`time_t mktime(`
`   struct tm *tmptr );`
	`#include <sys/time.h>`
	`struct tm { ... };`
	`struct tm *gmtime(`
	`   long *t);`
	`struct tm *localtime(`
	`   long *t);`

The functions `gmtime` and `localtime` convert an arithmetic calendar time returned by `time` to a "broken-down" form of type `struct tm`. The `gmtime` function converts to Greenwich mean time (GMT) while `localtime` converts to local time, taking into account the time zone and possible daylight saving time. The functions return a null pointer if they encounter errors. These functions are portable across UNIX systems and ANSI C. The structure `struct tm` includes the fields listed in the table below. The type of all fields is `int`.

Fields in struct tm type

Name	Units	Range
tm_sec	seconds after the minute	0..61[1]
tm_min	minutes after the hour	0..59
tm_hour	hours since midnight	0..23
tm_mday	day of month	1..31
tm_mon	month since January	0..11
tm_year	years since 1900	≥0
tm_wday	day since Sunday	0..6
tm_yday	day since January 1	0..365
tm_isdst	daylight saving time flag	>0 if daylight daving dime; 0 if not; <0 if don't know

[1] The range allows up to 2 leap seconds.

In most implementations `gmtime` and `localtime` return a pointer to a single static data area that is overwritten on every call. Therefore, the returned structure should be used or copied before any subsequent call to either function.

The function `mktime` constructs a value of type `time_t` from the broken-down local time specified by the argument `tmptr`. The values of `tmptr->tm_wday` and `tmptr->tm_yday` are ignored by `mktime`. If successful, `mktime` returns the new time value and adjusts the contents of `*tmptr`, setting the `tm_wday` and `tm_yday` components. If the indicated calendar time cannot be represented as a value of `time_t`, then `mktime` returns the value `(time_t)-1`. An example of the use of `mktime` is shown in section 18.5.

18.5 DIFFTIME

ANSI C facilities	Traditional and alternate facilities

`#include <time.h>`
`double difftime(`
    `time_t t1,`
    `time_t t0);`	

The `difftime` function is found only in ANSI C; it subtracts calendar time `t0` from calendar time `t1`, returning the difference in seconds as a value of type `double`. Programmers cannot assume that calendar time is encoded in `time_t` as a scalar value such as a number of microseconds.

For example, the following function returns the number of seconds between midnight on April 15, 1990, and the current date and time.

```
#include <time.h>
...
double Secs_Since_Apr_15()
{
    struct tm Apr_15_struct = {0}; /* Init all fields to 0 */
    time_t Apr_15_t;
    Apr_15_struct.tm_year = 90;
    Apr_15_struct.tm_mon  = 3;
    Apr_15_struct.tm_mday = 15;
    Apr_15_t = mktime(&Apr_15_struct);
    if (Apr_15_t == (time_t)-1)
        return 0.0; /* error */
    else
        return difftime( time(NULL), Apr_15_t);
}
```

References `time_t` 18.2

18.6 STRFTIME

ANSI C facilities	Traditional and alternate facilities

`#include <time.h>`
`size_t strftime(`
`    char *s,`
`    size_t maxsize,`
`    const char *format,`
`    const struct tm *timeptr);`	

Like `sprintf` (section 15.11) `strftime` stores characters into the character array pointed to by the parameter `s` under control of the string `format`. However, `strftime` only formats a single date and time quantity specified by `timeptr` (section 18.4), and the formatting codes in `format` are interpreted differently from `sprintf`. (See table 18–1.) No more than `maxsize` characters (including the terminating null

Table 18–1: Formatting codes for strftime

Code	Replaced by
`%a`	abbreviated weekday name, e.g., `"Mon"`
`%A`	full weekday name, e.g., `"Lundi"`
`%b`	abbreviated month name, e.g., `"Jul"`
`%B`	full month name, e.g., `"Fevrier"`
`%c`	locale-specific date and time
`%d`	day of the month as a decimal integer (01–31)
`%H`	the hour (24-hour clock) as a decimal integer (00–23)
`%I`	the hour (12-hour clock) as a decimal integer (01–12)
`%j`	day of the year as a decimal number (001–366)
`%m`	month, as a decimal number (01–12)
`%M`	minute, as a decimal number (00–59)
`%p`	the locale's equivalent of AM/PM designation for 12-hour clock
`%S`	second, as a decimal number (00–61)[1]
`%U`	week number of the year (00–53)[2]
`%w`	weekday as a decimal number (0–6, Sunday=0)
`%W`	week number of the year[3]
`%x`	locale-specific date
`%X`	local-specific time
`%y`	year without century as a decimal number (00–99)
`%Y`	year with century as a decimal number, e.g., 1952
`%z`	time zone name or abbreviation, or none if not known
`%%`	a single %

[1] Allows for up to 2 leap-seconds (60 and 61).
[2] Week number 1 has the first Sunday; previous days are week 0.
[3] Week number 1 has the first Monday; previous days are week 0.

character) are placed into the array designated by s. The actual number of characters stored (not including the terminating null character) is returned. If maxsize is not large enough to hold the entire formatted string, zero is returned.

The formatting is locale-specific. (See setlocale, section 11.5.)

A plausible implementation of asctime (section 18.3) using strftime is shown below as an example. Since the formatting is locale-specific, the length of the output string (including the terminating null character) might be greater than 26, which is the case for the output from asctime:

```c
#include <time.h>
#define TIME_SIZE 26
char *asctime2( const struct tm *tm )
{
    static char time_buffer[TIME_SIZE];
    size_t len;
    len = strftime( time_buffer, TIME_SIZE,
        "%a %b %d %H:%M:%S %Y\n", tm);
    if (len == 0)
        return NULL;   /* time_buffer is too short */
    else
        return time_buffer;
}
```

19

Control Functions

Chapter summary

Name	Section	Name	Section	Name	Section
abort	19.3	gsignal	19.6	raise	19.6
alarm	19.7	jmp_buf	19.4	setjmp	19.4
assert	19.1	kill	19.6	signal	19.6
atexit	19.5	longjmp	19.4	sleep	19.7
exec	19.2	NDEBUG	19.1	ssignal	19.6
exit	19.3	psignal	19.6	system	19.2

The facilities in this chapter provide extensions to the standard flow of control in C programs. The functions `signal` and `raise` implement a primitive exception-handling mechanism; `assert` and `exit` provide program-termination capabilities; and `exec` and `system` allow other programs to be started from within a C program.

19.1 ASSERT, NDEBUG

ANSI C facilities	Traditional and alternate facilities
`#include <assert.h>`	`include <assert.h>`
`#ifndef NDEBUG`	`#ifndef NDEBUG`
`void assert(int expression);`	`void assert(`*scalar* `expression);`
`#else`	`#else`
`#define assert(x) ((void)0)`	`#define assert(x) ((void)0)`
`#endif`	`#endif`

The macro `assert` takes as its single argument a value of any integer type. (Many implementations allow any scalar type.) If that value is 0 (false) and if additionally the macro NDEBUG is not defined, then assert will print a diagnostic message on the standard output stream and halt the program by calling abort (in ANSI C) or exit (in traditional C). The assert facility is always implemented as a macro, and the header file assert.h must be included in the source file to use the facility. The diagnostic message should include the text of the argument, the file name (__FILE__) and the line number (__LINE__).

If the macro NDEBUG is defined when the header file assert.h is read, the assert facility is disabled, usually by defining assert to be the empty statement. No diagnostic messages are printed and the argument to assert is not evaluated.

The assert facility is typically used during program development to verify that certain conditions are true at run time. It provides reliable documentation to people reading the program and can greatly aid in debugging. When a program is operational, assertions can easily be disabled, after which they have no run-time overhead. In the example below, the assertion is better documentation than the English comment, which can be misinterpreted:

```
#include <assert.h>
int f(x)
  int x;
{
    /* x should be between 1 and 10 */
    assert(x>0 && x<10);
    …
}
```

References abort 19.3; exit 19.3

19.2 EXEC, SYSTEM

ANSI C facilities	Traditional and alternate facilities

`#include <stdlib.h>`
`int system(`
`    const char command);`
	`int system(char command);`
	`execl(char *name,`
	`    char *argi, …, NULL );`
	`execlp(char *name,`
	`    char *argi, …, NULL );`
	`execle(char *name,`
	`    char *argi, …, NULL,`
	`    char *envp);`
	`execv(char *name, char *argv[] );`
	`execvp(char *name, char *argv[] );`
	`execve(char *name, char *argv[],`
	`    char *envp[]);`

The function system passes its string argument to the operating system's *command processor* for execution in some implementation-defined way. In UNIX systems, the command processor is the shell. The value returned by system is implementation-defined but is usually the completion status of the command. In ANSI C, `system` may be called with a null argument in which case 0 is returned if there is no command processor provided in the implementation and a nonzero value is returned if there is.

The various forms of `exec` are found mainly in UNIX systems; they are not included in ANSI C. In all cases, they transform the current *process* into a new process by executing the file `name` (typically created by the linker or loader). They differ in how arguments are supplied for the new process:

1. The functions `execl`, `execlp`, and `execle` take a variable number of arguments, the last of which must be a null pointer. By convention, the first argument should be the same as `name`; that is, it should be the name of the program to be executed.
2. The functions `execv`, `execvp`, and `execve` supply a pointer to a null-terminated vector of arguments, such as is provided to function `main`. By convention, `argv[0]` should be the same as `name`; that is, it should be the name of the program to be executed.
3. The functions `execle` and `execve` also pass an explicit "environment" to the new process. The parameter `envp` is a null-terminated vector of string pointers. Each string is of the form `"name=value"`. (In the other versions of `exec`, the environment pointer of the calling process is implicitly passed to the new process.)
4. The functions `execlp` and `execvp` are the same as `execl` and `execv`, respectively, except that the system looks for the file name in the set of directories normally searched for commands (usually the value of the environment variable `path` or `PATH`).

When the new process is started, the arguments supplied to `exec` are made available to the new process's `main` function.

References `main` 20.1

19.3 EXIT, ABORT

ANSI C facilities	Traditional and alternate facilities
`#include <stdlib.h>`	
`#define EXIT_FAILURE …`	
`#define EXIT_SUCCESS …`	
`void exit(int status);`	`void exit(int status);`
	`void _exit(int status);`
`void abort(void)`	`void abort(void)`

The `exit`, `_exit`, and `abort` functions cause the program to terminate. Control does not normally return to the caller of these functions.

The function `exit` terminates a program normally, with these cleanup actions:

1. (ANSI C only) All functions registered with the `atexit` function are called in the reverse order of their registration as many times as they were registered.
2. Open output steams are flushed. All open steams are closed.
3. Files created by the `tmpfile` function are removed.
4. Control is returned to the host environment with a status value signifying success or failure.

By convention in many systems, a `status` value of 0 signifies successful program termination and nonzero values are used to signify various kinds of abnormal termination. In ANSI C the value 0 and the value of the macro `EXIT_SUCCESS` will signify successful termination, and the value of the macro `EXIT_FAILURE` will signify unsuccessful termination; the meaning of other values is implementation-defined. Returning an integer value from the function `main` with a `return` statement acts like calling `exit` with the same value.

The function `_exit`, provided in some traditional C implementations, differs from `exit` in that cleanup activities are not performed.

The `abort` function causes "abnormal" program termination. Whether or not `abort` causes cleanup actions is implementation-defined. The status value returned to the host system is implementation-defined but must denote "unsuccessful." In ANSI C and many traditional implementations the call to `abort` is translated to a special signal (SIGABRT in ANSI C) that can be caught. If the signal is ignored or if the handler returns, then ANSI C implementations will still terminate the program, but other implementations may allow the `abort` function to return to the caller.

References `fflush` 15.2; `atexit` 19.5; `main` function 9.9; `return` statement 8.9; `signal` 19.6; `tmpfile` 15.16

19.4 SETJMP, LONGJMP, JMP_BUF

ANSI C facilities	Traditional and alternate facilities
`#include <setjmp.h>`	`include <setjmp.h>`
`typedef … jmp_buf;`	`typedef … jmp_buf;`
`int setjmp(jmp_buf env);`	`int setjmp(jmp_buf env);`
`void longjmp(`	`void longjmp(`
`    jmp_buf env,`	`    jmp_buf env,`
`    int status);`	`    int status);`

The `setjmp` and `longjmp` functions implement a primitive form of nonlocal jumps, which may be used to handle abnormal or exceptional situations. This facility is traditionally considered more portable than `signal` (section 19.6), but the latter has also been incorporated into ANSI C.

The macro `setjmp` records its caller's environment in the "jump buffer" `env`, an implementation-defined array, and returns 0 to its caller. (The type `jmp_buf` must be implemented as an array type so that a pointer to `env` is actually passed to `setjmp`.)

The function longjmp takes as its arguments a jump buffer previously filled by calling setjmp and an integer value, status, that is usually nonzero. The effect of calling longjmp is to cause the program to return from the call to setjmp again, this time returning the value status. Some implementations, including ANSI C, do not permit longjmp to cause 0 to be returned from setjmp, and will return 1 from setjmp if longjmp is called with status 0.

The setjmp and longjmp functions are notoriously difficult to implement, and the programmer would do well to make minimal assumptions about them. When setjmp returns with a nonzero value, the programmer can assume that static variables have their proper value as of the time longjmp was called. Automatic variables local to the function containing setjmp are guaranteed to have their correct value in ANSI C only if they have a volatile-qualified type or if their values were not changed between the original call to setjmp and the corresponding longjmp call. Furthermore, ANSI C requires that the call to setjmp either be an entire expression statement (possibly cast to void), the right-hand side of a simple assignment expression, or be used as the controlling expression of an if, switch, do, while, or for statement in one of the following forms:

```
(setjmp(...))
(!setjmp(...))
(exp relop setjmp(...))
(setjmp(...) relop exp)
```

where *exp* is an integer constant expression and *relop* is a relational or equality operator. ANSI C requires that longjmp operate correctly in nonnested signal (interrupt) handlers, but in some older implementations a call to setjmp or longjmp during interrupt processing or signal handling will not operate correctly.

If the jump buffer argument to longjmp is not set by setjmp, or if the function containing setjmp is terminated before the call to longjmp, the behavior is undefined.

Below is a typical use of setjmp and longjmp.

```
#include <setjmp.h>
jmp_buf ErrorEnv;
...
int guard()  /* Return 0 if successful; else longjmp code. */
{   int status = setjmp(ErrorEnv);
    if ( status != 0) return status;   /* error */
    process();
    return 0;
}

int process()
{   ...
    if (error_happened) longjmp(ErrorEnv, error_code);
    ...
}
```

The `longjmp` function is to be called when an error is encountered in function `process`. The function `guard` is the "backstop," to which control will be transferred by `longjmp`. The function `process` is called directly or indirectly from `guard`; this ensures that `longjmp` cannot be called after `guard` returns, and that no attempt is made to depend on the values of local variables in the function containing `longjmp`. (This is a conservative policy.) Note that the return value from `setjmp` must be tested to determine if the return was caused by `longjmp` or not.

19.5 ATEXIT

ANSI C facilities	Traditional and alternate facilities
`#include <stdlib.h>` `int atexit(void (*func)(void));`	

The `atexit` function is found in ANSI C. It "registers" a function so that the function will be called when `exit` is called or when the function `main` returns. The functions are not called when the program terminates abnormally, as with `abort` or `raise`. Implementations must allow at least 32 functions to be registered. The `atexit` function returns zero if the registration succeeds and returns a nonzero value otherwise.

The registered functions are called in the reverse order of their registration, before any standard cleanup actions are performed by `exit`. Each function is called with no arguments and should have return type `void`. A registered function should not attempt to reference any objects with storage class `auto` or `register` (e.g., through a pointer) except those it defines itself. Registering the same function more than once will cause the function to be called once for each registration.

Some C implementations define a related function, `onexit`.

In the following example, the `main` function opens a file and then registers the `cleanup` function that will close the file in case `exit` is called. (In fact, `exit` closes all files, but perhaps the programmer wants to close this one first.)

```
#include <stdlib.h>
FILE *Open_File;

void cleanup() { if (Open_File != NULL) fclose(Open_File); }

int main()
{
    int status;
...
    Open_File = fopen("out.dat","w");
    status = atexit(cleanup);
    assert(status == 0);
    ...
}
```

References abort 19.3; exit 19.3; main function 9.9; raise 19.6; void type 5.9

19.6 SIGNAL, RAISE, GSIGNAL, SSIGNAL, PSIGNAL

ANSI C facilities	Traditional and alternate facilities
```#include <signal.h>```	```#include <signal.h>```
```#define SIG_IGN …```	```#define SIG_IGN …```
```#define SIG_DFL …```	```#define SIG_DFL …```
```#define SIG_ERR …```	```#define SIG_ERR … /* ANSI */```
```#define SIGxxx …```	```#define SIGxxx …```
...	...
```void (*signal(```	```void (*signal(```
``` int sig,```	``` int sig,```
``` void (*func)(int)))(int);```	``` void (*func)(int)))(int);```
```int raise(int sig);```	```int raise(int sig) /* ANSI */;```
```typedef … sig_atomic_t;```	```int kill(int pid, intsig);```
	```int (*ssignal(```
	``` int softsig,```
	``` int (*func)(int)))(int);```
	```int gsignal(int softsig);```
	```void psignal(int sig,char```
	```*prefix);```

Signals are (potentially) asynchronous events that may require special processing by the user program or by the implementation. Signals are named by integer values, and each implementation defines a set of signals in header file `signal.h`, spelled beginning with the letters `SIG`. Signals may be triggered or *raised* by the computer's error-detection mechanisms, by the user program itself via `kill` or `raise`, or by actions external to the program. Software signals used by the functions `ssignal` and `psignal` are user-defined, with values generally in the range 1 through 15; otherwise they operate like regular signals.

A signal handler for signal `sig` is a user function that is invoked when signal `sig` is "raised." The handler function is expected to perform some useful action and then return, generally causing the program to resume at the point it was interrupted. Handlers may also call `exit` or `longjmp`. Signal handlers are normal C functions taking one argument, the raised signal:

```
void my_handler(int the_signal)
{
    …
}
```

Some non-ANSI implementations may pass extra arguments to handlers for certain predefined signals.

The function `signal` is used to associate signal handlers with specific signals. In the normal case `signal` is passed a signal value and a pointer to the signal handler for that signal. If the association is successful, then `signal` returns a pointer to the previous signal handler (which may be `SIG_DFL` if there was no handler); otherwise it returns the value −1 (`SIG_ERR` in ANSI C) and sets `errno`:

```
void new_handler(int sig) { … }
void (*old_handler)();
…
old_handler = signal( sig, &new_handler );
if (old_handler==SIG_ERR)
    printf("?Couldn't establish new handler.\n");
…
if (signal(sig,old_handler)==SIG_ERR)
    printf("?Couldn't put back old handler.\n")
```

The function argument to `signal` may also have two special values, `SIG_IGN` and `SIG_DFL`. A call to `signal` of the form `signal(sig, SIG_IGN)` means that signal `sig` is to be ignored. A call to `signal` of the form `signal(sig, SIG_DFL)` means that signal `sig` is to receive its "default" handling, which usually means ignoring some signals and terminating the program on other signals.

The `ssignal` function (found in UNIX System V) works exactly like `signal` but is used only in conjunction with `gsignal` for user-defined software signals. Handlers supplied to `ssignal` may return integer values that become the return value of `gsignal`.

The `raise` and `gsignal` functions cause the indicated signal (or software signal) to be raised in the current process. The `kill` function causes the indicated signal to be raised in the specified process; it is less portable.

When a signal is raised for which a handler has been established by `signal` or `gsignal`, the handler is given control. ANSI C (and most other implementations) either reset the associated handler to `SIG_DFL` before the handler is given control or in some other way block the signal; this is to prevent unwanted recursion. (Whether this happens for the signal SIGILL is implementation-defined for historical and performance reasons.) The handler may return, in which case execution continues at the point of interruption, with the following caveats:

1. If the signal was raised by `raise` or `gsignal`, those functions return to their caller.
2. If the signal was raised by `abort`, ANSI C programs are terminated. Other implementations may return to the caller of `abort`.
3. If the handled signal was `SIGFPE` or another implementation-defined computational signal, the behavior upon return is undefined.

Signal handlers should refrain from calling library functions other than `signal` itself, since some signals could arise from library functions and since library functions (other than `signal`) are not guaranteed to be reentrant.

ANSI C defines the macros listed in the table on the next page to stand for certain standard signals. These signals are common to many implementations of C.

Standard signals

Macro name	Signal meaning
SIGABRT	abnormal termination, such as is caused by the abort facility
SIGFPE	an erroneous arithmetic operation such as an attempt to divide by zero
SIGILL	an error caused by an illegal computer instruction
SIGINT	an attention signal, as from an interactive user striking a special keystroke
SIGSEGV	an invalid memory access
SIGTERM	a termination signal, from a user or another program

The psignal function (not in ANSI C) prints on the standard error output the string prefix (which is customarily the name of the program) and a brief description of signal sig. This function may be useful in handlers that are about to call exit or abort.

References exit 19.3; longjmp 19.4

19.7 SLEEP, ALARM

ANSI C facilities	Traditional and alternate facilities
	void sleep(unsigned seconds);
	unsigned alarm(unsigned seconds);

The alarm function sets an internal system timer to the indicated number of seconds and returns the number of seconds previously on the timer. When the timer expires, the signal SIGALRM is raised in the program. If the argument to alarm is 0, then the effect of the call is to cancel any previous alarm request. The alarm function is useful for escaping from various kinds of deadlock situations.

The sleep function suspends the program for the indicated number of seconds, at which time the sleep function returns and execution continues. Sleep is typically implemented using the same timer as alarm, and if the sleep time exceeds the time already on the alarm timer, sleep will return immediately after the SIGALRM signal is handled. If the sleep time is shorter than the time already on the alarm timer, then sleep will reset the timer just before it returns so that the SIGALARM signal will be received when expected.

Implementations will generally terminate sleep when any signal is handled; some, including System V UNIX, supply the number of unslept seconds as the return value of sleep (of type unsigned).

Some implementations may define these functions as taking arguments of type unsigned long. These functions are not part of ANSI C, since they are peripheral to the C language and more properly the concern of an operating systems standard such as POSIX.

References signal 19.6

20

Miscellaneous Functions

Chapter summary

Name	Section	Name	Section	Name	Section
bsearch	20.5	getcwd	20.3	main	20.1
ctermid	20.2	getenv	20.4	qsort	20.6
cuserid	20.2	getwd	20.3		

The facilities in this section allow the C programmer to interrogate, and in some cases modify, the environment in which the program is running. The function main, which programmers must to establish an entry point in their C programs is also described, as are the functions bsearch and qsort, which provide general searching and sorting capabilities.

20.1 MAIN

ANSI C facilities	Traditional and alternate facilities

`int main(void);`
`int main(`
`   int argc,`
`   char *argv[]);`
	`int main(void);`
	`int main(`
	`   int argc,`
	`   char *argv[]);`
	`int main(`
	`   int argc,`
	`   char *argv[],`
	`   char *env[]);`
	`extern char *environ[];`

The function main is not a library function; it is a function that the programmer defines to designate the entry point of his program and to serve as a vehicle for obtaining information about the program's execution environment. Among all the source files making up a C program, there must be exactly one definition of main. Most C implementations, including ANSI C, permit `main` to be defined with zero or two parameters, customarily called `argc` and `argv`. Some implementations provide a third parameter, `env`. The arguments to `main` are set up by the execution environment and are not directly under control of the C programmer.

The parameter `argc` is the count of the number of "program arguments" or "options" supplied to the program when it was invoked by a user or another program.

The parameter `argv` is a vector of pointers to strings representing the program arguments. The first string, `argv[0]`, is the name of the program itself; if the name is not available, `argv[0][0]` must be `'\0'`.. The string `argv[i]`, i=0, …, `argc`−1, is the ith program argument. The value of `argv[argc]` may be a null pointer, but is not so in all implementations. The vector `argv` and the strings to which it points must be modifiable, and their values must not be changed by the implementation or host system during program execution.

Some implementations permit a third argument to `main`, `env`, which points to a null-terminated vector of "environment values," each one a pointer to a null-terminated string of the form `"name=value"`. In some UNIX implementations an external variable, `environ`, holds the environment pointer. For example, the following short program prints out its name and arguments, and its environment:

```
#include <stdio.h>
int main(argc,argv,envp)
    int argc;
    char *argv[],*envp[];
{
    int i;
    printf("Invocation: ");
    for( i=0; i<argc; i++)
        printf("%s ",argv[i]);
    printf("\nEnvironment:\n");
    for( i=0; envp[i] != NULL; i++)
        printf("%s\n",envp[i]);
    return 0;
}
```

20.2 CTERMID, CUSERID

ANSI C facilities	Traditional and alternate facilities
	`#include <stdio.h>`
	`char *ctermid(char *s);`
	`char *cuserid(char *s);`
	`#define L_ctermid …`
	`#define L_cuserid …`

The function `ctermid` computes a file name that corresponds to the controlling terminal for the current process. This file name can be passed to `fopen` to establish an I/O connection with the terminal. The concept of treating I/O devices like terminals as files is central to UNIX but may be less natural in other systems. However, many C implementations provide a similar facility.

The argument s may be null, in which case the terminal file name is stored in an internal buffer whose address is returned as the value of the call. The next call to ctermid might overwrite the buffer. If s is not null, it is assumed to point to a character array at least L_ctermid characters long, into which the name is stored. The value of s is then returned.

The function cuserid retrieves the name of the user who "owns" the current process. The argument s may be null, in which case the user name is stored in an internal buffer whose address is returned as the value of the call. The next call to cuserid will overwrite the buffer. If s is not null, it is assumed to point to a character array at least L_cuserid characters long, into which the name is stored. The value of s is returned.

20.3 GETCWD, GETWD

ANSI C facilities	Traditional and alternate facilities

	`#include <sys/parm.h>`
	`char *getcwd(char *buf,`
	`  int size);`
	`char *getwd(char *pathname);`
	`#define MAXPATHLEN …`

The functions getcwd or getwd (depending on the implementation) are used to determine the "current working directory," which is generally the file system directory in which file I/O will take place if a specific directory is not specified in a file name.

The getcwd function returns a pointer to the current working directory name. If the argument buf is null, then size bytes of storage are allocated by malloc, the working directory name is copied into that storage, and its address is returned. If the argument buf is not null, it should point to at least size characters of space into which the working directory name will be copied and the address buf will be returned. In some implementations, size must be larger than the longest pathname to be returned (e.g., 2 bytes longer). If an error occurs, a null pointer is returned and errno is set.

The getwd function copies into the character array at pathname the working directory name. The array should be at least MAXPATHLEN characters long. If an error occurs, a null pointer is returned and a message is placed in pathname.

References errno 11.2; malloc 16.1

20.4 GETENV

ANSI C facilities	Traditional and alternate facilities

`#include <stdlib.h>`
`char * getenv(`
`  const char *name );`
	`char * getenv(`
	`  char *name );`

The `getenv` function takes as its single argument a pointer to a string which is interpreted as a name understood by the execution environment. The function returns a pointer to another string, which is the "value" of the argument `name`. If the indicated name has no value, a null pointer is returned. The value string should not be modified by the programmer, and it may be overwritten by a subsequent call to `getenv`. The set of (*name,value*) bindings may also available to the `main` function (section 20.1).

20.5 BSEARCH

ANSI C facilities	Traditional and alternate facilities
`#include <stdlib.h>`	
`void *bsearch(`	`char *bsearch(`
`   const void *key,`	`   char *key,`
`   const void *base,`	`   char *base,`
`   size_t count,`	`   unsigned count,`
`   size_t size,`	`   int size,`
`   int (*compar)(`	`   int (*compar)(`
`      const void *the_key,`	`      char *the_key,`
`      const void *a value));`	`      char *a value));`

The function `bsearch` searches an array of `count` elements whose first element is pointed to by `base`. The size of each element in characters is `size`. `compar` is a function whose arguments are a pointer to the key and a pointer to an array element ; it returns a negative, zero, or positive value depending if the key is less than, greater than, or equal to the element. The array must be sorted in ascending order (according to `compar`) at the beginning of the search. `bsearch` returns a pointer to an element of the array that matches the the `key`, or a null pointer if no such element is found.

Example   The function `fetch` below uses `bsearch` to search `Table`, a sorted array of structures. The function `key_compare` is supplied to test the key values. Notice that `fetch` first embeds the key in a dummy element (`key_elem`); this allows `key_compare` to be used with both `bsearch` and `qsort` (section 20.6):

```
#include <stdlib.h>
#define COUNT 100
struct elem {int key; int data; } Table[COUNT];

int key_compare(e1,e2)
    const void * e1, *e2;
{
    int v1 = ((struct elem *)e1)->key;
    int v2 = ((struct elem *)e2)->key;
    return (v1<v2) ? -1 : (v1>v2) ? 1 : 0;
}
```

```
int fetch(key)
    int key;
/* Return the data item associated with key in
   the table, or 0 if no such key exists. */
{
    struct elem *result;
    struct elem key_elem;
    key_elem.key = key;
    result = (struct elem *)
            bsearch(
                (void *) &key_elem, (void *) &Table[0],
                (size_t) COUNT, sizeof(struct elem),
                key_compare);
    if (result == NULL)
        return 0;
    else
        return result->data;
}
```

20.6 QSORT

ANSI C facilities	Traditional and alternate facilities
`#include <stdlib.h>`	
`void qsort(`	`void qsort(`
`   const void *base,`	`   char *base,`
`   size_t count,`	`   unsigned count,`
`   size_t size,`	`   int size,`
`   int (*compar)(`	`   int (*compar)(`
`      const void *element1,`	`      char *element1,`
`      const void *element2));`	`      char *element2));`

The function qsort sorts an array of count elements whose first element is pointed to by base. The size of each element in characters is specified by size. compar is a function that takes as arguments pointers to two elements and returns −1 if the first element is "less than" the second, 1 if the first element is "greater than" the second, and 0 if the two elements are equal. The array will be sorted in ascending order (according to compar) at the end of the sort.

The function sort_table on the next page uses qsort to sort the table in the example from section 20.5. Function key_compare from that example is used to compare table elements:

```
void sort_table()
/* Sorts Table according to the key values */
{
    qsort(
        (void *)Table,
        (size_t) COUNT,
        sizeof(struct elem),
        key_compare );
}
```

A

The ASCII Character Set

Hex.	Octal	Dec.	Char	Name	Dec.	Char.	Dec.	Char.	Dec.	Char.
					0x20		0x40		0x60	
					040		0100		0140	
0	0	0	^@	NUL	32	SP	64	@	96	`
1	1	1	^A	SOH	33	!	65	A	97	a
2	2	2	^B	STX	34	"	66	B	98	b
3	3	3	^C	ETX	35	#	67	C	99	c
4	4	4	^D	EOT	36	$	68	D	100	d
5	5	5	^E	ENQ	37	%	69	E	101	e
6	6	6	^F	ACK	38	&	70	F	102	f
7	7	7	^G	BEL, \a	39	'	71	G	103	g
8	010	8	^H	BS, \b	40	(	72	H	104	h
9	011	9	^I	TAB,\t	41	)	73	I	105	i
0xA	012	10	^J	LF, \n[1]	42	*	74	J	106	j
0xB	013	11	^K	VT, \v	43	+	75	K	107	k
0xC	014	12	^L	FF, \f	44	,	76	L	108	l
0xD	015	13	^M	CR, \r	45	-	77	M	109	m
0xE	016	14	^N	SO	46	.	78	N	110	n
0xF	017	15	^O	SI	47	/	79	O	111	o
0x10	020	16	^P	DLE	48	0	80	P	112	p
0x11	021	17	^Q	DC1	49	1	81	Q	113	q
0x12	022	18	^R	DC2	50	2	82	R	114	r
0x13	023	19	^S	DC3	51	3	83	S	115	s
0x14	024	20	^T	DC4	52	4	84	T	116	t
0x15	025	21	^U	NAK	53	5	85	U	117	u
0x16	026	22	^V	SYN	54	6	86	V	118	v
0x17	027	23	^W	ETB	55	7	87	W	119	w
0x18	030	24	^X	CAN	56	8	88	X	120	x
0x19	031	25	^Y	EM	57	9	89	Y	121	y
0x1A	032	26	^Z	SUB	58	:	90	Z	122	z
0x1B	033	27	^[	ESC	59	;	91	[	123	{
0x1C	034	28	^\	FS	60	<	92	\	124		
0x1D	035	29	^]	GS	61	=	93	]	125	}
0x1E	036	30	^^	RS	62	>	94	^	126	~
0x1F	037	31	^_	US	63	?	95	_	127	DEL

[1] The use of '\012' for '\n' is common, but some systems use other values, such as '\023'.

B

Syntax of the C Language

This appendix summarizes the grammar for the ANSI C language. The productions are listed in alphabetical order and are accompanied by the section numbers in this book where each production is first presented. The topmost production of the grammar is *translation-unit*.

abstract-declarator :   5.12
       pointer
       pointer$_{opt}$ direct-abstract-declarator

add-op : one of   7.6.2
       +   −

additive-expression :   7.6.2
       multiplicative-expression
       additive-expression add-op multiplicative-expression

address-expression :   7.5.6
       & *unary-expression*

array-declarator :   4.5.3
       declarator [*constant-expression$_{opt}$*]

assignment-expression :   7.9
       conditional-expression
       unary-expression assignment-op assignment-expression

assignment-op : one of   7.9
       =   +=   −=   *=   /=   %=
       <<=   >>=   &=   ^= |=

bit-field :   5.6
        declarator$_{opt}$: *width*

bitwise-and-expression :   7.6.6
        equality-expression
        bitwise-and-expression & *equality-expression*

bitwise-negation-expression :   7.5.5
        ~ *unary-expression*

bitwise-or-expression :   7.6.6
        bitwise-xor-expression
        bitwise-or-expression | *bitwise-xor-expression*

bitwise-xor-expression :   7.6.6
        bitwise-and-expression
        bitwise-xor-expression ^ *bitwise-and-expression*

break-statement :   8.8
        `break ;`

c-char :   2.7.3
        any source character except the apostrophe ',
           backslash \, or newline character, or
        escape-character

c-char-sequence :   2.7.3
        c-char
        c-char-sequence c-char

case-label :   8.7
        `case` *constant-expression*

cast-expression :   7.5.1
        (*type-name*)   *unary-expression*

character-constant :   2.7.3
        ' *c-char-sequence* '
        `L`' *c-char-sequence* '

character-escape-code : one of   2.7.5
        `a  b  f  n  r  t  v  \  '  "  ?`

character-type-specifier :   5.1.3
        `char`
        `signed char`
        `unsigned char`

comma-expression :   7.10
       assignment-expression
       comma-expression ,   *assignment-expression*

component-declaration :   5.6
       type-specifier component-declarator-list ;

component-declarator :   5.6
       simple-component
       bit field

component-declarator-list :   5.6
       component-declarator
       component-declarator-list ,   *component-declarator*

component-selection-expression :   7.4.2
       direct-component-selection
       indirect-component-selection

compound-statement :   8.4
       { *inner-declaration-list*$_{opt}$ *statement-list* $_{opt}$ }

conditional-expression :   7.8
       logical-or-expression
       logical-or-expression   ?   *expression*   :   *conditional-expression*

conditional-statement :   8.5
       if-statement
       if-else-statement

constant :   2.7
       integer-constant
       floating-point-constant
       character-constant
       string-constant

constant-expression :   4.5.3
       expression

continue-statement :   8.8
       `continue ;`

decimal-constant :   2.7.1
       nonzero-digit
       decimal-constant digit

declaration :   4.1
       declaration-specifiers initialized-declarator-list ;

declaration-list :   8.4, 9.1
         declaration
         declaration-list declaration

declaration-specifiers :   4.1
         storage-class-specifier declaration-specifiers$_{opt}$
         type-specifier declaration-specifiers$_{opt}$
         type-qualifier declaration-specifiers$_{opt}$

declarator :   4.5
         pointer-declarator
         direct-declarator

default-label :   8.7
         `default`

digit : one of   2.5
         `0   1   2   3   4   5   6   7   8   9`

digit-sequence :   2.7.2
         digit
         digit digit-sequence

direct-abstract-declarator :   5.12
         (*abstract-declarator*)
         direct-abstract-declarator$_{opt}$ [*constant-expression$_{opt}$*]
         direct-abstract-declarator$_{opt}$ (*parameter-type-list$_{opt}$*)

direct-component-selection :   7.4.2
         postfix-expression **.** *name*

direct-declarator :   4.5
         simple-declarator
         (*declarator*)
         function-declarator
         array-declarator

do-statement :   8.6.2
         `do` *statement* `while` (*expression*) `;`

dotted-digits :   2.7.2
         digit-sequence **.**
         digit-sequence **.** *digit-sequence*
         . *digit-sequence*

enumeration-constant :   5.5
         identifier

enumeration-constant-definition :   5.5
   enumeration-constant
   enumeration-constant = *expression*

enumeration-definition-list :   5.5
   enumeration-constant-definition
   enumeration-definition-list , *enumeration-constant-definition*

enumeration-tag :   5.5
   identifier

enumeration-type-definition :   5.5
   enum *enumeration$_{opt}$-tag* { *enumeration-definition-list* }

enumeration-type-reference :   5.5
   enum *enumeration-tag*

enumeration-type-specifier :   5.5
   enumeration-type-definition
   enumeration-type-reference

equality-expression :   7.6.5
   relational-expression
   equality-expression equality-op relational-expression

equality-op : one of   7.6.5
   == !=

escape-code :   2.7.5
   character-escape-code
   octal-escape-code
   hex-escape-code   (ANSI C)

exponent :   2.7.2
   e *sign-part$_{opt}$ digit-sequence*
   E *sign-part$_{opt}$ digit-sequence*

expression :   7.10
   comma-expression

expression-list :   7.4.3
   assignment-expression
   expression-list , *assignment-expression*

expression-statement :   8.2
   expression ;

field-list :   5.6
   component-declaration
   field-list component-declaration

floating-constant :   2.7.2
        digit-sequence exponent floating-suffix$_{opt}$
        dotted-digits exponent$_{opt}$ floating-suffix$_{opt}$

floating-suffix : one of   2.7.2
      `f    F    l    L`

floating-type-specifier :   5.2
      `float`
      `double`
      `long double`

following-character :   2.5
      letter
      underscore
      digit

for-expressions :   8.6.3
      (expression $_{opt}$; expression $_{opt}$; expression $_{opt}$)

for-statement :   8.6.3
      `for` *for-expressions statement*

function-call :   7.4.3
      postfix-expression (expression-list$_{opt}$)

function-declarator :   4.5.4, 9.1
      direct-declarator (parameter-type-list)
      direct-declarator (identifier-list$_{opt}$)

function-definition :   9.1
      function-specifier   compound-statement

function-specifier :   9.1
      declaration-specifiers$_{opt}$ declarator declaration-list$_{opt}$

goto-statement :   8.10
      `goto` *identifier ;*

hex-digit : one of   2.7.1
      `0    1    2    3    4    5    6    7    8    9`
      `A    B    C    D    E    F    a    b    c    d    e    f`

hex-escape-code :   2.7.5
      `x` *hex-digit*
      hex-escape-code hex-digit

hexadecimal-constant :   2.7.1
      0x *hex-digit*
      0X *hex-digit*
      hexadecimal-constant   hex-digit

identifier   :   2.5
      underscore
      letter
      identifier following-character

identifier-list :   4.5.4, 9.1
      identifier
      identifier-list , identifier

if-else-statement :   8.5
      if (*expression*) *statement* else *statement*

if-statement :   8.5
      if (*expression*) *statement*

indirect-component-selection :   7.4.2
      postfix-expression −> name

indirection-expression :   7.5.7
      * *unary-expression*

initialized-declarator :   4.1
      declarator initializer-part$_{opt}$

initialized-declarator-list :   4.1
      initialized-declarator
      initialized-declarator-list , initialized-declarator

initializer :   4.6
      expression
      { *initializer-list , $_{opt}$* }

initializer-list :   4.6
      initializer
      initializer-list , initializer

integer-constant :   2.7.1
      decimal-constant integer-suffix$_{opt}$
      octal-constant integer-suffix$_{opt}$
      hexadecimal-constant integer-suffix$_{opt}$

integer-type-specifier :   5.1
> *signed-type-specifier*
> *unsigned-type-specifier*
> *character-type-specifier*

iterative-statement :   8.6
> *do-statement*
> *while-statement*
> *for-statement*

label :   8.3
> *named-label*
> *case-label*
> *default-label*

labeled-statement :   8.3
> *label* : *statement*

letter : one of   2.5
```
A   B   C   D   E   F   G   H   I   J   K   L   M
N   O   P   Q   R   S   T   U   V   W   X   Y   Z
a   b   c   d   e   f   g   h   i   j   k   l   m
n   o   p   q   r   s   t   u   v   w   x   y   z
```

logical-and-expression :   7.7
> *bitwise-or-expression*
> *logical-and-expression* && *bitwise-or-expression*

logical-negation-expression :   7.5.4
> ! *unary-expression*

logical-or-expression :   7.7
> *logical-and-expression*
> *logical-or-expression* || *logical-and-expression*

long-suffix : one of   2.7.1
> l   L

mult-op : one of   7.6.1
> *   /   %

multiplicative-expression :   7.6.1
> *unary-expression*
> **multiplicative-expression mult-op unary-expression**

named-label :   8.10
> *identifier*

nonzero-digit : one of   2.7.1
       1   2   3   4   5   6   7   8   9

null-statement :   8.11
    ;

octal-constant :   2.7.1
    0
    octal-constant octal-digit

octal-digit : one of   2.7.1
    0   1   2   3   4   5   6   7

octal-escape-code :   2.7.5
    octal-digit
    octal-digit octal-digit
    octal-digit octal-digit octal-digit

parameter-declaration :   4.5.4, 9.1
    declaration-specifiers declarator
    declaration-specifiers abstract-declarator$_{opt}$

parameter-list :   4.5.4, 9.1
    parameter-declaration
    parameter-list , parameter-declaration

parameter-type-list :   4.5.4, 9.1
    parameter-list
    parameter-list , . . .

parenthesized-expression :   7.3.3
    (*expression*   )

pointer: 4.5.2, 5.12
    ⋆ *type-qualifier-list$_{opt}$*
    ⋆ *type-qualifier-list$_{opt}$ pointer*

pointer-declarator :   4.5.2
    pointer direct-declarator

postdecrement-expression :   7.4.4
    postfix-expression --

postfix-expression : 7.4
    primary-expression
    subscript-expression
    component-selection-expression
    function-call
    postincrement-expression
    postdecrement-expression

postincrement-expression : 7.4.4
    postfix-expression ++

predecrement-expression : 7.5.8
    -- *unary-expression*

preincrement-expression : 7.5.8
    ++ *unary-expression*

primary-expression : 7.3
    name
    literal
    parenthesized-expression

relational-expression : 7.6.4
    shift-expression
    relational-expression relational-op shift-expression

relational-op : one of 7.6.4
    <   <=   >   >=

return-statement : 8.9
    return *expression* $_{opt}$;

s-char-sequence : 2.7.4
    s-char
    s-char-sequence s-char

s-char : 2.7.4
    any source character except the double quote ",
        backslash \, or newline character
    escape-character

shift-expression : 7.6.3
    additive-expression
    shift-expression shift-op additive-expression

shift-op : one of 7.6.3
    <<   >>

signed-type-specifier :   5.1.1
        `short` *or* `short int` *or* `signed short` *or* `signed short int`
        `int` *or* `signed int` *or* `signed`
        `long` *or* `long int` *or* `signed long` *or* `signed long int`

simple-component :   5.6
        declarator

simple-declarator :   4.5.1
        identifier

sizeof-expression :   7.5.2
        `sizeof` (*type-name*)
        `sizeof` *unary-expression*

statement :   ch. 8
        expression-statement
        labeled-statement
        compound-statement
        conditional-statement
        iterative-statement
        switch-statement
        break-statement
        continue-statement
        return-statement
        goto-statement
        null-statement

statement-list :   8.4
        statement
        statement-list statement

storage-class-specifier : one of   4.3
        `auto  extern  register  static  typedef`

string-constant :   2.7.4
        " *s-charr-sequence$_{opt}$* "
        `L`" *s-char-sequence$_{opt}$* "

structure-tag :   5.6
        identifier

structure-type-definition :   5.6
        `struct` *structure-tag$_{opt}$* { *field-list* }

structure-type-reference :   5.6
        `struct` *structure-tag*

structure-type-specifier :   5.6
      structure-type-definition
      structure-type-reference

subscript-expression :   7.4.1
      postfix-expression [*expression*]

switch-statement :   8.7
      `switch` (*expression*) *statement*

top-level-declaration :   9.1
      declaration
      function-definition

top-level-declaration-list :   9.1
      top-level-declaration
      top-level-declaration-list top-level-declaration

translation-unit :   9.1
      top-level-declaration
      translation-unit   top-level-declaration

type-name :   5.12
      declaration-specifiers abstract-declarator$_{opt}$

type-qualifier :   4.4
      `const`
      `volatile`

type-qualifier-list :   4.5.2
      type-qualifier
      type-qualifer-list type qualifier

type-specifier :   4.4
      enumeration-type-specifier
      floating-point-type-specifier
      integer-type-specifier
      structure-type-specifier
      typedef-name
      union-type-specifier
      void-type-specifier

typedef-name :   5.10
      identifier

unary-expression :   7.5
        postfix-expression
        cast-expression
        sizeof-expression
        unary-minus-expression
        unary-plus-expression
        logical-negation-expression
        bitwise-negation-expression
        address-expression
        indirection-expression
        preincrement-expression
        predecrement-expression

unary-minus-expression :   7.5.3
        - *unary-expression*

unary-plus-expression :   7.5.3
        + *unary-expression*

underscore :   2.5

        _

union-tag :   5.7
        identifier

union-type-definition :   5.7
        `union` *union-tag$_{opt}$* { *field-list* }

union-type-reference :   5.7
        `union` *union-tag*

union-type-specifier :   5.7
        union-type-definition
        union-type-reference

unsigned-suffix : one of   2.7.1
        `u   U`

unsigned-type-specifier :   5.1.2
        `unsigned short int`$_{opt}$
        `unsigned int`$_{opt}$
        `unsigned long int`$_{opt}$

void-type-specifier :   5.9
        `void`

while-statement :   8.6.1
        `while` (*expression*) *statement*

width :   5.6
        expression

C

Answers to the Exercises

This appendix contains solutions to the exercises in chapters 2–9.

CHAPTER 2

1. Reserved words, hexadecimal constants, wide string constants, and parentheses are lexical tokens. Comments and whitespace serve only to separate tokens. Trigraphs are removed before token recognition.

2. The number of tokens for each string is:

    (a) 3 tokens

    (b) 2 tokens; – is an operator, not part of the constant

    (c) 1 token

    (d) 3 tokens; the second one is "FOO"

    (e) 1 token

    (f) 4 tokens; ** is not a single operator

    (g) not a token; same as "X\", which is an unterminated string constant

    (h) not a token; identifiers cannot have $

    (i) 3 tokens; *= is an operator

    (j) either none or 3; ## is not a lexical token, but it happens to be a preprocessor token

3. The result is ***/; the comments are identified below between parentheses. Quotation marks inside a comment do not have to balance.

    ```
    /**/*/*"*/*/*"//*//**/*/
    (--) (---) (-----) (--)
    ```

4. The order is:
    1. converting trigraphs
    2. processing line continuation
    3. removing comments
    4. collecting characters into tokens

5.   Some possible objections:
   (a) difficult to identify (read) the multiple words in the identifier; use upper case or underscores
   (b) the identifier's spelling is very close to a reserved word
   (c) closely resembles a numeric literal (the first letter is an "oh")
   (d) if the compiler accepted this identifier, it would be an extension

CHAPTER 3

1.   (a) The space before the left parenthesis is not permitted in ANSI or traditional C. Instead of a macro with one parameter, `ident` will be a macro with no parameters that expands to "`(x) x`".
   (b) The = and ; characters are not necessary and are probably wrong. In some traditional C compilers the space after # might cause problems.
   (c) This definition is all right.
   (d) This definition is all right; you can define reserved words as macros.

2.   *ANSI C*   *Traditional C*
   (a) `b+a`   `b+a`
   (b) `x 4`   (two tokens)   `x4` (one token)
   (c) `"a book"`   `# a book`
   (d) `p?free(p):NULL`   `p?p?p?p?…:NULL:NULL:NULL` (infinitely)

3.   The result after preprocessing (ignoring whitespace) is these three lines:
```
int blue = 0;
int blue = 0;
int red = 0;
```

4.   Because the arguments and body are not parenthesized, the result of expanding the macro could be misinterpreted in a larger expression. A safer definition would be
```
#define DBL(a)     ((a)+(a))
```

5.   The macro is expanded in the following steps:
```
M(M)(A,B)
MM(A,B)
A = "B"
```

6.   This solution depends on the presence of `defined` and `#error`:
```
#if !defined(SIZE) || (SIZE<1) || (SIZE>10)
#error "SIZE not properly defined "
#endif
```

7.   In the preprocessor command `#include </a/file.h>`, the sequence `/a/file.h` is considered a token (a single file name); it would not be a token to the compiler.

8.   Presumably the programmer wishes to print an error when `x==0`. However, `x==0` is a run-time test, whereas `#error` is a compile-time command. If this program were compiled, the error message would always appear and halt compilation, regardless of the value of x.

CHAPTER 4

1. The function will return the value of its argument each time it is called. Only if the `static` storage class specifier is used on the declaration of i inside P will the return value change in successive calls.

2. The declarations of f as a function, integer variable, type name, and enumeration constant all conflict with each other; eliminate all but one of those declarations. The use of f as both a structure tag and a union tag conflict; eliminate the union so that f is also declared as a structure component. The use of f as a label does not conflict with any other declarations except in a few older C implementations.

3.

Code	`int i;`	`long i;`	`float i;`
`1  int i;`	(defined)		
`2  void f(i)`		(defined)	
`3      long i;`		(defined)	
`4  {`			
`5      long l = i;`		(used)	
`6      {`			
`7          float i;`			(defined)
`8          i = 3.4;`			(used)
`9      }`			
`10     l = i+2;`		(used)	
`11 }`			
`12 int *p = &i;`	(used)		

4. (a) `extern void P(void)`
    (b) `register int i;`
    (c) `typedef char *LT;`
    (d) `extern Q(int i, const char *cp);`
    (e) `extern int R( double *(*p)(long i) );`
    (f) `static char STR[11];` (Note: leave room for the null character.)
    (g) `const char STR2[] = INIT_STR2;` Braces around INIT_STR2 are optional.. Also acceptable would be: `const char *STR2=INIT_STR2;` (No braces.)
    (h) `int *IP = &i;`

5. `int m[3][3] = {{1,2,3},{1,2,3},{1,2,3}};`

CHAPTER 5

1. Note that none of these types should involve type `int`, since the size of `int` might be no larger than `short` anyway.
    (a) `long` or `unsigned long` (`unsigned short` might not handle 99999)
    (b) a structure containing two components: type `short` (for the area code) and type `long` (for the local number) (or the unsigned versions of these types)
    (c) `char` (any variant)
    (d) `signed char` in ANSI C; `short` in other implementations (`char` might be unsigned)
    (e) `signed char` in ANSI C; `short` in other implementations (`char` might be unsigned) (characters are guaranteed to have positive values in type `signed char`)
    (f) `double` would work, but less space would be occupied by using type `long` and storing the balance as a number of cents

2. The type of `UP_ARROW_KEY` is `int` and has the value `0x86` (134). If the computer uses a `signed` type for `char`, the values for the extended characters will be negative, so if the argument to `is_up_arrow` really is `0x86`, the `return` statement test will be $-122==134$, which is false instead of true. The correct way to write the function is to coerce the character code to be of type `char` or coerce the argument to be of type `unsigned char`. That is, use one of the following return statements:

```
return c == (char) UP_ARROW_KEY;
return (unsigned char) c == UP_ARROW_KEY;
```

The first solution is probably better since it allows the most freedom in defining a value for `UP_ARROW_KEY`.

3. (a) legal
    (b) legal
    (c) illegal; cannot dereference a `void *` pointer
    (d) illegal; cannot dereference a `void *` pointer

4. (a) `*(iv + i)`
    (b) `*(*(im+i)+j)`

5. 13. The cast is not necessary in ANSI C, but it makes the intent clearer and may be needed in some older compilers.

6.  ```
    x.i   =  0;
    x.F.s = 0;              (0 and 1 are the only legal values.)
    x.F.e = 0;
    x.F.m = 0;
    x.U.d = 0.0;            (or x.U.p = NULL; , but not x.U.a[0] = '\0';,
                            which leaves some elements of a undefined)
    ```

7. The sketches are shown below. The number of bits occupied by each field is indicated, and markers along the bottom indicate word boundaries. Note particularly the order of the bit fields.

Big endian, right-to-left bit packing

increasing memory addresses ⟶

Little endian, right-to-left bit packing

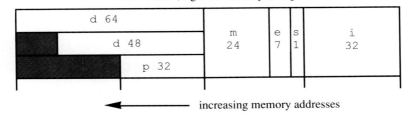

⟵ increasing memory addresses
    ```

8.  ```
    typedef int *fpi();  /* type definition */
    fpi *x;              /* variable declaration */
    int *fpi()           /* function; can't use typedef in header */
    {
        return (fpi *)0;
    }
    ```

CHAPTER 6

1. All the casts are permitted in ANSI and traditional C except (c) and (e), which are disallowed in ANSI C.

2. In this solution, we assume the traditional C compiler allows mixed pointer assignments but otherwise follows ANSI rules. However, for some traditional C compilers the answers will be the same as for question 1.
    (a) Permitted in ANSI and traditional C.
    (b) Disallowed in ANSI C; permitted in traditional C.
    (c) Disallowed in ANSI C; permitted in traditional C.
    (d) Disallowed in ANSI C and traditional C.
    (e) Disallowed in ANSI C; permitted in traditional C.
    (f) Permitted in ANSI and traditional C.

3. (a) `unsigned`
    (b) `unsigned long` in traditional C; `long` or `unsigned long` in ANSI C
    (c) `double`
    (d) `long double` in ANSI C;
    (e) `int *` (the usual unary conversions are applied to `int []`)
    (f) `short (*) ()`, because the usual unary conversions are applied first. Here is a plausible situation in which this could happen:
    ```
    extern short f1(), f2(), (*pf)();
    extern int i;
    pf = (i>0 ? f1 : f2);  /* binary conv on f1 and f2 */
    ```

4. It is permitted (if wasteful) for an implementation to use 32 bits to represent type `char`. Regardless of the representation, the value of `sizeof(char)` is always 1. The range of type `int` cannot be smaller than that of type `char`; it can be the same or it can be arbitrarily larger.

5. There is not necessarily any relationship between them. They could be the same or one could be larger than the other.

6. The value 128 can be expressed as the 32-bit hexadecimal number 00000080_{16}. Since computer A is a big endian, the bytes are stored in the order 00_{16}, 00_{16} 00_{16}, 80_{16}. On the little endian computer, the bytes are reassembled from the low-order end, yielding 80000000_{16}, or -2,147,483,648. The result is the same if A is the little endian and B is the big endian.

CHAPTER 7

1. (a) `char *`
    (b) `double` (`float` in ANSI C)
    (c) `float`
    ```

    (d) `int`
    (e) `double` (`float` in ANSI C)
    (f) `int`
    (g) `int`
    (h) `int`
    (i) illegal
    (j) `float`

2. (a) `p1+=1; p2+=1; *p1=*p2;`
    (b) `*p1=*p2; p1-=1; p2-=1;`

3. (a) `#define low_zeroes(n)    (-1<<n)`
    (b) `#define low_ones(n)  (~low_zeroes(n))`
    (c) `#define mid_zeroes(width,offset) \`
              `(low_zeroes(width+offset) | low_ones(offset))`
       (The + operator could be used in place of |.)
    (d) `#define mid_ones(width,offset (~mid_zeroes(width,offset))`

4.   The expression `j++==++j` is legal but its result is undefined in ANSI C because `j` is modified twice in the same expression. Depending on which operand of `==` is evaluated first, the result could be 0 or 1, although the final value of `j` is likely to be 2. On the other hand, `j++&&++j` is legal and defined; its result is 0 and `j` has the value 1 at the end of the expression.

5. (a) allowed, since the types are compatible
    (b) not allowed (the referenced type on the left does not have enough qualifiers)
    (c) allowed, since only one type specifies a size
    (d) allowed, since qualification is irrelevant if the right side is not an lvalue
    (e) not allowed, only because `float` is not compatible with its promoted type (`double`)
    (f) allowed, since the referenced types are compatible

6.   No. The assignment is illegal because each structure definition creates a new type. If the definitions are in different source files, the types are compatible, but this is a technicality that permits programs compiled in separate pieces to have well-defined behavior.

CHAPTER 8

1. (a)
```
n = A;
L1:
if (N>=B) goto L2;
sum+=n;
n++;
goto L1;
L2:;
```
    (b)
```
L:
if (a<b) {
    a++;
    goto L;
}
```
    (c)
```
L:
sum += *p;
if (++p < q) goto L;
```

2. The value of j is 3. "j is undefined" is incorrect; although the program jumps into a block, the fact that i has storage class `static` means that it will be properly initialized before the program begins.

3. The value of sum is 3. i takes on the values 0, 1,... each time around the loop. When i is 0, 1, and 3, `sum` is incremented and the `continue` statement causes another loop iteration. When i is 2, `sum` is not altered but the loop is continued. However, when i is 4, the `break` within the `switch` causes control to reach the `break` statement in the loop, which causes termination of the loop. Therefore `case 5:` is never executed.

CHAPTER 9

1. (a) valid prototype
   (b) legal declaration, but not a prototype; must have a parameter type list within parentheses
   (c) illegal declaration; must have at least one parameter declaration before ellipsis
   (d) illegal declaration; must have at least one type specifier, storage class specifier, or type qualifier before each parameter name
   (e) valid prototype; parameter name is not necessary
   (f) legal definition, but not a prototype; must have parameter types within parenthses

2. (a) not compatible; prototype's parameter type is not compatible with the usual argument conversions, which is required when the definition is not in prototype form
   (b) not compatible; it does not matter that the prototype appears in the definition
   (c) compatible; the parameter names do not have to be the same
   (d) not compatible; the two prototypes do not agree in the use of the ellipsis
   (e) compatible; neither is a prototype, so promoted argument types are passed
   (f) compatible

3. (a) not legal; cannot convert short * to int * under the assignment conversions
   (b) legal; s will be converted to type int and ld will be unchanged
   (c) legal; ld will be converted to type short
   (d) legal; the first parameter is unchanged, the second is converted to type int, and the third is unchanged
   (e) legal; the parameter is converted to type int before the call, and back to type short at the beginning of the called function
   (f) legal, but probably wrong; the parameter is unchanged but will be interpreted as being of type int by the caller

4. The call is governed by the prototype appearing on the first line. The latter declaration does not hide the former, because P has external linkage.

5. (a) OK; the value will be converted to type short before being returned
   (b) OK; the value will be converted to type short before being returned
   (c) illegal; the expression cannot be converted to the type of the return value
   (d) illegal; the expression cannot be converted under the assignment conversion rules

Index